The Illustrated Encyclopedia of Active New Religions, Sects, and Cults

Benjamin Beit-Hallahmi

The Rosen Publishing Group, Inc.
New York

Published in 1993 by The Rosen Publishing Group, Inc.
29 East 21st Street, New York, NY 10010

First Edition

Manufactured in the United States of America

Library of Congress Cataloging-in Publication Data

Beit-Hallahmi, Benjamin
The illustrated encyclopedia of active new religions, sects, and
cults / Benjamin Beit-Hallahmi.
   p.   cm.
   Includes bibliographical references and index.
   ISBN 0-8239-1505-0
  1. Religions–Encyclopedias   I. Title
BL80.2.B385   1993
291.9'03–dc20   93-18928
                           CIP

Photographs courtesy: The Bettmann Archive, Inc., The Associated Press, United Press
International, and Reuters News Service.
Photo Research by Vera Ahmadzadeh.

ABOUT THE AUTHOR

BENJAMIN BEIT-HALLAHMI, currently professor of psychology at the University of Haifa, was born in Tel-Aviv in 1943. In 1970 he received a Ph.D. in clinical psychology from Michigan State University. Since then he has held full-time appointments at The University of Michigan and the University of Haifa and visiting appointments at universities and research institutions in the United States, Israel, and France.

Beit-Hallahmi is the author of *Psychoanalysis and Religion: A Bibliography* (1978), *Prolegomena to the Psychological Study of Religion* (1989), *Despair and Deliverance: Private Salvation in Contemporary Israel* (1992), and *The Psychoanalytic Study of Religion* (1993). He is coauthor of *The Social Psychology of Religion* (with Michael Argyle, 1975), *Twenty Years Later: Kibbutz Children Grown Up* (with A.I. Rabin, 1982), and *The Kibbutz Bibliography* (with S. Shur, J.R. Blasi, and A.I. Rabin, 1981). In addition, he edited *Research in Religious Behavior* (1973), and coedited *Tradition, Conflict, and Continuity: Judaism in Israel*, and *Religion, Coping, and Pathology* (1993). Besides his publications in psychology, Beit-Hallahmi has written widely about political affairs, including the books *The Israeli Connection* (1987) and *Original Sins* (1992).

ACKNOWLEDGMENTS

Several organizations and many individuals have made this work possible. I would like to mention the help and facilities provided by the University of Haifa library, the Elmer Holmes Bobst Library at New York University, The New York Public Library, the Columbia University libraries, the University of Haifa Research Authority, and the Liberal Studies Program at New York University. Among the individuals whose help was vital, I would like to mention Shlomo Abramovitch, Hanni Amit-Kochavi, Jim Andrea, Yigal Arens, Robert Balch, Eileen Barker, Avner Ben-Ner, Yoram Bilu, Alan Black, Lisa Cohen, Simon N. Coleman, Thadeusz Doktor, Ronald Enroth, Daniele Friedlander, Daniel Friedmann, Yvonne Haddad, Michael Hill, Maxine Gold, Judy Klein, Rachael L.E. Kohn, Yolanda Lazo, Burton Levine, Efrat Levy, Shqipe Malushi, Jean-François Mayer, Leonard Prager, Roger Rosen, Roy A. Rosenberg, Ulysses Santamaria, Michal Sherbak, Shanee Stepakoff, James D. Tabor, Madeleine Tress, Michael Valenti, Anthony van Fossen, Cynthia L. Ward, and Leonard Zeskind.

Errors, ambiguities, redundancies, and omissions are unavoidable accompaniments of any attempt to gather such an enormous quantity of facts and names, many of which are controversial, and few beyond dispute. I alone am responsible for all errors and omissions and will appreciate corrections.

GENERAL BIBLIOGRAPHY

Further information on many entries can be found in the following:

Barker, E. *New Religious Movements: A Practical Introduction.* London: Her Majesty's Stationery Office, 1989.

Barrett, D.B. *World Christian Encyclopedia.* New York: Oxford University Press, 1982.

Brandon, S.G.F. *Dictionary of Comparative Religion.* New York: Scribner's, 1970.

Choquette, D. *New Religious Movements in the United States and Canada : A critical Assessment and Annotated Bibliography.* Westport, CT & London: Greenwood Press, 1985.

Clark, E.T. *The Small Sects in America.* New York: Abingdon, 1965.

Desroche, H. *Dieux D'Hommes.* Paris: Mouton, 1969.

Ellwood, R.S. *Religious and Spiritual Groups in Modern America.* Englewood Cliffs, NJ: Prentice-Hall, 1973.

Hinnels, J.R. *The Penguin Dictionary of Religions.* New York: Penguin, 1984.

La Barre, W. *The Ghost Dance.* New York: Doubleday, 1970.

Mathison, R. *Faiths, Cults and Sects of America.* Indianapolis: Bobbs-Merrill, 1960.

Mead, F.S. *Handbook of Denominations in the United States.* Nashville: Abingdon, 1970.

Melton, J.G. *A Directory of Religious Bodies in the United States.* New York: Garland, 1977.

————. *The Encyclopedia of American Religions.* Wilmington, NC: McGrath Publishing Co., 1978.

————. *Magic, Witchcraft and Paganism in America: A Bibliography Compiled from the Files of the Institute for the Study of American Religion.* New York: Garland Publishing, 1982.

————. *The Encyclopedia of American Religions.* Supplement to the First Edition. Detroit: Gale Research Co., 1985.

————. *Encyclopedic Handbook of Cults In America.* New York and London: Garland Publishing Inc., 1986.

————. *Biographical Dictionary of American Cult and Sect Leaders.* New York and London: Garland Publishing Inc., 1986.

————. *The Encyclopedia of American Religions.*, 2d ed. Detroit: Gale Research Co., 1987.

————. *The Encyclopedia of American Religions.* Supplement to the Second Edition. Detroit: Gale Research Co., 1988.

————. *The Encyclopedia of American Religions*, 3d ed. Detroit: Gale Research Co., 1989.

Piepkorn, A.C. *Profiles in Belief: The Religious Bodies of the United States and Canada*, vol. I. New York: Harper & Row, 1977.

Pike, E.R. *Encyclopedia of Religion and Religions.* London: George Allen & Unwin, 1951.

Ram Dass. *Journey of Awakening.* New York: Bantam, 1978.

Rice, E. *Eastern Definitions.* Garden City, NY: Doubleday & Company, 1978.

Sandri, D. *À La Recherche des Sectes et Sociétés Secrètes d'Aujourdhui.* Paris: Presse de la Renaissance, 1978.

Schultz, T., ed. *The Fringes of Reason.* New York: Harmony Books, 1989.

Sutherland, S., Houlden, L., Clarke, P., and Hardy, F., eds. *The World's Religions.* London: Routledge, 1988.

Thiollier, M.-M. *Dictionnaire des Religions.* Paris: Larousse, 1966.

HOW TO USE THIS ENCYCLOPEDIA

The listings in this *Encyclopedia* include:

A group name, with information about it; *e.g.* JEHOVAH'S WITNESSES.

A group leader's name with cross reference to the group name; *e.g.,* Joseph Smith, Jr., see MORMONS.

A group's unofficial name, with cross reference to the main entry; *e.g.,* Moonies, see UNIFICATION CHURCH.

The name of an organization related to a religious movement; *e.g.,* American Freedom Coalition, see UNIFICATION CHURCH.

Major ideas or concepts, often related to numerous movements; *e.g.,* FUNDAMENTALISM.

Note that unattributed quotations in entries come from publications of the group in question: pamphlets, posters, and advertisements of all kinds. Bibliographic sources given in entries list only books based on scholarly research, not publications representing the group itself.

INTRODUCTION

This Encyclopedia is designed to serve as a reference guide for persons seeking basic information about modern religious movements, and to be accessible to a wide variety of users, from students at all levels to media professionals and scholars.

What does the Encyclopedia cover? To be included in it, a group must espouse a religious belief system; *i.e.*, a belief system referring to an invisible, "supernatural" world inhabited by deities, the souls of the dead and the unborn, and sometimes other entities such as angels and devils.

To be classified as a new religious movement, a group must demonstrate novelty in both organization and beliefs, some doctrinal discontinuity with its environment. There must be a clear distinction from existing religious groups in new leadership and new claims to divine truth.

To be classified as "modern," a group must have come into existence in the last two hundred years. The entries include groups most likely to be encountered in academic literature and in the media when modern religious movements are discussed.

Some of the groups are clearly small and eccentric. Our main reason for giving them attention is that there is no way of predicting which will succeed and grow.

In the scholarly literature, a group is defined as a *sect* when it has had an earlier connection with another religious organization; *i.e.*, it arose from a schism. A *cult* is in a way more deviant, having no ties to earlier tradition and existing outside the religious establishment and its boundaries. Both terms are today reserved for religious groups that are outside the mainstream of society and culture. They are often small in membership and lack social standing because of size and because of deviance from majority belief systems. Use of the terms implies nothing pejorative.

The information about the groups covered was gathered first from the scholarly literature, ranging from specialized research monographs to standard reference works. Writings produced by the groups themselves were consulted, and such writings are often quoted to present their beliefs faithfully. Media reports were used in some cases. Last but not least, direct contact with various groups and their members has been a constant source of information. We are grateful to countless members of new religious movements, and in many cases to the official leadership, for their readiness to provide information and insights.

A

AARONIC ORDER

Dissident Mormon group founded in 1945 in Utah by Maurice Lerrie Glendenning, who became a Mormon in 1929 but was excommunicated a few years later for publishing dissident ideas. Group scriptures include traditional Mormon publications together with the writings of its founder. The organization is based in Salt Lake City.
See also MORMONS

Source:
Baer, H.A. *Recreating Utopia in the Desert: A Sectarian Challenge to Modern Mormonism.* Albany: SUNY Press, 1988.

Hamaas Abdul-Khaalis, see HANAFI MADH-HAB CENTER

Roger Abergal, see ROOT OF DAVID MINISTRIES

Donald Abernathy, see APOSTOLIC GOSPEL FAITH OF JESUS CHRIST

ABILITISM

Known also as the Institute of Ability and the Santana Dharma Foundation, this group is an offshoot of SCIENTOLOGY founded by H. Charles Berner (1929–) in California in 1965. Its doctrine combines Scientology with Hindu concepts. Meditation, tai chi, vegetarianism, and body exercises are used. Headquarters are in Lucerne Valley, California.

ABODE OF THE MESSAGE, THE

Also known as the Abode community, this is a Sufi Order commune made up of nu-clear families, founded by Pir Vilayat Inayat Khan in 1975 in an old SHAKER village in New Lebanon, New York. It operates AEgis, a school for "Spirituality in Our Time," and the "Alchemical Retreat Process," developed by its founder.
See also SUFI ORDER IN THE WEST

A COURSE IN MIRACLES (ACIM)

Christian-NEW THOUGHT belief system transmitted by numerous teachers conducting many groups across the United States. The book *A Course in Miracles* was published in 1975 by Helen Schucman (?–1981), who claimed to have been only the medium for a divine revelation from Christ. According to other versions of the book, it is the joint work of Schucman and William Theiford. ACIM has also been used by some Jewish groups.

The ACIM message is based on the notion that death is an illusion, sin unreal, and guilt to be avoided. Only the spirit is real. Thought is all-powerful, and through positive, nonjudgmental thinking most human problems will be solved.
See also FOUNDATION FOR "A COURSE IN MIRACLES" (FACIM); FOUNDATION FOR INNER PEACE; INTERFAITH FELLOWSHIP

ACTUALISM

NEW THOUGHT healing group founded in 1960 in California by Russell Paul Schofield, whose declared goal is "to enlighten awareness to the interdependence and interaction of body, mind, identity, and spirit. This results in a continuously renewing force which brings about the transformation of the personality to the point of wholeness." The group offers "life-energy" and "abundance" courses.

Boto Adai, see ÉGLISE ADAISTE

Barry Adams, see RAINBOW FAMILY OF LIVING LIGHT

John Quincy Adams, see CHURCH OF THE LITTLE CHILDREN

Lucy Adeoti, see NEW SALEM CHURCH (ALADURA)

ADVANCED ABILITY CENTER (AAC)

Also known as the Church of the New Civilization, this international SCIENTOLOGY splinter group is based in California and was formed in the early 1980s by David Mayo, former Scientology leader. The group was sued by Scientology for using its ideas. The case was won by the AAC after a legal struggle. Branches have operated in Europe.

See also ABILITISM; DUGA (ABILITY)

ADVENT CHRISTIAN CHURCH

Adventist group created when, following the Great Disappointment of 1844 among the SECOND ADVENTISTS in the United States, various groups tried to maintain and revise Millerite predictions about the impending Second Coming. One group believed that Miller was mistaken by ten years in his calculations, and so the Second Coming would occur in 1854. In 1855 the Advent Christian Church was formed in Worcester, Massachusetts, by a group under the leadership of Jonathan Cummins. Members still follow the Millerite notion of an imminent Coming. They do not believe in the immortality of the soul, but in a conditional immortality dependent on individual salvation. The wicked do not enjoy soul immortality and would not share in the final resurrection of the dead.

See also ADVENTISTS; CHURCH OF GOD (ABRAHAMIC FAITH); PRIMITIVE ADVENT CHRISTIAN CHURCH

ADVENTISTS, SECOND

U.S. 19th-century movement founded by William Miller (1781–1849). Miller announced the Second Coming of Jesus Christ for 1831; later the Second Coming was expected in 1843–1844. Finally the date was set for October 22, 1844. Miller based his calculations on a close reading of selected Bible phrases with apocalyptic flavor. He started with Daniel 8:14: "Unto two thousand and three hundred days; then shall the sanctuary be cleansed." He found the exact meaning of this number in Ezekiel 4:6: "I have appointed thee each day for a year." The starting point for this period of 2,300 years was determined, with the help of Ezra 7:12–26 and Daniel 9:22–27, to be 457 BCE. Then a few more steps led to fixing 1844 as the year of the Second Advent.

The Millerite version of the movement died out when the prophecy of the Second Coming failed to materialize, but at least thirty-three religious movements in the United States can be traced back to the "Great Disappointment" of October 22, 1844. Some ADVENTISTS still kept hoping and reformulating their prophecies. In 1858 the American Millenial Association was organized, and a few years later the name Evangelical Adventists was chosen. The Great Disappointment led eventually to the formation of several well-known religious movements, such as the SEVENTH-DAY ADVENTIST CHURCH and JEHOVAH'S WITNESSES.

See also SECOND ADVENT CHRISTIANS; SEVENTH DAY ADVENTISTS

Sources:

Cohen, D. *Waiting for the Apocalypse.* Buffalo: Prometheus Books, 1983.

Cross, W. *The Burned-Over District.* New York: Harper & Row, 1965.

Gaustad, E.S. *The Rise of Adventism.* New York: Harper & Row, 1974.

Harrison, J.F.C. *The Second Coming, Popular Millenarianism 1780–1850.* London: Routledge & Kegan Paul, 1979.

ADVENT SABBATH CHURCH

African-American Adventist, Sabbath-keeping congregation founded in 1941 in New York City by Thomas I.C. Hughes, a former Seventh-Day Adventist. In 1956 it joined with other groups to form THE UNIFICATION ASSOCIATION OF CHRISTIAN SABBATH KEEPERS.

See also ADVENTISTS; SEVENTH-DAY ADVENTISTS

AETHERIUS SOCIETY

International "UFO"-Christian group founded in 1954 in England by George King (1919–), known to followers as His Eminence Sir George King. King is a second-generation spiritualist medium and occultist who at the time reported receiving a call from the Interplanetary Parliament. Later he was contacted by "Master Aetherius" from the planet Venus. He has

A member of the Millerite sect prepares to survive the end of the world in a specially constructed refrigerator.

claimed to receive messages from Aetherius as well as from "Master Jesus." Group members claim to communicate with Space Masters, who give help, advice, and love to the faithful. Visits by space-ships and movements of cosmic energies are reported and celebrated. Group branches, as well as a College of Spiritual Science, have operated in Great Britain and the United States.

Source:

Evans, C. *Cults of Unreason*. London: Harrap, 1973.

AFRICAN APOSTOLIC CHURCH OF JOHANE MARANKE (AACJM)

Known sometimes as the Apostolic Church of Johanes Maranke, and also as VaPostori, this syncretistic, nativist African movement was started in 1932 in Southern Rhodesia (now Zimbabwe) by Muchabaya Mom-berume (1912–1963), later known by his religious name Johane Maranke, and spread to Zambia. The group's doctrine is based on the founder's revelations, received after a period of illness, seclusion, and symbolic "death." Members are supposed to avoid both Western medicine and traditional magic and to rely solely on faith healing. They take part in public confession of sins followed by judgment by the group's prophets. Physical illness is considered to be caused by witchcraft, and deviant, sinful behavior is sometimes judged to be the result of "spirit possession" and treated by exorcism. In recent years the movement has operated most strongly in Zaire, Zambia, and Zimbabwe.

Source:

Jules-Rosette, B. *African Apostles: Ritual and Conversion in the Church of John Maranke*. Ithaca: Cornell University Press, 1975.

AFRICAN METHODIST EPISCOPAL CHURCH (A.M.E.)

African-American Christian church founded in 1816 in Philadelphia by Richard Allen (1760–1831), who in 1787 left the Methodist Church because of its racial segregation policy. The A.M.E. started mission work in Liberia in 1820 and had much influence on the development of independent native churches in Africa, especially in South Africa.

AFRICAN METHODIST EPISCOPAL ZION CHURCH (AMERICAN ZION CHURCH)

African-American Christian group incorporated in New York City in 1800.

AFRICAN ORTHODOX CHURCH

U.S. Eastern Orthodox church with an African-American membership, founded in 1921 by George Alexander McGuire (1866–1934). McGuire first founded the Inde-pendent Episcopal Church to serve black Americans and then left the Episcopal fold when thwarted in his aspirations for promotion.

AFRO-ATHLICAN CONSTRUCTIVE GAATHLY

South African independent native "Ethiopian" church, founded in the 1930s in Kimberley. It has a strong African nationalist ideology influenced by the Ethiopia myth and by the back-to-Africa movement led by Marcus Garvey in the early 20th century.

Marcus Garvey in 1922. He led the back-to-Africa movement in the early 20th century.

Gregorio Aglipay, see PHILIPPINE INDEPENDENT CHURCH

AGNI YOGA SOCIETY

International Theosophical group started in the 1920s by Nicholas Roerich (1874–1947). The founder published messages received from Master Morya, one of the Ascended Masters discussed by Helena Petrovna Blavatsky (as well as by many others since the 19th century). This group later inspired the WELT-SPIRALE movement in Europe.
See also THEOSOPHY

AHMADIYYA ANJUMAN ISHA'AT ISLAM

Heterodox Moslem sect, the smaller section of the AHMADIYYA MOVEMENT, formed in 1914 after a schism that followed the death of its founder. The dispute arose out of differing beliefs about the true nature of the Ahmadiyya Movement's founder. The majority views him as a true prophet, whereas the minority considers him only a great teacher. World headquarters are in Lahore, Pakistan, with branches in other countries.

AHMADIYYA MOVEMENT

Popularly known as Ahmadis, Quadianis, or Mirzais, and officially titled the Ahmadiyyat Movement in Islam, this schismatic Islamic Shia movement was founded by Ghulam Ahmad (1835–1908), known as el-Qadiani, of Qadian in Punjab, India. In 1889 he claimed to have had a divine revelation. Later he claimed to be the Messiah expected by various traditions, among others the Mahdi of Islam, Jesus of Christianity, and an avatar of Krishna, as well as the fulfillment of Zoroastrian and Buddhist traditions. Such claims naturally led to negative, sometimes violent, reactions on the part of orthodox Moslems. On Ahmad's death a disciple was chosen as the khalifa. When that khalifa died in 1914 a split ensued, with the majority of believers following the founder's son, Mirza Bashir-ud-Din Mahmud Ahmad. The group is head-quartered in Rabwah, Pakistan. It has engaged in missionary activities in Africa, Asia, and America and has spread to many parts of the world, with branches in the U.S., Europe, and Israel in addition to Pakistan and India.

The group presents itself as the "Renaissance of Islam." Its doctrine is a sectarian version of Sunni Islam, claiming that divine revelation was not ended with Muhammad and the Quran and that Mirza Ghulam Ahmad was either a prophet or a major reformer. Christian ideas are influential, and the myth of Jesus Christ plays a role. According to Ahmadiyya doctrine, Jesus prophesied the coming of the movement. He did not die on the cross, but was taken alive to India and preached in Kashmir until he died at 120. Otherwise Islamic doctrine is followed with few changes (tobacco is banned). Ahmadis believe their founder's prophecy that an apocalypse will soon take place on earth and only they will survive. Pacifism is emphasized, but aggressiveness in missionary work is advocated. The Movement is led by a khalifa, usually a descendant of the prophet. A minority of the membership formed the AHMADIYYA ANJUMAN ISHA'AT ISLAM.

"Sister" Aimee, see FOURSQUARE GOSPEL, INTERNATIONAL CHURCH OF

Omraam Mikhael Aivanhov, see

FRATERNITÉ BLANCHE UNIVERSELLE

Ajaib Singh (Sant), see SANT BANI ASHRAM

AKHANANANDA SARASWATI, SWAMI

Hindu leader and holy man, born July 25, 1911, to a Brahmin family in northern India as Shantanu Behari. His ashram in Vrindaban has attracted both Indian and foreign followers since the 1940s. Several founders of new religious groups have claimed him as a teacher.

Swami Akhilananda, see RAMA-KRISHNA VEDANTA SOCIETY

ALADURA

Nativist Christian PENTECOSTAL movement in Nigeria that developed into a large number of churches. It was started in 1918 by Josiah O. Oshitelu, then expanded in the 1930s under Joseph Babalola. Aladura in Yoruba means "prayer people," and the movement was so named because of its emphasis on prayer and faith healing. It advocates a modest life-style and responsible work habits. Smoking and drinking alcohol are forbidden. Doctrine is syncretistic, with Christian practices and ideas of salvation combined with African traditions. Thus, polygyny in marriage is the rule, and traditional divination methods and amulets are used.

The movement operates schools, factories, food stores, health centers, and other essential services. The Nigeria Association of Aladura Churches had 55 member groups in 1982, and the movement has spread all over West Africa and to Great Britain.

Sources:

Peel, J.D.Y. *Aladura: A Religious Movement among the Yoruba.* London: Oxford University Press, 1968.

Turner, H.W. *History of an Independent African Church.* Oxford: Clarendon Press, 1967.

ALAMO CHRISTIAN FOUNDATION

Sometimes known as the Holy Alamo Christian Church, Consecrated; the Alamo Christian Church; the Tony and Susan Alamo Foundation; or the Alamo Foundation/Music Square Church, this conservative Christian group was part of the JESUS MOVEMENT of the late 1960s–early 1970s. Officially known as the Christian Foundation, the group was started in the late 1960s and incorporated in 1969 in Los Angeles, California, by Tony and Susan Alamo. Susan Alamo, who was born in the late 1920s in Arkansas as Edith Opal Horn, came from a Christian background. She met Tony Alamo, who was nominally Jewish and was born Bernard Lazar Hoffman, in Missouri while teaching a Bible class. The two went to southern California in search of success in the entertainment world. Both converted to evangelical Christianity in the early 1960s. The group espouses Christian Fundamentalist and anti-Communist doctrine; it takes an active anti-abortion stand.

In 1970 the group moved to Saugus, California, and in 1975 to Dyer, Arkansas. Susan Alamo died in 1982. Group members often live together, and most of them are employed by the Foundation, which operates several businesses. The group was sued by the U.S. government for not paying wages to member employees, and in 1983 it was ordered to pay minimum wages. In 1985 the order was upheld by the U.S. Supreme Court.

In 1986 the Foundation was reorganized as the Alamo Christian Church, headed by Tony Alamo and based in Alma, Arkansas. Alamo is also president of the American Association of Non-Denominational Christian Schools. He has presented himself as an "Israelite," a Hebrew Christian, and has engaged in vehement anti-Catholic propaganda. The group has operated several successful corporations. In the late 1980s it was involved in serious legal troubles, and Tony Alamo was a fugitive wanted by the F.B.I.

See also SUSAN LIPOWITZ FOUNDATION

Muzaffer al-Ashki, see HALVETI-JERRAHI ORDER OF NEW YORK

Ada Albrecht, see NEW ACROPOLIS

ALETHEIA PSYCHO-PHYSICAL FOUNDATION

Occultist group founded in 1969 in California by Jack Schwartz. Practices include meditation, diagnosing the human "aura," and tarot and I Ching readings. The group is based in Grant's Pass, Oregon.

Asa Alonzo Allen, see MIRACLE REVIVAL FELLOWSHIP

Allen-Michael, see ONE WORLD FAMILY

ALL FAITHS CHURCH/SCIENCE OF MIND

NEW THOUGHT group based in El Monte,

Tony Alamo leaves Federal Court in Florida after his arrest on charges of child abuse.

California, founded by David Thompson in the 1950s.

Frank Alper, see ARIZONA METAPHYSICAL SOCIETY

ALPHA AND OMEGA CHRISTIAN CHURCH

PENTECOSTAL group based in Hawaii, founded in 1962 by Alezandro B. Faquaragon. Membership is drawn from the Filipino community, with connection to similar groups in the Philippines.

ALPHA AND OMEGA PENTECOSTAL CHURCH OF GOD OF AMERICA, INC.

African-American   PENTECOSTAL

group, initially known as the Alpha and Omega Church of God Tabernacles. Based in Baltimore, it was founded in 1944 by Magdalen Mabel Phillips, who withdrew from the UNITED HOLY CHURCH OF AMERICA. A schism in the group in 1964 created the TRUE FELLOWSHIP PENTECOSTAL CHURCH OF GOD OF AMERICA.

AMANA CHURCH SOCIETY

Sometimes known as Amana (Faithfulness) Church Society, or the Church of True Inspiration, this U.S. Protestant group was founded in Germany in 1714 as the Community of True Inspiration. A large section of the membership moved to the United States in 1842 and settled near Buffalo, New York, organized as the Ebenezer Society. The settlements were communes in which all property was held collectively. In 1855 the Society moved to Iowa, where the villages of Amana, East Amana, South Amana, Middle Amana, High Amana, West Amana, and Homestead were founded. In 1932 the settlements were reorganized as a cooperative corporation, producing electrical appliances under the Amana name. The group doctrine is pietistic, with members admitted at age fifteen and no ordained ministry.

Source:

Barthel, D.L. *Amana, From Pietist Sect to American Community.* Licoln: University of Nebraska Press, 1984.

AMERICAN CATHOLIC CHURCH

U.S. group, part of the OLD CATHOLIC movement, which follows Roman Catholic traditions but rejects papal authority and infallibility. It was founded in 1915 by Joseph Rene Vilatte. The church has several branches in the United States and Canada. It follows a Theosophical Christianity, which makes it similar in beliefs and practices to the LIBERAL CATHOLIC CHURCH.

AMERICAN CATHOLIC CHURCH ARCHDIOCESE, THE

North American Eastern Orthodox church with an African-American membership, founded in 1927 by James F.A. Lashley as an outgrowth of the AFRICAN ORTHODOX CHURCH.

AMERICAN CATHOLIC CHURCH (SYRO-ANTIOCHEAN)

U.S. OLD CATHOLIC group created through a secession from the AMERICAN CATHOLIC CHURCH by Herbert F. Wilkie in the 1950s.

American Citizens for Honesty in Government, see SCIENTOLOGY

AMERICAN CONFERENCE OF UNDENOMINATED CHURCHES

U.S. conference of Fundamentalist churches founded in 1922 by R. Lee Kirkland and others, which was superseded in 1930 by the INDEPENDENT FUNDAMENTAL CHURCHES OF AMERICA.

American Cryonics Society, Inc., see VENTURISM

AMERICAN EVANGELICAL CHRISTIAN CHURCHES

U.S. association of Fundamentalist ministers that offers doctrinal freedom on questions of predestination within a strictly Fundamentalist framework.

Founded in 1944, it is based in Pineland, Florida.

AMERICAN EVANGELISTIC ASSOCIATION, THE

PENTECOSTAL group founded in 1954 in Baltimore, Maryland, by John E. Douglas. It licenses ministers and operates overseas missions, mainly in Asia.

American Freedom Coalition (AFC), see UNIFICATION CHURCH

AMERICAN INDIAN EVANGELICAL CHURCH

PENTECOSTAL group based in Minneapolis, Minnesota, with membership of native Americans. First organized in 1945, the group adopted its current name in 1956.

AMERICAN MESSIANIC FELLOWSHIP

Formerly known as the Chicago Hebrew Mission, this Hebrew Christian group was founded in the 1940s.
See also HEBREW CHRISTIANITY

American Muslim Mission, see NATION OF ISLAM (NOI)

AMERICAN ORTHODOX CATHOLIC CHURCH

OLD CATHOLIC group founded in 1962 by Robert S. Zeiger and having a few parishes across the United States. The clergy work full time in secular occupations.

AMERICAN RESCUE WORKERS

Conservative Protestant group formed in 1882 as the result of a secession from the SALVATION ARMY and incorporated in 1896. The cause for secession was the wish of American members for more national independence. Following the Salvation Army in practice and doctrine with few exceptions, the group engages in providing emergency aid but also functions as a church. The doctrine is Protestant Fundamentalist. The military pattern of the Salvation Army is retained.

AMERICAN TEILHARD ASSOCIATION

Christian group committed to the teachings of the Jesuit Pierre Teilhard de Chardin, who attempted an interpretation of evolution within a Christian framework.

AMERICAN UNIVERSALIST TEMPLE OF DIVINE WISDOM

Christian-Theosophical group founded in 1966 in Escondido, California.

AMIS DE LA CROIX GLORIEUSE DE DOZULÉ

French Christian group founded in 1982 in Saint-Quentin by Albert Delbauche. The founder has predicted the occurrence of various catastrophes and claimed many apparitions. In 1981 he announced that he would have a son who would liberate France. A daughter was born, whom he described as Joan of Arc, who would reestablish the French monarchy.

AMIS DE L'HOMME

French Millenarian group started after a schism in the THE CHURCH OF THE KINGDOM OF GOD, PHILANTHROPIC ASSEMBLY, around 1950. Founded by Lydie Sartre (1898–1963), known as "Dear Mother" to her followers, it is based in the department of Lot-et-Garonne. Adherents

come mostly from southern France. Members live communally and follow a tightly regimented life.
See also JEHOVAH'S WITNESSES

AMMAL'S GARDEN

Religious commune based in Tucson, Arizona, and founded in the early 1970s. Its doctrine and practices combine Western and Hindu traditions, including meditation.

AMORC ROSICRUCIAN ORDER

Known officially as the Ancient and Mystical Order Rosae Crucis, this international occultist group was founded in 1909 in New York by Harvey Spencer Lewis (1883–1939), who combined traditional European occultism with turn-of-the-century enthusiasm for ancient Egyptian civilization. AMORC teachings include belief in black magic and "mental poisoning," reincarnation, and "auras." Christianity plays a special role in Lewis's teachings, as he claimed to know the true messages contained in the New Testament and offered a new version of the events described therein. In it, he connected early Christianity with "ancient Egyptian" traditions. AMORC headquarters were moved to San Jose, California, before World War I. After the founder's death the group was led by his son, Ralph Maxwell Lewis (1904–), and in recent years by Gary Stewart. The group does most of its work by mail, offering correspondence courses to members around the world.
See also EMIN; ROSICRUCIANS; THEOSOPHY

ANANDA ASHRAMA

Hindu group, originally the Boston branch of the VEDANTA SOCIETY. It was founded in 1909 as the Boston Vedanta Center by Swami Paramananda (1884–1940), a disciple of Swami Vivekananda who followed him from India to the United States. In 1923 Swami Paramananda started a monastic community in California. He was succeeded by Srimata (Reverend Mother) Gayati Devi (1906–) in 1940. The group follows the teachings of Sri Ramakrishna.
See also RAMAKRISHNA MATH AND MISSION

ANANDA COOPERATIVE VILLAGE

Also known as Ananda World Brotherhood Village, this Hindu-Christian commune was founded in 1968 by James Donald Walters (1926–), also known as Swami Kriyananda. It is based in North San Juan, California. Members are followers of Paramahansa Yogananda, founder of the SELF-REALIZATION FELLOWSHIP, who was Swami Kriyananda's teacher. They practice Yogananda's technique of kriya yoga. Their doctrine is syncretistic and combines Hindu and Christian as well as occultist traditions such as astrology. Ananda Cooperative Village operates The Expanding Light, which offer programs to nonmembers. Commune branches operate in Italy and the Western United States.

ANANDA MARGA

Officially known in the West as the Ananda Marga Yoga Society, this Hindu revival movement was founded in India in 1955 by Prabhat Ranjan (P.R.) Sarkar (1921–1990), a former railway employee. The founder is known to his followers as Shrii Anandamurti, Anandamurtiji, or "Baba." The Ananda Marga scripture is the

Ananda Sutra, written by the founder. It prescribes the group's practices, which include meditation several times a day. Sexual intercourse is permitted only for procreation in marriage, but devout members are celibate. Ananda Marga promotes a two-pronged program of individual salvation through meditation and social reform through the total restructuring of human institutions.

Sarkar had developed a radical political ideology in addition to his religious teachings, and this kept getting him in trouble with the Indian government and other governments as well. His followers say, "The movements he founded— Ananda Marga, Prout, and Neo-Humanism—have championed the removal of caste, racial, nationalistic, and religious barriers between people while supporting the preservation of cultural expression and unity of all animate and inanimate beings." Sarkar advocated a world government, a world language, and a world army; his social vision is known as PROUT, which stands for Progressive (pro), Utilization (u), Theory (t).

The movement's political arm, the Proutist movement, took part in Indian elections in 1967 and 1969 but failed to achieve representation. Ananda Marga has been accused of violence toward members and nonmembers. Two members were convicted of political assassination in Australia. Sarkar and other members were accused of conspiracy to commit murder in 1971. He was sentenced to life imprisonment in 1976 but was released in 1978. Ananda Marga was declared an illegal organization by the Indian government in 1975, but this was rescinded in 1977. As a way of protesting their treatment by gov-

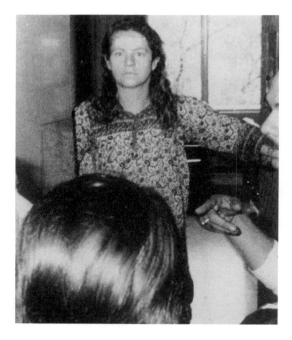

In Calcutta, a member of Ananda Marga in police custody in a hospital because of her connection with the secretive group.

ernment authorities, eight adherents committed self-immolation in the 1960s and 1970s. In 1982 seventeen members were killed by a mob in Calcutta.

In 1987 a U.S. member of the group, Ravi Batra (1943–), published a best-selling book (*The Great Depression of 1990.* New York: Simon & Schuster) predicting a major economic depression and basing his prediction on Sarkar's "law of social cycles." In 1989 Batra published *Regular Economic Cycles* (New York: St. Martin's Press), also based on insights gained from Sarkar, identified only as an "Indian philosopher."

Ma Anandamayi, see SRI MA ANANDAMAYI MONASTERY

ANCHOR BAY EVANGELISTIC ASSOCIATION

Pentecostal offshoot of the FOURSQUARE GOSPEL CHURCH. Formally incorporated in 1940, it was founded by Roy John Turner, who joined Pentecostalism in 1916 and worked with Aimee Semple McPherson in the 1930s. The group is based in New Baltimore, Michigan, and is a member of the PENTECOSTAL FELLOWSHIP OF NORTH AMERICA.

Cay Andersen, see COMMUNITY OF JESUS

Lester B. Anderson, see SALEM ACRES

James F. Andrews, see FULL SALVATION UNION

ANDROMEDA, THE CHAPEL OF THE OPEN DOOR

Christian-occultist group founded in 1969 in Long Lake, Minnesota. It is connected with the CONGREGATIONAL CHURCH OF PRACTICAL THEOLOGY.

ANGLICAN CATHOLIC CHURCH IN NORTH AMERICA

U.S. Anglican group started in 1977 in secession from the Protestant Episcopal Church in protest over the ordination of women.

ANGLO-SAXON FEDERATION OF AMERICA

U.S. British-Israelist group founded by Howard B. Rand of Haverhill, Massachusetts, in 1928. In 1930 W.J. Cameron became president of the Federation. The group was most active in the 1930s and 1940s, disseminating literature containing the BRITISH-ISRAELISM message.

Anishinabe, see CENTER OF FIRST LIGHT

Ansaaru Islaam, see NUBIAN ISLAAMIC HEBREWS

ANTHROPOSOPHICAL SOCIETY

Western occultist movement founded through the defection from the THEOSOPHICAL SOCIETY of Rudolf Steiner (1861–1925), an Austrian. Steiner joined the Theosophical Society in 1902 and became secretary of its German branch, but in 1912 he withdrew in protest against the formation by Annie Besant of the Order of the Star in the East.

All German members of THEOSOPHY and some Swiss members joined Steiner in the new group. The world center is in Dornach, Switzerland.

Steiner called his theory Christian Occultism and regarded Jesus Christ as the "central happening of all history." He regarded the Christian Trinity as the ultimate reality, and the Second Coming of Jesus Christ was to lead to the "respiritualization of the cosmos." Steiner created an eclectic system based on Theosophy, other occult traditions, especially Rosicrucianism, and Christianity. According to Steiner's teachings, the universe, including humankind, has evolved through three stages. The early stages were dominated by intuitive and "clairvoyant" forms of consciousness (and matter). These were "astral," or "etheric" stages of development. These forms of consciousness can be recovered by following Steiner's techniques of meditation. Steiner was a prolific writer,

Rudolf Steiner, founder of the Anthroposophical Society, with Marie von Sivers.

and his numerous books contain information on nutrition (vegetarianism is recommended), organic farming known as bio-dynamic agriculture, child care, education, and cures for cancer and other diseases. Steiner had his own theory of evolution through reincarnation, and his own theories of Atlantis, Lemuria, and Egyptian mythology. The movement has been known for its educational work, especially with the retarded.

See also CAMPHILL MOVEMENT; CHRISTIAN COMMUNITY CHURCH; ROSICRUCIANS

ANTOINISME
Officially incorporated as the Société des Antoinistes and named for its founder, Louis Antoine (1845–1912), known as *le Guérisseur*, "the Healer," this healing-spiritualist group has about sixty branches in France and Belgium. Antoine was born to a poor Catholic family and worked as a miner and metalworker. His reputation as a healer kept growing during his lifetime. Like other 19th-century healing cults (see CHRISTIAN SCIENCE), Antoiniste doctrine denies the existence of evil, or even the existence of matter, and assumes the existence of "fluids" that control the world and the human body. Evil, suffering, and death exist only in human imagination and are based on fallible human perceptions. Antoine founded the New Spiritualism in 1906 and died in 1912. Healing practitioners today dress in black, lay their hands on the locus of pain, and pray.

APOCALYPSE SOCIETY, INC., THE
Monotheistic group founded in the 1980s in New York City by Romiche Henry. Its doctrine is based on the "Virgin Life Principle of God which is a catalyst to achieve the individual highest level of spiritual awareness." It is opposed to any kind of sexuality.

APOSTLES OF INFINITE LOVE
Originally known as the Order of the Mother of God, this Roman Catholic traditionalist splinter group was founded in 1952 in Canada by Jean-Grégoire de la Trinité. In 1968 the founder declared himself Pope Gregory XVII, reported divine revelations (especially apparitions of the Virgin Mary), and spoke against reforms in the official Church. The movement is based in Quebec, where it has established several monasteries and centers. Branches

have operated in the United States and in the Caribbean, especially in Guadeloupe and Puerto Rico. The group doctrine denounces reforms in the Roman Catholic Church since 1960.

In the 1960s and 1970s the group collaborated with the RENOVATED CHURCH OF CHRIST. Later it was tied to the PALMARIAN CATHOLIC CHURCH. In North America the group is sometimes known as the Catholic Church of the Apostles of the Latter Times.

APOSTOLIC CHURCH

International PENTECOSTAL group with branches in North America and in Great Britain. It was founded by Daniel Powell Williams in 1916 in Wales after a split in the APOSTOLIC FAITH CHURCH.

APOSTOLIC CHURCH OF GOD

Sabbath-keeping Adventist group formed in 1949 by Dewey E. Skagg, formerly of the CHURCH OF GOD (SEVENTH-DAY, SALEM, WEST VIRGINIA), in dissent from the doctrine of his former church. It is based in Edgewater, Florida.
See also GENERAL CONFERENCE OF THE CHURCH OF GOD; SEVENTH-DAY ADVENTIST CHURCH

APOSTOLIC CHURCH OF JESUS

PENTECOSTAL group founded by Raymond P. Virgil and based in Pueblo, Colorado. Membership is drawn from Hispanic communities.

APOSTOLIC CHURCH OF JESUS CHRIST

PENTECOSTAL group with African-American membership, based in Indianapolis, Indiana. It was formed in 1924 after the white members of the PENTECOSTAL ASSEMBLIES OF THE WORLD left the originally integrated group.

APOSTOLIC FAITH

U.S. PENTECOSTAL group founded by Charles and Ada Lochbaum in 1923 and based in Hawaii. Doctrine emphasizes healing, tithing, and the coming of the millennium.

APOSTOLIC FAITH CHURCH (KANSAS)

PENTECOSTAL group founded by Charles Parham in Topeka, Kansas. Parham founded the Bethel Healing Home in 1898 and the Bethel Bible College in 1900. Twentieth-century Pentecostalism is said to have started in the winter of 1900–1901 in the Bethel Bible College. Later Parham spent his time traveling around the South, and in 1905 he established a Bible school in Houston, Texas. The group's doctrine emphasizes healing and tithing. A schism during the late 1940s resulted in the formation of the FULL GOSPEL EVANGELICAL ASSOCIATION.

APOSTOLIC FAITH MISSION (AFM)

PENTECOSTAL group started by Minnie Hanson in Topeka, Kansas, in 1907. It emphasizes faith healing and speaking in tongues.

APOSTOLIC FAITH MISSION OF PORTLAND, OREGON, U.S.A.

Known also as the Apostolic Faith, this PENTECOSTAL, evangelical group was founded in 1907 by Mrs. Florence L. Crawford. A "born again" experience is required for membership, and worldly amusements are banned.

APOSTOLIC GOSPEL FAITH OF JESUS CHRIST

PENTECOSTAL group founded in 1963 in California by Donald Abernathy. In 1968 the founder had a vision in which the destruction of the West Coast in an earthquake was predicted. As a result the members moved to cities on the East Coast. The group's doctrine emphasizes faith healing and pacifism. A strict dress code is followed.

APOSTOLIC OVERCOMING HOLY CHURCH OF GOD (AOH CHURCH OF GOD)

Formerly known as the Ethiopian Overcoming Holy Church of God, this U.S. PENTECOSTAL group was founded by William Thomas Phillips (1893–1973) in 1919. Membership has been made up mostly of African-Americans. Worship includes faith healing and speaking in tongues. The group's doctrine is influenced by "black-Jewish" ideas, in which Ethiopia plays a special role.

APOSTOLIC UNITED ORDER

Known also as Apostolic United Brethren, this Mormon splinter group is committed to the practice of polygamy. Founded by Joseph Musser in the early 1950s, it has been led by members of the Allred family. See also THE CHURCH OF THE FIRST BORN OF THE FULLNESS OF TIMES; CONFEDERATE NATIONS OF ISRAEL; REORGANIZED CHURCH OF JESUS CHRIST OF LATTER DAY SAINTS; UNITED ORDER EFFORT

Source:
Bradlee, B., Jr. and Van Atta, D. *Prophet of Blood*. New York: G.P. Putnam's Sons, 1981.

AQUARIAN EDUCATIONAL FOUNDATION

Theosophical-occultist group founded in California in 1963. It follows the teachings of the ARCANE SCHOOL started by Alice B. Bailey, augmented by the teachings of the group's founder, Haroutiun Saraydarian. The message of Christianity also plays some role in its teachings.
See also LUCIS TRUST; THEOSOPHY

AQUARIAN FOUNDATION

Spiritualist-Theosophical group founded in 1955 in Seattle, Washington, by Keith Milton Rhinehart. Its doctrine includes many elements familiar from THEOSOPHY, such as The Great White Brotherhood and reincarnation. Masters of the Great White Brotherhood are said to communicate with the group. The founder has also claimed to carry the Christian stigmata on his body.

AQUARIAN MINYAN OF BERKELEY

Jewish revival group started in the 1970s in Berkeley, California. It combines traditional Jewish ideas with Eastern practices such as meditation. In the 1980s it became affiliated with the P'NAI OR RELIGIOUS FELLOWSHIP.

AQUARIAN RESEARCH FOUNDATION (ARF)

Occultist commune founded in 1969 in Philadelphia by Arthur Rosenblum. Practices included "plant telepathy and flying saucers," as well as astrological birth control.

ARCANA WORKSHOPS

Occultist group in the Alice Bailey tradition, based in southern California. It oper-

ates mainly through correspondence.
See also LUCIS TRUST

ARCHDIOCESE OF THE OLD CATHOLIC CHURCH IN AMERICA

OLD CATHOLIC group founded in 1941 by Francis X. Resch, a former priest in the NORTH AMERICAN OLD ROMAN CATHOLIC CHURCH. It has headquarters in Milwaukee, Wisconsin.

Raymond Allen Archer, see THEOCRATIC COMMUNE NATURAL HEALTH SERVICE

Edward J. Arens, see UNIVERSITY OF THE SCIENCE OF SPIRIT

ARICA INSTITUTE

U.S. occultist group started in the 1960s in Arica, Chile, and formally founded by Oscar Ichazo in New York City in 1971. It is a system of religious psychotherapy combining Christian concepts, Eastern religious concepts taken from Hindu traditions and Sufism, Gurdjieff ideas, and secular psychotherapy techniques.
See also GURDJIEFF GROUPS

ARIEL MINISTRIES

Hebrew Christian group founded in the 1980s by Arnold Fruchtenbaum, with headquarters in California.
See also HEBREW CHRISTIANS

ARISING SUN IFO (IDENTIFIED FLYING OBJECTS)

UFO-Christian group based in Milwaukee and founded around 1970 by June Young, known as Bright Star. Messages are reported from Jesus Christ, the Virgin Mary, and Elvis Presley.

ARIZONA METAPHYSICAL SOCIETY

U.S. NEW THOUGHT group founded by Frank Alper in the 1970s. Beliefs include traditional Western occultism, spiritualism, and Hindu ideas. Meditation, "spiritual healing," and "channeling" are practiced. The group is affiliated with the CHURCH OF TZADDI.

ARMAGEDDON, CHURCH OF, see LOVE FAMILY

ARMAGEDDON TIME ARK BASE (A.T.A. BASE)

Christian-UFO group founded in the 1970s in Texas by O.T. Nodrog. Group members predict the coming of an apocalyptic S-Day, when only they will be saved by spaceships.

Raymond Armin, see EMIN SOCIETY

Garner Ted Armstrong, see CHURCH OF GOD INTERNATIONAL

Herbert W. Armstrong, see WORLD-WIDE CHURCH OF GOD

Hunt Armstrong, see DEFENDERS OF THE CHRISTIAN FAITH, INC.

Eberhard Arnold, see BRUDERHOF

Andras Corban Arthen, Deirdre Pulgram Arthen, see EARTHSPIRIT COMMUNITY

ARUNACHALA ASHRAMA BHAGAVAN SRI RAMANA MAHARSHI CENTER, INC.

North American Hindu group devoted to the teachings of Sri Bhagavan Ramana Maharshi (1879–1950). The group's ashramas follow the schedule of activities in the original RAMANA MAHARSHI ashrama on the sacred hill Arunachala in Tiruvannamalai, India. Its doctrine of "Self-abidance" is based on "the wholehearted practice of Self-Enquiry and submission and surrender to the supreme Self as taught by Bhagavan Sri Ramana Maharshi."

Aryan Nations, see CHURCH OF JESUS CHRIST CHRISTIAN—ARYAN NATIONS

ARYA SAMAJ

This name, which means Noble Society, denotes a reform group within Hinduism, founded on April 10, 1875, in Bombay by Dayananda Sarasvati (1824–1883). He was a Hindu follower of Siva who became disillusioned at age fourteen; between the ages of twenty-one and thirty-nine he was a wandering religious mendicant in India. The last twenty years of his life were spent on preaching tours around India.

Both Hindus and Sikhs eventually joined the group, which was strongly anti-Moslem and anti-Christian. The doctrine was unitarian, egalitarian, and nationalistic. The group's slogan was "Back to the Vedas!" It interpreted Hinduism in a strictly monotheistic way, claiming a return to the purity of early Vedic tradition. The founder preached that the Vedas, properly interpreted (*i.e.*, by himself), were sufficient for achieving salvation. He denounced the Hindu traditions of caste, image worship, and child marriage. After his death a schism occurred, but the group is still active in education and charity.

Source:
Farquhar, J.N. *Modern Religious Movements in India.* New York: Macmillan, 1919.

Shoko Asahara, see AUM SUPREME TRUTH

Muzaffer al-Ashki, see HALVETI-JERRAHI ORDER OF NEW YORK

R.H. Askew, see GENERAL CONFERENCE OF THE EVANGELICAL BAPTIST CHURCH

ASSEMBLIES OF GOD

U.S. PENTECOSTAL group with branches in seventy-two countries, started in 1914 by E.N. Bell and J. Roswell Flowers in Hot Springs, Arkansas, and now based in Springfield, Missouri. It has been one of the largest Pentecostal churches, operating eleven colleges, an active publishing outfit, and a large missionary organization out of which came many splinter groups and independent movements such as the LATTER RAIN MOVEMENT, the MANIFEST SONS OF GOD, and the CHRISTIAN GROWTH MINISTRIES.

ASSEMBLIES OF THE LORD JESUS CHRIST, INC.

U.S. PENTECOSTAL group formed in 1952 through the merger of the Asemblies of the Church of Jesus Christ, the Jesus Only Apostolic Church of God, and the Church of the Lord Jesus Christ. It is based in Memphis, Tennessee.

A huge crowd throngs to an Assembly of God annual rally in Winter Park, Florida, to hear Christian celebrities give testimony to their faith.

ASSEMBLIES OF YAHWEH

Adventist group founded in 1966 in Baltimore by Jacob O. Meyer. The group is totally Old Testament–oriented, keeping all its commandments, and being non-Trinitarian. Tithing, nonviolence, and conscientious objection to military service are also advocated. The Sacred Name Broadcast, a radio ministry, is a major part of the group's activities. It is headquartered in Bethel, Pennsylvania.

See also SACRED NAME MOVEMENT

ASSEMBLIES OF YAHWEH (MICHIGAN)

Adventist, Sabbatarian group founded in 1939 in Holt, Michigan. It ascribes special importance to the sacred name Yahweh, which members believe has been corrupted and neglected and should be put back into daily use. In addition they advocate the Old Testament dietary laws, the Jewish festivals, tithing, and divine healing.

See also SACRED NAME MOVEMENT

ASSEMBLY OF CHRISTIAN CHURCHES, INC., THE

Spanish-speaking PENTECOSTAL group founded in New York City in 1939 when BETHEL CHRISTIAN TEMPLE joined other Spanish-speaking groups to form the new group. It engages in missionary activities all over the world.

See also CONCILIO OLAZABAL DE IGLESIAS LATINO AMERICANO

19

Edgar Cayce, known as the "sleeping prophet."

ASSEMBLY OF CHRISTIAN SOLDIERS

U.S. Christian group, affiliated with the Ku Klux Klan, and committed to white supremacy and racial segregation.

See also IDENTITY MOVEMENT

ASSEMBLY OF YAHVAH

Adventist group started in 1949 in Emory, Texas, by Lorenzo Dow Snow (1913–   ) and E.B. Adam. Snow was a member of the ASSEMBLIES OF YAHWEH (MICHIGAN) but disagreed with that group over the spelling of the sacred name. In 1968 Wilburn Stricklin became the group leader. Doctrines include adherence to Old Testament dietary laws, tithing, and faith healing. The group operates Missionary Dispensary Bible Research, which produced the *Restoration of Original Sacred Name Bible*. The book uses Yahvah, Elohim, and Yashua as sacred names in its text.

See also SACRED NAME MOVEMENT

ASSOCIATED CHURCHES OF GOD

Group founded in 1974 by former members of the WORLDWIDE CHURCH OF GOD who disagreed with church policies. Specifically, the dissenters rejected tithing in favor of free-will offerings, and the theocratic government maintained by Herbert W. Armstrong in favor of a congregational governing structure.

ASSOCIATED GOSPEL CHURCHES

U.S. Fundamentalist group founded by W.O.H. Garman. Its membership came from former Methodist Protestant congregations that refused to enter the Methodist merger of 1939. The group believes in DISPENSATIONALISM. Group head-quarters are in Pittsbugh, Pennsylvania, and its missions operate all over the world.

ASSOCIATION FOR RESEARCH AND ENLIGHTENMENT, INC. (A.R.E)

Occultist organization with a strong Christian bent, headquartered in Virginia Beach, Virginia, and devoted to the teachings of Edgar Cayce, known as the "sleeping prophet." Cayce (1877–1947) became famous among U.S. occultists for his "readings," given in a trance state, during which he made "medical diagnoses" as well as prophecies.

Founded in 1931, the group describes itself as "made up of individuals interested in spiritual growth, parapsychological research, and the work of Edgar Cayce...Central to the philosophy of these (Cayce's) readings is the premise that man is a spiritual being whose purpose on earth is to reawaken and apply this knowledge. Meditation as well as other principles of physical, mental and spiritual attunement are studied and practiced."

The A.R.E. doctrine combines belief in reincarnation, "auras," Christianity, astrology, and a variety of "psychic discoveries." Since the 1950s the Association has been headed by Hugh Lynn Cayce (1906–1983), son of the founder, and then by Charles Thomas Cayce, his grandson.

See also LOGOS WORLD UNIVERSITY

ASSOCIATION FOR THE UNDERSTANDING OF MAN, THE

U.S. spiritualist-Christian group founded by Ray Stanford in the 1960s. Stanford's "readings," which have been published in several volumes, deal with illness and healing, meditation, psychic communications, the supraphysical functions of endocrine glands, marriage, and death.

ASSOCIATION INTERNATIONALE DES CLUBS ARCHEDIA SCIENCES & TRADITIONS

Also known as "Clubs Archedia," this international occultist movement was founded in Geneva, Switzerland, in 1984 by Luc Jouret (1947–). The group is devoted to "natural healing" as well as to reviving the medieval Templar Order. Branches have operated in Europe and North America.

ASSOCIATION OF PENTECOSTAL ASSEMBLIES

PENTECOSTAL group founded in 1921 in Atlanta, Georgia. In 1936 it merged with the National and International Pentecostal Missionary Union to form THE INTERNATIONAL PENTECOSTAL ASSEMBLIES.

ASSOCIATION OF SANANDA AND SANAT KUMARA

U.S. Christian-occultist group founded by Dorothy Martin (known as Sister Thedra). Her early group became famous under the name Lake City Group after being portrayed in a well-known psychological study. Mrs. Martin (named Marian Keech in the study) claimed to have received messages from a space being named Sananda warning her about a flood that would destroy most of North America. The date was announced as December 1953, and members expected the end of the world and their own salvation. After the prophecy failed, some of the group members maintained their faith. Mrs. Martin claimed that the world was saved by that

faith. She made predictions about various other disasters that also failed to materialize. These events took place in Chicago in late 1953, but the leader continued her extraterrestrial contacts. She joined the BROTHERHOOD OF THE SEVEN RAYS for several years, and in 1965 she founded the Association, which distributes her communications from various masters, mainly Sananda, otherwise known as Jesus Christ.

Source:

Festinger, L., Riecken, H.W., and Schachter, S. *When Prophecy Fails.* New York: Harper & Row, 1956.

ASSOCIATION OF SEVENTH-DAY PENTECOSTAL ASSEMBLIES

International PENTECOSTAL group with branches in the United States, Canada, Ghana, and Nigeria, founded in 1967 by members of several Sabbatarian churches. Members follow Old Testament commandments and practice faith healing.

ASTARA FOUNDATION

Spiritualist-Theosophical-Christian group founded in 1951 in Santa Monica, California, by Robert and Earlyne Chaney with the goal of being "a center of all religions and philosophies, a school of the ancient mysteries and an institute of psychic research." The group also promotes "healing."

Robert Chaney (1913–) was earlier a founder of the SPIRITUALIST EPISCOPAL CHURCH and a prominent medium at Camp Chesterfield, near Anderson, Indiana, one of the most important centers of spiritualism in the United States. The group has had branches in Europe and Africa.

Source:

Judah, J.S. *The History and Philosophy of the Metaphysical Movements in America.* Philadelphia: Westminster, 1967.

ATHANOR FELLOWSHIP

Neo-pagan group founded in the 1970s in Boston by Andras Corban Arthen and Deirdre Pulgram Arthen, which describes itself as "...a family of traditional magical groups which follow the practice of the GLAINN SIDHR ORDER." The Fellowship is affiliated with the COVENANT OF THE GODDESS.

See also EARTHSPIRIT COMMUNITY

ATLANTEANS

British spiritualist-occultist group founded in 1957 in London and led by Jacqueline Murray. Members of the group believe in the existence of the ancient island of Atlantis, which was populated by earthmen with Venusian souls. Messages have been reported from Helio-Aracnophus, high priestess of Atlantis. "Spiritual healing" is practiced, and occult traditions such as astrology and palmistry are taught.

Source:

Evans, C. *Cults of Unreason.* London: Harrap, 1973.

ATMANIKETAN ASHRAM

U.S. Hindu monastic residence founded in 1971 by Sadhu Loncontirth in Pomona, California. It is devoted to the teachings of SRI AUROBINDO.

See also CALIFORNIA INSTITUTE OF ASIAN STUDIES; MATAGIRI

ATOM FOUNDATION

Christian-occultist group founded by Michael Francis in Anchorage, Alaska, in the early 1980s. It is loosely affiliated with the LOGOS WORLD UNIVERSITY CHURCH.

AUM CENTER FOR SELF-REALIZATION

Religious commune founded by Ken and Mona Piller around 1970 in Kalispell, Montana. It is devoted to Eastern yoga, meditation, and "natural healing."

AUM SUPREME TRUTH (Aum Shinrikyo)

International Buddhist-Taoist-Hinduist group with branches in Japan and the United States, founded in 1986 and led by Shoko Asahara. It offers its members "real Initiation," "Astral Initiation," and "Causal Initiation." The goal of the group is "spiritual enlightenment." According to its publications, "After passing through Earthly Initiation which purifies one's consciousness, Astral Initiation which purifies one's subconsciousness, over 2,000 members in Japan have promoted their spiritual growth remarkably, and experienced astral projection and feelings of supreme bliss within half a year." Members are encouraged to leave their families and adopt a monastic life. In 1989 Shoko Asahara ran unsuccessfully in the elections for the Japanese parliament.

Samael Aunweur, see GNOSTIC ASSOCIATION OF ANTHROPOLOGY AND SCIENCE

Aurobindo Ghose, see SRI AUROBINDO

AUSAR AUSET SOCIETY

Rosicrucian group founded by R.A. Straughn, also known as Ra Un Nefer Amen, around 1975 in New York. The name is derived from the supposed ancient alternate names of the Egyptian gods Isis and Osiris. Straughn was a member of the ROSICRUCIAN ANTHROPOSOPHIC LEAGUE in the 1970s and formed the Society specifically to serve African Americans. The group operates on the East Coast.

See also ROSICRUCIANS

AVALON COMMUNITY

JESUS MOVEMENT evangelical group founded around 1970 in Akron, Ohio. It has been very active in media productions.

B

Babaji, see INTERNATIONAL BABAJI KRIYA YOGA SANGAM

Babaji Nagaraj, see HAIDAKHAN SAMAJ; INTERNATIONAL BABAJI KRIYA YOGA SANGAM

BABA LEAGUE THE

Sufi-oriented syncretistic group based in Berkeley, California. In existence since the 1960s, it is devoted to the teachings of Meher Baba.

See also MEHER BABA, FRIENDS OF; SUFISM REORIENTED

Joseph Babalola, see ALADURA

BABISM

Millenarian Islamic sect that developed out of the messianic Shiite tradition, founded by Mirza Ali Muhammad (1819–1850) of Shiraz, Iran, known as the Bab. Muhammad proclaimed himself to be the Bab (Gate) in 1844, a thousand years after the disappearance of the 12th imam, according to Islamic Shiite tradition. (In the Shiite Muslim tradition, Muhammad ibn al-Hannifiya, who disappeared or died in 880 C.E., is the Hidden Imam, who is in hiding and will come back one day to restore peace and justice.) The Bab, in Shiite lore, was supposed to announce the coming of one greater than himself, who would open a new era of peace and justice. At first Mirza's claim was welcomed, but when he started deviating from the Islamic tradition the reaction was violent. In 1848 the Babis declared publicly their secession from Is-lam, and two years later Muhammad was executed by a firing squad.

The leadership was then assumed by two half-brothers, Yahia Nuri (1830–1912), known as Sabh-i Azal, and Mirza Husayn Ali Nuri (1817–1892), known as Baha Allah. Later a split in the movement occurred when the former claimed to be the appointed successor while the latter said that he was the prophet foretold by the Bab. Followers of Baha Allah started a new movement, BAHAI. The followers of Yahia Nuri, known as Azalis or Bayanis, continued the tradition of Babism.

The sacred book is *al-Bayan*, written by Ali Muhammad. According to that book, some elements of traditional Islamic law are abolished, and a promise is made of a prophet to come. The number nineteen has central significance. A calendar of nineteen months, having nineteen days each, was created.

Source:

Smith, P. *The Babi and the Bahai Religions: From Messianic Shiism to a World Religion.* Cambridge: Cambridge University Press, 1987.

BAHAI

Heterodox Moslem sect developed in the late 19th century out of the BABISM movement in Iran. It has proselytized successfully in the West, so that now most members are Westerners and Bahaism is an international religion with followers on all continents.

The founder, Mirza Husayn Ali Nuri (1817–1892), known as Baha Allah ("Glory of God"), was a Babist who, while in exile and in prison, became convinced that he himself was the prophet or the Messenger of God whose coming was announced by the Bab. He wrote the group's scripture, *Kitab-i-Aqdas*. In 1863 he announced that he was the promised "Manifestation of God." After his death, his son Abbas Effendi (1844–1921), known as Abdu'l-Baha ("Servant of Baha"), was recognized as leader. Beginning in 1908, when he was released from prison after the "Young Turks" political changes in the Ottoman Empire, he undertook successful missionary work all over the world, especially in English-speaking countries, but also in India and Japan. In 1921 the leadership passed to the founder's grandson, Shoghi Effendi (1897–1957). After the latter's death in 1957 the movement was reorganized and placed under a nine-member body known as the Universal House of Justice. The world center of Bahaism and its holy places is in Israel. Its holiest shrines are concentrated in the Haifa area, where the founder worked and died; the Shrine of the Bab, with its golden dome, is one of Haifa's best-known landmarks. The Bahai organization in the United States is known as the National Spiritual Assembly (NSA) of Bahais in the United States. A National Spiritual Assembly (NSA) exists in more than 100 countries.

Bahaism, having distanced itself from Islam, claims to be a universalist religion proclaiming the religious unity of mankind and human equality. The religious prophecies of all past religions are supposedly being fulfilled through Bahaism.

Baha Allah is described as the messianic figure expected by Judaism, Christianity, Islam, Zoroastrianism, Hinduism, and Buddhism. Earlier prophets are recognized, but with the coming of Baha Allah, the "Manifestation of God," a new era is

said to have begun, to last 5,000 years. It is to lead to the Bahai Cycle, lasting 500,000 years, but only after a global catastrophe, the disintegration of the present world order.

The sect has rules covering prayers, fasting, marriage, divorce, and burial and prohibitions against political activity, homosexuality, and the use of drugs. Bahais of Middle Eastern origin are expected to follow special rules and to pay 19 percent of their savings to the group. Bahais meet on the first day of each of the nineteen months, each having nineteen days, in the Bahai calendar, which started in 1844. The meetings are devoted to scripture readings. Local congregations are tightly knit, and the private lives of members are closely supervised by the congregation and its leaders. Although there is no involvement in politics, Bahais support the ideal of a world government and the activities of the United Nations. Bahais have suffered persecution in various Islamic countries.

See also NEW HISTORY SOCIETY

Sources:

Miller, W.M. *What Is the Bahai Faith?* Grand Rapids, MI: Eeerdmans, 1977.

Smith, P. *The Babi and the Bahai Religions: From Messianic Shiism to a World Religion.* Cambridge: Cambridge University Press, 1987.

BAHAIS UNDER THE HEREDITARY GUARDIANSHIP

Known also as Orthodox Bahais, or Remeyites, this international BAHAI splinter group was founded in 1960 by Charles Mason Remey (1875–1974). Following the

Abdu'l–Baha (Courtesy U.S. Baha'i Office of Public Information)

A Bahai house of worship in Wilmette, Illinois, one of seven in the world.

death of Shoghi Effendi in 1957, Remey became a member of the Bahai collective leadership, known as Hands of the Cause and Chief Stewards. In 1960 he proclaimed himself the Second Guardian of the Faith and was declared a Covenant-Breaker by the other members of the leadership, thus being excommunicated.

According to the group's doctrine of the great global catastrophe, major changes in the earth's crust would lead to the rise of the seas and the death of two thirds of humanity. Remey predicted in 1960 that a catastrophic flood would inundate most of the United States and urged his followers to move to the Rocky Mountains. This catastrophe was initially prophesied for 1963 and then postponed to 1995.

Source:

Smith, P. *The Babi and Bahai Religions: From Messianic Shiism to a World Religion.* Cambridge: Cambridge University Press, 1987.

BAHAIS UNDER THE PROVISIONS OF THE COVENANT (BUPC)

U.S. schismatic BAHAI group founded in 1971 by Leland ("Doc") Jensen (1913–   ), a chiropractor. Jensen left the official United States Bahai organization in 1960 and joined the BAHAIS UNDER THE HEREDITARY GUARDIANSHIP. Noting the predictions of Charles Mason Remey about the impending flood that would cover the low-lying areas of the United States in 1963, Jensen moved to Missoula, Montana, where he opened a chiropractic office in 1964. He then dropped out of the Bahai faith altogether. In 1969 he was convicted of sex offenses and sentenced to twenty years in prison. In prison, Jensen reported having a series of revelations and claimed several identities mentioned in the Bible. Jensen combined Bahai teachings, occult ideas, and Christian eschatology to create the BUPC credo. He predicted a nuclear holocaust in 1980, followed by a thousand years of peace for those who would join BUPC and save themselves from destruction. He was paroled in 1973 and immediately started recruiting followers.

April 29, 1980, at 5:55 pm was the time specified by Jensen for a nuclear war to destroy one third of humanity. That would be followed by twenty years of further upheavals, starvation, revolutions, and natural disasters, and in the year 2000 God's Kingdom would be established and 1,000 years of peace would follow.

About 150 followers made preparations for the nuclear holocaust. When it did not take place, revised predictions were issued. The group entered a period of crisis and decline, but managed to survive.

BAHAI WORLD FEDERATION
BAHAI dissident organization uniting various groups in opposition to the official leadership of Shoghi Effendi, founded in 1950 in Acre, Israel, by Amin Effendi, the last surviving grandson of Mirza Husayn Ali Nuri, known as Baha Allah, the founder of the Bahais.

BAHAI WORLD UNION
Known also as the World Union of Universal Religion and Universal Peace, this international BAHAI dissident group was founded in 1930 by followers of the American Ruth White and the German Wilhelm Herrigel. Based mainly in Germany, it was in existence until May 1937, when all Bahai activities in Germany were banned by the Nazis. In 1948 it was revived by Hermann Zimmer in Stuttgart, Germany. See also NEW HISTORY SOCIETY

Frederick Bailes, see SCIENCE OF MIND CHURCH

Frank and Martha Baker, see WISDOM INSTITUTE OF SPIRITUAL ACTION

George Baker, see FATHER DIVINE MOVEMENT

Jim Bakker, see PRAISE THE LORD

Guy and Edna Ballard, see "I AM"

Bambi Baaba, see SSERULANDA SPIRITUAL PLANETARY COMMUNITY

Bamulonda, see WATCHMAN HEALING MISSION

Sasipada Banerjea, see SADHARANA DHARMA SABHA

John Gayner Banks, see INTERNATIONAL ORDER OF ST. LUKE THE PHYSICIAN

Baptist Church of Christ, see DUCK RIVER (AND KINDRED) ASSOCIATION OF BAPTISTS

BAPTIST MOVEMENT OF DIVINE HEALING-MEDIATION, THE

Christian-spiritualist group founded in 1953 in Jacksonville, Florida, which believes that the Bible gives proof of reincarnation.

Harrison D. Barrett, see NATIONAL SPIRITUALIST ASSOCIATION OF CHURCHES

Don Basham, see CHRISTIAN GROWTH MINISTRIES

BASIC BIBLE CHURCHES OF AMERICA

U.S. Protestant organization, offering ministry ordination by mail.

Basketmakers, see MASOWE APOSTLES

Muhaiyaddeen M.R. Bawa, see GURU BAWA FELLOWSHIP

Ern Baxter, see CHRISTIAN GROWTH MINISTRIES

BEIT ASSAPH

Israeli MESSIANIC JUDAISM group founded in the early 1980s in Netanya by David Loden. Its doctrine and practices are PENTECOSTAL.

BEIT IMMANUEL

Israeli Hebrew Christian charismatic group established in the 1970s in Tel-Aviv by Henry Knight, who went to Israel as an Anglican missionary. A branch known as HaMa'ayan was founded in the 1980s in Kfar Saba, 20 miles north of Tel Aviv.
See also HEBREW CHRISTIANITY

BELIEVERS IN THE COMMANDMENTS OF GOD

African-American, Adventist, Sabbath-keeping congregation in New York City, which existed independently prior to 1956. In that year it became part of THE UNIFICATION ASSOCIATION OF CHRISTIAN SABBATH KEEPERS.
See also SEVENTH-DAY ADVENTISTS

E.N. Bell, see ASSEMBLIES OF GOD

Anthony Benik, see UNIVERSAL CHRIST CHURCH

Elbert Benjamine, see CHURCH OF LIGHT

John G. Bennett, see CLAYMONT SOCIETY; COOMBE SPRINGS; GURDJIEFF GROUPS; INSTITUTE FOR THE COMPARATIVE STUDY OF HISTORY, PHILOSOPHY, AND THE SCIENCES

Roger Benson, see FINDHORN FOUNDATION

BEREAN BIBLE FELLOWSHIP

Fundamentalist, Dispensationalist group, centered in the U.S. Pacific Southwest.
See also DISPENSATIONALISM; FUNDAMENTALISM

BEREAN BIBLE FELLOWSHIP (CHICAGO)

U.S. Fundamentalist, Dispensationalist group founded in 1970 by Cornelius Stam

as a result of schism with the GRACE GOS-PEL FELLOWSHIP.
See also DISPENSATIONALISM; FUNDA-MENTALISM

BEREAN BIBLE STUDENTS CHURCH
Offshoot of JEHOVAH'S WITNESSES started in Cicero, Illinois, in the 1960s.

Berean Fellowship International, see WORLD RENEWAL, INCORPORATED

BEREAN FUNDAMENTAL CHURCHES
Fundamentalist, evangelical group started in 1936 by Ivan E. Olsen, with headquarters in North Platte, Nebraska.

Moses Berg ("David," "Mo"), see CHILDREN OF GOD

Diane Berke, see INTERFAITH FELLOWSHIP

H. Charles Berner, see ABILITISM

Oskar Ernst Bernhardt, see GRAIL MESSAGE

Erika Bertschinger, see ORDEN FIAT LUX

Annie Besant, see THEOSOPHICAL ORDER OF SERVICE; THEOSOPHICAL SOCIETY

BESHARA TRUST
Western Sufi school founded in 1971 in England by Bulent Rauf (?–1987) in cooperation with J.G. Bennett. It is devoted to the teachings of Muhyiddin Ibn Arabi (1165–1240), a 12th-century Sufi from Anadalusia. The group teaches the prac-tices of meditation and of *Zikr* or "Rememoration," the classical Sufi ceremony described as "the naming and rememoration of God in His singleness and in His aspects of universality." Trust branches have operated in the United States, Europe, Australia, and Israel.
See also SUFI ORDER IN THE WEST

BETHANY BIBLE CHURCH AND RELATED INDEPENDENT BIBLE CHURCHES
Fundamentalist, Dispensationalist group started in the 1950s in the Phoenix, Arizona, area.

Betty Bethards, see INNER LIGHT FOUNDATION

BETH BNAI ABRAHAM (BBA)
African-American Jewish group founded by Arnold Josiah Ford, an associate of Marcus Garvey, in 1924 in New York City. Ford earlier had headed a similar organization, known as the Moorish Zionist Church. The group disbanded after Ford left the United States and disappeared in 1931. It was succeeded by the COM-MANDMENT KEEPERS CONGREGATION OF THE LIVING GOD.

Source:
Brotz, H.M. *The Black Jews of Harlem.* New York: Schocken Books, 1970.

BETHEL CHRISTIAN TEMPLE
Spanish-speaking PENTECOSTAL group founded in 1931 in New York City by Francisco Olazabal. In 1939 it joined other Spanish-speaking groups to form THE ASSEMBLY OF CHRISTIAN CHURCHES, INC.

See also CONCILIO OLAZABAL DE IGLESIAS LATINO AMERICANO

BETHEL MINISTERIAL ASSOCIATION

Formerly known as the Evangelistic Missionary Alliance, the Bethel Assembly, and the Bethel Baptist Assembly, this PENTECOSTAL group was founded in 1934 by A.F. Varnell in Evansville, Indiana. The group doctrine emphasizes faith healing; it puts less emphasis on speaking in tongues.

BETHEL TEMPLE

U.S. PENTECOSTAL group formed in 1914, based in the Northwest.

BETH MESSIAH

MESSIANIC JUDAISM group founded in Cincinnati in 1970 by Martin Chernoff.

BETH MESSIAH

MESSIANIC JUDAISM group based in Virginia Beach, Virginia, and founded by Joseph Rosenfarb in the 1970s.

BETH MESSIAH

MESSIANIC JUDAISM group based in New Hanover, New Jersey, and founded by Larry Feldman in the 1970s.

BETH MESSIAH CONGREGATION

MESSIANIC JUDAISM group that serves as headquarters of the UNION OF MESSIANIC JEWISH CONGREGATIONS, founded in the 1970s by Daniel C. Juster in Gaithersburg, Maryland.
See also HEBREW CHRISTIANITY

BETH YESHUA

U.S. Hebrew Christian group founded in 1972 by Raymond Cohen, a former associate of the American Board of Missions to the Jews Inc. Beth Yeshua has branches in New York City, Philadelphia, and Florida. It is operated and financed by American Messianic Missions, Inc.
See also CHOSEN PEOPLE MINISTRIES; HEBREW CHRISTIANITY

Paul V. Beyerl, see LOTHLORIEN

Yogi Bhajan, see HEALTHY HAPPY HOLY ORGANIZATION

Clifford Bias, see FIRST UNIVERSAL SPIRITUALIST CHURCH OF NEW YORK CITY; UNIVERSAL SPIRITUALIST ASSOCIATION

BIBLE CHURCHES (CLASSICS EXPOSITOR)

Independent Fundamentalist, Dispensationalist group in Oklahoma, founded by C.E. McLain in the 1940s. It publishes *The Classics Expositor.*

BIBLE FELLOWSHIP UNION

British offshoot of JEHOVAH'S WITNESSES founded in 1945 by A.D. Hudson, which claims to follow the original teachings of Charles Taze Russell (1852–1916). It is similar in doctrine to the U.S.-based PASTORAL BIBLE INSTITUTE.

BIBLE HOLINESS MOVEMENT

Conservative Protestant group with headquarters in Vancouver, British Columbia, organized in 1949 as the Bible Holiness Mission by Wesley H. Wakefield. Like the SALVATION ARMY, out of which it grew, it engages in social welfare activities. It also promotes interracial cooperation and integration.

BIBLE MISSIONARY CHURCH
U.S. conservative Protestant group founded in 1955 by Glenn Griffith, a former minister in the CHURCH OF THE NAZARENE. Doctrine emphasizes strict adherence to a simple life-style and behavior and bans television.

BIBLE PRESBYTERIAN CHURCH
U.S. Fundamentalist group founded in 1937 by Carl McIntire (1906–   ), in dissent from the ORTHODOX PRESBYTERIAN CHURCH, which McIntire and his followers considered too liberal. The group became known for its militant conservative stance and its anti-Communist crusades. In 1941 McIntire formed the American Council of Christian Churches (ACCC), and in 1948 the International Council of Christian Churches (ICCC), to unite churches with similar conservative views. In 1956 the majority of the members left to form the Evangelical Presbyterian Church, in protest against McIntire's policies. In 1969 McIntire was removed from the leadership of the ACCC and formed the American Christian Action Council (ACAC). Another group of members then left the Bible Presbyterian Church to form the WESTMINSTER BIBLICAL FELLOWSHIP.

See also FUNDAMENTALISM

Dr. Carl McIntire (left center) leads a parade in Chicago in 1975, urging America to resist further Communist takeovers in Southeast Asia and elsewhere.

BIBLE TEMPLE

PENTECOSTAL, Fundamentalist group founded in the 1980s in Portland, Oregon. It has been one of the centers of the RESTORATION MOVEMENT in North America.

BIBLE WAY CHURCH OF OUR LORD JESUS CHRIST WORLD WIDE

U.S. PENTECOSTAL group with African-American membership, founded in 1957 by Smallwood E. Williams and other former members of the CHURCH OF OUR LORD JESUS CHRIST OF THE APOSTOLIC FAITH.

Essie Binkley, see OLD TIME FAITH, INC.

BLACK HEBREWS (THE KINGDOM OF GOD NATION)

Known also as the Hebrew Israelites, or the Original Hebrew Israelite Nation, this African-American Jewish group was founded in Chicago, Illinois, in the 1960s. Its leader, Ben-Ami Carter, sometimes known as Ben-Ami Ben-Israel, was born in Chicago in 1940 as Gerson Parker. In the 1960s he became a storefront preacher of Abeita Culture Center, an evangelical church on Chicago's South Side. There he developed his theology of Black Hebrews. The basis of the faith is the claim that the original Israelites, written about in the Old Testament and exiled from Israel 4,000 years ago, were blacks. Descendants of those blacks should now go back to that land and claim it. The real heirs to ancient Judaism are said to be not contemporary Jews, but contemporary blacks.

The Black Hebrews' faith also includes belief in immortality. Their leader is

Ben-Ami Carter, founder and leader of the Kingdom of God Nation (Black Hebrews).

quoted as saying, "We are phasing out death and are on the path toward solving the mysteries of everlasting life. The Bible shows that some of the prophets lived to be 900 years old. I am positive that, following the way of righteousness, some of our people will live to be 600." With a view toward such longevity, presumably, the group does not consume meat, dairy products, tobacco, sugar, or alcohol. Members fast every Saturday and abstain from movies and television. They change their "slave names" to Hebrew names and practice polygamy. Before 1977, Ben-Ami Carter prophesied that year as the time of the final battle of Armageddon, after which his sect would dominate the world.

In the late 1960s Carter led his followers first to Liberia, then to Israel. The

Ben-Ami Carter holds a press conference on Mount Zion after Israeli authorities had ordered him and his followers to leave the country.

first Black Hebrew families arrived in Israel by late 1969. Not surprisingly, the Israeli government and the Israeli public have not taken kindly to their presence. According to Israeli law, most of them have entered Israel illegally. The government has tried to stop Black Hebrews from entering the country. Many have been denied entry.

Source:

Lounds, M., Jr. *Israel's Black Hebrews: Black Americans in Search of Identity.* Washington, DC: University Press of America, 1981.

Dorothe Blackmere, see CHURCH OF TZADDI

Jesse N. Blakeley, see UNDENOMI-

NATIONAL CHURCH OF THE LORD

Daniel Blanchard, see FAMILLE DE NAZARETH (COMMUNE DE NAZARETH)

Helena Petrovna Blavatsky, see THEOSOPHY

BLUE ROSE MINISTRY

Occultist group founded in Arizona in the 1970s, offering messages from extraterrestrials.

B'NAI NOACH ("Children of Noach")

Also known as the Noachide movement, and officially known as Agudat Keren B'nai No'ach, this Jewish-oriented group was started in the 1970s by Vendyl Jones, a former Baptist minister, in Fort Worth,

Texas. Members are "Gentiles who follow the Laws of Noah, and practice Torah faith for non-Jews as defined by orthodox Judaism."

The group proclaims the value and superiority of Judaism, which should be recognized by all Christians. Members call upon gentiles to keep the "Seven Laws of Noah" according to Jewish traditions. A special Jewish liturgy, including a marriage ceremony and a prayerbook, are being prepared. The movement has been recognized and encouraged by Orthodox Jewish organizations in the United States and Israel. Branches have been started in Europe and West Africa.

See also EMMANUEL; FRAZIER CHAPEL

B'nai Or, see P'NAI OR

BO AND PEEP

Christian-UFO group started in 1975 by a former music professor, Marshall Herff Applewhite (1932–   ), and a registered nurse, Bonnie Lu Trousdale Nettles (1928–1985?), in Los Angeles. They called themselves Bo and Peep and were also known as "the Two," in reference to a New Testament prophecy about two witnesses. The group had at the height of its success about two hundred members. Its doctrine was known as Human Individual Metamorphosis (HIM), aiming at the liberation of humans from the endless cycle of reincarnation. The leaders claimed that they would fulfill the ancient prophecy by being assassinated and coming back to life three and a half days later. Following the resurrection, they would be lifted up by a UFO to the divine kingdom in outer space. The followers agreed, in preparation for the journey, to get rid of most material possessions and worldly attachments, including family and work.

Members of the group traveled around the United States recruiting members and proclaiming their prophecies. Followers were promised immortality, androgeneity, and perfection, provided they followed the rules and ideas of the leaders. Bonnie Nettles died in the mid-1980s of cancer, and no further details are known, since the group has been operating in complete secrecy.

BODY OF CHRIST

International Protestant Fundamentalist organization founded in Argentina in 1970 by Juan Carlos Ortiz, former Assembly of God minister. The organization is structured according to the "shepherding" principle, which provides for an authoritarian leadership and close supervision of members. This style has been the basis of the SHEPHERDING movement, which also includes CHRISTIAN GROWTH MINISTRIES and CHRISTIAN RESTORATION MINISTRIES.

BODY OF CHRIST, THE

Known officially as the Endtime Body—Christian Ministries, Inc., and also as the End Times Ministry, The Movement, or The Body, this U.S. PENTECOSTAL Adventist group was founded in the late 1960s by Sam Fife (1925–1979), a minister from Miami, and C.E. ("Buddy") Cobb, an airline pilot. Fife referred to himself as "the light of the world" and called on followers to separate themselves from their communities and families in preparation for the "fullness of time." To separate its members from the world in preparation for the Second Coming, The Body opened "wilder-

ness" farms in Mississippi, South America, Canada, and Alaska. Local chapters were quite autonomous and known by different names. Thus, the chapter in Green-town, Ohio, has been known as Christian Ministries, and the one in Hollywood, Florida, as Word Mission. Doctrine includes belief in de-mons and possession by demons, as well as the expectation of an imminent Second Coming.

See also MANIFEST SONS OF GOD

Giorgio Bongiovanni, see NON-SIAMOSOLI

William Booth, see SALVATION ARMY

BOSTON CHURCH OF CHRIST

Fundamentalist organization founded in Boston in 1980 by Kip McKean, growing out of the Lexington Church of Christ. It is a branch of the CROSSROADS CHURCHES OF CHRIST and is structured according to the SHEPHERDING principle, which provides for an authoritarian leadership and close supervision of members. This style has been the basis of the shepherding movement, or "discipleship," which includes the BODY OF CHRIST, CHRISTIAN GROWTH MINISTRIES, and CHRISTIAN RESTORATION MINISTRIES. The group has operated branches and missions in the United States, Latin America, and Europe.

See also NEW YORK CHURCH OF CHRIST

Lewis Bostwick, see CHURCH OF DIVINE MAN

Enid Brady, see MARA LA ASPARA

BRAHMA KUMARIS (RAJA YOGA)

Officially known as the Brahma Kumaris World Spiritual University (BKWSU), this international Hindu revival movement was founded in 1937 in Karachi by Dada Lekh Raj (1877–1969). A wealthy diamond merchant, he started having visions at the age of sixty and adopted the name of Prajapita Brahma. The group teaches the practice of Raja Yoga meditation, which does not require the use of mantras, special postures, or breathing exercises. Most active members of the group are celibate women. Brahama Kumaris operates the Brahma Kumaris World Spiritual University, which has branches all over the world, with most members in Europe and the United States and international headquarters in Mount Abu, India. The group operates the Global Co-Operation for a Better World, engaged in charity work around the world.

BRAHMA SAMAJ

Also known as Brahmo Samaj (the God Society or the Fellowship of Believers of the One True God), the Theistic Church of India, and the Unitarian Union, this Hindu revitalization movement was founded in 1828 by Ram Mohan Roy (1774–1833) in Calcutta. Roy was born into a wealthy Indian family and held a high position in the Indian civil service. After retiring at age forty-two, he devoted his life to religious writing, translations, and leadership. The Brahma Samaj developed out of the British India Unitarian Association, founded in 1827. The founder was first exposed to Islamic teachings and then studied Western languages and religions, which led him to found the Unitarian Association; followers of all theistic faiths met weekly for common prayers. He regarded contemporary Hinduism as a degeneration of earlier monotheism and promoted a return to the original unitarian doctrines.

After the founder's death, Debendranath Tagore (1817–1905) became leader, but the movement suffered a split in 1865 when the majority of members followed Kehsab Chandra Sen (1838–1884) into a new organization known as Brahma Samaj of India. Tagore represented more conservative Hindu views, since he was opposed to intercaste marriages and to the remarriage of widows. Unlike Roy, he was committed to a return to the ancient Vedas rather than to a rapprochement with Christianity. The group under the Tagore leadership, which became known as the Adi Brahma Samaj, concentrated on trying to reform Hinduism. Sen's followers represented less conservative views. The Brahma Samaj of India was later split into the SADHARAN BRAHMO SAMAJ (Universal Society of God) and THE CHURCH OF THE NEW DISPENSATION.
See also ARYA SAMAJ; PRATHANA SAMAJ

BRANCH DAVIDIANS (BRANCH SEVENTH-DAY ADVENTISTS)

Adventist group started near Waco, Texas, in 1935. Members of the Branch in its various organizational forms have followed the teachings of Victor T. Houteff, which deviated from those of the SEVENTH-DAY ADVENTIST ASSOCIATION. After Houteff's death and the discrediting of his wife because of the failure of a prophecy, Ben Roden (d. 1978) renamed the group the Branch Davidians. Roden's son, who took over from his mother, was challenged in 1987 by Vernon Howell, an ousted member. Howell's trial on charges of attempted murder ended in mistrial; the charges were later dropped.

Howell in 1990 changed his name to Koresh. He recruited intensively, combining biblical exhortation with rock music. He fathered numerous children by women members. He stockpiled Mount Carmel with a formidable arsenal. On February 28, 1993, more than 100 federal officers attempted to arrest Koresh on a weapons charge. After a 45-minute gun battle, four officers were dead and many wounded. A 51-day standoff ensued, puncuated by hours of telephone negotiations and intermittent release of children and a few adults. On April 19, the F.B.I. began firing tear gas into the compound. Within hours, members of the cult set the frame buildings afire. Of some 80 persons, including at least 17 children, only nine persons escaped the inferno. The compound was utterly destroyed.

BRANHAM TABERNACLE

Known also as Branhamites, or END TIME BELIEVERS, this PENTECOSTAL group was founded by William Marrion Branham (1909–1965) in Indiana in 1946. Branham became known during his lifetime for his claims of visions and angelic voices speaking to him. He also became known as a faith healer. His doctrine, as presented in many sermons, deviated from mainstream Christianity in rejection of Trinitarianism and emphasis on belief in Jesus Christ as God. Missions around the world have made his message internationally known, especially in Asia and Africa.

BRIDGE CENTER FOR SPIRITUAL STUDIES, THE

Christian-Theosophical, "New Age" group founded in 1975 in Wheaton, Illinois, by

Brent D. Ferré. In 1985 it moved to Arizona. It is "... devoted to facilitating Self-Awareness and Spiritual Empowerment through the Christine Philosophy." Its doctrine includes mostly Theosophical concepts. The group has operated mainly by mail.

See also THEOSOPHY

BRIDGE MEDITATION CENTER, THE

Occultist group based in Georgia and founded around 1970, with practices and beliefs combining "meditation, new thought principles, aquarian age living, Christ truth teaching, Zen and Tibetan Buddhist philosophy, and universal scriptures."

BRIDGE TO FREEDOM, THE

Known today as the New Age Church of the Christ, U.S. Theosophical group founded in the 1950s in New York by Geraldine Innocente and other members of the "I AM" group.

The group's teachings are based on messages received from the Ascended Masters. The Bridge to Freedom has inspired several similar groups around the world.

See also LICHTKREIS MICHAEL; SUMMIT LIGHTHOUSE

Charlotte Bright, see TEMPLE OF UNIVERSAL LAW

John Bright, see CHURCH OF GOD BY FAITH

George Brinkman, see PENTECOSTAL CHURCH OF GOD OF AMERICA

BRITISH ISRAELISM

Known also as Anglo-Israelism, this belief system is shared by numerous Christian groups and individuals; it states that the modern "Celto-Saxon" nations (*i.e.*, Great Britain and the United States) are the "racial" and true descendants of the biblical "Children of Israel." This is related to the idea of the "Ten Lost Tribes," which were supposed to have existed in the ancient Kingdom of Israel and were then dispersed. British Israelism claims that some of them reached Britain.

Such ideas were held by the 17th-century Levellers, but the movement really started in the 19th century, following the visions of Richard Brothers (1757–1824), and with the writings of John Wilson (?–1870), F.R.A. Glover (1800–1881), and Edward Hine (1825–1891). In 1875 the Anglo-Israel Association was founded in London, and in 1919 the British Israel World Federation. These groups have promoted British Israelism through publications and lectures.

British Israelism represents a Fundamentalist position, asserting the literal truth of the Bible. Some of the groups have adopted Sabbatarianism. Numerous British-Israelist groups have operated in the United States, where the movement had its own seminary, the Dayton Theological Seminary, between 1947 and 1953.

The movement has attracted attention because of its racist prejudices and assertions in regard to all groups that are not considered Anglo-Saxon, be they African-Americans, Jews, or other "inferior races." British-Israelists in the United States have been the inspiration for the related, but not identical, IDENTITY MOVEMENT, which is a loose designation for a number of small groups.

Source:
Roy, R.L. *Apostles of Discord.* Boston: Beacon Press, 1953.

Eva Broch, see PATHWORK

Henry C. Brooks, see WAY OF THE CROSS CHURCH

Nona Brooks, see DIVINE SCIENCE CHURCH

BROTHERHOOD OF LIGHT

U.S. occultist group dating to 1876, when Emma Harding Britten presented it to the public in her book *Art Magic.* The group was headed by a scribe, an astrologer, and a seer, and astrology played a major role. Under the leadership of the astrologer Elbert Benjamine (1882–1951), also known as C.C. Zain, between the two World Wars, it developed into an international organization, also known as Church of Light, with branches across the United States and in Great Britain, Mexico, Canada, and Chile.

BROTHERHOOD OF THE CROSS AND STAR

Sometimes known as the Holy Apostles Community, this syncretistic African movement has strong Christian elements and some Hindu ones. It was started in Nigeria in 1954 by Offu Ebongo (1918–), known as the Father or Olumba Olumba Obu. The founder is believed to be an incarnation of Jesus Christ, and in that a successor to Krishna, and to protect members from disease and trouble. He is considered omnipotent and omniscient, in possession of "spiritual X-rays," which his followers also can operate. The mere mention of his initials, O.O.O., is believed to preserve from danger. "The Kingdom of God, which our Lord Jesus Christ had promised, has now been established." Members are called upon to follow a modest life-style and to avoid smoking, drinking, and fornication.

In Western Nigeria the Brotherhood founded the Aiyetoro ("happy city"), a socioreligious community that includes industry, hospitals, and schools and provides its members with the highest living standard of any village in the country. The Brotherhood also operates plantations and trade organizations. It has operated branches in the United States and Great Britain.

BROTHERHOOD OF THE WHITE TEMPLE

Communal Theosophical group founded in the 1930s by Maurice Doreal in Denver, Colorado. He claimed to be relying on the advice of Tibetan teachers through "soul travel" to Tibet; relayed messages dealing with Atlantis, Lemuria, and the Great Pyramid, and predicted an impending world catastrophe.
See also THEOSOPHY

BROTHER JULIUS

U.S. Christian-inspired group founded and led by Julius Schacknow (1924–). During his U.S. Navy service in World War II he experienced considerable difficulties, ending up in psychiatric hospitals. In 1947 he heard the "voice of God" and converted from Judaism to Christianity. He has

claimed to be Jesus Christ, back on earth for the Second Coming. Brother Julius practices faith healing. The group started in 1968 in New York City and in 1971 moved to Meriden, Connecticut. Since 1976 it has operated several successful business enterprises, specializing in real estate and construction. The founder has been accused of having sexual relations with underage female followers.

William Henry Francis Brothers, see OLD CATHOLIC CHURCH IN AMERICA

Charles Paul Brown and Berna-Deane Brown, see THE ETERNAL FLAME FOUNDATION

BRUDERHOF

Known officially as the Hutterian Brethren, and also as the Hutterian Society of Brothers, this Christian, communal, pacifist movement was founded in 1920 in Germany by Eberhard Arnold (1883–1935). Arnold's Christian Anabaptist ideas led to a merger with the Hutterites, which lasted until 1956. The group migrated to Great Britain, Paraguay, and then the United States, where it has remained since 1954 in several communal settlements. A British commune has been in existence since 1971.

Source:
Zablocki, B. *The Joyful Community*. Baltimore: Penguin, 1971.

David Bruggman, see CHURCH OF THE COVENANTS

Brunton Philosophic Foundation, see PAUL BRUNTON PHILOSOPHIC FOUNDATION

Frank N.D. Buchman, see MORAL REARMAMENT

Raymond Buckland, see SEAX-WICA SEMINARY

Zsuasznna Budapest, see DIANIC WICCADIANIC WICCA

BUILDERS, THE

Also known as Sunburst Farms, this syncretistic commune was founded, as Brotherhood of the Sun, by Norman Paulsen (known as Brother Norman), at Sunburst Ranch near Santa Barbara, California, in 1971. Paulsen had been a member of the SELF-REALIZATION FELLOWSHIP, and his beliefs combine Hindu ideas with Christianity. According to Paulsen, the Second Coming occurred on January 1, 1961, together with the coming of the Aquarian Age. "The Builders derives its name from the ancient ones referred to in Genesis as the Sons of God, who were on earth before the creation of man. These beings are Christ-conscious entities, responsible for the evolution of life forms in the expanding spheres of creation. The Builders of old and of present are the true Sons and Daughters of Divine Spirit." The group practices "the SUN meditation technique," vegetarianism, and the avoidance of drugs and alcohol.

BUILDERS OF THE ADYTUM (BOTA)

Occultist group inspired by the HERMETIC ORDER OF THE GOLDEN DAWN, founded in 1920 in New York by Paul Case (1894–1954). Its teachings, which are

mostly transmitted by correspondence, include use of Tarot, "healing, Kabbalah, and alchemy." They also include messages from the Masters in the Theosophical tradition.
See also THEOSOPHY

Source:
Ellwood, R.S. *Religious and Spiritual Groups in Modern America.* Englewood Cliffs, NJ: Prentice-Hall, 1973.

Robert Burton, see FELLOWSHIP OF FRIENDS

D.J. Bussell, see CHIROTHESIAN CHURCH OF FAITH

BUSSHO GOHNEN KAI

Japanese new religion, coming out of the Nichiren Shu tradition, started after World War II. It has been involved in politics since the 1960s and has taken a right-wing, nationalistic stance. In the 1970s it formed a right-wing religious group together with SEICHO-NO-IE and SEKAI KYUSEI-KYO. See also RISSHO KOSEI KAI

Richard Girnt Butler, see CHURCH OF JESUS CHRIST CHRISTIAN–ARYAN NATIONS

C

Eileen Caddy, Peter Caddy, see FINDHORN FOUNDATION

CAFH SPIRITUAL CULTURE SOCIETY
International Gurdjieff-inspired group devoted to "spiritual unfolding." According to official Cafh history, the group was founded in 1937 in Buenos Aires, Argentina, by Santiago Bovisio, known as Don Santiago, who acquired a following in the Spanish-speaking world and in the United States, Australia, and Israel. Members study the writings of Jorge Waxemberg, an Argentinian mystic who published the book *De La Mistica y Los Estados de Conciencia* in Buenos Aires in 1971.
See also GURDJIEFF GROUPS

Caillaux, see EVADISME

California Institute of Asian Studies, see CULTURAL INTEGRATION FELLOWSHIP

CALUMET PAGAN TEMPLE
Neo-pagan group founded by Richard Clarke in the 1960s, based in Calumet City, Illinois. The group is a member of the MIDWEST PAGAN COUNCIL.

CALVARY CHAPEL
U.S. Fundamentalist organization incorporating numerous independent congregations, especially on the West Coast, started by Chuck Smith in Costa Mesa, California, in 1965. There is some use of glossolalia and an active outreach ministry under the name of The Word for Today. Overseas operations have been extensive, including branches in Latin America, Europe, and West Africa.

CALVARY PENTECOSTAL CHURCH
PENTECOSTAL group founded in 1931 and active in the northwestern United States, with headquarters in Bellingham, Washington.

Alexander Campbell, see DISCIPLES OF CHRIST

CAMP FARTHEST OUT
Fundamentalist-NEW THOUGHT group devoted to prayer and faith healing, founded in 1930 by Glenn Clark, a member of the Plymouth Congregational Church in Minneapolis, Minnesota. The group has developed branches in Canada, Great Britain, and India.

CAMPHILL MOVEMENT
International ANTHROPOSOPHY subsidiary movement, devoted to taking care of retarded persons through "curative education" in cooperative farming communities. Founded in Scotland in 1940 by Karl Konig, in 1990 the movement had sixty communities in Europe, the Americas, South Africa, and Israel. The quality and the results of the work with the retarded have been considered remarkable by experts in the field. Farming is "byo-dynamic," or organic, using no chemicals, and following Steiner's ideas of "nature cycles." The Camphill Association of North America, founded in 1983, is made up of five communities.

CANDOMBLÉ
Syncretistic neo-African movement in Brazil, started in the 19th century. Its

Members of a Brazilian spiritualist movement, perform a ritual in honor of their goddess of the sea. In a Catholic country, they combine Catholicism with African and native Indian rituals.

pantheon of saints and spirits combines African and Roman Catholic figures, which guide the believers in seeking answers to life's problems.

CAO DAI

Vietnamese syncretistic, millenarian movement started as a secret society and growing into a large-scale movement after World War I. Begun in 1919 by Nguyen Van Chieu, a colonial civil servant, it was officially founded in 1926 by Le Van Trung. Membership was drawn from the lower middle class around Saigon. The doctrine is elaborate and is matched by a well-developed bureaucracy modeled

after the Roman Catholic Church and headed by a pope. The group claims to represent the final manifestation of God and combines Taoist, Buddhist, Confucian, and Christian traditions. Asian leaders, Europeans (*e.g.*, Victor Hugo), and Vietnamese personages are numbered among its saints. Membership is divided into nine levels, and moving up the scale requires devotion and self-denial. Members are vegetarian, but children are allowed meat several days a month.

Cao Dai was supported by church-owned corporations and members' contributions and operated a well-developed social welfare system. It was first tied to the French colonial administration. During the Japanese occupation the group's second pope, Pham Long Tac, supported Japan against the French and then supported the Bao Dai regime. The group had its own military force, fighting for the Japanese and then the French; in the early 1950s it fought against the Vietminh.

When Ngo Dinh Diem came to power in 1954, the Cao Dai controlled an entire province in South Vietnam. In April 1954 Ngo Dinh Diem defeated the Cao Dai militia, which was completely dissolved in 1956, but the local organizations survived. Cao Dai was neutral during the years of United States involvement in Vietnam, and since 1975 it has been free to operate.
See also HOA HAO

Carmel Henry Carfora, see NORTH AMERICAN OLD ROMAN CATHOLIC CHURCH

CARGO CULT

Collective term for a variety of nativist, syncretistic movements that have appeared most often in Oceania. They promote belief in obtaining "cargo," *i.e.,* manufactured goods and wealth, through spiritual means. Sometimes the expectation is that ancestors will return, delivering the "cargo."
See also GHOST DANCE

Sources:

Lanternari, V. *The Religions of the Oppressed.* New York: Knopf, 1963.

Maher, R.F. *New Men of Papua: A Study of Culture Change.* Madison: University of Wisconsin Press, 1961.

Worsley, P. *The Trumpet Shall Sound.* New York: Schocken, 1968.

CAROLINA EVANGELISTIC ASSOCIATION

PENTECOSTAL group founded in 1930 in Charlotte, North Carolina, by A.G. Garr (1874–1944), a former missionary for the CHURCH OF GOD (CLEVELAND, TENNESSEE) and a traveling revival preacher. The group is a member of the PENTECOSTAL FELLOWSHIP OF NORTH AMERICA.

Paul Case, see BUILDERS OF THE ADYTUM (BOTA)

Frank and William Casle, see FREE GOSPEL CHURCH, INC.

CATHEDRAL OF TOMORROW

Fundamentalist congregation founded in 1958 by Rex Humbard, Jr. Humbard came from a family of radio preachers and became one himself at an early age. In 1953 he founded the Calvary Temple in Akron, Ohio, and in 1958 decided to build the Cathderal in the same place. The main activity of the Cathedral was a television service broadcast over hundreds of stations in the United States. In the 1970s the organization ran into serious financial difficulties, but it recovered later.

CATHOLIC APOSTOLIC CHURCH

Known also as the Irvingites, after Edward Irving (1792–1834), whose teachings inspired it, this is an international millenarian movement. Irving, minister of the Caledonian Church in Hatton Garden, London, in 1825 started offering apocalyptic preaching that proclaimed the Second Coming of Jesus Christ, fixed for 1864. In preparation he called for a restructuring of the Christian church. In 1829 a larger church, the Regent Square Presbyterian

Church, was built for him, but his popularity was already in decline. In 1830 he was charged with heresy, and in 1833 he lost his pulpit. The group was actually organized in 1831, its main supporter being Henry Drummond (1786–1860), a wealthy Member of Parliament, whose estate became the center of the movement.

The doctrine rejected apostolic succession as adopted by most Christian churches, in favor of living apostles. Twelve apostles were designated, and in 1835 they were sent to inform the world of the Second Coming, addressing the Pope, among others. Their message was received with little enthusiasm. The Church attempted to revive the early practices of the Christian church by adopting the ritual and ornaments of the Roman Catholic Church as well as those of the Anglican and Greek churches. Practices include speaking in tongues and healing. During the 19th century the group experienced some success in Great Britain, Holland, Germany, and the U.S. The first U.S. branch was opened in 1851 in Potsdam, New York. In 1863 the group experienced its worse schism when German members who doubted the 1864 prediction defected to create the NEW APOSTOLIC CHURCH.

See also OLD APOSTOLIC CHURCH

CATHOLIC CHARISMATIC RENEWAL (CCR)

North American movement within the Roman Catholic Church, which started in California in 1958 and in Indiana in 1967. It involves introducing the historically Protestant traditions of Pentecostalism ("Baptism in the Spirit") into Catholic parishes. Glossolalia (speaking in tongues) is the most distinctive feature of the movement. Others include belief in healing and prophecy as gifts of the "Holy Spirit." The movement is sometimes referred to as Catholic Pentecostalism.

See also PENTECOSTAL

Source:

McGuire, M. *Pentecostal Catholics: Power, Charisma, and Order in a Religious Movement*. Philadelphia: Temple University Press, 1982.

Edgar Cayce, see ASSOCIATION FOR RESEARCH AND ENLIGHTENMENT; HOLISTIC COMMUNITY

Martin Cecil, see EMISSARIES OF DIVINE LIGHT

CENTER FOR CONSCIOUSNESS

NEW THOUGHT group based in New York City, founded in the 1980s by Theodore Smith.

CENTER FOR SPIRITUAL AWARENESS (CSA)

U.S. Hindu-inspired group created in 1962 by a merger of the CHURCH OF THE CHRISTIAN SPIRITUAL ALLIANCE and NEW LIFE WORLDWIDE. The group is headed by Roy Eugene Davis (1931–   ), who was a disciple of Paramahansa Yogananda of the SELF-REALIZATION FELLOWSHIP in Los Angeles in the 1950s. It is based in northeast Georgia, with branches elsewhere in the United States and in Europe. CSA's official doctrine is based on "man's certain destiny to spiritually awaken and consciously live in harmony with natural laws. Transcending the boundaries of sectarianism, while honoring all useful traditions, it encourages sincere seekers to enter into a process of needed self-transformation and to experi-ence the reality of God." The group practices Yogananda's technique of kriya yoga and collaborates with RELIGIOUS SCIENCE, NEW THOUGHT groups, and Hindu-oriented groups.

See also ANANDA COOPERATIVE VILLAGE; THE TEMPLE OF KRIYA YOGA

CENTER OF FIRST LIGHT, THE

New York City center founded by Turtle Heart (Anishinabe) in the 1980s, devoted to the preservation and propagation of Native American religious traditions. It is affiliated with the XAT AMERICAN INDIAN MEDICINE SOCIETY.

CENTER OF LIGHT COMMUNITY, THE

Occultist commune founded in Great Barrington, Massachusetts, in the late 1970s by Gene and Eva Graf. It is devoted to "healing" and growing "herbal remedies." The commune is affiliated with the Church of Christ-Consciousness, "a healing church believing in the divinity of the entire human family."

Robert Chaney, see ASTARA FOUNDATION; SPIRITUALIST EPISCOPAL CHURCH

Lewis Stuyvesant Chanler, see NEW HISTORY SOCIETY

Charismatic, see PENTECOSTAL

Ureal Vercilli Charles, see UNIVERSAL BROTHERHOOD

Haridas Chaudhuri, see CULTURAL INTEGRATION FELLOWSHIP

Martin Chernoff, see BETH MESSIAH

F.S. Cherry, see CHURCH OF GOD (BLACK JEWS)

Swami Chetananda, see NITYANANDA INSTITUTE

Chen Ye-su Chiao Hui, see TRUE JESUS CHURCH

Swami Chidananda, see DIVINE LIFE SOCIETY

Chidvilasananda, see SYDA FOUNDATION (SIDDHA YOGA DHAM ASSOCIATES)

CHILDREN OF GOD (COG)

Also known officially, since 1977, as the Family of Love (FOL), this Fundamentalist group was founded in California in 1968 by David Brandt Berg (1919–), who has adopted the names Moses Berg, Moses David, or "Mo." Berg started his leadership career as an evangelist for the CHRISTIAN AND MISSIONARY ALLIANCE. In 1964 he began work with radio and television evangelist Fred Jordan. In 1969 he had a group of followers called Revolutionaries for Jesus, in Huntington Beach, California, and became visible as part of what was known as the JESUS MOVEMENT or the Jesus Children. Until the end of 1971, Berg and his followers appeared regularly on a religious program, *Church in the Home*, run by Jordan. They also operated the American Soul Clinic, Inc.

In 1972, COG members started moving

to Europe. In the mid-1970s, finding himself in trouble with U.S. authorities and charged with various offenses, Berg found refuge in Libya, praising Muammar Khadafy as the "most remarkable voice of the Third World." Berg has communicated with his followers through the "MO letters," which contain "divine revelations" and secret knowledge. The group's teachings are contained in these letters by the leader, who is the sole authority over all matters. The teachings, though representative of evangelical Protestantism, are critical of the religious establishment, as they are of the political establishment. According to Berg, COG constitutes the latter-day Israel, heir to biblical promises to ancient Israel. Berg has been predicting a Great Confusion and Tribulation, to take place soon (1993?), after which Christ will rule on earth. The family of the founder is considered the Royal Family, divinely inspired and appointed to rule. There is a Council of Ministers and twelve bishops. The world is divided into twelve areas under the regional bishops. Berg believes that most of the world's resources and media are controlled by Jews, and that this worldwide conspiracy should, and will, be defeated.

Sources:
Davis, D. (Linda Berg). *The Children of God.* Grand Rapids: Zondervan, 1984.
Wallis, R. *The Elementary Forms of the New Religious Life.* London: Routledge & Kegan Paul, 1984.

John Chilembwe, see PROVIDENCE INDUSTRIAL MISSION

CHILTERN YOGA FOUNDATION
International Hindu organization founded in the 1980s by Swami Venkatesananda. Devoted to the teaching of "integral yoga," it has branches in North America, Australia, and South Africa.
See also SIVANANDA YOGA VEDANTA CENTERS

Chimnoy, see SRI CHIMNOY

CHINMAYA MISSION
International Hindu revival movement founded by Swami Chinmayananda in India in the 1950s. Branches in the West started developing in the 1960s in Europe and North America, but most followers are in India.

CHINOOK COMMUNITY
Syncretistic commune founded in the 1970s in Clinton, Washington, by Fritz Hull, a former Presbyterian minister, and Vivian Hull. It combines such themes as "Planetary Consciousness" with Christianity, in order to develop connections with mainline churches. Practices include silent meditation and prayer.

CHIROTHESIAN CHURCH OF FAITH
Theosophical-Christian group founded in 1917 in Los Angeles by D.J. Bussell. The group does not proselytize, but some meetings are open to the public.

Chitawala, see KITAWALA

Gurudev Shree Chitrabhanu, see JAIN MEDITATION INTERNATIONAL CENTER

Yonggi Cho, see FULL GOSPEL CENTRAL CHURCH

Members of the Children of God, wearing sackcloth and a yoke around the neck, march in "warning and mourning." They believe that theirs is the last generation to survive on earth.

Chogyam Trungpa, Rinpoche, see VARADHATU

CHOSEN PEOPLE MINISTRIES

Also known as Beth Sar Shalom, or Beth Sar Shalom Hebrew Christian Fellowship, this North American Hebrew-Christian organization was founded in 1894 in New York City by Leopold Cohn, a former Orthodox rabbi, as the American Board of Missions to the Jews (A.B.M.J.). Branches have operated in the United States and Canada.

CHRISTADELPHIANS

Also known as Brethren of Christ, this millenarian group was founded in 1844 in Birmingham and London by John Thomas, an English physician who also lived in the United States. It grew out of the DISCIPLES OF CHRIST. According to its doctrine, the millennium will be inaugurated by a resurrection, as the elect will gain everlasting life and the damned will be annihilated in hell. Christ will reign in Jerusalem, and the twelve tribes will be reunited there. The doctrine rejects Trinitarianism, and the group has no formal clergy. Members are pacifists and do not vote or hold political office. Branches have operated in Great Britain and the United States.

CHRISTANANDA YOGA ASHRAM

Syncretistic group based in California and founded by Sri Yogi Raj Evangelos Alexandrou. The group's doctrine combines Hindu, Islamic, and Eastern Christianity traditions. Practices included "deep meditation techniques from Tantra Yoga, Tao, Zen, Sufi, dancing and singing in joyous celebration and Christian mysticism."

CHRIST BROTHERHOOD

Known sometimes as the Messianic Brotherhood, this Christian commune was founded by Thomas Paterson Brown (1939–), known as "Paterson" and reportedly a former philosophy professor, in Eugene, Oregon, in 1968. The commune members, never numbering more than 50, moved around the United States, living in Santa Fe, New Mexico, Colorado, and Missoula, Montana, then returning to Eugene in 1981. There, in September 1981, the founder was convicted of third-degree rape and third-degree sodomy and sentenced to five years in prison. He broke his parole conditions in 1985 and disappeared. Group members then resurfaced in Europe and Israel.

CHRIST CATHOLIC CHURCH (DIOCESE OF BOSTON)

OLD CATHOLIC group founded in Boston in 1965 by Karl Pruter. In 1974 its base was moved to Phoenix, Arizona.

CHRIST CENTER FOR POSITIVE LIVING

NEW THOUGHT group founded by John McClain in Mesa, Arizona, in the early 1980s. The group's doctrine follows: "It is God's will that every individual on the face of the earth live a healthy happy and prosperous life; life is within the reach of each one of us and the way to its attainment begins with the realization that the Kingdom of God is within us, waiting for us to bring it into expression; we can bring this kingdom forth by practicing the universal principles handed down through the ages by Jesus Christ; the basis for right thinking is Love."

Alice Christensen, see LIGHT OF YOGA SOCIETY

CHRIST FAITH MISSION
PENTECOSTAL group founded by Finis E. Yoakum (?–1920) in Los Angeles in 1908 as the Old Pisgah Tabernacle. Yoakum also established a model Christian commune named Pisgah Grande in 1914; it was in existence until the 1920s. The group emphasizes faith healing.

CHRISTIAN AND MISSIONARY ALLIANCE (CMA or C & MA)
U.S. evangelical "HOLINESS" group founded in 1897 by Albert Benjamin Simpson, a former Presbyterian minister. It emphasizes cooperation with other Christian groups and the practice of faith healing and has operated missions around the world.
See also CHRISTIAN NATION CHURCH, U.S.A.

CHRISTIAN ASSEMBLY
Christian-NEW THOUGHT group founded by William Farwell in 1900 in San Jose, California, as a branch of the HOME OF TRUTH. In 1920 it separated from that movement, seeking a stronger Christian emphasis.

CHRISTIAN BELIEVERS CONFERENCE
Also known as the Christian Believers Assembly, this millenarian group was founded in 1910 in Chicago by a group of dissenters from the teachings of Charles Taze Russell in the Watch Tower Bible and Tract Society, led by H.C. Hennings, M.L. McPhail, and A.E. Williamson. There were several doctrinal disagreements over the status of Russell himself and over the meaning of the Lord's supposed presence on earth since 1874.
See also JEHOVAH'S WITNESSES

CHRISTIAN CATHOLIC APOSTOLIC CHURCH IN ZION
Earlier known as the Universal Christian Church, this U.S. millenarian group was founded by John Alexander Dowie (1847–1907) in 1896. Born in Edinburgh, Dowie emigrated to Australia in 1860, becoming a Congregational minister in Sydney and then a "spiritual healer" in Melbourne. In 1890 he moved to Chicago, and in 1901 he founded Zion City on Lake Michigan, north of Chicago. The group's doctrine emphasized the imminent Second Coming, and the main practice was "divine healing." The government structure was a "theocracy." Dowie also called himself "Elijah the Restorer," considering John the Baptist the Second Elijah, and himself the third. Dowie was charged with polygamy and embezzlement in 1906, but the movement survived his death a year later. Missionary efforts by Dowie's disciples in South Africa around the turn of the century led to the creation of the nativist "ZIONIST" movement and to the appearance of thousands of "Zionist" churches that follow the charismatic and healing aspect of the Church.

CHRISTIAN CHURCH OF NORTH AMERICA, THE
U.S. PENTECOSTAL group with membership of Italian-Americans, created from a merger of the UNORGANIZED ITALIAN CHRISTIAN CHURCHES OF NORTH AMERICA and the ITALIAN PENTECOSTAL ASSEMBLIES OF GOD.

CHRISTIAN COMMUNITY CHURCH (CHRISTENGEMEINSCHAFT or CG)

Known also as the Christian Community, this international Christian organization affiliated with ANTHROPOSOPHY was founded in 1922 by Rudolf Steiner (1861–1925) and Friedrich Rittelmeyer (1872–1938), a Lutheran pastor from Berlin. It expresses the connection between the occultist innovations of Anthroposophy and conventional Christianity. Worship services follow Protestant traditions, although clergy are known as priests. Organizationally, the group is separate from the ANTHRO-POSOPHICAL SOCIETY, but most priests are members of the Society. Branches operate throughout Western Europe and the English-speaking world.

CHRISTIAN COMMUNITY OF BOSTON

Christian mystical commune founded around 1970 and devoted to "Christianity as a vehicle for the expression of Light, Life, and Love" and to the teaching of "inner Christian mysteries and their application to one's daily living situation."

CHRISTIAN CONSERVATIVE CHURCH OF AMERICA

U.S. Identity, white-supremacist, and militarist group, founded by John R. Harrell in 1959. The founder has often been in trouble with the law, and the group has been noted for its racist and anti-Semitic positions.
See also IDENTITY MOVEMENT

Christian Crusade, see CHURCH OF THE CHRISTIAN CRUSADE

CHRISTIAN DEFENSE LEAGUE

Identity group founded by Wesley Swift and Bill Gale, a U.S. Army colonel in World War II, in the Los Angeles area in the late 1950s. It is connected with the CHURCH OF JESUS CHRIST—CHRISTIAN and the NEW CHRISTIAN CRUSADE CHURCH.
See also IDENTITY MOVEMENT

CHRISTIAN FELLOWSHIP INTERNATIONAL

Canadian offshoot of JEHOVAH'S WITNESSES, founded in 1981 by M. James Penton in Alberta.

CHRISTIAN GROWTH MINISTRIES (CGM)

PENTECOSTAL group based in Fort Lauderdale, Florida, known for its SHEPHERDING or "discipleship" doctrine, which creates a highly authoritarian structure of discipline in the group. Growing out of the Charismatic Renewal movement within mainline Protestant churches, it was founded in 1972 by Bob Mumford, and later led by Mumford, Charles Simpson, Derek Prince, Don Basham, and Ern Baxter. It was influenced by the BODY OF CHRIST, the Fundamentalist organization founded in Argentina in 1970 by Juan Carlos Ortiz.
See also CHRISTIAN RESTORATION MINISTRIES; LATTER RAIN MOVEMENT

CHRISTIAN HOLY GHOST CHURCH OF EAST AFRICA (CHGC)

African independent Christian PENTECOSTAL group, formed in 1934 among the Kikuyu tribe out of the conservative wing of the Aroti revival movement. It is part of the WAKORINO group of churches.

CHRISTIAN ISRAELITES

British millenarian group started in 1822 by John Wroe (1782–1863) among the SOUTHCOTTITES, the disappointed followers of Joanna Southcott, who prophesied in 1814 that she would give birth to a divine child named Shiloh. Joanna, sixty-four at the time, was never pregnant and died soon thereafter.

Wroe joined a Southcottite group led by John Turner, known as TURNERITES, and after Turner's death in 1821 claimed to be his successor. Wroe then announced that Shiloh, the divine child, had disappeared and would return but was testing their faith. They had to observe Old Testament laws of purity. Males were circumcised, and there was total abstinence from tobacco and alcohol. Wroe traveled widely in the English-speaking world, gaining many converts. The Christian Israelites group was formed in 1830 as a result of a schism within the Southcottites.

The church exists today only in the American Midwest and in Australia as the Christain Israelite Church.

See also NEW AND LATTER HOUSE OF ISRAEL; NEW HOUSE OF ISRAEL; PANACEA SOCIETY

Source:

Balleine, G.R. *Past Finding Out: The Tragic Story of Joanna Southcott and Her Successors.* New York: Macmillan, 1956.

CHRISTIAN MOBILIZERS

U.S. religious-political group started in the 1930s, combining Fundamentalism with right-wing, anti-Semitic, and pro-Nazi views.

CHRISTIAN NATIONALIST CRUSADE

U.S. British-Israelist group started in 1947 by Gerald L.K. Smith. It became known for its anti-Semitic and anti-black propaganda, and Smith became the most visible spokesman for BRITISH ISRAELISM. The group published *The Cross and the Flag*, which advocated shipping all blacks back to Africa and exhorted against "Jewish Gestapo organizations."

Source:

Roy, R.L. *Apostles of Discord.* Boston: Beacon Press, 1953.

CHRISTIAN NATION CHURCH, U.S.A.

Protestant evangelical group founded in 1895 in Marion, Ohio. Identical in doctrine to the CHRISTIAN AND MISSIONARY ALLIANCE, it advocates a strict code of behavior.

CHRISTIAN PATRIOTS DEFENSE LEAGUE (CPDL)

Identity group formed in the early 1980s in Flora, Illinois, by John Harrell. It advocates anti-Semitic and racist views and recruits members among Midwest farmers. Members have been preparing themselves for a race war that would devastate the United States.

See also IDENTITY MOVEMENT

CHRISTIAN RESEARCH, INC.

British-Israelist group founded by Gerka Koch, based in Arkansas after moving from Minneapolis. The group distributes British-Israelist literature and is active in support of conservative poilitical candidates.

See also BRITISH-ISRAELISM; LORD'S COVENANT CHURCH

CHRISTIAN RESTORATION MINISTRIES

Known also as the House Church Movement, Church of the Great Shepherd, or the Pyramid Church, this international PENTECOSTAL group was founded in the 1970s and is based in Wheaton, Maryland. It is known for its SHEPHERDING or "discipleship" doctrine, which creates a highly authoritarian structure of discipline in the group. It was inspired by the BODY OF CHRIST, an international Protestant Fundamentalist organization founded in Argentina in 1970 by Juan Carlos Ortiz. The Restoration movement has been most visible in North America and Great Britain. See also CHRISTIAN GROWTH MINISTRIES

CHRISTIAN REVOLUTIONARY BROTHERHOOD

Fundamentalist group founded by Barry I. Hyman in New York City in the 1980s, advocating social revolution based on Christianity. It communicates with the public via posters and leaflets; any membership in addition to the founder is in doubt.

CHRISTIAN SCIENCE

Officially known as Church of Christ, Scientist, this healing sect was founded in 1883 by Mary Baker Eddy (1821–1910). Mrs. Eddy became convinced of the healing power of faith after being cured of chronic illness by the hypnotist Phineas Parkhurst Quimby in 1862. In 1879 the Church of Christ, Scientist, was founded and in 1892 the First Church of Christ, Scientist, was organized in Boston. According to doctrine, Jesus Christ was a prophet and healer. The doctrine deviates from orthodox Christianity in regard to the Trinity, the divinity of Jesus Christ, and the nature of the Holy Ghost. God alone is worshiped. Jesus is the Guide, Holy Ghost, and Comforter. Christ, as distinguished from Jesus the prophet, is often equated with Truth. These differences have been the cause of attacks and controversies. The doctrine focuses on the secret of health, which is that of avoiding false thinking; *i.e.*, taking matter for reality. These ideas were developed in the founder's book *Science and Health with Key to the Scripture* (1875), which became the Church scripture. Members are enjoined to reject medical care in favor of healing through prayer. They also avoid smoking and alcohol. According to several studies, most members have been urban, middle-aged females who suffer from physical or mental difficulties.

Over the years some members have been involved in legal cases when their children have died because of the absence of medical care.

Since 1908 the Church has published a daily newspaper, *The Christian Science Monitor*, which enjoys a well-deserved reputation for its foreign affairs reporting.

The Church has been in serious decline since 1930, but it still has branches all over the world, mainly in English-speaking countries.

See also JEWISH SCIENCE, SOCIETY OF; NEW THOUGHT MOVEMENT; UNITED CHRISTIAN SCIENTISTS

Sources:

Braden, C.S. *Christian Science Today.* Dallas: Southern Methodist University Press, 1958.

Gottschalk, S. *The Emergence of Christian

Mary Baker Eddy.

Science in American Religious Life. Berkeley: University of California Press, 1973.

Peel, R. *Christian Science, Its Encounter with American Culture.* Garden City, NY: Doubleday, 1965.

CHRISTIAN SYNAGOGUE

Canadian Hebrew-Christian group founded in Toronto in 1915 by S.B. Rohold.

See also HEBREW CHRISTIANITY

CHRISTIAN UNION

Charismatic group founded by R.G. Sperling in North Carolina in the late 1880s, following the LATTER RAIN MOVEMENT.

CHRISTIAN UNION

Fundamentalist group founded in 1984 in Columbus, Ohio, and operating in the U.S. Midwest as well as in Africa, South America, and Japan.

CHRISTIAN WAY

Group of former CHRISTIAN SCIENCE members who have become evangelical Christians and oppose their former church. It is based in Lancaster, California.

Christian Workers for Fellowship, see CHURCH OF THE LIVING GOD, CHRISTIAN WORKERS FOR FELLOWSHIP (C.W.F.F.)

CHRIST MINISTRY FOUNDATION

Esoteric Christianity group founded in 1935 in Oakland, California, by Eleanore Mary Thedick (1883–1973). In 1970 the group merged with the SEEKER'S QUEST, but the groups separated again in 1972

Mary Baker Eddy (on balcony), founder of Christian Science, greets visitors to her home, Pleasant View, in New Hampshire in 1901.

Morning Glory Zell, a member of the neo-pagan Church of All Worlds, performs a witchcraft ritual to celebrate Halloween.(see p. 58)

after the founder's retirement. Healing through "spiritual work" is a major practice, and the group believes in reincarnation.

CHRIST'S CHURCH

Fundamentalist commune founded in the 1970s, based in Grand Rapids, Michigan.

CHRIST'S GOSPEL FELLOWSHIP

U.S. Fundamentalist, PENTECOSTAL group, connected with BRITISH ISRAELISM. It is based in Spokane, Washington, where it was founded by Robert Thornton in the 1960s.

Christ the Savior Brotherhood, see HOLY ORDER OF MANS

CHRIST TRUTH LEAGUE

NEW THOUGHT group founded in the 1950s by Alden (?–1985) and Nell (?–1971) Truesdell and inspired by various New Thought and Unity traditions. It has been based in Fort Worth, Texas.
See also UNITY SCHOOL OF CHRISTIANITY

CHRISZEKIAL ELIAS

U.S. self-proclaimed Pope, whose former name was Chester Olszewaski (1943–). A former Episcopal priest, he proclaimed himself Pope in 1977 and was ordained by Bishop Edward M. Stahlik of Milwaukee.

Chu Hui So, see LOCAL CHURCH MOVEMENT

CHURCHES OF CHRIST IN CHRISTIAN UNION OF OHIO, THE

Fundamentalist group founded in 1909 in Marshall, Ohio.

Churches of God (Adventist) Unattached Congregations, see GENERAL CONFERENCE OF THE CHURCH OF GOD

CHURCHES OF GOD, HOLINESS

Afro-American PENTECOSTAL group founded in 1920 in Atlanta, Georgia, by King Hezekiah Burrus (?–1963).

CHURCH OF ALL NATIONS

PENTECOSTAL group in Scrabble Creek, West Virginia, noted for its use of snakes during services. Its members, popularly known as "snake handlers," follow a strict code of conduct. Snake handling and the drinking of poison are regarded both as signs of the "Holy Spirit" and as tests of faith. In practice, snake handling is only rarely accompanied by drinking poison.
See also DOLLEY POND CHURCH OF GOD WITH SIGNS FOLLOWING; THE ORIGINAL PENTECOSTAL CHURCH OF GOD

Source:
La Barre, W. *They Shall Take Up Serpents.* New York: Schocken, 1969.

CHURCH OF ALL WORLDS

Neo-pagan U.S. group founded in 1961 by Tim Zell, who in 1976 changed his name to Otter G'Zell following a vision. The group was for many years the best known of U.S. Neo-pagan churches.

CHURCH OF APHRODITE

U.S. Neo-pagan group founded in 1938, aiming at a reconstruction of ancient pagan traditions.

CHURCH OF BASIC TRUTH

Occultist group founded in Phoenix, Arizona, in 1961 by George H. Hepker. The group teaches Hawaiian Huna and faith healing.

See also HUNA RESEARCH ASSOCIATES

CHURCH OF BIBLE UNDERSTANDING (COBU)

Also known as We People, and formerly known as the Forever Family, this Christian Fundamentalist group was founded in 1971 by Stewart Traill (1936–), a former salesman, in Allentown, Pennsylvania as part of the JESUS MOVEMENT of that period.

COBU's teachings are Adventist and Fundamentalist, based on its own system of Bible interpretation. The Second Coming is considered imminent.

The group attracted hundreds of young Americans and established communes all over the East Coast in its first five years of existence. It then declined, by 1985 having only the center in Philadelphia and residences in Baltimore, Arlington, Virginia, Tacoma Park, Maryland, and New York City. Beginning in 1984 the group encountered legal difficulties because of living conditions in the New York residences, in which minors lived.

From the late 1970s the group operated the Christian Brothers Cleaning Company, a carpet cleaning service.

CHURCH OF CHRIST AT HALLEY'S BLUFF, THE

U.S. Mormon splinter group that left the CHURCH OF CHRIST (TEMPLE LOT) in the 1950s.

See also MORMONS

CHURCH OF CHRIST (BIBLE AND BOOK OF MORMON TEACHING)

Mormon splinter group founded in 1946 by Pauline Hancock in Independence, Missouri. It represents a return to orthodox Christianity among members of the CHURCH OF CHRIST (TEMPLE LOT), and its doctrine rejects the Book of Mormon.

See also MORMONS

CHURCH OF CHRIST (FETTINGITE)

U.S. Mormon splinter group growing out of a schism in the CHURCH OF CHRIST (TEMPLE LOT) in 1930. Its founder, Otto Fetting (?–1933), in 1927 started claiming revelations, which eventually led to the schism. In 1947 a schism occurred in the new body, which led to the founding of the CHURCH OF CHRIST WITH THE ELIJAH MESSAGE.

See also MORMONS

THE CHURCH OF CHRIST (HOLINESS) U.S.A.

African-American HOLINESS group founded in 1894 in Jackson, Mississippi, by C.H. Mason. A schism in the group in 1908 led to the creation of the CHURCH OF GOD IN CHRIST.

Church of Christ, Scientist, see CHRISTIAN SCIENCE

CHURCH OF CHRIST (TEMPLE LOT)

U.S. Mormon splinter group founded in 1852 in opposition to polygamy and the baptism of the dead, as practiced then by a majority of MORMONS. The group still owns the Temple Lot in Independence, Missouri, designed by Joseph Smith, Jr., to be the future city of New Zion.

The Reverend Paul Lindstrom (right), founder of the Church of Christian Liberty, chats with families of crewmen shot down over North Korea in 1969.

See also APOSTOLIC UNITED ORDER; THE CHURCH OF JESUS CHRIST IN SOLEMN ASSEMBLY; THE CHURCH OF THE FIRST BORN OF THE FULLNESS OF TIMES; UNITED ORDER EFFORT

CHURCH OF CHRIST, THE CONGREGATION OF ALL SAINTS OF SOUTH AFRICA

South African independent "ZIONIST" church founded by the Zulu prophet George Khambule (1884–1949), who became active in 1925, making claims to divinity and appointing apostles. His visions were inspired by Christianity.

Sources:

Sundkler, B.G.M. *Bantu Prophets in South Africa.* London: Oxford University Press, 1961.

Sundkler, B.G.M. *Zulu Zion and Some Swazi Zionists.* London: Oxford University Press, 1976.

CHURCH OF CHRISTIAN LIBERTY, THE

Fundamentalist group founded in 1965 in Prospect Heights, Illinois, by Paul Lindstrom. It has been involved in right-wing political activities to an extent unusual for religious groups. Combating socialism and communism is one of its goals. Lindstrom has started such organizations as the Christian Defense League, and the Douglas MacArthur Brigade, formed to free U.S. war prisoners in Vietnam.

See also FUNDAMENTALISM

CHURCH OF CHRIST WITH THE ELIJAH MESSAGE

Known also as Dravesites, this U.S. Mormon splinter group grew out of a schism in the CHURCH OF CHRIST (FETTINGITE) in 1947. Its founder, W.A. Draves, started in 1937 to claim various revelations, which eventually led to the schism.

See also MORMONS

Church of Jesus Christ at Armaggedon, see LOVE FAMILY

CHURCH OF DANIEL'S BAND

Protestant conservative group founded in 1893 in Marine City, Michigan. The doctrine advocates evangelism and a modest life-style. Practices include "healing" and the "gift of the Holy Spirit."

CHURCH OF DIVINE MAN

Occultist group founded in 1972 by Lewis Bostwick (1918–) in Berkeley, California. Practices include "healing," "aura readings," and meditation.

CHURCH OF GOD (ABRAHAMIC FAITH)

Adventist group formed in the late 1880s in the United States by Adventists who continued to operate in small groups after the Great Disappointment of 1844. The Church is unitarian, denying the Christian trinity and the divinity of Jesus. It operates the Oregon Bible College in Oregon, Illinois, where headquarters are located, and several overseas missions.

See also ADVENT CHRISTIAN CHURCH; ADVENTISTS

CHURCH OF GOD (APOSTOLIC)

Originally known as the Christian Faith Band, this U.S. PENTECOSTAL group was started in 1877 by Thomas J. Cox in Danville, Kentucky. The current name was adopted in 1919. The group is otherworldly and strict in standards.

CHURCH OF GOD (BLACK JEWS)

African-American Jewish group founded in the early 20th century by F.S. Cherry, also known as Prophet Cherry. Its doctrine regards only blacks as true Jews, whereas Jews are regarded as usurpers of the legacy. All personages referred to in the early chapters of Genesis were black. Blacks were driven out of ancient Palestine to Africa by the Romans and then sold into slavery. The year 2000 will bring about the millennium and the final victory of black Jews.

Source:

Fauset, A.H. *Black Gods of the Metropolis.* Philadelphia: University of Pennsylvania Press, 1944.

CHURCH OF GOD, BODY OF CHRIST

Sabbath-keeping Adventist group with headquarters in Mocksville, North Carolina. It combines a strong Old Testament orientation with belief in the gifts of the Holy Spirit and faith healing. Members abstain from pork and believe in the imminent return of Christ.

See also ADVENTISTS; GENERAL CONFERENCE OF THE CHURCH OF GOD; SEVENTH-DAY ADVENTIST CHURCH

CHURCH OF GOD BY FAITH

PENTECOSTAL group based in Alachua, Florida, founded by John Bright in 1919.

CHURCH OF GOD (CLEVELAND, OHIO)

U.S. Fundamentalist, Adventist group founded in 1974 by Carl O'Brien, a former WORLDWIDE CHURCH OF GOD minister, in dissent against Herbert W. Armstrong.

CHURCH OF GOD (CLEVELAND, TENNESSEE)

Originally known as the Christian Union, this PENTECOSTAL group was founded in

1886 by Richard G. Spurling in Monroe County, Tennessee. Later the name was changed to Holiness Church. The name Church of God was adopted in 1907, under the leadership of A.J. Tomlinson. Since 1917 the group has operated three colleges. Schisms have led to the founding of (ORIGINAL) CHURCH OF GOD, INC., THE CHURCH OF GOD OF PROPHECY, THE CHURCH OF GOD (WORLD HEAD-QUARTERS), THE CHURCH OF GOD (JERUSALEM ACRES), and THE CHURCH OF GOD, THE HOUSE OF PRAYER.

CHURCH OF GOD IN CHRIST

African-American PENTECOSTAL group founded in 1908 by Charles H. Mason as a result of schism in THE CHURCH OF CHRIST (HOLINESS) U.S.A. The group emphasizes faith healing. It is based in Memphis, Tennessee.

CHURCH OF GOD IN CHRIST, CONGREGATIONAL

U.S. African-American PENTECOSTAL group (with branches in Great Britain and Mexico), founded in 1932 by J. Bowe, who dissented from the CHURCH OF GOD IN CHRIST. Members of the group are conscientious objectors.

CHURCH OF GOD IN CHRIST, INTERNATIONAL, THE

U.S. African-American PENTECOSTAL group created in 1969 in Kansas City through a schism in the CHURCH OF GOD IN CHRIST.

THE CHURCH OF GOD IN CHRIST (PENTECOSTAL)

U.S. PENTECOSTAL group founded in the early 1930s in Bluefield, West Virginia.

CHURCH OF GOD, INTERNATIONAL

Founded in 1978 by Garner Ted Armstrong, son of Herbert W. Armstrong, following his (second) suspension from his father's organization, the WORLD-WIDE CHURCH OF GOD. The Church is based on a radio ministry; headquarters are in Tyler, Texas. Doctrine is similar to that of the Worldwide Church of God.

CHURCH OF GOD (JERUSALEM)

Known also as Congregation of Elohim, and Family of Elohim, the Church was founded in 1955 by A.N. Dugger (?–1975), a former Seventh-Day Adventist. Dugger's doctrinal emphasis was Adventist; he was convinced that the founding of the State of Israel had eschatological significance and that after 1948 the Second Coming was imminent. Dugger's son, Charles Andy Dugger, established another group, WORKERS TOGETHER WITH ELOHIM. See also GENERAL CONFERENCE OF THE CHURCH OF GOD

CHURCH OF GOD (JERUSALEM ACRES), THE

U.S. PENTECOSTAL group created through dissension from THE CHURCH OF GOD OF PROPHECY. It was founded by Grady R. Kent in 1957. The doctrine, known as "New Testament Judaism," ignores all traditional Christian holidays in favor of a totally new holiday calendar following a newly created mythology. It is based in Jerusalem Acres, Cleveland, Tennessee.

CHURCH OF GOD OF PROPHECY

U.S. PENTECOSTAL group founded in 1921 following a leadership struggle in the CHURCH OF GOD (CLEVELAND, TEN-

NESSEE) by A.J. Tomlinson (1865–1943), who had lost in the struggle. It was first known as the Tomlinson Church of God; the current name was adopted in 1952.

Following Tomlinson's death in 1943, his son, Milton A. Tomlinson, became the leader. A leadership struggle led to the founding of THE CHURCH OF GOD (WORLD HEADQUARTERS). Branches of the Church of God of Prophecy have operated in Africa and Europe.

CHURCH OF GOD OF THE APOSTOLIC FAITH

PENTECOSTAL group founded in 1914 near Ozark, Arkansas, now based in Tulsa, Oklahoma. Its doctrine is similar to that of the CHURCH OF GOD (CLEVELAND, TENNESSEE).

CHURCH OF GOD OF THE MOUNTAIN ASSEMBLY, THE

PENTECOSTAL group founded in 1906 in Tennessee. Based in Jellico, Tennessee, it is active in the South and Midwest.

CHURCH OF GOD (SABBATARIAN)

Sabbath-keeping Adventist group that split off from the GENERAL CONFERENCE OF THE CHURCH OF GOD in 1969. It was originally led by Roy Marrs of Los Angeles and R.F. Marrs of Denver. The Denver group became known as the Remnant Church of God.
See also SEVENTH-DAY ADVENTIST CHURCH

Church of God (Seventh-Day), see GENERAL CONFERENCE OF THE CHURCH OF GOD

CHURCH OF GOD (SEVENTH-DAY, SALEM, WEST VIRGINIA)

Adventist, Sabbath-keeping group formed in 1933 as a result of a schism in the GENERAL CONFERENCE OF THE CHURCH OF GOD.
See also SEVENTH-DAY ADVENTIST CHURCH

CHURCH OF GOD SEVENTH ERA

U.S. Adventist group founded by Larry Gilbert Johnson, another result of the 1974 schism in the WORLDWIDE CHURCH OF GOD.

CHURCH OF GOD, THE ETERNAL

Adventist group founded by Raymond C. Cole in 1975 in dissent from the WORLD-WIDE CHURCH OF GOD. The church is based in Eugene, Oregon, where Herbert W. Armstrong founded the Radio Church of God in 1934. Cole claimed that divine truth was revealed to Armstrong only in the early years of the Radio Church. This divine truth is unchangeable, and the doctrinal changes instituted by Armstrong as the head of the Worldwide Church of God in 1974 were unacceptable. Branches of the group have operated in Western Europe.

CHURCH OF GOD, THE HOUSE OF PRAYER, THE

PENTECOSTAL group created as a result of a schism in THE CHURCH OF GOD (CLEVELAND, TENNESSEE). It was founded in Cleveland, Tennessee, by Harrison W. Poteat in 1939.

CHURCH OF GOD (WORLD HEADQUARTERS), THE

PENTECOSTAL group founded around

Homer A. Tomlinson, founder of the Church of God (World Headquarters), proclaims himself "King of Germany." The globe he holds is the symbol of his claim to be king of twenty-seven nations.

1945 in New York City by Homer Tomlinson (?-1968) after losing a leadership struggle with his brother, Milton A. Tomlinson, over the CHURCH OF GOD OF PROPHECY. As part of its program to create the Kingdom of God on earth, the group has sponsored the Theocratic Party, which has taken part in U.S. elections. It has established branches in Europe, Asia, and Africa.

CHURCH OF HANUMAN

Syncretistic group founded in the late 1960s and based in Palo Alto, California. It combines Christian, occult, and Eastern traditions, including Hindu and Sufi ideas and practices.

CHURCH OF INNER WISDOM

NEW THOUGHT group founded in 1968 in San Jose, California, by Joan Gibson, a former member of the AMORC ROSICRUCIAN ORDER.

CHURCH OF INTEGRAL LIVING

NEW THOUGHT group based in New York City, founded in the 1980s by Valerie Seyffert.

CHURCH OF ISRAEL, THE

White-supremacist, Identity group started in 1972 as a result of a split in the CHURCH OF CHRIST AT HALLEY'S BLUFF, a Mormon group, and led by Daniel Gayman, a former pastor of the Church of Christ who declared himself a bishop. Between 1974 and 1981 the new group was known as the Church of Christian Heritage.

According to Gayman's teachings, humanity is descended from the biblical Cain and Seth (Abel's brother and substitute) and represents either Satan or God. White gentiles are descended from Seth; blacks and Jews, from Cain.

See also CHURCH OF CHRIST (TEMPLE LOT); IDENTITY MOVEMENT; MORMONS

CHURCH OF ISRAEL, THE

British-Israelist group based in Missouri and led by Gordon Winrod, son of Gerald B. Winrod, founder of DEFENDERS OF THE FAITH.

See also BRITISH ISRAELISM

CHURCH OF JESUS CHRIST, THE

White-supremacist, Identity group founded by Thomas Arthur Robb, a chaplain for the Ku Klux Klan, and based in Bass, Arkansas.

CHURCH OF JESUS CHRIST—CHRISTIAN

British-Israelist group founded in 1946 by Wesley Swift (?–1970), a member of the Ku Klux Klan, in Lancaster, California. Swift is considered the real founder of the IDENTITY MOVEMENT. In addition to BRITISH ISRAELISM, the group doctrine includes belief in Atlantis and Lemuria, typical of THEOSOPHY and ANTHROPOSOPHY.

See also CHURCH OF JESUS CHRIST CHRISTIAN—ARYAN NATIONS.

CHURCH OF JESUS CHRIST CHRISTIAN—ARYAN NATIONS

An outgrowth of the CHURCH OF JESUS CHRIST—CHRISTIAN, formed in 1974 as Richard Girnt Butler inherited Swift's mantle and moved the group headquarters to Hayden Lake, Idaho. Butler was indicted on conspiracy charges in 1988, together with other members. The group is connected with other IDENTITY MOVE-

Richard G. Butler, founder of the Church of Jesus Christ Christian–Aryan Nations, a neo-Nazi organization in Idaho.

MENT groups and has been linked to THE ORDER.

See also BRITISH ISRAELISM; MOUNTAIN CHURCH OF JESUS CHRIST THE SAVIOUR

Source:

Coates, J. *Armed and Dangerous.* New York: Hill & Wang, 1987.

Church of Jesus Christ of Latter-Day Saints, see MORMONS

CHURCH OF MARY MYSTICAL ROSE OF PERPETUAL HELP

OLD CATHOLIC group founded in 1937 in Chicago and led by John Skikiewicz.

See also AMERICAN CATHOLIC CHURCH

CHURCH OF MERCAVAH

Occultist group founded in 1982 in Louisiana by James A. Montandon.

CHURCH OF PEACE AND HEALING

"Alternative, holistic Christian ministry," founded in New York City in the 1980s.

CHURCH OF RELIGIOUS PHILOSOPHY

Theosophical, "New Age" group founded by Jacob M. Sober and Miriam M. Sober in Arizona in the early 1980s. It operates the

President Efraim Rios Montt, military dictator of Honduras, a prominent member of the Church of the Complete Word. He is shown here during a 1983 visit by then President Ronald Reagan. (see page 68)

New Age Learning Center.
See also THEOSOPHY

CHURCH OF THE CHRISTIAN CRUSADE

Known also as the Christian Echoes Ministry, this Fundamentalist, evangelical group was founded in 1948 in Tulsa, Oklahoma, by Billy James Hargis. The group and its leader became notorious for their militancy in right-wing causes. In the mid-1970s Hargis was accused of gross immorality; he resigned from the movement but then came back. The Church has operated a number of outreach organizations such as the David Livingstone Missionary Foundation and Evangelism in Action.

CHURCH OF THE CHRISTIAN SPIRITUAL ALLIANCE (CSA)

U.S. Hindu-inspired group founded in the late 1950s by H. Edwin and Lois O'Neal and William Arnold Lapp. In 1962 it merged with the NEW LIFE WORLDWIDE to form the CENTER FOR SPIRITUAL AWARENESS (CSA).

CHURCH OF THE COMPLETE WORD

Known also as the Word Church, this Fundamentalist group was founded in Eureka, California, in the early 1970s by Jim Durkin, a reformed alcoholic, as the Lighthouse Ranch Commune. Later the group developed an active missionary program in Central America, especially in Guatemala. Efrain Rios Montt, military dictator in Guatemala from March 1982 to August 1983, was the best-known member of the group.

CHURCH OF THE COVENANTS

Fundamentalist, PENTECOSTAL group connected with BRITISH ISRAELISM, founded by David Bruggman in 1940, with headquarters in River Forest, Illinois. A branch in Dayton, Ohio, was headed by Millard J. Flenner, who operated the Dayton Theological Seminary (1947–1951).

CHURCH OF THE ETERNAL SOURCE

Neo-pagan group dedicated to the worship of ancient Egyptian gods, based in Burbank, California.
See also CHURCH OF ALL WORLDS; COVENANT OF THE GODDESS

CHURCH OF THE FIRST BORN OF THE FULLNESS OF TIMES

U.S. Mormon group committed to polygamy, founded in 1955 by Joel LeBaron (murdered in 1972). The founder claimed to have been visited by two divine messengers, who appointed him a prophet. Before that he was a member of the APOSTOLIC UNITED ORDER.
See also THE CHURCH OF THE LAMB OF GOD; CONFEDERATE NATIONS OF ISRAEL; MORMONS; REORGANIZED CHURCH OF JESUS CHRIST OF LATTER DAY SAINTS; UNITED ORDER EFFORT

CHURCH OF THE FULLER CONCEPT

NEW THOUGHT group founded by Bernese Williamson in Washington, D.C., in the 1960s. It operated the Hisacres New Thought Center.

CHURCH OF THE GIFT OF GOD

Christian-occultist group founded in the 1970s by James A. Dooling, III, in Magnolia, Massachusetts. The group operates the New England Conservatory of Health.

Practices include "medical astrology," "color therapy," and "psychic healing."

CHURCH OF THE GOSPEL, THE

Millenarian group founded in Pittsfield, Massachusetts in 1911.

CHURCH OF THE HEALING CHRIST (DIVINE SCIENCE), THE

NEW THOUGHT group, officially part of DIVINE SCIENCE, founded in New York City by Albert C. Grier (who also founded CHURCH OF THE TRUTH) but led by Emmet Fox (1886–1959) soon afterward, starting in 1925. Fox was born in Ireland in a Roman Catholic family, studied engineering in England, and then joined the New Thought movement in the United States. His version of New Thought was heavily Christian, and he claimed that the Bible contained a hidden metaphysical message.

CHURCH OF THE HUMANITARIAN GOD

Christian group founded in Florida in 1969, devoted to promoting nonviolence.

CHURCH OF THE KINGDOM OF GOD, PHILANTHROPIC ASSEMBLY, THE

Known also as the Philanthropic Assembly of the Friends of Man, this Fundamentalist, millenarian group was founded in 1921 by F.L. Alexander Freytag (1870–1947) in Switzerland. Freytag was the leader of the Swiss branch of the Watch Tower Tract and Bible Society (JEHOVAH'S WITNESSES) but began to dissent from its official teachings. The doctrine still follows some Jehovah's Witnesses ideas. It claims that Freytag was the "messenger of the eternal," chosen to announce the Second Coming. It also claims that two days (which equal 2,000 years) passed between the appearance of Jesus Christ and the year 1918, and since 1918 a new day (*i.e.,* millennium) has begun in which a new earth is to be created and eternal life is to be achieved, partly through a special health diet. After the founder's death the movement was split into a French branch (AMIS DE L'HOMME) and a Swiss one (Kirche des Reiches Gott/ Menschenfreunde). The Swiss branch, known today as the Assembly, has gained followers in Western Europe and the United States.

CHURCH OF THE LAMB OF GOD

Mormon splinter group formed in 1971 by Ervil LeBaron, who left the CHURCH OF THE FIRST BORN OF THE FULLNESS OF TIMES, claiming leadership over all polygamist groups and individuals. Ervil LeBaron resorted to murder in his war against other groups and leaders. On August 20, 1972, members of the Church of the Lamb of God killed Joel LeBaron, who was then the leader of The Church of the First Born, on orders of his brother Ervil. On December 14, 1972, group members attacked the settlement of Los Molinos in Mexico, where members of the Church of the First Born lived. Two persons were killed. On May 10, 1977, members of the Church of the Lamb of God killed Rulon C. Allred, leader of the APOSTOLIC UNITED ORDER. Ervil LeBaron was sentenced to life imprisonment and died in prison on August 16, 1981. The group no longer exists.

See also CONFEDERATE NATIONS OF

ISRAEL; MORMONS; REORGANIZED CHURCH OF JESUS CHRIST OF LATTER DAY SAINTS; UNITED ORDER EFFORT

Source:
Bradlee, B., Jr. and Van Atta, D. *Prophet of Blood*. New York: G.P. Putnam's Sons, 1981.

CHURCH OF THE LITTLE CHILDREN

North American PENTECOSTAL group founded in 1916 by John Quincy Adams (1890–1951), former Baptist minister, in Abbott, Texas. The group rejects as pagan belief in the Trinity, Sunday Sabbath, Christmas, Easter, neckties, and the names of the days of the week. Followers are conscientious objectors.

Church of the Living, see THE NEVERDIES

CHURCH OF THE LIVING GOD

Independent African-American church led by the black "Messiah," St. John the Vine, whose real name was John Hickerson and who was active in Baltimore, Maryland, and later in Harlem, New York City, in the early 20th century. FATHER DIVINE is reported to have been among his followers, later borrowing some of his teachings.

CHURCH OF THE LIVING GOD, CHRISTIAN WORKERS FOR FELLOWSHIP (C.W.F.F.)

African-American PENTECOSTAL group founded originally in 1889 in Wrightsville, Arkansas, by William Christian (1856–1928), a former slave. The group claims that biblical figures such as Jesus Christ were actually African and relies on revela-

tions provided to its (hereditary) leadership. Tithing is required.

CHURCH OF THE LIVING GOD, GENERAL ASSEMBLY

Originally known as Church of the Living God, Apostolic Church, this African-American PENTECOSTAL group was founded in 1902 as a result of a schism in the CHURCH OF THE LIVING GOD (CHRISTIAN WORKERS FOR FELLOWSHIP). In 1926 the group merged with the Church of the Living God, The Pillar and Ground of Truth to form THE HOUSE OF GOD WHICH IS THE CHURCH OF THE LIVING GOD, THE PILLAR AND GROUND OF TRUTH.

Church of the Living Word, see THE WALK

CHURCH OF THE LORD JESUS CHRIST OF THE APOSTOLIC FAITH

PENTECOSTAL group founded in 1933 by A.C. Johnson, formerly of the CHURCH OF OUR LORD JESUS CHRIST OF THE APOS-TOLIC FAITH. The group views Christmas and Easter as pagan and enforces a strict dress code. It is based in Philadelphia.

CHURCH OF THE LOVING SERVANT

U.S. "non-denominational church dedicated to service through healing," founded in the late 1970s by John Harvey Gray. The main practice is Reiki, which is described as "healing through energy."

CHURCH OF THE NAZARENE

"HOLINESS" group founded in Pilot Point, Texas, in 1908. Its doctrine includes the notion of Perfectionism, according to which Christians become perfect through baptism of the Holy Spirit.

CHURCH OF THE REDEEMER COMMUNITY

Christian commune founded by W. Graham Pulkingham, a Roman Catholic priest and a leader in the CATHOLIC CHARISMATIC RENEWAL movement, in Houston, Texas, in the 1960s.

CHURCH OF THE SACRED ALPHA, THE

Group based in California and founded in the 1960s, whose ritual involved "biofeedback" and supposed manipulation of alpha electrical activity in the brain. See also FEEDBACK CHURCH; HOLY FEEDBACK CHURCH

CHURCH OF THE SAVIOUR

Christian communal group founded in 1946 in Washington, D.C., by Gordon Cosby. It describes itself as a "...nondenominational, interracial church. It requires a rigorous preliminary course of Christian studies for all potential members. Commitment to certain minimum spiritual disciplines is expected. Each person is considered a minister to the world and belongs to a mission group dedicated to Christian outreach. There is no church edifice..." Members express their religious commitment through ser-vice to the poor and the oppressed in their immediate vicinity, and the group has been working in poor neighborhoods.

CHURCH OF THE TRINITY (INVISIBLE MINISTRY)

NEW THOUGHT group founded in 1972 in California by Friend Stuart (A. Stuart Otto), who started his activities in the movement in the 1950s following a "religious awakening." The group's doctrine is specifically Christian, and faith healing is emphasized.

CHURCH OF THE TRUTH

North American NEW THOUGHT group founded in 1913 in Spokane, Washington, by Albert C. Grier, a former Universalist minister.

Source:
Braden, C.S. *Spirits in Rebellion*. Dallas: Southern Methodist University Press, 1963.

CHURCH OF TZADDI

Occultist organization, self-described as a "non-denominational, metaphysical as well as spiritual church," founded in 1964 by Amy Kees (1914–) and her daughter Dorothe Jean Blackmere (1936–), with headquarters in Boulder, Colorado. Around 1940, Mrs. Kees reported hearing the voice, and then seeing the figure, of "Adonis, who had taught in a healing room—called Tzaddi—in King Solomon's Temple." Later she reported many contacts with other "Masters." In 1959 she joined the UNITY SCHOOL OF CHRISTIANITY and then formed her own group. The Church ministers offer "past life readings" and "Akashic records," as well as palmistry, handwriting analysis, and numerology. The Church has offered affiliation to similar groups.
See also ARIZONA METAPHYSICAL SOCIETY

CHURCH TRIUMPHANT

CHRISTIAN SCIENCE schismatic group in New York City under the leadership of Augusta Stetson (1842–1928), which was

James Francis Marion Jones, leader of The Church of Universal Triumph/The Dominion of God.

started after the death of Mary Baker Eddy in 1910.

CHURCH OF UNIVERSAL TRIUMPH/THE DOMINION OF GOD, THE

African-American millenial group founded in 1938 in Detroit by James Francis Marion Jones (1908–1971), known as Prophet Jones, a former minister of the TRIUMPH THE CHURCH AND KINGDOM OF GOD IN CHRIST. Members are forbidden tobacco, tea, coffee, and alcohol and are enjoined to follow a strict code of behavior. Doctrine predicts the coming of the millennium in the year 2000, when all persons alive will become immortal.

Prophet Jones was known in the 1940s and 1950s for his extravagant wealth. His personal charisma was compared to that of FATHER DIVINE and Daddy Grace.

"THE CHURCH WHICH IS CHRIST'S BODY"

Fundamentalist group founded by Maurice M. Johnson in 1925 in Los Angeles. Members refuse to incorporate or use any formal designations; they are active evangelizers.
See also FUNDAMENTALISM

CIRCLE OF ANGELS

Known also as the Metanoian Order, this Gurdjieff commune was founded in 1976 and based on Walden Farm in East Hardwick, Vermont.
See also GURDJIEFF GROUPS

CIRCLE OF LIGHT

Christian occultist group founded by Shirlee Dunlap in Lombard, Illinois, in the early 1980s. It is loosely affiliated with the LOGOS WORLD UNIVERSITY CHURCH.

CIRCLE SANCTUARY

Formerly known as the CHURCH OF CIRCLE WICCA, this neo-pagan group is self-described as a Wiccan Church. Founded in 1974 in Wisconsin by Selena Fox (1949–) and Jim Alan, and headquartered in Mt. Horeb, Wisconsin, it holds every summer a Pagan Spirit Gathering, among other pagan festivals. The Church is committed to the worship of the Great Mother Goddess as well as a male consort and an additional pantheon of pagan deities. "The Wiccan religion is pantheistic in that the Divine is seen as everywhere and in everything. The Wiccan religion also is animistic in that every human, tree, animal, stream, rock, and other forms of life is seen to have a Divine Spirit within. The Wiccan religion is monotheistic in that there is an honoring of Divine Unity. It also is polytheistic in that Wiccans honor the Divine through a variety of female and male deity forms— Goddesses and Gods which are aspects of the Divine Female and Divine Male and their Unity." The group has operated the Pagan Spirit Alliance (PSA), a network of self-declared pagans in North America and Great Britain.
See also CHURCH OF ALL WORLDS; COVENANT OF THE GODDESS

Citizens Commission on Human Rights, see SCIENTOLOGY

Glenn Clark, see CAMP FARTHEST OUT

Richard Clarke, see CALUMET PAGAN TEMPLE

CLAYMONT COURT

Formerly known as The Claymont Society for Continuous Education, Inc., this Gurdjieff group was founded in 1975 and headquartered in Charles Town, West Virginia. It is devoted to "the principles and techniques of Spiritual Psychology, according to the ideas of George I. Gurdjieff, and John G. Bennett." It operates the American Society of Continuous Education.

See also COOMBE SPRINGS; GURDJIEFF GROUPS; INSTITUTE FOR THE COMPARATIVE STUDY OF HISTORY, PHILOSOPHY, AND THE SCIENCES

Robert Clement, see EUCHARISTIC CATHOLIC CHURCH

Clement XV, see RENOVATED CHURCH OF CHRIST

R. Swinburne Clymer, see FRATERNITAS ROSAE CRUCIS

Victoria Coanda, see SIVANANDA YOGA VEDANTA CHURCH

C.E. Cobb, see BODY OF CHRIST

Srimati Margaret Coble, see ICSA (INTEGRAL CENTER OF SELF-ABIDANCE)

Raymond Cohen, see BETH YESHUA

Leopold Cohn, see CHOSEN PEOPLE MINISTRIES

Francisco Coll, see INNER PEACE MOVEMENT

Michel Collin, see RENOVATED CHURCH OF CHRIST

COLONY, THE

Christian commune founded by Brother John in the 1970s and based in northern California.

COMMANDMENT KEEPERS CONGREGATION OF THE LIVING GOD

Known also as Ethiopian Hebrews, this African-American Jewish group was founded in 1919 in New York City by Wentworth Arthur Matthew (1892–1973). Doctrine teaches that ancient Jews were all black and that Orthodox Judaism is the true religion and culture of Africans. Practices follow closely those of Orthodox Judaism. The group operates the Israelite Rabbinical Academy, which trains its rabbis.

Source:
Brotz, H.M. *The Black Jews of Harlem.* New York: Schocken Books, 1970.

COMMUNION PHALANGISTE (LA PHALANGE)

French traditionalist Roman Catholic group. Founded by Georges de Nantes as the Ligue de la Contre Réforme Catholic (C.R.C.), it assumed the current name in 1970. The group's doctrine regards the Roman Catholic Church as heretic, controlled by the Jews and the Masons. It opposes democracy and advocates a religious dictator who would establish Catholicism in France.

COMMUNITY CHAPEL AND BIBLE TRAINING CENTER

Fundamentalist, PENTECOSTAL group founded by Donald Lee Barnett in Burien, Washington, in 1967. Barnett (1930–), born in Idaho, was an aerospace engineer at the Boeing company and a part-time ASSEMBLY OF GOD preacher before starting his own church. He rejected the doctrine of the Trinity and promoted belief in demons, which he claimed to exorcise. Members were subject to a strict dress code. In March 1986 a group member drowned her five-year-old daughter in a motel swimming pool, claiming that a "hyperactivity demon" was possessing the child. In the same year Barnett was involved in legal charges by former members having to do with his authoritarian style and beliefs. In 1987 he was disfellowshipped by church elders because of alleged sexual affairs with women members. In 1988 he was legally forced to give up his rights to group property.

COMMUNITY OF JESUS

First known as Bethany House, this charismatic Christian group based in Cape Cod, Massachusetts, was started in 1969 by Cay Andersen and Judy Sorensen, former Episcopalians. It operates the 3D program—Discipleship, Discipline, and Diet—for overweight Christian women.

COMPANY AT KIRKRIDGE, THE

Christian ecumenical group founded in 1976 in Pennsylvania by John Oliver Nelson. Members can retain their membership in other Christian groups and attend only four weekend meetings a year with the Company.

Bertrand L. Comparet, see YOUR HERITAGE

CONCEPT-THERAPY INSTITUTE

Occultist-Theosophical group founded by Thurman Fleet in the 1970s, teaching Conceptology and "the laws of Life." It is based at the Aum-Sat-Tat Ranch in San Antonio, Texas.

CONCILIO LATINO-AMERICANO DE LA IGLESIA DE DIOS PENTECOSTAL DE NEW YORK, INCORPORADO

Known also as the Latin-American Council of the Pentecostal Church of God of New York, this Spanish-speaking PENTECOSTAL group was founded in 1957 in connection with the Puerto Rican IGLESIA DE DIOS PENTECOSTAL. Healing and tithing are emphasized in the group's doctrine.

CONCILIO OLAZABAL DE IGLESIAS LATINO AMERICANO

U.S. Spanish-speaking PENTECOSTAL group with branches in Mexico, founded by Francisco Olazabal (1886–1937), a former Methodist minister, in Los Angeles in 1923.

CONFEDERATE NATIONS OF ISRAEL

Originally known as THE CHURCH OF JESUS CHRIST IN SOLEMN ASSEMBLY, this Mormon splinter group committed to polygamy was founded by Alexander Joseph in 1974, after he left the APOSTOLIC UNITED ORDER. It is based in Big Water, Kane County, Utah, where most members live.

See also THE CHURCH OF THE FIRST BORN OF THE FULLNESS OF TIMES;

MORMONS; REORGANIZED CHURCH OF JESUS CHRIST OF LATTER DAY SAINTS; UNITED ORDER EFFORT

CONFRATERNITY OF DEISTS, INC.

Monotheistic group founded in 1967 by Paul Englert in St. Petersburg, Florida. The group's doctrine was one of belief in one God and opposition to established churches and accepted scriptures. At the same time, Deists were opposed to atheism.

CONGREGATIONAL CHURCH OF PRACTICAL THEOLOGY

Christian-occultist group founded in 1969 in Valley, Nebraska, by E. Arthur Winkler, a former United Church of Christ and United Methodist minister. It operates the Eastern Nebraska Christian College and is connected with ANDROMEDA, THE CHAPEL OF THE OPEN DOOR. Practices include meditation and "success through thought."

CONGREGATIONAL HOLINESS CHURCH

PENTECOSTAL group founded in 1920 in Georgia by Watson Sorrow, following a dispute over healing in the Georgia Conference of the PENTECOSTAL HOLINESS CHURCH. The majority slighted the need for human medicine and believed only in divine healing. The minority, led by Sorrow, recommended reliance on human medicine. Sorrow later founded the FIRST INTERDENOMINATIONAL CHRISTIAN ASSOCIATION.

CONGREGATION BEIT SHECHINAH

Jewish "spiritual renewal group" founded in the late 1980s in northern California by Leah Novick. Practices include "guided visualisations" and meditation.

CONGREGATION OF MARY THE IMMACULATE QUEEN

Traditionalist Catholic group started in 1971 in Idaho by Francis K. Schuckardt; it later moved its center to Spokane, Washington. The group believes that the Roman Catholic Church has been taken over by the Freemasons, who they claim had murdered Pope Pius XII, and that reforms in the Church since 1965 reflect that takeover. The founder left the group in 1984, and it has come under the guidance of George J. Musey of the SERVANTS OF THE SACRED HEART OF JESUS AND MARY.

CONGREGATION OF THE MESSIAH

MESSIANIC JUDAISM group started in Philadelphia in the 1960s.

CONSERVATIVE JUDAISM

U.S. Jewish renewal movement that originated among Jewish intellectuals in Central Europe in the 19th century, but that can best be dated to the founding in 1886 of the Jewish Theological Seminary in New York by Solomon Schechter (1848–1915). The Rabbinical Assembly of America was founded at the same time. The United Synagogue of America was founded in 1913. Today this is the largest Jewish grouping in the United States, with more followers than either REFORM JUDAISM or the historical Orthodox Judaism. It is virtually unknown outside the United States.

In doctrine, the Conservatives stand midway between Orthodoxy, the complete adherence to traditional Jewish practices, and Reform Judaism, which initially

The Jewish Theological Seminary, teaching center of the Conservative Jewish movement (courtesy Library of the Jewish Theological Seminary of America).

rejected almost all practices and preserved only a few central beliefs. It began as a reaction to Reform Judaism, and refused to espouse modernity as the only ideal.

Source:

Sklare, M. *Conservative Judaism: An American Religious Movement.* Glencoe, IL: The Free Press, 1955.

Continental Brethren, see PLYMOUTH BRETHREN

Mozella Cook, see SOUGHT OUT CHURCH OF GOD IN CHRIST AND SPIRITUAL HOUSE OF PRAYER, INC.

Grace Cooke, see WHITE EAGLE LODGE

COOMBE SPRINGS

British Gurdjieff group founded in the 1930s by John G. Bennett (1897–1974).
See also CLAYMONT SOCIETY; GURDJIEFF GROUPS; INSTITUTE FOR THE COMPARATIVE STUDY OF HISTORY, PHILOSOPHY, AND THE SCIENCES; SHERBORNE SCHOOL

COPTIC FELLOWSHIP OF AMERICA

"Esoteric Christianity" group founded in 1927 in Los Angeles by Hamid Bey (?–1976), who claimed to have studied in the hidden Christian temples of Egypt.

Isador Coriat, see EMMANUEL MOVEMENT

George and Mary Cornelius, see PACIFIC INSTITUTE OF SCIENCE AND HUMANITIES

Gordon Cosby, see CHURCH OF THE SAVIOUR

COSMIC CIRCLE OF FELLOWSHIP

UFO-Christian group founded by William A. Ferguson (?–1962) in 1954 in Chicago. Ferguson, a former mailman, reported his first extraterrestrial contact in 1938, when his soul traveled to Mars. He was convicted of fraud in 1947 for selling a "clarified water device" and spent a year in prison.

COSMIC STAR TEMPLE

UFO-Theosophical group founded in 1960 by Violet Gilbert and based near Roseburg, Oregon. The founder claimed first contact with "space brothers" in 1937 and a first visit to Venus in 1939.
See also THEOSOPHY

Course in Miracles, see A COURSE IN MIRACLES

COVENANT COMMUNITY FELLOWSHIP

Fundamentalist group started in the 1980s in Rensselaer, Indiana.

COVENANT OF THE GODDESS

International association of Wiccan (neopagan) groups dedicated to the worship of the Great Mother Goddess and her male consort, founded in 1975 in California. Members, known as "witches," are organized in covens and celebrate solar festivals such as the Spring Equinox (March 21), Fall Equinox (September 21), Summer Solstice (June 21) and Winter Solstice (December 21). Headquarters are in Berkeley, California.

THE COVENANT, THE SWORD, THE ARM OF THE LORD (CSA)

Identity communal group established in 1976 by James D. Ellison in Zaraphath-Horeb, Arkansas. The founder was inspired by the Ku Klux Klan ideology of white supremacy, with emphasis on military training. There was also the notion of "survivalism"; *i.e.*, preparing for civil war or major natural disaster that would destroy U.S. society. In April 1985 the group was raided by federal authorities, and its arms were seized. Ellison was subsequently sentenced to 20 years in prison on weapons charges, with two elders of the group. The group was disbanded in 1986. See also CHRISTIAN PATRIOTS DEFENSE LEAGUE; IDENTITY MOVEMENT

COVEN OF ARIANHU

Witchcraft group associated with the CHURCH AND SCHOOL OF WICCA, founded by Louise and Loy Stone in Texas.

Thomas J. Cox, see CHURCH OF GOD (APOSTOLIC)

Norman Craemer, see SCHOOL OF LIGHT AND REALIZATION (SOLAR)

Malinda Cramer, see DIVINE SCIENCE CHURCH

Jean-Michel Cravanzola, see JEAN-MICHEL ET SON ÉQUIPE

Florence L. Crawford, see APOSTOLIC FAITH MISSION OF PORTLAND, OREGON, U.S.A.

Benjamin Creme, see WORLD TEACHER

Robert Crosbie, see UNITED LODGE OF THEOSOPHISTS

CROSSROADS CHURCHES OF CHRIST

Fundamentalist organization founded in 1973 by Chuck Lucas at the University of Florida in Gainesville and growing out of the CHURCH OF CHRIST. The organization is structured according to the SHEPHERDING principle, which provides for authoritarian leadership and close supervision of members. This style has been the basis of the "shepherding movement," which includes the BODY OF CHRIST, CHRISTIAN GROWTH MINISTRIES, and CHRISTIAN RESTORATION MINISTRIES. Branches have operated across the United States and the Western Hemisphere. See also BOSTON CHURCH OF CHRIST; NEW YORK CHURCH OF CHRIST

Aleister Crowley, see ORDO TEMPLI ORIENTIS

James Christian Crummer, see UNIVERSAL EPISCOPAL COMMUNION

A.B. Crumpler, see PENTECOSTAL HOLINESS CHURCH

CRUSADE FOR CHRIST AND COUNTRY

Identity group founded by Gordon "Jack" Mohr in the 1970s and based in Mississippi. See also IDENTITY MOVEMENT

Hugh de Cruz, see NEW AGE CHRISTIANITY WITHOUT RELIGION

CRYSTAL CATHEDRAL

Protestant-NEW THOUGHT church

Part of the cache of arms seized by police at a survivalist camp of the Covenant, the Sword, and the Arm of the Lord in a 1985 raid. Also found was the photograph of Adolf Hitler in the background. (see p. 79)

The Crystal Cathedral of television evangelist Robert Schuller in California.

founded in southern California in 1955 by Robert Schuller (1927–), former Reformed Church of America minister. The Cathedral's message is one of positive thinking, making a connection between religious salvation and symbols of material success. It defines itself as a place where "...positive attitudes are developed, good people become better, hurts are healed, lessons are learned, friendships are developed, marriages are strengthened, families are bonded, the restless find peace, love is alive, God is understood, Jesus is Lord." The Cathedral operates mostly through television programs and books, which have reached millions.

CULTURAL INTEGRATION FELLOWSHIP

Hindu-oriented group devoted to the teachings of SRI AUROBINDO, founded in 1951 by Haridas Chaudhuri (1913–1975) in San Francisco. It operates the California Institute of Asian Studies, founded in 1968.

Jonathan Cummins, see ADVENT CHRISTIAN CHURCH

D

DA'AT

Israeli new religion founded in 1987 by Shlomo Kalo (1922–), based on his personal vision of life and the universe. The group's name is an acronym of Da Et Atzmecha Tamid ("Always Know Thyself"). Kalo claims to be an entity from the star Sirius, created thirteen million years ago and now descended to earth in human form to show humanity the road to enlightenment. His mission to earth follows those of Moses of the Old Testament, Jesus of the New Testament, and Muhammad of the Koran. When his mission is over, Kalo will again assume the form of light radiation, nurtured by pure energy. He advocates celibacy and the avoidance of meat, wine, anger, envy, and all sensual enjoyment and encourages his followers to live communally in small groups. Kalo's writings before the surfacing of his claim to be an emissary from Sirius include about fifteen books devoted to explicating classical Buddhism and his interpretations and additions to it.

Mikkel Dahl, see DAWN OF TRUTH

DAMASCUS CHRISTIAN CHURCH

Spanish-speaking PENTECOSTAL group started in 1939 in New York City, with branches in the Caribbean.

Anthony Damiani, see WISDOM'S GOLDENROD CENTER FOR PHILOSOPHIC STUDIES

Lillian K. Daniel, see UNIVERSAL PEACE INSTITUTE

John Nelson Darby, see PLYMOUTH BRETHREN

Baba Hari Dass, see LAMA FOUNDATION; SRI RAMA FOUNDATION

DAVIDIAN SEVENTH-DAY ADVENTIST ASSOCIATION

U.S. Adventist group founded by Victor T. Houteff (1885–1955), a dissenting member of the SEVENTH-DAY ADVENTISTS. In the early 1930s he proclaimed himself a divine messenger charged with the task of gathering the 144,000 souls destined for salvation according to the New Testament Book of Revelation. In 1935 he moved with eleven followers to Mount Carmel Center, near Waco, Texas, to gather the 144,000. The next step was to have been a move to Palestine and the establishment of a Davidian kingdom prior to the Second Coming of Christ. The group was first known as the BRANCH SEVENTH-DAY ADVENTISTS, but in 1942 it took the present name.

When Houteff died his wife took over the leadership. She later announced that the Davidian kingdom would arrive on April 22, 1959, when both Arabs and Israelis would disappear forever from the Holy Land. The faithful gathered at Mount Carmel to await this event, and in their disappointment most left the group. In December 1961, Mrs. Houteff confessed her error and the error of the group's teachings. In an even more unusual step, in March 1962 the association was officially dissolved. However, a few members were committed to reviving it, and in 1970 it was set up in Exter, Missouri.

Gordon Davidson, see SIRIUS COMMUNITY

J. David Davis, see EMMANUEL

Roy Eugene Davis, see CENTER FOR SPIRITUAL AWARENESS (CSA)

R.E. Dawkins, see GOSPEL ASSEMBLIES (DAWKINS)

DAWN BIBLE STUDENTS ASSOCIATION

U.S. outreach ministry organization started in the late 1920s in secession from JEHOVAH'S WITNESSES, which distributes the teachings of Charles Taze Russell (1852–1916) through printed publications, radio, and television. Based in New York City, the group works in the United States, Great Britain, Western Europe, and Oceania.

See also PASTORAL BIBLE INSTITUTE

DAWN OF TRUTH

North American Christian-occultist group founded by Mikkel Dahl in Windsor, Ontario, in 1961. Teachings include the "power of the Great Pyramid" and "spiritual laws of successful living."

Baba Dayal, see NIRANKARI

DEATH ANGELS

U.S. Islamic group started in the 1970s as a splinter group from the NATION OF ISLAM (NOI).

Paul Decelles, see PEOPLE OF PRAISE (POP)

DEFENDERS OF THE CHRISTIAN FAITH, INC.

U.S. Fundamentalist group founded in 1925 by Gerald B. Winrod (1898–1957) as an interdenominational organization. It is politically conservative and anti-Semitic. Several publications, mainly *The Defender*, promote its views. Reaching the height of its growth in the 1930s, the group declined after Winrod's death and then recovered somewhat in the 1960s under the leadership of G.H. Montgomery and Hunt Armstrong.

Source:
Roy, J.L. *Apostles of Discord.* Boston: Beacon Press, 1953.

DEFENDERS OF THE FAITH, THE (Iglesia Defensores de La Fe)

North American Spanish-speaking Fundamentalist group, started in 1931 in Puerto Rico during a visit by Gerald B. Winrod, founder of the DEFENDERS OF THE CHRISTIAN FAITH, INC. In 1944 the group began recruiting members in the Spanish-speaking communities of the continental United States.

Albert Delbauche, see AMIS DE LA CROIX GLORIEUSE DE DOZULÉ

Alexander Demaras, see NEW YORK METAPHYSICAL SOCIETY

DENVER AREA WICCAN NETWORK (DAWN)

Neo-pagan group based in Denver, Colorado, and founded in the late 1980s.

Christopher de Peyer, see FOUNDATION FAITH OF THE MILLENNIUM

Karen DePolito, see TEMPLE OF THE ETERNAL LIGHT

Amrit Desai, see KRIPALU YOGA ASHRAM

DESTINY OF AMERICA FOUNDATION

British-Israelist organization founded by Conrad Gaard and based in his Christian Chapel Church in Tacoma, Washington. Gaard was an active author and radio speaker until his death in 1969.
See also BRITISH ISRAELISM

Source:
Roy, R.L. *Apostles of Discord*. Boston: Beacon Press, 1953.

DEVA COMMUNITY

U.S. Theosophical commune founded in the 1970s in Maryland.

Swami Vishnu-Devananda, see SIVANANDA YOGA VEDANTA

Robert Devine, see UNITED LEADERSHIP COUNCIL OF HEBREW ISRAELITES

Walter De Voe, see ELOHISTS

Dharmadhatu, see VAJRADHATU

DIANIC WICCA

U.S. neo-pagan, witchcraft, feminist organization, founded by Zsuasznna Budapest in the mid-1970s. Based in California, it calls for lesbian separatism, prescribes all-female membership of covens, and practices the worship of a monotheistic goddess.
See also COVENANT OF THE GODDESS; TEMPLE OF THE GODDESS WITHIN

DIANOLOGY AND EDUCTIVISM

Also known as Church of Eductivism, Church of Spiritual Science, Association of International Dianologists, and the Personal Spiritual Freedoms Foundation. This U.S. group is an offshoot of SCIENTOLOGY founded in 1965 by Jack Horner (1927–), the first person to be awarded the "Doctor of Scientology" degree, and one of L. Ron Hubbard's earliest associates.

Kenneth G. Dickkerson, see POSITIVE THINKING MINISTRY

Edwin John Dingle, see INSTITUTE OF MENTALPHYSICS

Ding Le Mei, see INSTITUTE OF MENTALPHYSICS

Dirya Sandesh Parishad, see DIVINE LIGHT MISSION (DLM)

"Discipleship," see SHEPHERDING

DISCIPLES OF CHRIST

Sometimes known as the Restoration Movement, or Campbellites, this Protestant millenarian denomination was started in 1830 by Alexander Campbell (1788–1866), an Irish Presbyterian minister who moved to the United States in 1807. Campbell preached a return to "primitive Christianity" and the abolition of all formal creeds. In 1829 he predicted the "purification of the Sanctuary" to take place in 1847. Then he became convinced that the year 1866 would be decisive, and in 1862 he computed the millennium to occur 1996–2996. In 1812 in Washington, Pennsylvania, he founded the Christian Association, which later became the Disciples of Christ. In several English-speaking countries outside the United States the movement is known as the Churches of Christ.

DISCIPLES OF FAITH
NEW THOUGHT group based in Nashville, Tennessee, operating strictly by mail. It offers followers prayers that guarantee health and prosperity.

Disciples of Jesus, see TWO-BY-TWO'S

DISPENSATIONALISM
The belief in seven dispensations, or ages, of history, which is found in many millenarian Protestant groups. According to the most common version, the seven dispensations are: Innocence, Conscience, Government, Promise, Law, Grace, and the Personal Reign of Christ.
See also PLYMOUTH BRETHREN

Source:
Ehlert, A.D. *A Bibliographic History of Dispensationalism.* Grand Rapids, MI: Baker Book House, 1965

DIVINE LIFE SOCIETY (Divine Love Consciousness)
International Hindu group founded in 1936, devoted to the teachings of Swami Sivananda Saraswati (1887–1963), a noted 20th-century Hindu guru who was the teacher of Swami Satchidananda and Swami Vishnu Devananda. Sivananda worked in a hospital for ten years before taking the vows of holiness and renouncing the world. In 1924 he opened a small free dispensary, which later became a hospital, and preached selfless service to humanity as the highest calling. In 1945 he founded an All World Religious Federation, and later the Yoga Vedanta Forest Academy, known as The Forest Academy. The Society is based in Shivanandanagar, Tehri-Garhwal, India. Its activities in the West started in 1954, when the European Divine Life Society was established in Switzerland. In 1959 branches were established in the United States following a visit by Swami Chidananda.
See also INTEGRAL YOGA INSTITUTE; SIVANANDA YOGA VEDANTA

DIVINE LIGHT MISSION (DLM)
Known also as Dirya Sandesh Parishad, and more recently as Elan Vital, this international Hindu movement was founded in 1960 in India. It became known all over the world in the 1970s under the leadership of Pratap Singh Rawat-Balyogeshwar, better known as Guru Maharaj Ji (the full title is Satguru Balyogeshwar Shri Sant Ji Maharaj), who was born in 1958 in India. He was the youngest of four sons born to Prem Nagar, also known as Shri Hans Maharaj Ji, who founded the Divine Light Mission in 1960. Shri Hans Maharaj Ji claimed to have reached enlightenment through the knowledge given to him by his guru Shri Sarupanand Ji in the 1920s. When the founder died in 1966, the eight-year-old Pretap stood up at the funeral to announce his ascent to the throne and became the movement's recognized leader. Guru Maharaj Ji went on a world tour in 1971, visiting Great Britain, France, Germany, Australia, South Africa, and the United States. His brothers were also active in the movement.

Maharaj Ji was considered *satguru*, or the Perfect Master. Members of the group, known as *premies* (devotees), were those who had received "the Knowledge" from the Master, including four meditation procedures leading to ecstasy and perfection. The four procedures are known as Light, Music, Nectar, and Word; two hours a day were devoted to them, but continuous meditation on the Word was recommended. Meetings in which members were recruited, known as *satsang*, were held in local ashrams.

In addition to meditation and *satsang*, the *premies* were supposed to spend their time at *darshans* (talks by the satguru) and in service to the group. One form of *darshan* was *pranam*, in which the *premies* prostrated themselves in front of the satguru. Service activities included seeking donations and distributing group literature.

There were ashrams, communal houses, in which members of both sexes lived monastically and celibately. *Premies* living in ashrams gave all their material possessions to the satguru and obeyed strict discipline. They abstained from alcohol, meat, tobacco and other drugs, and food not provided by the ashram. Some members not living in ashrams lived communally but with no hierarchy, with laxer discipline and mutual support by members themselves. DLM's best-known recruit in the U.S. in the early 1970s was Rennie Davis, a cofounder of the radical Students for a Democratic Society (S.D.S.) in the 1960s, and a codefendant in the Chicago Seven trial in 1969. Davis became a DLM member in 1972.

In November 1973 DLM organized a gathering known as Millennium '73 in Houston's Astrodome. *Premies* expected the millennium to arrive and all the world's problems to be solved at the *darshan* given during the gathering, but the event was a failure even in attendance and media attention; and it started the group's decline. At the height of its life cycle, in the mid-1970s, the Divine Light Mission had thirty ashrams in the United States, with headquarters in Denver, and a score of ashrams in Europe and Israel. In the early 1980s the organization was dismantled by Guru Maharj Ji himself. He left his followers with "the Knowledge," the four practices of meditation and ecstasy, which they could use and teach, but he freed them of any allegiance to him or to the movement. He was no longer the guru. DLM became The Knowledge, and the movement, based in the U.S., became known as Elan Vital.

Source:

Downton, J.V. Jr. *Sacred Journeys: The Conversion of Young Americans to Divine Light Mission*. New York: Columbia University Press, 1979.

DIVINE SCIENCE CHURCH

NEW THOUGHT group started by Malinda Cramer (?–1907), who chartered The Home College of Divine Science in 1888 in San Franciso. Her work was followed and expanded by Nona Brooks (1863–1945). In 1896 the College of Divine Science was founded in Denver, Colorado. The International Divine Science Association was founded in 1892, and in 1957 the Divine Science Federation International was organized. According to the group's doctrine, illness and poverty can be avoided by a return to oneness with the "Divine Omnipresence."

Sources:

Braden, C.S. *Spirits in Rebellion*. Dallas: SMU Press, 1963.

Guru Maharaj Ji, leader of the Divine Light Mission, with his bride and former secretary, the former Karolyn Lois Johnson. At the time, in 1974, the Mission had thirty centers in the United States, with headquarters in Denver, Colorado.

Judah, J.S. *The History and Philosophy of the Metaphysical Movements in America.* Philadelphia: Westminster Press, 1967.

DIVINE SCIENCE OF LIGHT AND SOUND, THE

Syncretistic group founded in 1980 by Jerry Mulvin (1936–), a former leader of ECKANKAR in Marina del Rey, California. The doctrine and practices focus on "traveling into the inner world" as well as "out-of-body travel."

Dodrup Chen, Rinpoche, see MAHA-SIDDHA NYINGMAPA

Jules Doinel, see GNOSTIC CHURCH

DOLLEY POND CHURCH OF GOD WITH SIGNS FOLLOWING

U.S. PENTECOSTAL group noted for its use of snakes during services, founded in the 1930s by Thomas Harden. Its members are popularly known as "snake handlers." Members follow a strict code of conduct. Snake handling and the drinking of poison are regarded both as signs of the "Holy Spirit" and as tests of faith. In practice, snake handling is only rarely accompanied by drinking poison. Cases of death from snake bites have occurred since the practice started in 1909, and laws have been passed against snake handling, but bites are not a common occurrence.

See also CHURCH OF ALL NATIONS; ORIGINAL PENTECOSTAL CHURCH OF GOD

Members of a Pentecostal group popularly known as "snake handlers" performing a funeral ritual.

Source:
La Barre, W. *They Shall Take Up Serpents*. New York: Schocken, 1969.

Clemente Dominguez y Gomez, see PALMARIAN CATHOLIC CHURCH

James A. Dooling,III, see CHURCH OF THE GIFT OF GOD

DOOR OF FAITH CHURCHES OF HAWAII

U.S. PENTECOSTAL group founded in 1940 by Mildred Brostek. It operates overseas missions in addition to its activities in Hawaii.

Maurice Doreal, see BROTHERHOOD OF THE WHITE TEMPLE

DOR HASHALOM

Jewish-NEW THOUGHT group based in New York City and founded in the 1980s by Burt Aaron Siegel. It later merged with THE NEW SYNAGOGUE.

DORJE KHYUNG DZONG

Tibetan Buddhist retreat center founded in the 1970s in Colorado.

John E. Dougla, see AMERICAN EVANGELISTIC ASSOCIATION

John L. Douglas, see GENERAL PSIONICS, CHURCH OF

DOUKHOBORS

The name, which means "spirit-wrestlers," refers to an anarchist religious group started in Russia at the end of the 18th century. Its doctrine opposes all civil authority and supports communal living. Members believe in reincarnation, and an early leader, Sergei Kapoustin, claimed to be an incarnation of Jesus Christ. They suffered persecution in Czarist Russia, and so a migration to Canada was arranged in 1898. The leader changed the group's name to the Christian Community of Universal Brotherhood. Since settling in Canada they have been involved in many clashes with authorities, in which they often use nudism as a form of protest. One of several internal schisms created a group known as SONS OF FREEDOM.

Sources:
Maude, A. *A Peculiar People*. New York: Funk & Wagnalls, 1904.
Woodcock, G., and Abakumovic, I. *The Doukhobors*. Toronto: McClelland and Stewart, 1977.

W.A. Draves, see CHURCH OF CHRIST WITH THE ELIJAH MESSAGE

DREADS, THE

Nativist African-American nationalist movement based in Dominica, inspired by the RASTAFARIANS of Jamaica. The term "dread" is used by Rastafarians to mean "the power that lies within any man." The movement was subject to suppression by the government of Dominica in the 1970s.

Timothy Drew, "Noble Drew Ali," see MOORISH SCIENCE TEMPLE OF AMERICA

DROMENON

Syncretistic "non-residential transformational community," founded by Jean Houston and Robert Masters in the late 1970s and based in New York City. Doctrine combines Western and Eastern mythology.

Henry Drummond, see CATHOLIC APOSTOLIC CHURCH

Murshida Ivy O. Duce, see SUFISM REORIENTED, INC.

DUCK RIVER (AND KINDRED) ASSOCIATION OF BAPTISTS (BAPTIST CHURCH OF CHRIST)

Conservative Protestant group founded in 1825 as the result of a split with the Elk River Baptist Association in the hill country of Tennessee and Alabama.

Peter Duenov, see FRATERNITÉ BLANCHE UNIVERSELLE

Caroline Duke, see AQUARIAN BROTH-ERHOOD OF CHRIST; INDEPENDENT ASSOCIATED SPIRITUALISTS

Shirlee Dunlap, see CIRCLE OF LIGHT

Lawrence, Pamela, and Olivia Durdin-Robertson, see FELLOWSHIP OF ISIS

Steve Durkee, see LAMA FOUNDATION

Jim Durkin, see CHURCH OF THE COMPLETE WORD

DZOGCHEN ORYGEN CHO LING

U.S. Tibetan Buddhist group connected with the XIV Dalai Lama, founded in the 1980s.

E

EARTHSPIRIT COMMUNITY

Neo-pagan group founded in 1980 in Boston by Andras Corban Arthen and Deirdre Pulgram Arthen, who are members of the ATHANOR FELLOWSHIP, the inner circle of the group. Its credo is that "all things in the Universe interact in both a physical and spiritual relationship." During its meetings and festivals, "drumming, chanting, tarot, vision questing, healing, dancing" are practiced.

EAST-WEST CULTURAL CENTER

Hindu-oriented group devoted to the teachings of SRI AUROBINDO, founded in 1953 in Los Angeles by Judith M. Tyberg.

Offu Ebongo, see BROTHERHOOD OF THE CROSS AND STAR

ECCLESIA

U.S. Fundamentalist group founded in the early 1980s by Eldrige Broussard, Jr.

ECKANKAR

Occultist Sikh-inspired group founded in California in 1964 by John Paul Twitchell (1908–1971), who was a member of the SELF-REVELATION CHURCH OF ABSOLUTE MONISM between 1950 and 1955 and then joined RUHANI SATSANG and SCIENTOLOGY. The group refers to itself as the Ancient Science of Soul Travel, and its teachings reflect closely the Sikh tradition of Kirpal Singh. Followers are expected to follow a Living Eck Master, who is able to deliver them from the wheel of reincarnation. The Living Eck Master is believed to be "the God man of the age...omnipotent, omniscient and omnipresent. He is all powerful, all wise, and is in all places simultaneously...He has appeared as Krishna, Buddha, or Vishnu...He is Zeus to the Greeks; Jupiter to the Romans;...Jehovah to the old Judean...Jesus to the Christians; and Allah to the Mohammedans." The group teaches "Spiritual travel of the soul body."
See also SAWAN KIRPAL RUHANI MISSION

F.S. Edgell, see NEW JERUSALEM FELLOWSHIP

Clyde Edminster, see CALVARY FELLOWSHIP, INC.

Alexis Edwards, see FINDHORN FOUNDATION

Église Catholic Française, see GALLICAN CHURCH

ÉGLISE DE LA SAINTE FAMILLE

French traditionalist Catholic group founded in 1974 by Pierre Poulain (1924–   ). The founder has announced the coming of great catastrophes as a divine punishment for the sins of the world. In 1979 he predicted the birth of his daughter Marie. A son was born and named "Jesus-Pierre, the Savior and Redeemer of humanity." Coronation of a future king is predicted for 1999, and a golden crown is being prepared.

Frederick Eikerekoetter II ("Reverend Ike"), see UNITED CHURCH AND SCIENCE OF LIVING INSTITUTE

Okano Eizo, see GEDATSU-KAI

Ulf Ekman, see WORD OF LIFE

ELIJAH VOICE SOCIETY
U.S. offshoot of JEHOVAH'S WITNESSES, which broke away from the Stand Fast Bible Students in 1923.

ELIM FOURSQUARE GOSPEL
Christian Fundamentalist, PENTECOSTAL group founded in 1915 in Belfast by George Jeffreys (1889–   ). For 25 years the founder was active in preaching his message throughout the British Isles, but he left in 1940 to start the BIBLE PATTERN FELLOW-SHIP, also Fundamentalist. The group practices speaking in tongues and healing. Members believe in spirit guidance and the rapidly approaching Second Coming.

Elim Ministerial Fellowship, see ELIM MISSIONARY ASSEMBLIES

ELIM MISSIONARY ASSEMBLIES
First known as the Elim Ministerial Fellowship, this U.S. PENTECOSTAL group was founded in 1932 and adopted the current name in 1947. The group operates the World Missionary Assistance Plan in foreign countries.

Michael El-Legion, see EXTRA-TERRESTRIAL COMMUNICATIONS NETWORK

James Ellison, see THE COVENANT, THE SWORD, THE ARM OF THE LORD

ELOHISTS
Syncretistic group founded in 1918 by Walter De Voe in Brookline, Massachusetts. In the early 1900s he was a student of NEW THOUGHT and started the Elohist Ministry, focused on "healing". It "... evolved into a ministry devoted to the rescue, education and revival of earth-bound spirits through the assistance of mediums and 'angelic helpers'." In the late 1930s De Voe discovered *OAHSPE: A New Bible*, published in 1882 by John Ballou Newbrough (1828–1891). The group then became closely connected to the UNIVERSAL FAITHISTS OF KOSMON (U.F.K.).

Source:
Goodspeed, E.J. *Modern Apocrypha*. Boston: Beacon Press, 1956.

EMBASSY OF THE GHEEZ-AMERICANS
Africanist, occultist group founded by the "Empress Mysikiitta Fa Sennato," who runs the Mt. Helion Sanctuary in Long Eddy, New York. The "Empress" supposedly arrived from outer space and reports many adventures there. She calls for the revival of the Gheez-Nation, the ancient people of Ethiopia, who are truly the chosen people.

Harold Davis Emerson, see MAYAN TEMPLE

EMIN SOCIETY, THE
First known as the Eminent Way, the Faculty of Colour, and the Church of the Eminent Way, this international occultist-syncretistic group was founded in 1971 in London by Raymond Schertenlieb (1924–   ), also known as Raymond John Armin and to members of the Society as Leo. The group operates through "choirs, herbal groups, tarot groups, Bible study classes, poetry groups, mumming groups, theatrical groups, bands, vocal groups, music composition, dancing troups, healers, astrology

groups, palmistry, graphology, phrenology and other detection groups...." It has branches in Israel, Canada, Australia, and the United States in addition to the center in London. The Church of Emin Coils is the Florida branch of the Emin Society, organized in 1978 by Leo and his emissaries. The Emin University of Life has operated in New York City as a branch of the Society.

Many of the beliefs and practices in the Emin lore are similar to those of other modern occult groups, especially the ROSICRUCIANS, the GURDJIEFF GROUPS, and ANTHROPOSOPHY. These include belief in the existence of three human brains. The practices of the Society include reading "auras," diagnosing individuals on the basis of "aura colors," and a rite of exorcism that "...arrests any hostile, degenerative or unreasonable essence, practice, mind or mental projection; which stands against anything which tries to prevent the given right of human life to become enhanced over its planatary station;...It is processed and dealt with entirely in the occult, electrical and electro-magnetic fields of human precincts, dwelling precincts, location precincts and all concentrated ground or dimensions." Major concerns expressed in Emin writings are those of becoming electrically polluted and the means to avoid or rectify this pollution; and "...electrical stumps traveling through the astral light can attach themselves, in the way of a barnacle or limpet, to the human aura. Understand that all sorts of electrical filth can be released by people which then moves through the astral light looking for a human host which is higher than itself upon whose aura it can attach itself, and from which it can electrically feed, and even grow. But there is worse to come, for at close quarters someone can stick upon you one of those electrical barnacles or limpets deliberately, through spite, malice, hatred, jealousy, sexual projection.... Now, this can become even more serious, in that once an electrical barnacle or limpet has attached itself to a person's aura, it can then work like modern radar, acting as a beacon to that from which it came...this indicates a very dangerous prospect should a 'branch office' be established on the very edge of your aura which is tranmitted into on a long-term basis." The solution for this worrisome state, according to Emin writings, is cleansing your aura.

For members of Emin, personal time is measured in Emin years, which are nine months long. "A normal seasonal life cycle is...72 Emin years; which then translates into 54 calendar years, which is, interestingly enough, the age at which Mohammed is recorded to have become divine. Any more birthdays or cycles after this time are considered to be grace of extension."

Standards of behavior in the Society include rules about symbols and sexual behavior. "It is forbidden ... to erect a pentagram or an aeneagram; and it is against God and creation to worship any symbol in an upside-down condition, or to practice a ceremony backwards. Any offender will be exorcised and excommunicated." This is, in part, because "...the two symbols become portals or terminal points of the arrival and despatch of inter-galactic electrical form..." causing death by "...spontaneous combustion, petrification, lack of energy (wasting) and electrical gangrene." Regarding sex, "At no time will homosexuality, lesbianism, transvestism, nymphonic or any other unnatural condition or freak practice...be permitted." Emin doctrine claims to be based on secret knowledge developed by ancient Egyptian culture.

EMISSARIES OF DIVINE LIGHT

Also known as the Ontological Society, Divine Light Emissaries, the Foundation of Universal Unity, the Universal Institute of Applied Ontology, and the Integrity Society, this international esoteric Christianity group was founded in 1932 in Tennessee by Lloyd Arthur Meeker, also known as Uranda. He was succeeded as group leader by Martin Cecil (1909–1988), who has been responsible for formulating most of the official doctrine.

The belief system of the Emissaries contains a combination of modern occult ideas, à la Gurdjieff, together with some traditional, old-fashioned Christianity. There is also the notion that humanity is undergoing a major change in consciousness and that this change is occurring all around us and is leading to revolutionary consequences. The main idea is the centrality of consciousness and the unity of body and mind. The group promotes "holistic healing." The International Emissary organization sponsored the "10th International Human Unity Conference," held at Warwick University, England, in July 1983. It was described as "Part of a global, creative shift which transcends human beliefs, fears, ambitions, and differences." The group also promotes communal living and has set up communes around the world in which most members live. Its headquarters are at the Sunrise Farm in Loveland, Colorado, and it has operated the Emissary Foundation International (EFI). Branches have operated in North America, Europe, Africa, and Israel.
See also GURDJIEFF GROUPS

EMMANUEL

B'NAI NOACH congregation started in the 1980s in Athens, Tennessee, by J. David Davis, a former Baptist minister.
See also FRAZIER CHAPEL

EMMANUEL ASSOCIATION

U.S. conservative Protestant group founded in 1937 by Ralph G. Finch (?–1949). Doctrine calls for a strict code of behavior and extreme simplicity in life-style. Members are conscientious objectors.

EMMANUEL CHURCH OF CHRIST ONENESS PENTECOSTAL

PENTECOSTAL group started in Dover, Tennessee, in the early 1930s. Practices include faith healing and glossolalia. The group attracted much media attention when John David Terry (1944–), who had served as leader since 1969, was convicted of murder in 1988 and sentenced to death.

EMMANUEL HOLINESS CHURCH

PENTECOSTAL group with branches in the United States and Great Britain, formed in 1953 as a result of a schism in the PENTECOSTAL FIRE-BAPTIZED HOLINESS CHURCH, which in turn was created by a schism in the Pentecostal Holiness Church. Disputes over dress standards (wearing neckties) led to the original schism and the founding of Emmanuel Holiness Church. Doctrine is similar to that of the parent body.

EMMANUEL MESSIANIC CONGREGATION

Originally known as Emmanuel Presbyterian Hebrew Christian Congregation, this Hebrew Christian group based in Baltimore

was founded in the first quarter of the 20th century. It has been connected with LEDERER MESSIANIC MINISTRIES.
See also HEBREW CHRISTIANS

EMMANUEL MOVEMENT

Faith healing group, influenced by CHRISTIAN SCIENCE and NEW THOUGHT, which attempted to reconcile religious beliefs with medical views. It was started in Boston in 1904 around the Emanuel Episcopal Church by Elwood Worcester, Samuel McComb, and Isador Coriat. The movement extended to other large cities in the United States. The group's doctrine claimed to offer "sound psychology, sound medicine, and sound religion."

Sheldon Emry, see THE LORD'S COVENANT CHURCH

END TIME MINISTRIES

Adventist group started in Sioux Falls, South Dakota, in the late 1970s, which has preached reliance on faith healing and rejection of modern medicine. One case of death was reported in 1989 as a result.

EPIPHANY BIBLE STUDENTS ASSOCIATION

U.S. Adventist group formed by John J. Hoefle (1895–1984) as a result of a schism in the LAYMEN'S HOME MISSIONARY MOVEMENT. The dispute started after the death in 1955 of Paul S.L. Johnson, founder of the Movement, and concerned accusations and counteraccusations betweem Hoefle and Raymond Jolly, Johnson's successor as leader. Hoefle was expelled in February 1956 and continued to express his dissenting view that other groups have dis-

torted the original message of Charles Taze Russell.
See also JEHOVAH'S WITNESSES

EQUIFRILIBRICUM WORLD RELIGION

Sometimes known as the Equality-Fraternity-Liberty Church, or Moncadistas, this independent Protestant church was started in 1925 among Filipinos in the United States. It has also operated in the Philippines.

Paul Erdman, see LOVE FAMILY

ERIE BIBLE TRUTH DEPOT

Group of PLYMOUTH BRETHREN founded by A.E. Booth in Erie, Pennsylvania, around 1930.

Source:
Ehlert, A.D. *A Bibliographic History of Dispensationalism.* Grand Rapids, MI: Baker Book House, 1965.

ESP PICTURE PRAYERS

NEW THOUGHT group founded by Murcie P. Smith in Gary, Indiana. It has operated by offering its followers prayers and "ESP readings" by mail.

ETERNAL FLAME FOUNDATION, THE

Known also as the Arizona Immortals, or the Forever People, this NEW THOUGHT group is "dedicated to building a deathless world." It was founded in Scottsdale, Arizona, in the late 1960s by Charles Paul Brown (1935–), a former Presbyterian minister and nightclub singer. In the spring of 1960 Brown had a vision of Jesus Christ and a revelation of physical immortality as a reality, or "cellular awakening." He was joined in leading the group by BernaDeane

Brown (1937–) and James R. Strole (1949–).

Doctrine is connected with Christian theology but claims that "...death is actually a fabrication or lie imposed on our minds and bodies by a ruling death consciousness in order to control the species of man and keep him in eternal bondage...there will never be lasting peace on earth until the *last enemy of man, which is death* is abolished...most religions believe that physical immortality will eventually take place in the bodies of mankind upon the earth. However, it is always projected into some future dispensation due to misconceptions and religious dogmas. We feel the time IS NOW for an immortal species of mankind to be birthed upon the planet."

ETHERIAN RELIGIOUS SOCIETY OF UNIVERSAL BROTHERHOOD

Esoteric Christian group founded in 1965 by E.A. Hurtienne in San Marcos, California. Practices include meditation and faith healing. It is affiliated with the LIVING CHRIST MOVEMENT.

ETHIOPIAN HEBREWS

"Black Jews" group started in Chicago in the 1940s by Abihu Reuben as an offshoot of the COMMANDMENT KEEPERS CONGREGATION OF THE LIVING GOD.

ETHIOPIAN ZION COPTIC CHURCH

International Rastafarian group incorporated in 1976 in White Horse, Jamaica, under the leadership of Keith Gordon, known as Nyah. Branches have operated in the United States, where members have run into legal trouble because of their use of marijuana.

See also RASTAFARIANS

"ETHIOPIANS"

South African independent church movement created in secession from European mission churches. "Africa for Africans" is the movement's slogan, but it otherwise follows the doctrines of mainline Protestants. In this case, as in other places, the special role of Ethiopia (Abyssinia) in black political consciousness is influential in developing a separate, positive identity. Ethiopia is viewed as an African, Christian, and sovereign kingdom, a source of inspiration for all Africans. The other major church movement in South Africa is the "ZIONISTS."

See also RASTAFARIANS

ETOISM

Officially known as the Christian Fellowship Church, this syncretistic-Pentecostal movement (CARGO CULT) was started as an independent Melanesian church in the New Georgia group of the Solomon Islands in 1960 by Silas Eto (1905–). Considered a messiah by his followers, who were former members of the Methodist Mission church, Eto was educated as a Methodist, but his dissatisfaction with the church organization led to the formation of an independent movement. The church built the Holy Village of Paradise, which serves as its center. Church practices include faith healing and speaking in tongues.

ETZBA ELOHIM (THE FINGER OF GOD)

Israeli new religion founded in 1981 by Rina Shani (1937–1983), born Rina Shomroni. Shani first made a name for herself in the 1960s as a poet and writer, and by 1970 she had three books of poetry to her credit. In 1981 she was again in the public eye, this time as a cult leader facing charges for the ritual use of marijuana. The metamorphosis, as she herself described it, started in 1970 when she first tasted cannabis. In 1973 Rina Shani had another illumination in the form of an encounter with a schizophrenic artist, whom she started treating through "awareness work," and she practiced as a self-styled "therapist" until 1979. In January 1979, following her arrest on drug charges, she had another mystical experience, another final illumination: "I was dead, and then I was born again. On that day, and the following one, I experienced infinity, and on the third day I experienced God. I enjoyed Jehovah's presence and unity with him."

After this revelation she changed her name to Rain Shine, moved to a new location, and started saving souls through her methods. By 1981 she had a score of devoted followers who took care of all her needs. In addition to marijuana, Rain Shine regarded LSD as a major sacrament. Group members used the sacraments and chose new names as symbols of their personal transformation. Seeing families as evil and parents as "crucifying" their children was among Rain's articles of faith. She declared herself totally opposed to marriage, parenting, and finally, sex. Rain Shine and members of her group were charged with illegal drug use. While her followers usually got in serious trouble for using drugs, Rain used her considerable charisma on Israeli judges and escaped punishment time and again. A fact that did not endear the group to the public was Rain's readiness to accept minors as disciples. Rain left Israel and went to India. In November 1983 she died of hepatitis on the banks of the Ganges River.

EUCHARISTIC CATHOLIC CHURCH

Christian homosexual group founded in 1970 in New York City by Robert Clement.

EVADISME

Occultist-Christian group founded in Paris around 1830 by Caillaux, known as Ganneau (?–1851), who called himself Le Mapah (a combination of *maman* and *papah*—mother and father) and proclaimed himself prophet and God. His teachings included emphasis on the importance of the feminine in religion, and he named his group after the androgynous Evadah (Eve+Adam). He also taught that Mary of the New Testament was the God-Mother, wife of the Man-God. Ganneau declared a new age starting in 1838, the age of Evadah, in which all forms of oppression would be opposed.

EVANGELICAL BIBLE CHURCH

PENTECOSTAL group founded by Frederick B. Marine in 1947 in Baltimore. A strict code of conduct is enforced, and members are conscientious objectors.

EVANGELICAL CHRISTIAN SCIENCE CHURCH

Independent CHRISTIAN SCIENCE group founded after the death of Mary Baker Eddy in 1910 by Oliver C. Sabin, Jr.

EVANGELICAL METHODIST CHURCH, THE

Fundamentalist group founded in 1946 in Memphis, Tennessee.

EVANGELICAL MINISTERS AND CHURCHES, INTERNATIONAL, INC.

Association of evangelical, Fundamentalist ministers, founded in 1950 in Chicago.
See also FUNDAMENTALISM

EWAM CHODEN TIBETAN BUDDHIST CENTER

Tibetan Buddhist group founded by Lama Kunga Thartse, Rinpoche in 1971 and based in northern California. The founder is believed by his disciples to be "the designated reincarnation of Sevan Repa, Heart Disciple of Milarepa." Beliefs and practices include studies of the Tibetan Book of the Dead and meditation.
See also VAJRADHATU

EXTRA-TERRESTRIAL COMMUNICATIONS NETWORK

"UFO" group founded in the 1980s in Arizona by Michael El-Legion. "Michael works extensively with the Intergalactic Confederation and Ascended Masters of the Spiritual Hierarchy."

F

FACIM, see FOUNDATION FOR "A COURSE IN MIRACLES" (FACIM)

FACTUM HUMANUM

Also known as the White Order, a European occultist group founded in the 1970s.

Faculty of Colour, see EMIN SOCIETY

FAITH ASSEMBLY, THE

Known initially as the Glory Barn Faith Assembly, this evangelical, PENTECOSTAL group was founded in North Webster, Indiana in 1963 by Hobart E. Freeman (1920–1984), a former professor at Grace Theological Seminary, and Melvin Greider (1937–   ). The Assembly had congregations in the Midwest and South. Freeman advocated the complete avoidance of modern medicine, relying instead on prayer. "Sickness and disease have been repeatedly defeated by maintaining a positive confession of faith in the face of all apparent evidence to the contrary... When genuine faith is present it alone will be sufficient, for it will take the place of medicines and other aids." At least 100 deaths occurred among members and their children in Indiana, Illinois, Ohio, Kentucky, Michigan, and Missouri as a result of medical neglect. Legal action was taken against members whose children died because of negligence, and several were convicted of reckless homicide and sentenced to prison terms.

Faithists, see UNIVERSAL FAITHISTS OF KOSMON

"FAITH" MOVEMENT

North American Fundamentalist, PENTECOSTAL organization founded in the 1970s by Kenneth Hagin in Oklahoma. A loose association of congregations and "media ministries," its theological message is sometimes called the "Health and Wealth Gospel," emphasizing the power of positive thinking. Faith healing is a major activity. The group is connected with the Swedish WORD OF LIFE CHURCH.

FAITH TABERNACLE

PENTECOSTAL group founded in California in 1924.

Faith Tabernacle, see CHRIST APOSTOLIC CHURCH

Theodore G. Falcon, see MAKOM OHR SHALOM

FAMILLE DE NAZARETH (COMMUNE DE NAZARETH)

French Catholic schismatic, monastic group founded in 1980 in Paris by Daniel Blanchard, a former Benedictine monk.

"The Family," see THE PROCESS

Family of Elohim, see CHURCH OF GOD (JERUSALEM)

Family of Love, see CHILDREN OF GOD

FANSCIFIAROAN CHURCH OF WICCA

Neo-pagan group started in the 1970s in Connecticut by Franklin Hedgecock. FANSCIFIAROAN stands for FANtasy, SCIence, FIction, ARt, and ROAN—the color reddish brown. The founder states, "Wicca is a religion of joy and love... The

David and Kathleen Bergmann, members of Faith Assembly, arrive at court for their trial on charges of reckless homicide and child neglect in the death of their infant daughter in 1984.

goal of the craft is to live in harmony with nature and the spirit world on the other side. The other side or the spirit world has a leader who created all things."

Alezandro B. Faquaragon, see ALPHA AND OMEGA CHRISTIAN CHURCH

W.D. Fard, see NATION OF ISLAM

FARM, THE

Syncretistic commune near Summerton, Tennessee, founded in 1971 by Stephen Gaskin (1936–   ) and his followers. The leader has preached "love, peace, telepathy, vibrations, meditation, honesty, truth and unity of human beings through spiritual enlightenment." Doctrine combines Christian and Buddhist ideas with meditation under the influence of marijuana. Members are vegetarian. The use of marijuana has caused legal difficulties, and four members, including Gaskin, served prison terms in the early 1970s. Since then use of illegal drugs has been prohibited.

Source:

Hall, J.R. *The Ways Out: Utopian Communal Groups in an Age of Babylon.* London: Routledge & Kegan Paul, 1978.

Abdul Haleem Farrakhan, see NATION OF ISLAM (FARRAKHAN)

(Louis) Farrakhan, see NATION OF ISLAM (FARRAKHAN)

William Farwell, see CHRISTIAN ASSEMBLY

FATHER DIVINE MOVEMENT

Officially known as the Universal Peace

Followers of Father Divine parade in New York City, celebrating his accomplishments on their behalf.

Mission Movement, this unique U.S. movement, with mostly black membership, saw enormous growth and gained much attention between the two World Wars. Its founder, whose real name was George Baker, was known as the Messenger, as Major Morgan J. Devine, and later as Father Major Jealous Divine (1880?–1965). He is reported to have been a follower and assistant of several African-American "Messiahs" before launching his own effort. The movement first became visible around 1914; it attracted greater interest during the Great Depression of the 1930s because of its economic success. Father Divine initiated several profit-making businesses and was able to lift his followers out of poverty through his code of ideal conduct. The group was based in New York City during its first thirty years, but in 1942 headquarters was moved to Philadelphia. Since the death of Father Divine the movement has been led by Mother Divine, the former Edna Rose Ritchings of Montreal (1925–), who married Father in 1946. The marriage was celibate.

The movement's doctrine specifies that Father Divine and his wife are the personifications of God as father and mother, and that Father Divine has fulfilled all the biblical prophecies about the Coming of the Messiah and the Second Coming of Christ. It prescribes communal living and the International Modesty Code prohibiting smoking, drinking, obscenity, vulgarity, profanity, and the receiving of gifts and tips. Celibacy is expected of truly committed followers.

Father Divine was active in the struggle for equality for U.S. blacks, preached and practiced integration, and held up the U.S. Constitution as the basis for just government. The movement has operated several corporations that provide employment for members, and Father Divine exhorted his followers to pay only cash for expenses, so as to avoid debt.

In addition to branches on the East Coast and in California, the Movement has operated missions in Europe, Australia, and Africa.

See also FATHER JEHOVAH; ST. JOHN THE DIVINE

Father Divine (next to railing) and Mother Divine cheer as they inspect their newly acquired "Heaven," a donated estate near West Park, New York.

Sources:

Burnham, K.E. *God Comes to America.* Boston: Lambeth, 1979.

Cantril, H. *The Psychology of Social Movements.* New York: Wiley, 1941.

Fauset, A.H. B*lack Gods of the Metropolis.* Philadelphia: University of Pennsylvania Press, 1944.

Harris, S. *Father Divine.* New York: Macmillan, 1971.

Parker, R.A. T*he Incredible Messiah.* Boston: Little, Brown, 1937.

Weisbrot, R. *Father Divine and the Struggle for Racial Equality.* Urbana: University of Illinois Press, 1983.

FÉDÉRATION UNIVERSELLE DES ORDRES ET SOCIETES INITIATIQUES (F.U.D.O.S.I)

Known also in Latin as Federatio Universalis Dirigens Ordines Societatesque Initiationis, this international organization of fourteen Rosicrucian groups was founded in 1934.

See also ROSICRUCIANS

Thomas Fehervary, see TRADITIONAL CHRISTIAN CATHOLIC CHURCH

Larry Feldman, see BETH MESSIAH

FELLOWSHIP IN PRAYER

Syncretistic group founded in 1949 in New Jersey, whose main practice is ecumenical prayer.

FELLOWSHIP OF CHRISTIAN BELIEVERS

Also known as the Body of Christ Movement, this U.S. PENTECOSTAL group was founded in the 1960s in Grand Rapids, Minnesota, by Charles P. and Dorothy Schmitt. Doctrine emphasizes the imminent coming of Jesus Christ, following the Latter Rain awakening of the 1940s.

FELLOWSHIP OF FRIENDS (FOF)

International Gurdjieff group founded in 1969 by Robert Burton in northern California. Branches have operated worldwide. Unlike most Gurdjieff groups, the FOF recruits members by advertising in newspapers. It charges a membership fee of 10 percent of gross monthly income. In French-speaking countries the group is known as Rassemblement des amis.

See also GURDJIEFF GROUPS

FELLOWSHIP OF INDEPENDENT EVANGELICAL CHURCHES

U.S. Fundamentalist group founded in 1949. Members believe in Satanic forces and in angels.

See also FUNDAMENTALISM

FELLOWSHIP OF ISIS (F.O.I.)

International neo-pagan group founded in 1976 by Lawrence, Pamela, and Olivia Durdin-Robertson. It is devoted to worship of the Egyptian goddess Isis and other ancient goddesses. The founders are considered hereditary priests, "from an hereditary line of the Robertson from Ancient Egypt." The grouo operates the College of Isis, which confers magi degrees.

FELLOWSHIP OF THE INNER LIGHT

Also known as Inner Light Consciousness (ILC), this Christian-spiritualist group was founded in 1974 by Paul Solomon, a former Baptist minister, in Virginia Beach, Virginia. Solomon offers "readings," which include advice on illness and healing, information about past lives and about Atlantis and Lemuria, and prophecies about the fate of the world, all within a Christian framework. The content of the "readings" is similar to those of Edgar Cayce. A related organization headed by Solomon is the Association of the Light Morning.

See also ASSOCIATION FOR RESEARCH AND ENLIGHTENMENT

Pat Fenske, see SPIRITUAL FELLOWSHIP OF AMERICA

FERAFERIA

"Witchcraft" group founded in 1967 in Los Angeles, devoted to the "Magic Maiden of the Aquarian Age" and to the worship of the processes of nature.

Joseph T. Ferguson, see UNIVERSAL CHURCH OF SCIENTIFIC TRUTH

William Ferguson, see COSMIC CIRCLE OF FELLOWSHIP

Michel Fernandez, see FRATERNITÉ "SALVE REGINA" DU FRÉCHOU

Brent D. Ferré, see BRIDGE CENTER FOR SPIRITUAL STUDIES

John Todd Ferrier, see ORDER OF THE CROSS

Otto Fetting, see CHURCH OF CHRIST (FETTINGITE)

Sam Fife, see BODY OF CHRIST

FILIPINO ASSEMBLIES OF THE FIRST BORN

PENTECOSTAL group founded by Julian Barnabe in 1933 in California. Membership consists of Filipino immigrants in California and Hawaii.

Charles S. Fillmore, Myrtle Fillmore, see NEW THOUGHT; UNITY SCHOOL OF CHRISTIANITY

FINDHORN FOUNDATION

British Christian-Anthroposophical group describing itself as a "theocratic democracy," founded in 1963 in northern Scotland by Eileen Caddy, Peter Caddy, Alexis Edwards, and Roger Benson. The founders claim to receive direct and detailed messages from the Christian God dealing with every aspect of life. They also report communications from "devas," elves, fairies, and gnomes, as well as the nature god Pan. The stated aim of the group is "... to usher in the New Age; to raise the vibrations by the awareness of the Christ Consciousness within each one ..." A major inspiration seems to be ANTHROPOSOPHY. The Foundation operates the Onearth Network of Resource People, also known as the Network of Light.

FIRE BAPTIZED HOLINESS CHURCH OF GOD OF THE AMERICAS

U.S. African-American PENTECOSTAL group based in Atlanta, founded by W.E. Fuller (1875–1958) in 1908, after he withdrew from the mostly white Fire Baptized Holiness Association because of dicrimination.

FIRST COMMUNITY CHURCH OF AMERICA

U.S. Fundamentalist group founded by Robert Taylor in the 1970s.

FIRST HEBREW PRESBYTERIAN CHRISTIAN CHURCH

Hebrew-Christian congregation founded by David Bronstein in Chicago in 1934. It later separated from the Presbyterian Church and became nondenominational.
See also HEBREW CHRISTIANS

FIRST INTERDENOMINATIONAL CHRISTIAN ASSOCIATION

PENTECOSTAL group founded in 1946 in Atlanta, Georgia, by Watson Sorrow, following a dispute over healing in the Georgia Conference of the PENTECOSTAL HOLINESS CHURCH.
See also CONGREGATIONAL HOLINESS CHURCH

FIRST SPIRITUALIST CHURCH OF NEW YORK

Spiritualist congregation based in New York City and led by Arthur Ford (1897–1971), part of the INTERNATIONAL GENERAL ASSEMBLY OF SPIRITUALISTS.

FIRST UNIVERSAL SPIRITUALIST CHURCH OF NEW YORK CITY

Spiritualist congregation founded by Clifford Bias in 1959 and led by him until his death in 1987.
See also UNIVERSAL SPIRITUALIST ASSOCIATION

FISHERFOLK COMMUNITIES OF CELEBRATION

International Christian Fundamentalist group of communes, with branches in Colorado, England, and Scotland.

Fletcher Fist, see MU FARM

Robert Fitzgerald, see UNIVERSAL CHURCH OF THE MASTER

FIVE PERCENTERS

U.S. Islamic group started in the 1970s as a splinter from the NATION OF ISLAM (NOI).

Thurman Fleet, see CONCEPT-THERAPY INSTITUTE

Cathy Florida, see LIGHTHOUSE UNIVERSAL LIFE CHURCH

Amanda Flowers, see INDEPENDENT SPIRITUALIST ASSOCIATION

J. Roswell Flowers, see ASSEMBLIES OF GOD

Ralph P. Forbes, see SWORD OF CHRIST GOOD NEWS MINISTRIES

Arnold Josiah Ford, see BETH BNAI ABRAHAM

Arthur Ford, see FIRST SPIRITUALIST CHURCH OF NEW YORK; INTERNATIONAL GENERAL ASSEMBLY OF SPIRITUALISTS; SPIRITUAL FRONTIERS FELLOWSHIP

Julia O. Forrest, see SPIRITUAL SCIENCE CHURCH

FORT WAYNE GOSPEL TEMPLE

Millenarian group founded by B.E. Rediger, a former Mennonite, in Fort Wayne, Indiana, in the 1920s.

FOUNDATION CHURCH OF DIVINE TRUTH

Christian-spiritualist group founded in Washington, D.C., in 1985, succeeding the Foundation Church of the New Birth. The earlier group, founded in 1958 by John Paul Gibson, espoused the teachings of James E. Padgett (1852–1923), who had claimed to have received 2,500 messages from "Jesus and his Celestial co-workers." In addition, it espoused the teachings of Daniel G. Samuels, who claimed similar revelations. The church was dissolved in 1983 upon the death of Gibson.

FOUNDATION FAITH OF GOD

Formerly known as the Foundation Faith of the Millennium and Foundation Church of the Millennium, this U.S. occultist group was founded in 1974 by Christopher de Peyer and Peter McCormick, following a schism in THE PROCESS. Members expect the imminent coming of a messiah, who will lead humanity into a new age. Spiritual healing is practiced.

Sources:

Bainbridge, W.S. *Satan's Power: Ethnography of a Deviant Psychotherapy Cult.* Berkeley: University of California Press, 1978.

Evans, C. *Cults of Unreason.* London: Harrap, 1973.

FOUNDATION FOR "A COURSE IN MIRACLES" (FACIM)

Formerly known as the Inner Miracle Partnership, this occultist-Christian group was founded around 1980 by Gloria and Kenneth Wapnick and based in New York State. It is devoted to teaching "A Course in Miracles." The book *A Course in Miracles* was published in 1975 by Helen Schucman, who claimed to have been only the medium for a divine revelation.

See also FOUNDATION FOR INNER PEACE; INTERFAITH FELLOWSHIP

FOUNDATION FOR INNER PEACE

Occultist-Christian group founded by Judith Skutch in 1975 in New York City, devoted to the teaching of "*A Course in Miracles.*"

See also A COURSE IN MIRACLES; FOUNDATION FOR "A COURSE IN MIRACLES"; INTERFAITH FELLOWSHIP

FOUNDATION OF HUMAN UNDERSTANDING

Christian-occultist group founded in 1961 in Los Angeles by Roy Masters (1928–   ). Masters was born in London to a Jewish family and came to the United States in 1949. In the 1950s he opened an Institute for Hypnosis but was imprisoned for practicing medicine without a license. Since then he has been teaching meditation, operating mainly through radio broadcasts and literature.

FOUNDATION OF I, INC. (FREEDOM OF THE COSMOS)

Occultist group founded in the 1980s and based in New York City. It claims to employ ancient Hawaiian processes to teach its followers "… the art of resolving problems and releasing blocks to your *Self-Identity*— the *Self* or *Mind* in partnership with the *Divine* creator."

FOUNDATION OF RELIGIOUS TRANSITION

Christian-occultist group founded in 1969 by James A. and Diane Pike. James A. Pike

The Very Reverend James Pike, Dean of the Cathedral of St. John the Divine. He later left the Protestant Episcopal Church over doctrinal differences and established the Foundation of Religious Transition.

was the Episcopal Bishop of California, who left his church because of doctrinal disagreements that led to his trial for heresy. Pike did not accept the idea of the Trinity or the inerrancy of the Bible, and became committed to spiritualism. He died unexpectedly in September 1969, and the group's name was changed to the Bishop Pike Foundation. In 1972 it merged with the LOVE PROJECT.

FOUNDATION OF REVELATION

Hindu-oriented group founded in 1971 in San Francisco. It is devoted to the mysterious prophecies of an unnamed Indian holy man, who predicted the coming of the new age of Siva Kalpa in 1966.

FOURSQUARE GOSPEL, INTERNATIONAL CHURCH OF

North American PENTECOSTAL, Adventist group founded in Los Angeles in 1923, as the Angelus Temple, by "Sister" Aimee Semple McPherson (1890–1944). The official name was adopted in 1927. Mrs. Semple McPherson was known for her flamboyant style and was much in the public eye during her lifetime. She also practiced "healing and tongues." The group operated the first church-owned radio station in the United States and has had an active publication program.

Source:
Thomas, L. *The Vanishing Evangelist.* New York: Viking, 1959.

Emmet Fox, see CHURCH OF THE HEALING CHRIST

Selena Fox, see CIRCLE SANCTUARY

Marianne Francis (Aleuti Francesca), see SOLAR LIGHT CENTER

Michael Francis, see ATOM FOUNDATION

Fransisters and Franbrothers, see ORDER OF FRANSISTERS AND FRANBROTHERS

FRATERNITAS ROSAE CRUCIS

Rosicrucian group founded in Boston in 1868 by Pascal Beverly Randolph (1825–1875). The founder developed a system of occult sexuality or "sex magick," to be practiced only by married couples. In the early 20th century the group was reorganized by R. Swinburne Clymer. Its doctrine combines monotheism with Hindu ideas of karma and reincarnation. Aiming at better health through positive thinking is a recommended practice.
See also ROSICRUCIANS

FRATERNITÉ BLANCHE UNIVERSELLE (F.B.U.)

Known in English-speaking countries as the Universal White Brotherhood, this international occultist-Theosophical-Christian group was founded in 1947 in Paris by Omraam Mikhael Aivanhov, or Ivanoff (1900–1986), who was born in Bulgaria and went to France in 1937. In 1978 the Fondation Pobeda Ouspech Universelle was founded in Vaduz, Lichtenstein, to promote worldwide propagation of the ideas of the group, which has been reported to have ties to neo-Nazi groups in Europe.

Aivanhov claimed to have been sent by his spiritual master, Peter Duenov, and to have had a secret Tibetan teacher, like Duenov, who is considered the "19th Grand

Master of Humanity." Group doctrine is reminiscent of THEOSOPHY ideas about "hidden wisdom" and "evolved beings" in addition to a melange of astrology, yoga, and Christian traditions. Intoxicants are forbidden, and meals are simple and vegetarian. Special physical exercises are designed to "balance electro-magnetic forces in the body." Sexual relations are forbidden. The group claims to prepare the new world order for the "Age of Aquarius." Branches have operated in Europe and North America.

FRATERNITÉ "SALVE REGINA" DU FRÉCHOU

French Catholic schismatic group founded in 1977 by Roger Kozic and Michel Fernandez. In 1977 Kozic started reporting apparitions of the Virgin Mary, who announced the coming of global chaos. Many miracles and visions have been reported at the site, which has become a pilgrimage spot. These actions have been denounced by the Roman Catholic Church.

FRATERNITY OF ST. PIUS X

International Catholic traditionalist movement founded in 1965 by Archbishop Marcel Lefebvre (1906–1991). Lefebvre, who was made archbishop by Pope Pius XII, started the movement after the Second Vatican Council (1962–1965), which introduced many reforms in Roman Catholic practices and doctrines. He was excommunicated in 1988, after consecrating four bishops.

The movement regards itself as the guardian of tradition against heresies and the deterioration of church authority and faith caused by "satanic" reforms. It protests the obligatory use of the 1965 revised ritual,

known as Novus Ordo, in place of the Tridentine Mass formulated by Pope Pius V in 1570. It is also opposed to the ecumenical movement, which encourages contacts with other religions, and it has taken strong right-wing political views. The movement has had branches in Europe, North America, South America, and Oceania. Its English-speaking branches have been known collectively as the Catholic Tridentine Church.
See also SOCIETY OF ST. PIUS V

Henry D. Frazier, see GENERAL PSIONICS, CHURCH OF

R.O. Frazier, see UNIVERSAL CHURCH, THE MYSTICAL BODY OF CHRIST

FRAZIER CHAPEL

U.S. B'NAI NOACH congregation started in the 1980s by Jack Saunders, a former Baptist minister.
See also EMMANUEL

FREE CHRISTIAN ZION CHURCH OF CHRIST, THE

African-American conservative Protestant group founded in Redemption, Arkansas, in 1906 by E.D. Brown.

FREE CHURCH OF GOD IN CHRIST

African-American PENTECOSTAL group founded in 1915 by E.J. Morris in Enid, Oklahoma.

FREE DAIST COMMUNION

Formerly known as the Crazy Wisdom Fellowship, Johannine Daist Community (JDC), the Laughing Man Institute, the Dawn Horse Communion, Free Primitive Church of Divine Communion, Free Com-

Roman Catholic dissident Archbishop Marcel Lefebvre ordains a priest at Econe, Switzerland. Lefebvre was the founder of the Fraternity of St. Pius X. (see page 109)

The Reverend Ian Paisley, founder of the Free Presbyterian Church, protests the British government's Anglo-Irish Agreement in 1987. (see page 112)

munion Church, Dawn Horse Fellowship, Da Free John, or Bubba Free John, this is a loose grouping of the followers of Free John (1939–), whose real name is Franklin Albert Jones. A native of New York City, a graduate of Stanford University, and a disciple of Rudi (Albert Rudolph or Swami Rudrananda), Jones started the group in 1972 in California. Free John has also claimed to be a disciple of Muktananda, Nityananda, and Ramana Maharshi. Free John claims to have achieved "spiritual enlightenment" and "a permanent awakening to God-Realization" on September 10, 1970. In 1979 he retired from active leadership of the group.

In 1985 Da Free John became Da Kalki (Heart Master Da Love-Ananda) or Avadhoota Da Love-Ananda Hridayam, and the group became the Free Daist Communion. More recently Da Kalki changed his name to Da Avabhasa (The "Bright"), known also as The Divine World-Teacher and True Heart Master. The various name changes of both the group and its leader are said to contribute to the followers' well-being. The group offers Hindu-inspired teachings, meditation, and a guru-disciple relationship. Members are promised "Realization" of a "Divine Condition" through "a sacred relationship with Da Kalki." "Bubba Free John elucidates all the philosophical and esoteric matters that must be considered in spiritual or real life. But Bubba is not a mere intellectual or speculative philosopher. His writings, like all his actions, express the elegance and conscious intensity of Divine Ignorance, of God-Realization, which is his constant Enjoyment."

FREE GOSPEL CHURCH, INC.
PENTECOSTAL group founded in 1916 by Frank and William Casley and based in western Pennsylvania.

Hobart E. Freeman, see FAITH ASSEMBLY

FREE PRESBYTERIAN CHURCH
Northern Ireland Protestant group founded in 1951 by Ian Paisley (1926–) in dissent from the established Presbyterian Church. It holds a strong anti-Catholic position and is linked with the Unionist position in Northern Ireland, which advocates union with Great Britain.

FREE PROTESTANT EPISCOPAL CHURCH
Britsh Protestant church formed in 1897 through the union of three small dissenting bodies. Branches have developed in the United States and Canada. Doctrine mostly follows that of the Protestant Episcopal Church, but members are conscientious objectors.

FREE WILL BAPTIST CHURCH OF THE PENTECOSTAL FAITH
PENTECOSTAL group formed in the 1950s in South Carolina.

FRIENDS OF ISRAEL (FOI)
Canadian Hebrew-Christian group based in Hamilton, Ontario, founded in 1892.
See also HEBREW CHRISTIANS

Neal Vincent Frisby, see MIRACLE LIFE REVIVAL, INC.

S.H. Froehlich, see APOSTOLIC CHRISTIAN CHURCH (NAZAREAN)

Arnold Fruchtenbaum, see ARIEL MINISTRIES

Frum, John, see JOHN FRUM

Daniel Fry, see UNDERSTANDING, INC.

F.U.D.O.S.I, see FÉDÉRATION UNIVERSELLE DES ORDRES ET SOCIÉTÉS INITIATIQUES (F.U.D.O.S.I)

W.E. Fuller, see FIRE BAPTIZED HOLINESS CHURCH OF GOD OF THE AMERICAS

FULL GOSPEL CENTRAL CHURCH
Also known as the S-Church, and originally known as the Full Gospel Revival Centre, this Korean Christian PENTECOSTAL movement was founded by Yonggi Cho (1936–), who at age nineteen reported a visit by Jesus Christ that made him a Christian for life. The movement started in 1958, and the present name was adopted in 1962. Branches have opened in the United States and Japan. The doctrine resembles that of the ASSEMBLIES OF GOD. Practices include glossolalia and faith healing. Followers are promised both physical health and material prosperity.

FULL GOSPEL CHURCH ASSOCIATION
Known also as the Full Gospel Church of God, this PENTECOSTAL group was founded by Dennis W. Thorn in 1952 in Amarillo, Texas. Its doctrine emphasizes healing and tithing.

FULL GOSPEL EVANGELICAL ASSOCIATION
U.S. PENTECOSTAL group resulting from a schism during the late 1940s in the APOSTOLIC FAITH CHURCH (KANSAS). The dissenting group was first known as the Ministerial and Missionary Alliance of the Original Trinity Apostolic Faith, Inc. In 1952 it formed the Association.

FULL GOSPEL FELLOWSHIP OF CHURCHES AND MINISTRIES INTERNATIONAL
U.S. PENTECOSTAL group emphasizing healing and mission work overseas, founded in 1949 by Gordon Lindsey (1906–1973) and officially incorporated in 1962. The UNITED PENTECOSTAL FAITH CHURCH is affiliated with this group.

FULL GOSPEL MINISTER ASSOCIATION
PENTECOSTAL group based in East Jordan, Michigan, which issues credentials to both ministers and churches. Members are conscientious objectors.

FULL GOSPEL TABERNACLE
British-Israelist group founded in the 1930s in Tulsa, Oklahoma, by Jonathan Ellsworth Perkins, former Methodist minister.
See also BRITISH ISRAELISM

FULL SALVATION UNION
Schismatic Christian group founded in Lansing, Michigan, in 1934 by James F. Andrews. No ceremonies are observed, according to the group's doctrine.

FUNDAMENTALISM
U.S. Protestant movement guided by the doctrine of complete faith in the five fundamentals: the inerrancy of the Bible, the virgin birth of Jesus, the supernatural atonement, the physical resurrection of Jesus,

and the authenticity of the Gospel miracles. Another version of the "five points" includes: the divine inspiration of the Bible, the depravity of man, redemption through the blood of Christ, the true church as a body composed of all believers, and the coming of Christ to establish his reign. In 1983 a convention of Fundamentalist Baptists in Kansas City, Missouri, affirmed the following five fundamentals: Inerrant scripture; Christ is God in the flesh; Christ died for the sins of mankind; Christ rose bodily; Christ will return bodily.

Sources:

Furniss, N.F. *The Fundamentalist Controversy, 1918–1931.* New Haven: Yale University Press, 1954.

Marsden, G.M. *Fundamentalism and American Culture.* Oxford: Oxford University Press, 1980.

Niebuhr, H.R. "Fundamentalism." In *Encyclopedia of the Social Sciences, VI.* New York: 1937.

Sandeen, E.R. *The Roots of Fundamentalism.* Chicago: The University of Chicago Press, 1970.

FUNDAMENTALIST ARMY, THE

Originally known as the Open Door Community Church (O.D.C.C.), this Fundamentalist, evangelical, semicommunal group was founded by Robert Leslie Hymers, Jr. (1941–   ), former Southern Baptist minister, in San Fernando Valley, California, in 1975. "Faith healing" and exorcism are practiced. The group operates the Open Door Messianic Jewish Congregation, started in 1977.

FUTURE FOUNDATION

Occultist group founded in Stenauer, Nebraska, by Gerald W. Gottula in 1969. Doctrine includes belief in the coming New Age. Practices include astrology, faith healing, and "psychic prophecy."

G

Conrad Gaard, see DESTINY OF AMERICA FOUNDATION

GALLICAN CHURCH (Église Gallicane, Église Catholic Française)

French Old Catholic group started in 1883 and reorganized in 1907 by Joseph René Vilatte. It follows Roman Catholic traditions but rejects papal authority and infallibility and follows a Theosophical Christianity. There is emphasis on gnosticism, occultism, and faith healing. The Theosophical influence makes it similar in beliefs and practices to the LIBERAL CATHOLIC CHURCH. It has had connections with other Old Catholic and traditionalist Catholic groups in Europe and North America.
See also AMERICAN CATHOLIC CHURCH; THEOSOPHY

Charles Gamble, see SEVENTH DAY PENTECOSTAL CHURCH OF THE LIVING GOD

GANDEN MAHAYANA CENTER

Known also as Ganden Tekchen Ling, this Tibetan Buddhist group based in Wisconsin was founded by Geshe Lhundup Sopa in the 1970s. It is devoted to spreading Tibetan Buddhism in the West.

Source:
Sopa, G., & Hopkins, J. *Practice and Theory of Tibetan Buddhism.* New York: Grove Press, 1976.

GANIENKAH

Native American religious commune founded by members of the Mohawk tribe in the Adirondack Mountains in 1974.

Juanita Garcia Peraga, see MITA

G. Garr, see CAROLINA EVANGELISTIC ASSOCIATION

Florence Garrique, see MEDITATION GROUP FOR THE NEW AGE

Gaskin, Stephen, see THE FARM

Srimata (Reverend Mother) Gayati Devi, see ANANDA ASHRAMA

Daniel Gayman, see CHURCH OF ISRAEL

GEDATSU CHURCH OF AMERICA

Branch of the Japanese Gedatsu movement brought to the United States in the 1940s and incorporated in 1951. It is based in California.
See also GEDATSU-KAI

GEDATSU-KAI (Salvation Society)

Japanese new religion founded in 1929 by Okano Eizo (1881–1948), also known as Seiken, and posthumously known as Gedatsu Kongo, a former priest in the Shugendo sect of Japanese Buddhism. The doctrine combines Christian, Shinto, and Buddhist ideas.

Source:
Earhart, H.B. *Gedatsu-Kai and Religion in Contemporary Japan.* Bloomington, IN: Indiana University Press, 1989.

Joseph H. Gelberman, see INTERFAITH TEMPLE; TREE OF LIFE

The XIV Dalai Lama of Tibet (left) greets Archbishop of Canterbury Robert Runcie in London during a visit in 1988. The Dalai Lama is a follower of the Gelug-Pa (Yellow Hat) sect of Tibetan Buddhism.

GELUG-PA ("Yellow Hat")

The largest of the four sects of Tibetan Buddhism, led by the 98th Ganden Tripa, known as Ganden Tri Rinpoche (1921–   ), who was crowned by the XIV Dalai Lama in 1984. The Dalai Lama is considered a follower of this tradition.
See MANJUSHRI INSTITUTE

GENERAL ASSEMBLY AND CHURCH OF THE FIRST BORN

U.S. PENTECOSTAL group founded in 1907. Members deviate from standard Christian teachings (by denying original sin) and practice healing and speaking in tongues. They do not consult medical doctors. In 1976 a child of group members died after medical care was avoided by its parents. An Oklahoma court ruled that another child of the same family would be transferred to government care.

GENERAL ASSEMBLY OF SPIRITUALISTS (G.A.S.)

Group founded in 1931, when the New York State Association of the NATIONAL SPIRITUALIST ASSOCIATION OF CHURCHES left the N.S.A.C. The immediate cause was a statement condemning belief in reincarnation as unacceptable. The General Assembly follows other N.S.A.C. principles but also espouses reincarnation.

GENERAL CHURCH OF THE NEW JERUSALEM

U.S. Swedenborgian organization founded in 1840 after a schism in the GENERAL CHURCH OF THE NEW JERUSALEM.
See also SWEDENBORG FOUNDATION

GENERAL CONFERENCE OF THE CHURCH OF GOD (SEVENTH DAY)

Popularly known as the Church of God (Seventh-Day), this is a U.S. Sabbath-keeping, Adventist movement whose members reject the teachings of Ellen G. White and the SEVENTH-DAY ADVENTIST CHURCH. While the latter group was being organized in the mid-19th century and becoming the largest Adventist group, smaller congregations kept their independence. In 1906 these groups were incorporated as the Churches of God (Adventist) Unattached Congregations.

The group has a strong Old Testament orientation. In addition to keeping the Saturday Sabbath, it forbids the use of tobacco, alcohol, and pork. Major Christian festivals, including Christmas and Easter, are considered pagan and ignored.
See also ADVENTISTS

GENERAL CONFERENCE OF THE EVANGELICAL BAPTIST CHURCH

Originally known as the Church of the Full Gospel, Inc., this PENTECOSTAL group was founded in 1935 in Goldsboro, North Carolina, by R.H. Askew. Doctrine emphasizes healing, speaking in tongues, and tithing.

GENERAL CONVENTION OF THE NEW JERUSALEM

The first Swedenborgian organization in the United States, founded in 1817, with headquarters in Newton, Massachusetts.
See also SWEDENBORG FOUNDATION

GENERAL COUNCIL OF THE CHURCHES OF GOD

Formed in 1950 as a result of dissent within

Sioux Chieftain Sitting Bull, who was killed in the massacre at Wounded Knee, South Dakota, following the Ghost Dance movement of 1890. The movement was in reaction against oppression by the encroaching Europeans.

the GENERAL CONFERENCE OF THE CHURCH OF GOD, this Sabbath-keeping Adventist group has headquarters in Meridian, Idaho.

See also ADVENTISTS; SEVENTH-DAY ADVENTIST CHURCH

GENERAL PSIONICS, CHURCH OF

Occultist group founded by John L. Douglas and Henry D. Frazier in Redondo Beach, California, in 1968. It has operated mainly by mail.

Genshifukuin - Kami - No - Makuya - Kyokai, see MAKUYA

GEORGIAN CHURCH, THE

Neo-pagan U.S. group founded by George Patterson (?–1984) in the mid-1970s and originally known as the Church of Wicca of Bakersfield. The doctrine and rituals are devoted to the worship of the Mother Goddess.

See also CHURCH OF ALL WORLDS; COVENANT OF THE GODDESS

Heinrich Geyer, see NEW APOSTOLIC CHURCH.

Nemi Chand Ghandi, see SARVA DHARMA SAMBHAVA KENDRA

Moshe Ghibbory, see UNITED ISRAEL WORLD UNION

Aurobindo Ghose, see SRI AUROBINDO

Chimnoy Kumar Ghose, see SRI CHIMNOY

GHOST DANCE

Generic name of revitalization movements (or waves of movements) in various nations and tribes of natives in North America during the 19th century. Scholars refer to the 1890 Ghost Dance in contrast to the 1870 Ghost Dance and the Prophet Dance. All agree that the Ghost Dance movements arose out of the deprivation, suffering, and decimation of North American natives resulting from European colonization. Thus, the phenomenon parallels similar native movements elsewhere (see CARGO CULTS).

The Ghost Dance represented a traditional response to externally imposed oppression and deprivation and to an internal crisis of authority. The doctrine was based on the theme of the coming triumph of the natives over the Europeans, material prosperity at their expense, the resurrection of the dead and return to precolonial conditions, and the return of the buffalo herds. The eventual outcome would be a renewal of native existence. To bring about this salvation, natives had to perform the sacred dance.

Ghost Dance of 1870

Started by the prophet Wodziwob of the Nevada North Paiute tribe. He had visions of the total disappearance of white people and their property being preserved for the natives. It was a limited movement compared to the second wave, but it spread westward to northern California and Oregon, ending by 1875.

Ghost Dance of 1890

The largest wave of the Ghost Dance movement occurred in the Western states among forty-five North American tribes: the Northern Arapaho, the Southern Arapaho,

Arikara, Assiniboin, Bannock, Caddo, Chemehuevi, Northern Cheyenne, Southern Cheyenne, Cohonino (Havasupai), Delaware, Gosuite, Gros Ventres (Atsina), Hidatsa (Minitari), Iowa, Kansas, Kichai, Kickapoo, Kiowa, Kiowa-Apache, Mandan, Oto-Missouri, California Paiute, Duck Valley Paiute, Pyramid Lake Paiute, Walker River Paiute, Nevada Paiute, Oregon Paiute, Pawnee, Pit River, Taos, Ft. Hall Shoshoni, Lemhi Shoshoni, Eastern Shoshoni, Western Shoshoni, Duck Valley Shoshoni, Teton Sioux, Yanktonais Sioux, Tule River, Uinta, and White River Ute, Uncompahgre Ute, Walapai, Washo, and Wichita.

The Ghost Dance of 1890 started during a solar eclipse in 1888 or 1889, when visions were announced by the prophet Wovoka (also known as Jack Wilson, 1858–1932), a Paiute from Nevada and the reputed son of Tavibo the medicine man (who assisted Wodziwob in the Ghost Dance of 1870). After his father's death, Wovoka was adopted by a Mormon named David Wilson and had much exposure to Mormon teachings. His prophetic messages are reported to have been received while he was ill and suffering from fever. The messages had four elements: equality of men and women in ritual, an end to intertribal war, distribution of lands to the natives in the coming messianic age, and the requirement of performing the sacred dance. In this vision the native dead appeared around God's throne, and Wovoka received an assurance that he was the messenger of a messianic Kingdom soon to be established under Jesus Christ. There the natives would recover their lands and their lost way of life, while the whites would disappear. The Ghost Dance itself was designed to secure communication with the dead, hasten the coming of the messianic age, and gain further assurances for Wovoka's messages. Men and women, dressed in white, danced in circles, singing "revealed" songs and reaching ecstasy. Wovoka's followers also believed that they were immune to bullets.

The Ghost Dance of 1890 ended with the massacre at Wounded Knee, South Dakota, on December 29. Chief Sitting Bull and 150 to 300 Sioux were killed.

In the 1970s the Oglala Sioux became embroiled in a dispute with the U.S. government over the Wounded Knee territory. As negotiations stalled, Sioux leaders Leonard Crow Dog and Wallace Black Elk organized a revival of the Ghost Dance to re-energize their people.

Sources:

Dubois, C. *The 1870 Ghost Dance*. Berkeley: University of California Press, 1939.

LaBarre, W. *The Ghost Dance*. New York: Dell, 1972.

Lanternari, V. *The Religions of the Oppressed*. New York: Knopf, 1963.

Miller, D.H. *Ghost Dance*. Lincoln, NB: University of Nebraska Press, 1985.

Mooney, J. *The Ghost Dance Religion and Wounded Knee*. New York: Dover, 1973.

Spier, L. *The Prophet Dance of the Northwest and Its Derivatives: The Source of the Ghost Dance*. New York: AMS Press, 1979.

Thornton, R. *We Shall Live Again: The 1870 and 1890 Ghost Dance Movements as Demographic Revitalization*. New York: Cambridge University Press, 1986.

GLAD TIDINGS MISSIONARY SOCIETY

North American PENTECOSTAL group growing out of the Glad Tidings Temple of Vancouver, British Columbia, and inspired by the LATTER RAIN MOVEMENT.

GLAINN SIDHR ORDER

International neo-pagan organization founded in the 1970s.
See also ATHANOR FELLOWSHIP; EARTHSPIRIT COMMUNITY

GLASTONBURY COMMUNITY

British mystical community founded in the 1960s, focusing on belief in angels and fairies and contacts with them. Glastonbury is the focus of many traditions ascribing to it the tomb of King Arthur and the first Christian church in Great Britain. It was the site of a great medieval Benedictine monastery, destroyed by order of Henry VIII in 1538.

Maurice Lerrie Glendenning, see AARONIC ORDER

GLIDE MEMORIAL METHODIST CHURCH

Radical Christian congregation started in San Francisco in the 1960s.

GNOSTIC ASSOCIATION OF ANTHROPOLOGY AND SCIENCE

Known sometimes as the Gnostic Association of Cultural and Anthropological Studies, this international Theosophical, Eastern-oriented group was founded by Samael Aunweur (or Samuel Aun Weor, ?–1977) in Mexico in 1952. The founder was a member of FRATERNITAS ROSICRUCIANA ANTIQUA, and his teachings include "alchemy, Tibetan psychology, and Zen meditation." Association branches have operated in Latin America, Europe, and the United States.
See also THEOSOPHY

GNOSTIC SOCIETY

Theosophical group based in Los Angeles, officially devoted to teaching the original works of H.P. Blavatsky.
See also THEOSOPHY

F.G. Goad, Sr., see FOREST GATE CHURCH

GOD'S HOUSE OF PRAYER FOR ALL NATIONS, INC.

PENTECOSTAL group founded in 1964 in Peoria, Illinois, by Tommie Lawrence, formerly of the CHURCH OF GOD IN CHRIST. The group emphasizes faith healing and has contacts with the MIRACLE REVIVAL FELLOWSHIP.

E.J. Gold, see INSTITUTE FOR THE HARMONIOUS DEVELOPMENT OF THE HUMAN BEING (IHDHB)

Joel S. Goldsmith, see INFINITE WAY SOCIETY

Keith Gordon, see ETHIOPIAN ZION COPTIC CHURCH

Jacob Goren, see HEBREW CHRISTIAN ASSEMBLY—JERUSALEM CONGREGATION

Marjoe Gortner, see OLD TIME FAITH, INC.

GOSPEL ASSEMBLIES

PENTECOSTAL group founded in 1914 by

121

William Sowders (1879–1952) in Louisville, Kentucky. Its doctrine is unique among Pentecostal groups in deviating significantly from the Fundamentalist Trinitarian position. It also follows a belief in DISPENSATIONALISM, which is the division of history into periods, and in 1914 as being the beginning of the last dispensation, the end of time. The latter idea was adopted from Charles T. Russell, founder of JEHOVAH'S WITNESSES. The group emphasizes its lack of formal membership or creed except for the Bible. Following the death of the founder, the group divided into several assemblies, each claiming the original name.

GOSPEL HARVESTERS EVANGELISTIC ASSOCIATION

Also known as the International Communion of Charismatic Churches, this PENTECOSTAL group was founded in 1961 in Atlanta, Georgia, by Earl P. Paulk, Jr. It promotes the "Kingdom Church" or "Kingdom Now" doctrine, which is critical of established churches and calls for the Christianization of society.

GOSPEL HARVESTERS EVANGELISTIC ASSOCIATION (BUFFALO)

North American PENTECOSTAL group founded in 1962 in Buffalo, New York, by Rose Pezzino. Branches operate in Canada and the southern United States.

Leon Gotlieb, see MORNINGSTAR

Gerald W. Gottula, see FUTURE FOUNDATION

Marcelino Manoel de Graca ("Sweet Daddy Grace"), see UNITED HOUSE OF PRAYER FOR ALL PEOPLE

GRACE GOSPEL EVANGELISTIC ASSOCIATION INTERNATIONAL, INC.

U.S. PENTECOSTAL group started in the mid-1930s. Its doctrine combines Pentecostalism with Calvinism, emphasizing predestination rather than free will in the achievement of grace.

GRACE GOSPEL FELLOWSHIP

U.S. Fundamentalist, Dispensationalist group founded in 1944 by J.C. O'Hair and Harry Bultema.
See also DISPENSATIONALISM; FUNDAMENTALISM

GRACE GOSPEL MISSIONS

U.S. Dispensationalist mission organization promoting Fundamentalist Christianity. It was first formed in 1939 under the name World Wide Grace Testimony.
See also DISPENSATIONALISM; FUNDAMENTALISM

Grace, "Sweet Daddy," see UNITED HOUSE OF PRAYER FOR ALL PEOPLE

Gene and Eva Graf, see CENTER OF LIGHT COMMUNITY

GRAIL MESSAGE (Gralsbewegung)

International occultist-syncretist movement founded in 1928 in Austria by Oskar Ernst Bernhardt (1875–1941) of Bischofswerda, Germany. In 1924 he started publishing his revelations under the name Abd-ru-shin. The Message is a combination of Western and Hindu ideas but without any Christian notions. Branches have operated in Western Europe, Australia, and the United States.

W.V. Grant, see INTERNATIONAL DELIVERANCE CHURCHES

Richard Grave, see UNIVERSAL LINK

John Harvey Gray, see CHURCH OF THE LOVING SERVANT

GREATER REFUGE TEMPLE
PENTECOSTAL group started in New York City in the 1950s, affiliated with the CHURCH OF OUR LORD JESUS CHRIST OF THE APOSTOLIC FAITH of Great Britain.

GREATER WORLD CHRISTIAN SPIRITUALIST LEAGUE, THE
International spiritualist group founded in London in 1920. It promotes a combination of Christianity and the practice of spirit communication and "spiritual healing." Branches operate all over the English-speaking world.

Great I Am, see I AM

GREAT SCHOOL OF THE MASTERS
Theosophical-occultist group based in California, founded in 1883 by John E. Richardson. Richardson claimed to have received messages from an Indian master named Hoo-Kna-ka. The group operates the School of Natural Science, which offers correspondence courses.

Joyce Green, see JOYA HOUSES

Gregory XVII, see APOSTLES OF INFINITE LOVE

Albert C. Grier, see CHURCH OF THE TRUTH

Glenn Griffith, see BIBLE MISSIONARY CHURCH

Simon Grimes, see PANSOPHIC INSTITUTE

Darwin Gross, see ECKANKAR

GURDJIEFF FOUNDATION
Occultist group founded in New York in 1953 by John Pentland (1907–1984), which has served as a center for Gurdjieff teaching and activities. In the late 1970s it was moved to San Francisco, to a branch that was started in 1955.

GURDJIEFF GROUPS
Georgei Ivanovich (G.I.) Gurdjieff (1874?–1949) was the creator of a twentieth-century occult tradition, sometimes known as the Fourth Way School, which has reached a special degree of fame and acceptance. Ideas connected with Gurdjieff seem to crop up in a variety of modern occult groups and new religions.

Gurdjieff was apparently born in Alexandropol, Armenia. According to some of his followers, he received his higher education in Kars and then "disappeared" for twenty years. Like Madame Blavatsky, Gurdjieff repeatedly claimed to have spent several years in Central Asia and Tibet, studying with mysterious "Masters" of "ancient wisdom" during his travels in the East, but neither the travels nor the Masters have been substantiated. In 1922 he founded the Institute for the Harmonious Development of Man, in Fontainebleau, near Paris, also

G. I. Gurdjieff, head of the Institute for the Harmonious Development of Man, arrives on a visit to the United States.

known as Le Prieuré, the Priory, which existed till 1933.

His teachings were put into writing by Pyotr Demainovitch (P.D.) Ouspensky (1878–1947), his most important disciple and exponent, who continued to teach his ideas after severing personal relations with the Master in 1932. The tradition is sometimes referred to as G-O, for Gurdjieff-Ouspensky; it is also known as The Fourth Way, The Gurdjieff Work, or just The Work.

He taught that although humans possess not one but four brains (instinctive, moving, emotional, and intellectual), these organs are uncoordinated, and so man is "asleep" and has to become conscious through various exercises. There are seven evolutionary levels and seven "psychological centers." The exercises include "cultivating the opposite" by going against one's ingrained habits, going against one's limits by fasting and sleep deprivation, long silences, meditation, and prayer. Infractions of rules and laxness in exercises lead to heavy fines. Followers celebrate Gurdjieff's birthday, January 13, and the day of his death, October 29.

Since there was only one Master and no real organization, and secrecy about special knowledge is of the essence, Gurdjieff followers are rather elusive. They meet privately in small groups with one teacher and his helpers, and do not normally wish to attract attention. However, several Gurdjieff groups do advertise their existence in an attempt to recruit members. In the United States one known group is the GURDJIEFF FOUNDATION. Another, the INSTITUTE FOR RELIGIOUS DEVELOPMENT, includes the disciples of W.A. Nyland, who at one point was affiliated with the Foundation.

See also CLAYMONT; COOMBE SPRINGS; FELLOWSHIP OF FRIENDS; INSTITUTE FOR THE COMPARATIVE STUDY OF HISTORY, PHILOSOPHY, AND THE SCIENCES; INSTITUTE FOR RELIGIOUS DEVELOPMENT; INSTITUTE FOR THE HARMONIOUS DEVELOPMENT OF THE HUMAN BEING; ORAGE GROUP; THE PROSPEROS; SHERBORNE SCHOOL; SHERBORNE STUDIES GROUP; SUBUD

Sources:

Ellwood, R.S. *Religious and Spiritual Groups in Modern America.* Englewood Cliffs, NJ: Prentice-Hall, 1973.

Webb, J. *The Harmonious Circle: The Lives and Work of G.I. Gurdjieff, P.D. Ouspensky, and Their Followers.* New York: G.P. Putnam, 1980.

GURU BAWA FELLOWSHIP

Also known as the Bawa Muhaiyaddeen Fellowship, this North American Islamic-oriented group was founded in 1974 around the personality of Muhaiyaddeen M.R. Bawa (?–1986), who had described himself as a "contemporary Sufi." Guru Bawa was a Tamil from Sri Lanka, who was reputed to have established a "spiritual school" there around 1940, teaching the unity of God and human unity in God. In 1971 he came to the United States and set up fellowship groups for his students. According to the Fellowship, "Guru Bawa emphasizes the living of Universal Divine Qualities and Characteristics." Bawa's doctrine includes belief in reincarnation, and he claims to carry on the work of twenty-five divine messengers, including Moses, Jesus, and Muhammad.

Gurudev Siddha Peeth, see SYDA FOUNDATION

Guru Ma, see SUMMIT LIGHTHOUSE

Guru Maharaj Ji, see DIVINE LIGHT MISSION

H

Issa Al Haadi, see NUBIAN ISLAAMIC HEBREWS

John Hackman, see TWELVE APOSTLES

Kenneth Hagin, see "FAITH" MOVEMENT

HAIDAKHAN SAMAJ
Western Hindu-inspired group devoted to the teachings of Haidakhan Baba, also known as Babaji Nagaraj (?–1984) of the Himalayas, with branches in Europe and North America.
See also INTERNATIONAL BABAJI KRIYA YOGA SANGAM

Franklin Hall, see HALL DELIVERANCE FOUNDATION

H. Richard Hall, see UNITED CHRISTIAN CHURCH AND MINISTERIAL ASSOCIATION

HALL DELIVERANCE FOUNDATION
PENTECOSTAL-healing group built around the personality of Franklin Hall, who started a "healing ministry" in 1946. Doctrine recommends prayer and fasting; Hall's book presenting it is titled *Atomic Power with God with Fasting and Prayer* (1973). The group is based in Phoenix, Arizona.

HALVETI-JERRAHI ORDER OF NEW YORK
Sufi group, based in New York City, founded in the 1970s and led by Muzaffer al-Ashki. The group claims to follow the teachings of Pir Nureddin Jerrahi, who founded the Jerrahi order in Istanbul in the 17th century. It operates the Massjid al-Farah al Ashki.

HaMa'ayan, see BEIT IMMANUEL

Hamid Bey, see COPTIC FELLOWSHIP OF AMERICA

Charles Hamilton, see KNIGHTS TEMPLAR NEW AGE CHURCH

HANAFI MADH-HAB CENTER
U.S. Moslem group, started in 1967. Historically, Hanafi is the most liberal of the four legal schools of Sunni Islam, the other three being Maliki, Shafii, and Hanbali. A group aligning itself with the Hanafi tradition was founded in the United States in 1967 by Hamaas Abdul-Khaalis (formerly Ernest Timothy McGee), who thus broke away from the NATION OF ISLAM; this group, made up of U.S. blacks, is known as the Hanafi Muslims.

The conflict between the Hanafis and the Nation of Islam led to lethal violence. On January 10, 1973, several members of the Nation broke into the home of Hamaas Abdul Khaalis, killed three of his children, and wounded his wife, who has remained paralyzed for life. In 1977 members of the Hanafi Muslims were involved in a takeover of a charitable Jewish organization in Washington, D.C., in order to draw attention to the 1973 killings and to their demands for retribution.

Pauline Hancock, see CHURCH OF CHRIST (BIBLE AND BOOK OF MORMON TEACHING)

HANDSOME LAKE RELIGION
Known also as Longhouse Religion, this

Hamaas Abdul Khaalis, leader of the Hanafi Muslims. (see page 127)

syncretistic Native American movement was founded in 1799 by the Seneca chief Ganiodayo (Handsome Lake, 1735–1815). After a long period of decline and demoralization, the Seneca were revitalized by the chief's visions, which called for the adoption of a "puritan" ethic. Handsome Lake was changed by the visions from an alcoholic to a prophet who saved his people. Later the movement spread among the Iroquois. Currently about 5,000 native Americans are active members in New York and Canada.

Source:
Wallace, A.F.C. *The Death and Rebirth of the Seneca*. New York: Knopf, 1970.

Otoman Zar-Adhust Hanish, see MAZDAZNAN MOVEMENT

Srila Hansadutta, see VEDIC CULTURAL CENTER

Minnie Hanson, see APOSTOLIC FAITH MISSION

HANUMAN FELLOWSHIP, THE

Hindu group based in California and founded in the 1970s. It is "based on the study and practice of Ashtanga Yoga as taught by Baba Hari Dass." Its practices include meditation, yoga, and charitable activities.

HANUMAN FOUNDATION

Hindu group founded by Baba Ram Dass in 1974 and devoted to promoting the knowledge of Hindu beliefs and practices in the West. Baba Ram Dass was born in 1931 in Boston as Richard Alpert. After earning a Ph.D. in psychology from Stanford University, in 1961 he had his first experience with LSD. In 1967 he went to India and found his guru, Neem Karoli Baba, who named him Ram Dass.

Source:
Ram Dass. *Be Here Now.* New York: Crown, 1971.

Hare Krishna, see INTERNATIONAL SOCIETY FOR KRISHNA CONSCIOUSNESS

Billy James Hargis, see CHURCH OF THE CHRISTIAN CRUSADE

Ernest Hargrove, see THEOSOPHICAL SOCIETY IN AMERICA

William Wade Harris, see HARRIS MOVEMENT

HARRIS MOVEMENT

Also known as the Harrist Church, this nativist Christian movement in West Africa was founded by William Wade Harris (c.1850–1929). A Liberian of the Grebo tribe, Harris took an active part in his tribe's struggle against foreign domination, supporting an insurrection against the American settlers that demanded British rule. Imprisoned, he gained the nickname "Old Man Union Jack," but he then had a Christian revelation. He claimed to have seen the Angel Gabriel, who instructed him to preach. His message, which he began preaching in 1913, was of an African Christianity based on the principles of Christian baptism and opposition to traditional "paganism" and to European clothes and customs. Between 1913 and 1915 he led some 120,000 people in the Ivory Coast and Ghana to leave traditional religions and join his movement. French authorities in the Ivory Coast reacted violently to Harris and his movement. Later some members joined Methodist (with the leader's encouragement) and Roman Catholic churches, but the movement survived and has continued to flourish in West Africa. After the founder's death, John Ahui and Albert Atcho continued his work in the Ivory Coast. There have been many schisms and groupings, each claiming the Harris legacy. The movement has also influenced several independent groups, such as the TWELVE APOSTLES.

Sources:
Haliburton, G.M. *The Prophet Harris.* London: Longman, 1971.
Walker, S.S. *The Religious Revolution in the Ivory Coast: The Prophet Harris and the Harrist Church.* Chapel Hill: University of North Carolina Press, 1983.

Harvester Church, see GOSPEL HARVESTERS EVANGELISTIC ASSOCIATION

George Hawtin, see LATTER RAIN MOVEMENT

HEALING ORDER OF THE SUFI ORDER

Known also as the Sufi Healing Order, this U.S. branch of the SUFI ORDER IN THE WEST is devoted to faith healing. It was founded by Himayat Inayati in the late

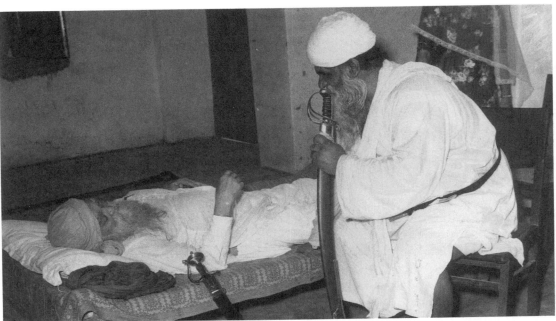

Sikh leader Tara Singh and his wife (top) are shown before he undertakes a "fast unto death" in the Golden Temple at Amritsar, India. Below, he begins his fast. He ended his protest, however, in expectation of government concessions to his demands.

1970s and based in Leicester, North Carolina.

HEALTHY, HAPPY, HOLY ORGANIZATION (3HO)

Officially known as the Sikh Dharma of the Western Hemisphere, and popularly known as the White Sikhs, orthodox Sikh movement was created for Western followers. It was founded in Los Angeles in 1969 by Harbhajan Singh Khalsa Yogiji (1929–), known also as Yogi Bhajan or Siri Singh Sahib. The 3HO is actually the educational arm of the movement.

Sikh doctrine, as developed by Guru Nanak (1439–1538), was inspired by both Islam and Hinduism. Nanak's writings, known as *Siri Guru Granth Sahib,* are the Sikh scripture. The religion is strictly monotheistic and utilizes mantras and meditation following Hindu traditions. Fish, meat, and drugs are avoided. Members are enjoined to carry out the five k's of Sikh tradition: *kesh*—tying the hair under a turban, *kangha*—using a comb, *kachera*—special underwear, *kara*—wearing a steel bracelet, and *kirpan*—wearing a dagger. Wearing the turban at all times has gotten Sikhs in legal trouble with military and police authorities all over the world.

Members adopt Punjabi names and practice meditation and "full moon celebrations." 3HO practices go beyond traditional Sikhism in the teaching of yoga techniques. The group's doctrine also includes belief in "electromagnetic fields," special energy in human hair, and magical mantras providing protection and prosperity. There have been some 3HO communes in the United States.

Sources:
Cole, W.O. and Piara Singh Sambhi. *The Sikhs.* London: Routledge & Kegan Paul, 1978.
Khushwant Singh. *A History of the Sikhs.* Princeton: Princeton University Press, 1963–1966.

HEART CONSCIOUSNESS CHURCH

Communal group founded in California in 1975 and based on "...that essence common to the Holistic Health Movement, the Human Potential Movement and Universal Spirituality...group sharing of spiritual energy; meditation; chanting...surrendering to the infinite (God, Brahma, Tao, the Void) without and within us all); respect for the wisdom of the great teachers..." It operates the Harbin Hot Springs Community in Middletown, California.

HEBREW CHRISTIAN ASSEMBLY— JERUSALEM CONGREGATION

Israeli Hebrew-Christian group based in Jerusalem, founded around 1970 by Ze'ev Kofsman, Jacob Goren, and Victor Smadja. The group's theology has been that of the OPEN BRETHREN.
See also HEBREW CHRISTIANITY; MESSIANIC ASSEMBLY OF ISRAEL

HEBREW CHRISTIANITY

International movement that developed out of the efforts of Christian groups to convert Jews in the 19th century.

The message proclaimed by Hebrew Christianity is the possibility of combining Jewish identity and Christian beliefs of the Fundamentalist variety. The rituals combine Jewish and Protestant elements. Members define themselves as Jews loyal to their people who have accepted Jesus as the true Messiah. They proclaim a double loyalty, to Jewish identity and to Christianity, although they reject the term Christian. Often the use of traditional Christian terms is avoided. Thus, the name Jesus Christ is replaced by Yeshua, and New Testament by Holy Scripture or New Covenant.

Although the Hebrew-Christian missionary movement was founded in Europe during the 19th century, it has existed in the United States since 1915 under various organizational forms. Leaders of the various groups have been ordained by Baptist churches and have had close contacts with Fundamentalist groups. Individual congregations have differed significantly in doctrine and rituals.

See also MESSIANIC JUDAISM

Sources:

Pruter, K. *Jewish Christians in the United States: A Bibliography.* New York: Garland Publishing, 1986.

Sobel, B.Z. *Hebrew Christianity: The Thirteenth Tribe.* New York: Wiley, 1974.

Franklin Hedgecock, see FANSCI-FIAROAN CHURCH OF WICCA

Kashavrao Baliram Hedgewar, see RASHTRIYA SWAYAMASEVAK SANGH

Max Heindel, see ROSICRUCIAN FELLOWSHIP

Sylvia Hellman, see YASODHARA ASHRAM SOCIETY

Romiche Henry, see APOCALYPSE SOCIETY, INC.

Kirby J. Hensley, see UNIVERSAL LIFE CHURCH

HEPHZIBAH FAITH MISSIONARY ASSOCIATION, THE

Evangelical, PENTECOSTAL group founded in Glenwood, Iowa, in 1892.

George H. Hepker, see CHURCH OF BASIC TRUTH

HEPZEBAH HOUSE

Fundamentalist group based in New York City, founded in the 1940s. It was was influenced by the ideas of T. Austin-Sparks, founder of the HONOR OAK CHRISTIAN FELLOWSHIP CENTRE in London.

See also FUNDAMENTALISM; THIS TESTIMONY

Wilhelm Herrigel, see BAHAI WORLD UNION

John Hickerson, see CHURCH OF THE LIVING GOD

HICKSITE FRIENDS

Society of Friends group that seceded from the main body of Quakers in the United States in 1828. It was named after Elias Hicks (1748–1830), who led the movement with his Unitarian tendencies. Hicks in 1826 denied the notion of the divinity of Jesus Christ, declaring that he recognized no Savior but the Inner Light. This group contrasted with the Conservative Friends, also known as Wilburites, after John Wilbur.

Robert Hieronimus, see SAVITRIA

Christopher Hills, see UNIVERSITY OF THE TREES

HIMALAYAN ACADEMY
Commune founded in 1962 in Virginia City, Nevada, which followed a combination of Hinduism and Christianity.

HIMALAYAN INSTITUTE
Hindu-oriented group founded in the 1970s, based in Schaumburg, Illinois.

HIMALAYAN INTERNATIONAL INSTITUTE OF YOGA SCIENCE AND PHILOSOPHY
Hindu group based in Honesdale, Pennsylvania, founded in 1971 by Sri Swami Rama (1925–   ), who teaches "the system of super-conscious meditation." Rama was born in India, became a monk as a young man, and came to the United States in 1969.

HINDU AMERICAN RELIGIOUS INSTITUTE, THE
Hindu group based in western Pennsylvania, founded by Shakaracharya Swami Swanandashram around 1970 and dedicated to spreading Hindu doctrines in the United States. The founder's doctrine follows: "That Unchangeable Eternal Consciousness you are, know thyself. We live to know what is the truth behind life. We hear the truth; we meditate upon the truth; and we realize the truth. That is the aim of life."

Hindu Visva Parisad, see VISHWA HINDU PARISHAD (VHP)

John-Roger Hinkins, see MOVEMENT OF SPIRITUAL INNER AWARENESS

HIS NAME MINISTRIES
PENTECOSTAL, evangelical group based in California, founded around 1970.

Hitonomichi, see PERFECT LIBERTY KYODAN

HOA HAO
Also known as Phat Giao Hoa Hao, this Vietnamese millenarian movement was founded in 1939 by Huyen Phu So (1919–   ), who was assassinated in 1947 by the Vietminh. The movement was puritanical, peasant-based, and centered in the western Mekong Delta. Its doctrine was based on a return to traditional Buddhism, with minimal theology and no ritual.

When Ngo Dinh Diem came to power in 1954 the Hoa Hao controlled an entire province in South Vietnam. In March 1954 Diem defeated its militia, but local organizations survived. In July 1956 the most important of the Hoa Hao military leaders, Ba Cut, was executed.
See also CAO DAI

James Hodge, see UNITED LEADERSHIP COUNCIL OF HEBREW ISRAELITES

Francis Hodur, see POLISH NATIONAL CATHOLIC CHURCH OF AMERICA

Christopher Hoffmann, see TEMPLE SOCIETY

G.W. Hoffmann, see KORNTALITES

HOHM
Hindu-occultist group founded in 1975 in New Jersey by Lee Lozowick, who woke up one morning to find himself *aware, i.e.,* able to transmit ultimate truths to followers through words or through his very presence. He has offered his followers thoughts on gurus, the Godlife, existence, and the meaning of life.

Members of a "holiness" sect pray for their ailing son, refusing medical help.

"HOLINESS"

U.S. groups known by this name expect (or require) their members to experience: (1) "conversion"; (2) "sanctification" (in lifestyle), and (3) "being filled with the Holy Spirit." Step 3 may consist of a vision, a dream, "healing," or glossolalia.

HOLISTIC COMMUNITY

Anthroposophical-occultist commune founded in Mt. Freedom, New Jersey, in the 1970s. Doctrine and practices are based on the teachings of Rudolf Steiner and Edgar Cayce.

See also ANTHROPOSOPHY; ASSOCIATION FOR RESEARCH AND ENLIGHTENMENT

Gilbert N. Holloway, see NEW AGE CHURCH OF TRUTH

Ernest S. Holmes, see CHURCH OF RELIGIOUS SCIENCE

Henry Holstine, see NEVERDIES

Holy Earth Assembly, see THE HOLY EARTH ASSEMBLY (T.H.E.A.)

HOLY FEEDBACK CHURCH

Group devoted to biofeedback, founded in California in the late 1960s.

See also CHURCH OF THE SACRED ALPHA; FEEDBACK CHURCH

HOLY GHOST REPAIR SERVICE, INC.

JESUS MOVEMENT center founded in the early 1970s in Denver, Colorado.

HOLY GROUND

Native American nativist-Christian group started in 1921 among the Apaches of New Mexico. Its doctrine emphasizes monotheism and combines New Testament figures, such as Jesus Christ, with traditional mythology.

Holy Jesus Society, see SEI IESU KAI

HOLY SHANKARACHARYA ORDER, THE

Hindu monastic group based in western Pennsylvania, founded in 1968. The group also operates the Shankaracharya Pitham Sadhanalaya Ashram in Virginia.
See also YOGIRAJ

HOME OF TRUTH MOVEMENT

Initially known as the Christian Science Home, this NEW THOUGHT group was founded in 1888 in San Francisco by Annie Rix Militz, a student of Emma Curtis Hopkins. Doctrine emphasizes the possibilities of "Christian mind healing" to overcome illness and death.
See also HOPKINS ASSOCIATION, EMMA C.

Source:

Braden, C.S. *Spirits in Rebellion.* Dallas: SMU Press, 1963.

HONBUSHIN

First known as Mirokukai, this Japanese new religion was created following a schism in HONMICHI after the founder's death in 1958. The group formed around his second daughter, Tama, who claimed to be his true successor. Honbushin means True Constitution.

HONMICHI-KYO

First known as Tenri Kenkyukai (Tenri Study Association) and then Tenri Honmichi (Tenri True Way), this Japanese Shinto-inspired new religion grew out of the TENRIKYO movement. It was founded in 1925 by a Tenrikyo missionary, Ajijiro Onishi (1881–1958). In 1913 Onishi became convinced that he had received a divine revelation, which led him to claim that he should reign over the Tenrikyo movement. Doctrine is millenarian, focusing on the figure of the founder.

HONOR OAK CHRISTIAN FELLOWSHIP CENTRE

British Fundamentalist Christian group founded in London around 1920 by T. Austin-Sparks, a former Baptist. His writings later inspired THIS TESTIMONY, a U.S. Fundamentalist group.
See also FUNDAMENTALISM; HEPZEBAH HOUSE; LOCAL CHURCH MOVEMENT; WESTMORELAND CHAPEL

HOPKINS ASSOCIATION, EMMA C.

NEW THOUGHT group founded by Emma Curtis Hopkins (?–1925), a former CHRISTIAN SCIENCE leader, in Chicago in 1886. In 1887 the Illinois Metaphysical College, also known as the Christian Science Theological Seminary, was founded. The Association influenced many similar groups such as the CHURCH OF RELIGIOUS SCIENCE, HOME OF TRUTH MOVEMENT, and the UNITY SCHOOL OF CHRISTIANITY, whose founders were all students of Mrs.

Hopkins. Her ideas were carried on through JOY FARM and the Ministry of the High Walls.

Jack Horner, see DIANOLOGY AND EDUCTIVISM

Ralph G. Horner, see STANDARD CHURCH OF AMERICA

David Horowitz, see UNITED ISRAEL WORLD UNION

Hosannas, see MASOWE APOSTLES

HOUSE OF GOD WHICH IS THE CHURCH OF THE LIVING GOD, THE PILLAR AND GROUND OF TRUTH WITHOUT CONTROVERSY

U.S. African-American PENTECOSTAL group founded in the 1930s as a result of a schism in the Church of the Living God, the Pillar and Ground of the Truth.

HOUSE OF JUDAH

African-American "Black Jews" group founded by William A. Lewis and based in Allegan County, Michigan. The group gained much publicity in 1982 when a child died as a result of beating and its mother was convicted of involuntary manslaughter. In 1986, group leaders were convicted of conspiring to enslave children. The group's doctrine calls for strong discipline and prescribes corporal punishment.
See also BLACK JEWS

HOUSE OF PRAYER FOR ALL PEOPLE, THE

Adventist, British-Israelist group founded in 1941 by William Lester Blessing (1900–1984) in Denver, Colorado. According to Blessing, Yashua the messiah is already here and will make himself known before the year 2000 by establishing his kingdom on earth. Blessing also promoted ideas about the Great Pyramid, UFOs, and "psychic phenomena." In the 1940s he distributed literature that was anti-Semitic, anti-black, and anti-Catholic.

Source:
Roy, J.L. *Apostles of Discord*. Boston: Beacon Press, 1953.

House of Prayer for All the People, see UNITED HOUSE OF PRAYER FOR ALL PEOPLE

HOUSE OF THE GODDESS (HOG)

British neo-pagan group founded by Shan, a "coven mother," in London in 1985 "...to provide contact, support, study and celebration for anyone interested in Paganism, and in particular, the Carft." It is led by women, and "...respect for the feminine is a priority."

HOUSE OF THE LORD

African-American PENTECOSTAL group founded in 1925 in Detroit by W.H. Johnson. The group advocates a strict conduct code, which forbids worldly amusements, fighting in wars, life insurance, and real estate ownership. Glossolalia is practiced.

Jean Houston, see DROMENON

Luther S. Howard, see PENTECOSTAL CHURCH OF ZION

Leonard Howell, see RASTAFARIANS

Lafayette Ronald (L. Ron) Hubbard, see SCIENTOLOGY

A.D. Hudson, see BIBLE FELLOWSHIP UNION

Fritz and Vivian Hull, see CHINOOK COMMUNITY

HUNA RESEARCH ASSOCIATES

U.S. occultist group founded around 1950 by Max Freedom Long (?–1971), which claims to have knowledge of the magical practices of the Hawaiian huna religion. Members study the teachings of Long, who claimed to have found connections between huna and Christianity.

See also CHURCH OF BASIC TRUTH

Percy Hunt, see LATTER RAIN MOVEMENT

Neva Dell Hunter, see QUIMBY CENTER

George Willie Hurley, see UNIVERSAL HAGAR'S SPIRITUAL CHURCH

E.A. Hurtienne, see ETHERIAN RELIGIOUS SOCIETY OF UNIVERSAL BROTHERHOOD

Barry I. Hyman, see CHRISTIAN REVOLUTIONARY BROTHERHOOD

I

"I AM"

Known originally as the Great I Am or Mighty I Am, this Theosophical group was founded in the 1930s in Los Angeles by Guy W. Ballard (1878–1939). The founder, who worked as a spiritualist in the 1920s, reported that in 1930, near Mt. Shasta, he had a meeting with "Master Saint-Germain," who gave him much arcane knowledge about karma and reincarnation. Unlike traditional Theosophical teachings, in Ballard's teachings the Ascended Masters (and Jesus of the New Testament) do not limit themselves to Central Asia, but visit the Western United States. Ballard worked with his wife Edna (?–1971) and his son Donald in propagating these ideas. In the 1940s the group was convicted of mail fraud but won acquittal at the U.S. Supreme Court. Group headquarters, known as the Saint Germain Foundation, are on Mt. Shasta.
See also SUMMIT LIGHTHOUSE; THEOSOPHY

ICSA (INTEGRAL CENTER OF SELF-ABIDANCE)

Formerly known as the Intercosmic Center of Spiritual Associations, and the International Center for Self-Analysis, this U.S. Hindu group was founded in 1958 by Shri Brahmananda Sarasvati and Rammurti Sriram Mishra in North Syracuse, New York, and has been directed by Srimati Margaret Coble. Doctrine emphasizes "the One Presence-Power-Reality." It "presents a clear message of the unity and common spirituality of humanity, summed up by the universal statement, I AM."

IDENTITY MOVEMENT

Also known as Christian Identity, this Christian theological movement is based on an unconventional interpretation of biblical mythology. That interpretation claims that the peoples of Northern Europe, referred to as "Anglo-Saxons," are the true Children of Israel, Jews are the Children of Satan, and Africans are "pre-Adamic." The Anglo-Saxons are descended from Adam, whereas Jews are the descendants of Cain.

Unlike BRITISH ISRAELISM, which represents "Anglo-Saxons" as descendants of ancient Jews, Identity claims that ancient Jews were identical with "Anglo-Saxons." Biblical references to "Israel as the chosen nation" are actually references to "Anglo-Saxons."

Groups associated with Identity theology have been anti-Semitic, blaming Jews for recent social and economic problems in the United States, and promoting the idea of an Aryan nation and racial purity.

Idries Shah, see INSTITUTE FOR CULTURAL RESEARCH

IGLESIA BANDO EVANGELICO GEDEON

Also known in the United States as the Gilgal Evangelistic International Church and as the Soldiers of the Cross of Christ, Evangelical International Church, this Spanish-speaking PENTECOSTAL group was founded as the Gideon Mission in the early 1920s in Havana, Cuba, by Ernest William Sellers (?–1953). The group follows Old Testament Sabbath and dietary laws and emphasizes prophecy and revelation in dreams. In the 1950s mission work was started in Latin America and the United States. In 1969, following the Cuban revolu-

Guy W. Ballard, founder of the Theosophical group the Great I Am, with his wife, Edna.

George A. Stallings sings as he celebrates mass at his Imani Temple, a breakaway Roman Catholic group in Washington, D.C.

tion, the group moved its headquarters to Miami, Florida.

IGLESIA DE DIOS PENTECOSTAL

Known also as the Pentecostal Church of God, this Puerto Rican PENTECOSTAL group was founded in the 1930s. Healing and tithing are emphasized.

See also CONCILIO LATINO-AMERICANO DE LA IGLESIA DE DIOS PENTECOSTAL DE NEW YORK, INCORPORADO

Iglesia Defensores de La Fe, see DEFENDERS OF THE FAITH

Iglesia Filipina Independiente, see PHILIPPINE INDEPENDENT CHURCH

IGLESIA NI CRISTO (MANALISTA, INC)

Officially known as the Church of Christ, this millenarian Christian group in the Philippines was founded in 1913 by Felix Manalo (1886–1963), a former Catholic who claimed a divine mission of recreating the original Christian church. It has been quite nationalistic in emphasis and has developed into a political force by directing members how to vote in national elections. The group has operated missions in North America and Europe since 1968.

"Reverend Ike," see UNITED CHURCH AND SCIENCE OF LIVING INSTITUTE

Daisaku Ikeda, see SOKA GAKKAI

IMANI TEMPLE

Known sometimes as the Afro-American Imani Temple, this breakaway Roman Catholic group was founded in 1989 in Washington, D.C., by George A. Stallings.

A Roman Catholic priest who sought to express African-American nationalism through the movement, Stallings has been accused of sexual and financial offenses.

Hazrat Inayat Khan, see SUFI ORDER IN THE WEST

Himayat Inayati, see HEALING ORDER OF THE SUFI ORDER

INDEPENDENT ASSEMBLIES OF GOD, INTERNATIONAL

North American PENTECOSTAL group developing out of the Scandinavian Assemblies of God in the United States, Canada, and Other Lands, formed in 1918 out of similar groups in Scandinavian communities in the northern United States. The Independent Assemblies of God was formed in 1935, and the current name was adopted in 1948 following a schism over predictions of the coming millennium. The dissenting group became THE INDEPENDENT ASSEMBLIES OF GOD (UNINCORPORATED).

INDEPENDENT ASSEMBLIES OF GOD (UNINCORPORATED), THE

North American PENTECOSTAL group founded in 1948 following a schism in the Independent Assemblies of God.

See also INDEPENDENT ASSEMBLIES OF GOD, INTERNATIONAL

INDEPENDENT CHURCH OF JESUS CHRIST OF LATTER DAY SAINTS

European branch of SONS AHMAN ISRAEL, U.S. polygamist Mormon group.

See also MORMONS

INDEPENDENT FUNDAMENTAL CHURCHES OF AMERICA (IFCA)

U.S. Fundamentalist group founded in 1922 by R. Lee Kirkland under the name AMERICAN CONFERENCE OF UNDENOMINATED CHURCHES. The group superseded the Conference in 1930.

INDEPENDENT FUNDAMENTALIST BIBLE CHURCHES, THE

Fundamentalist group formed in 1965 by Marion H. Reynolds, W.E. Standridge, Henry Campbell, and Kenneth L. Barth. Its headquarters are in Los Angeles, California.

INDEPENDENT SPIRITUALIST ASSOCIATION (I.S.A.)

U.S. spiritualist organization founded in 1924 by Amanda Flowers, who withdrew from the NATIONAL SPIRITUALIST ASSOCIATION. The I.S.A. allows members to follow belief in reincarnation.

Two leading members, John Bunker and Clifford Bias, left the I.S.A. to form the Spiritualist Episcopal Church.

Source:
Judah, J.S. *The History and Philosophy of the Metaphysical Movements in America.* Philadelphia: Westminster, 1967.

INDEPENDENT THEOSOPHICAL SOCIETY

Theosophical organization founded in 1923 by T.H. Martyn, who had been General Secretary of the Australian branch of the Theosophical Society.
See also THEOSOPHY

INDIAN SHAKER CHURCH

Native American nativist-Christian move- ment started by John Slocum, of the Squaxin tribe, in 1881 in Puget Sound. It replaced traditional shamanistic "healing" with shaking and dance rituals having an overall Christian bent. Over the years it has spread on the Pacific coast.

Source:
Barnett, H.G. *Indian Shakers.* Carbondale, IL: Southern Illinois University Press, 1957.

Daniel Inesse, see TAYU FELLOWSHIP

INFINITE WAY SOCIETY

North American dissident CHRISTIAN SCIENCE group founded in 1946 by Joel S. Goldsmith (1892–1964), a former Christian Science practitioner. Beyond healing practices, the group advocates contemplative meditation.

INNER CIRCLE KETHRA E'DA FOUNDATION

Spiritualist group based in California, founded in 1945 by Mark (?–1969) and Irene Probert. Teachings consist of messages from "ancient masters" long dead, who communicated them to Mark Probert while in trance.

INNER CIRCLE OF ENCHANTMENT INC. (I.C.E.)

Occultist, NEW THOUGHT group founded by Sally Stern in New Jersey in the 1980s and devoted to "psychic development" through home study.

INNER LIGHT FOUNDATION

Christian occultist group founded in 1967 in Novato, California, by the spiritualist medium Betty Bethards. "The principal objective of the Inner Light Foundation is to engage in spiritual, educational, charitable, and scientific activities which foster, develop, and achieve in mankind an awareness of his unity with God, the Universal Consciousness."

INNER PEACE MOVEMENT (IPM)

International occultist group founded in 1964 by Francisco Coll, a former member of the SPIRITUAL FRONTIERS FELLOWSHIP. The group teaches "self-realization."

Geraldine Innocente, see BRIDGE TO FREEDOM

INSIGHT MEDITATION SOCIETY

Buddhist-inspired group started around 1980 by Joseph Goldstein, Catherine Ingram, and Sharon Salzberg and based in Barre, Massachusetts. The main practice is "mindfulness meditation."

INSTITUTE FOR CULTURAL RESEARCH

British occultist group founded in 1965 in COOMBE SPRINGS, P.D. Ouspensky's estate in England, as the Society for Understanding Fundamental Ideas (SUFI). Its founders were John Godolphin Bennett (1897–1974) and Idries Shah (1924–   ), an Indian of Afghan descent who has been one of the most visible promoters of Sufism in the West since the 1950s. The Institute is now based at Langston Green, England.
See also GURDJIEFF GROUPS; SUFI ORDER IN THE WEST

INSTITUTE FOR PLANETARY SYNTHESIS (IPS)

Swiss occultist group founded in 1981 in Geneva by Rudolf Schneider (1932–   ). Its doctrines have been strongly influenced by the teachings of Alice Bailey of the LUCIS TRUST, as well as by the ideas of the WORLD TEACHER TRUST. The group proclaims a message of imminent salvation and world change.

INSTITUTE FOR RELIGIOUS DEVELOPMENT

Gurdjieff group founded by Wilhelm A. Nyland (?–1975) and based near New York City. Nyland was an associate of Gurdjieff from 1924 to 1949 and then went to the United States to spread Gurdjieff's message.
See also GURDJIEFF GROUPS

INSTITUTE FOR RESEARCH ON THE DISSEMINATION OF HUMAN KNOWLEDGE

U.S. group devoted to promoting the ideas of Idries Shah, founded in the late 1960s in Boulder, Colorado.
See also INSTITUTE FOR CULTURAL RESEARCH; SUFI ORDER IN THE WEST

INSTITUTE FOR THE COMPARATIVE STUDY OF HISTORY, PHILOSOPHY, AND THE SCIENCES

Founded in 1946 by John Godolphin Bennett (1897–1974) and other disciples of P.D. Ouspensky and based in Coombe Springs, P.D. Ouspensky's estate in England. Bennett was later involved in SUBUD but in 1968 converted to the Roman Catholic Church.
See also CLAYMONT COURT; GURDJIEFF GROUPS

INSTITUTE FOR THE HARMONIOUS DEVELOPMENT OF THE HUMAN BEING (IHDHB)

Gurdjieff group founded and directed by E.J. Gold in California. His teachings are eclectic, using ideas and practices from many traditions. The group's core belief includes reincarnation, "spiritual evolution," and a search for "control over the soul's destiny." Gold claims to be the direct successor to Gurdjieff, and also to be a Sufi. The group has also been referred to as Shakti.

See also GURDJIEFF GROUPS

Source:

Westley, F. *The Complex Forms of the Religious Life*. Chico, CA: Scholars Press, 1983.

INSTITUTE OF COSMIC WISDOM

Occultist group founded by Clark Wilkerson in the late 1940s in Playa del Ray, California. Doctrine combines NEW THOUGHT with Huna magic.

See also HUNA RESEARCH ASSOCIATES

INSTITUTE OF MENTALPHYSICS

Occultist group founded in 1927 in Los Angeles by Edwin John Dingle (1881–1972), also known as Ding Le Mei, who claimed to have studied the ancient wisdom of the "Aryans" in Tibet. The group is devoted to meditation, yoga, and "other spiritual practices," which were supposed to lead "to the highest development of the total person, body, mind, and spirit, one is evolutionarily able to achieve."

INSTITUTE OF PYRAMIDOLOGY, THE

British offshoot of JEHOVAH'S WITNESSES founded in 1940 in London by Adam Rutherford. Relying on the teachings of Charles Taze Russell, it claims that the Great Pyramid of Egypt is a major source of occult knowledge, or "the Bible in Stone."

INTEGRAL YOGA INSTITUTE (IYI)

International Hindu group with headquarters in the United States, founded by Sri Swami Satchidananda, also known as Narayan, who was a disciple of Sivananda. Swami Satchidananda came to the United States in 1966. He has advocated the use of yoga techniques, which include *hatha* (physical posture, breathing, and deep relaxation), *raja* (concentration and meditation, *japa*, repeating a mantra, *karma* ("selfless actions"), *bhakti* (devotional practices), and *jnana* (self-inquiry). Branches, sometimes known as Satchidananda Ashram-Yogaville, have operated in Sri Lanka, Australia, Europe, and Africa.

See also SIVENANDA YOGA VEDANTA

INTERFAITH FELLOWSHIP

Occultist-Christian group founded in the 1980s by Jon Mundy and Diane Berke and based in New York State, devoted to teaching A COURSE IN MIRACLES. The book *A Course in Miracles* was published in 1975 by Helen Schucman, who claimed to have been only the medium for a divine revelation.

See also FOUNDATION FOR "A COURSE IN MIRACLES"; FOUNDATION FOR INNER PEACE

INTER-FAITH MINISTRIES FOR RENEWAL

Fundamentalist group started as part of the JESUS MOVEMENT around 1970 in Des Moines, Iowa, active in media and outreach activities.

INTERFAITH TEMPLE or INTERFAITH, INC.

Jewish-syncretistic group based in New

York City, founded by Joseph H. Gelberman in the early 1970s. Its doctrine combines Jewish beliefs and practices with Hindu and Theosophical concepts. It operates the Institute of Personal Religion, the New Light Temple, and the New Seminary, which trains Interfaith ministers as well as rabbis. The group has worked with NEW THOUGHT organizations.

See also THEOSOPHY; TREE OF LIFE

INTERNATIONAL ASSOCIATION FOR LIBERAL CHRISTIANS AND RELIGIOUS FREEDOM (IARF)

Liberal Christian group founded in the United States in 1910 as the International Council of Unitarians and other Liberal Religious Thinkers and Workers, and in 1930 renamed the International Congress of Free Christians and other Religious Liberals.

INTERNATIONAL BABAJI KRIYA YOGA SANGAM

Hindu group founded in 1952. "Guided by Yogi S.A.A. Ramaiah, disciple of Master Babaji Nagaraj of the Himalayas. Kriya Yoga involves *hatha*, *kundalini*, *mantra*, *dhyana*, *pranayama*, and *bhakti yogas*."

See also HAIDAKHAN SAMAJ

INTERNATIONAL CHRISTIAN CHURCHES, THE

PENTECOSTAL group with members in Hawaii and the Philippines, founded in 1943 by Franco Manuel, former member of the Disciples of Christ Church in Hawaii.

INTERNATIONAL CHURCH OF SPIRITUAL VISION, INC.

Also known as Western Prayer Warriors, this U.S. PENTECOSTAL-Adventist, occultist group was founded in the 1960s by Dallas Turner, known in his career as a singer as Nevada Slim. The group keeps in contact with its members mostly by mail.

INTERNATIONAL COMMUNITY OF CHRIST

U.S. Christian-Theosophist organization founded in 1957 by Gene Savoy (1927–   ) and offering correspondence courses and other materials containing the message of the New Christianity. The message includes claims about "nuclear energy in the brain" and "electromagnetic force fields." The organization operates the "Jamilian University" in Reno, Nevada.

INTERNATIONAL DELIVERANCE CHURCHES

PENTECOSTAL group founded by W.V. Grant and based in Dallas, Texas. The group focuses on the practice of faith healing.

INTERNATIONAL EVANGELISM CRUSADES

PENTECOSTAL group founded in 1959 by Frank E. Stranges. The group's doctrine includes belief in extraterrestrial contacts. It has had branches in North America and Asia.

INTERNATIONAL GENERAL ASSEMBLY OF SPIRITUALISTS (IGAS)

Christian-spiritualist organization founded in New York City in 1931 and incorporated in Buffalo in 1936 by Arthur Ford (1897–1971). The group's doctrine emphasizes prayer, "healing, and spiritual development." Branches have operated in Asia and Africa.

INTERNATIONAL HEBREW CHRISTIAN ALLIANCE OF AMERICA

U.S. Hebrew-Christian organization founded in 1925.
See also HEBREW CHRISTIANITY

INTERNATIONAL METAPHYSICAL ASSOCIATION (IMA)

Independent CHRISTIAN SCIENCE group founded in 1955. Disputing the authority of the Church of Christ, Scientist, it is officially committed to the original teachings of Mary Baker Eddy.

INTERNATIONAL ORDER OF ST. LUKE THE PHYSICIAN

Christian-NEW THOUGHT group founded in 1946 by John Gayner Banks. It is devoted to "spiritual healing."

INTERNATIONAL PENTECOSTAL ASSEMBLIES, THE

PENTECOSTAL group founded in 1936 through the merger of the National and International Pentecostal Missionary Union and the ASSOCIATION OF PENTECOSTAL ASSEMBLIES. Members believe in healing and in a personal devil. The doctrine, which is similar to that of THE CHURCH OF GOD (CLEVELAND, TENNESSEE), formerly included a ban on military service.

INTERNATIONAL SCHOOL OF YOGA AND VEDANTA

Also known as the Yoga Research Foundation, this Hindu group was founded in 1969 in Miami by Swami Jyotir Maya Nanda (1931–), who studied under Swami Sivananda Saraswati.

INTERNATIONAL SOCIETY FOR KRISHNA CONSCIOUSNESS (ISKCON)

Known all over the world by the popular name Hare Krishna (HK), this Hindu revival movement reached the West and was formally organized in the United States in 1966. It was founded by A.C. Bhaktivedanta Swami Prabhupada, born in Calcutta as Abhay Charan De (1896–1977), who arrived in the United States in 1965.

ISKCON doctrine is based on the *Bhagavad-Gita* as interpreted by A.C. Bhaktivedanta. This interpretation emphasizes the priority of Krishna, who is defined as the Supreme Personality of Godhead. ISKCON rituals are classified as *bhakti*, that is, devotion. "The most perfect action is to serve Krishna." This sentence sums up the *bhakti* spirit. The holy name of Krishna must be pronounced 1,728 times a day. The chant, or *mantra*, for which members of the group have become known is: *Hare Krishna, Hare Krishna, Krishna, Krishna, Hare, Hare, Hare Rama, Hare Rama, Hare, Hare*. The rules of conduct include abstention from all intoxicants (tobacco, alcohol, coffee, tea, narcotics, and soft drugs), meat, fish, and eggs. All eating is an act of worship. Sex is allowed only for procreation within marriage.

Members are noticeable by their distinctive dress and grooming, which include saffron robes, color marks on their faces, and for men, shaved heads except for a topknot by which Krishna will pick them up when the world ends, and by *sankirtan*, *i.e.*, ritual begging. The group has often been accused of deceptive practices in fundraising.

The group's doctrine reflects the appearance of a revitalization movement that

A. C. Shaktivedanta Swami Prabhupada, spiritual leader of the Hare Krishna movement in San Francisco.

started in the 19th century within the traditional Caitanya (Gaudiya) Vaisnavism of India. According to this tradition, the last incarnation of Krishna appeared in 1486 in India, when Caitanya appeared. Then started a succession of disciples, down to Sri Srimad Bhakitisiddhanta Sarasvati Gosvami Maharaja in the early 20th century, the guru who initiated A.C. Bhaktivedanta Swami Prabhupada in 1933. ISKCON's vision of the ideal society includes an agrarian economy based on the protection of cows, and the division of society into four castes.

The group has sent missionaries to India and established centers there, but most of its members are Westerners. In 1972 an ISKCON temple opened in Mayapurand,

India. The Krishna Balaram Mandir in Vrndavana, India, now the official world center, opened in 1973. The North American branches of ISKCON established close contacts with immigrant Hindus there in the 1980s.

Sources:

Daner, F. *The American Children of Krishna.* New York: Holt, Rinehart & Winston, 1975.

Hubner, J., and Gruson, L. *Monkey on a Stick: Murder, Madness and the Hare Krishnas.* San Diego: Harcourt Brace Jovanovich, 1988.

Judah, J.S. *Hare Krishna and the*

Counterculture. New York: Wiley, 1974.

Rochford, E.B. Jr. *Hare Krishna in America.* New Brunswick, NJ: Rutgers University Press, 1985.

INTERNATIONAL SOCIETY OF DIVINE LOVE (I.S.D.L.)

Hindu group founded in 1980 by Prakashanand H.D. Saraswati (1929–), known as "His Divinity." "Spending most of his lifetime in the isolated retreats of Braj [India], Shree Swamiji, realizing the need of the souls, has introduced his visual experiences to the world, discriminately explaining all the five sciences of matter, mind, soul, God and DIVINE LOVE. Thus his teachings hold the authentic originality of the Ancient Indian Scriptures and his method of meditation is unbelievably effective." Branches of the group have operated in the United States, Europe, and New Zealand.

INTERNATIONAL SPIRITUALIST FEDERATION

Spiritualist organization based in London, with a membership of spiritualist groups in forty nations.

INTERNATIONAL YOGA FELLOWSHIP IN AMERICA

U.S. Hindu group founded by Eddie Brahmananda Shapiro, who was "empowered by Paramahansa Satyananda" during a trip to India in 1968.

INVITATION À LA VIE INTENSE (I.V.I.)

International Christian-occultist "healing" group founded in 1983 in Paris by Yvonne Trubert (1922–). "Pray-Love-Heal" is the group's slogan and goal. Its doctrine combines Roman Catholic elements with Hindu ideas of reincarnation. Group members are said to be reincarnations of early Christians. "Healing" consists of "harmonizing the three bodies: physical, enegetic, and astral," and members claim cures of all known diseases. Branches have operated in Western Europe.

Richard Ireland, see UNIVERSITY OF LIFE CHURCH

Edward Irving, see CATHOLIC APOSTOLIC CHURCH

ISHVARA (Lifewave)

British Eastern-inspired group started in the 1970s, led by John Herbert Yarr, known as "Divine Master Ishvara" or "the perfect master Yarr."

David Israel, see SONS AHMAN ISRAEL

ISRAELI SCHOOL OF U.P.K., THE

"Black Israelite" group based in New York City, which claims that African-Americans are the descendants of the mythological tribe of Judah and that Jews have usurped their identity from its rightful owners.

"ISRAELITES"

South African independent, millenarian separatist group, founded in 1918 by Enoch Mgijima (1858–1928), a former member of the Church of God and Saints of Christ who was excommunicated for preaching his end-of-the-world visions. His followers settled in a colony in Bullhoek, near Queenstown. The doctrine was Old Testament–oriented. Mgijima claimed to have been chosen as prophet by the God of Israel. The New Testament was regarded as a fiction created by the whites. The "Israel-ites" were Jehovah's elect, fighting for land against the Midianites and the Philistines, and He would deliver them from bondage and let them crush the Europeans. When the military approached the colony on May 24, 1921, Mgijima told his followers that they were immune to bullets. The outcome was that 117 "Israelites" were killed. The movement survived this tragedy and the death of its founder.

Source:
Sundkler, B.G.M. *Bantu Prophets in South Africa*. London: Oxford University Press, 1961.

ISRAEL SOODO WON (Israel Monastery)

Korean Christian monastic group founded in the 1940s by Paik Moon Kim, a self-proclaimed messiah. Sun Myung Moon, founder of the UNIFICATION CHURCH, is reported to have spent six months in this group in 1945.

ITALIAN PENTECOSTAL ASSEMBLIES OF GOD

U.S. PENTECOSTAL group started by John Santamaria and his son Rocco, who started evangelical work among Italian immigrants in 1904. The group was organized in 1907 and later merged with the UNORGANIZED ITALIAN CHRISTIAN CHURCHES OF NORTH AMERICA to form THE CHRISTIAN CHURCH OF NORTH AMERICA.

Shinjo Ito, see SHINYO-EN

ITTOEN ("Garden of Light")

Japanese new religion started after World War II by Nishida Tenko. Tenko was elected to the upper chamber of the Japanese Diet in 1947.

Omraam Mikhael Ivanoff, see FRATERNITÉ BLANCHE UNIVERSELLE

J

Moineddin Jablonski, see SUFI ISLAMIA RUHANIAT SOCIETY

O.L. Jaggars, see UNIVERSAL WORLD CHURCH

JAIN MEDITATION INTERNATIONAL CENTER

North American Jain group founded in New York City in 1975 by Gurudev Shree Chitrabhanu (1923–   ), a former Jain monk who immigrated to the United States in 1971. Devoted to spreading the Jain tradition of India in the West, it is connected with JAIN SAMAJ EUROPE.

Source:
Jaini, P.S. *The Jaina Path of Purification.* Berkeley: University of California Press, 1979.

JAIN SAMAJ EUROPE

International group dedicated to spreading the Jain tradition in Europe. Founded by Natubhai Shah in 1988, it is connected with the JAIN MEDITATION INTERNATIONAL CENTER.

JALA SANGHA

Hindu-oriented group founded in 1970 in Redondo Beach, California, by Yogi Yukteswar Sri Bbajhan.

JAMAA ("Family")

Zairian separatist Catholic movement started in the 1940s in Katanga province of the then Belgian Congo by Placide Tempels, a Belgian Franciscan priest. In 1953 it became officially independent of the Roman Catholic Church. Its doctrine emphasizes the importance of the nuclear family.

Source:
Fabian, J. *Jamaa: A Charismatic Movement in Katanga.* Evanston: Northwestern University Press, 1971.

Jana Sangh, see RASHTRIYA SWAYAMASEVAK SANGH

JAPPA TABERNACLE

Fundamentalist, PENTECOSTAL group connected with BRITISH ISRAELISM, founded by Otis B. Read in Baltimore in the 1940s.

JEAN-MICHEL ET SON ÉQUIPE (Jean-Michel and his team)

International Christian PENTECOSTAL group founded by Jean-Michel Cravanzola (1945–   ) in Switzerland in 1971. The founder moved to the United States in 1982 after being convicted of fraud in Lausanne in 1979. Group doctrine rejects belief in the Trinity and promotes faith healing. Branches have operated in France, Switzerland, and North America. The Swiss branch has used the name Action et Compassion.

George Jeffreys, see BIBLE PATTERN FELLOWSHIP; ELIM FOURSQUARE GOSPEL

JEHOVAH'S WITNESSES

Officially known, since 1939, as the Watchtower Bible and Tract Society, the International Bible Students Association, or Jehovah's Christian Witnesses, incorporated in 1884 as the Zion's Watch Tower

A soloist lifts her voice in prayer during an annual convention of Jehovah's Witnesses.

Tract Society, and sometimes known as Russellites, this Christian Adventist group with worldwide activities has been headquartered in Brooklyn, New York, since 1909. Officially, Witnesses regard their group as a world religion separate from all other traditions, but they still claim to be the true Christians. They often refer to themselves as Bible Students.

The history of the Witnesses starts with the work of Charles Taze Russell, born in 1852 in Pittsburgh, Pennsylvania. In 1870 he joined an Adventist group that followed the ideas of Jonas Wendell. Following predictions by Wendell naming 1874 as the time of the Second Coming, Russell believed that actually it was the presence of God on earth that began in 1874.

In 1879 Russell published the first issue of the *Watch Tower*, which became the organ of a movement known as "Millenial Dawn Bible Students"; in 1881 the Zion's Watch Tower Tract Society was founded.

According to Russell's doctrine, history is divided into three periods: from the biblical Creation to the biblical Flood, from the Flood to Jesus Christ's death, and from Jesus Christ's death to 1914, date of salvation for the 144,000 "elect." In 1886 Russell made public his timetable for the millennium. According to this divine plan, the millenial dawn period (1874–1914) would end with the establishment of God's direct rule on earth and the restoration of mankind to perfection. In 1914 the date was revised forward to 1918, and then Russell died in 1916.

Joseph Franklin Rutherford (1869–1941), known as "Judge," who succeeded the founder as leader, pronounced in 1920 what has become a well-known Witness slogan, "Millions now living will never die."

He kept announcing dates for the end of the days, first 1920, then 1925 and 1940. In 1931 the Watch Tower Bible and Tract Society became officially known as Jehovah's Witnesses. It experienced a significant revival during the Great Depression. In 1969 Nathan Homer Knorr (1905–1977), Rutherford's successor as spiritual leader of the group, stated that the Millennium of Christ's reign on earth would start in 1975. Later the date of October 2, 1984, was proclaimed.

The Witnesses' doctrine claims to be faithful to the Bible, as shown by the use of the name Jehovah for the deity and the belief in a literal Kingdom of God. Witnesses reject the notion of an immortal soul, believe in baptism by immersion, do not participate in politics, never vote, and refuse blood transfusions. Because of their refusal to bear arms or salute national flags, Witnesses have been subjected to persecution and imprisonment in many countries, including Nazi Germany, Malawi, Yugoslavia, China, Poland, and Israel.

Since World War II, Jehovah's Witnesses have experienced a tremendous growth in numbers and activity, and they are now found in most countries of the world. Their best-known publications, *The Watchtower* and *Awake!*, were said in 1987 to have a combined distribution of 23 million. They distribute literature and proselytize by visiting people at their homes. The British branch of Jehovah's Witnesses, founded in 1914, is known as the International Bible Students Association.

See also BEREAN BIBLE STUDENTS CHURCH; BIBLE FELLOWSHIP UNION; THE INSTITUTE OF PYRAMIDOLOGY; KITAWALA; LAYMEN'S HOME MISSIONARY MOVEMENT (LHMM); PASTORAL

BIBLE INSTITUTE; PROVIDENCE INDUS-
TRIAL MISSION; WATCH TOWER MOVE-
MENT; WATCHTOWER MOVEMENT

Sources:
Beckford, J. *The Trumpet of Prophecy: A Sociological Study of Jehovah's Witnesses.* Oxford: Blackwell, 1975.
Botting, H., and Botting, G. *The Orwellian World of the Jehovah's Witnesses.* Toronto: University of Toronto Press, 1984.
Penton, J. *Apocalypse Delayed.* Toronto: University of Toronto Press, 1985.
Rogerson, A. *Millions Now Living Will Never Die.* London: Constable, 1969.
Sterling, C.W. *The Witnesses.* Chicago: Henry Regnery, 1975.
Stroup, H.H. *The Jehovah's Witnesses.* New York: Columbia University Press, 1945.

JESUS FELLOWSHIP CHURCH

British PENTECOSTAL, Fundamentalist group started in 1969 by Noel Stanton. Many of its members have lived in communal households.

Jesus Freaks, see JESUS MOVEMENT

JESUS MOVEMENT

Known also as Jesus Children or Jesus Freaks, this collection of Fundamentalist Christian groups sprang up in the United States in the late 1960s to the mid-1970s. At the height of its success the movement was said to have 200 communes in California alone. Only a few of the groups survived past the mid-1970s, among them THE CHURCH OF BIBLE UNDERSTANDING.

Sources:
Ellwood, R.S. *One Way: The Jesus Movement and Its Meaning.* Englewood Cliffs, NJ: Prentice-Hall, 1973.
Richardson, J.T., Stewart, M.W., and Simmonds, R.B. *Organized Miracles.* New Brunswick, NJ: Transaction Books, 1979.
Streiker, L.D. *The Jesus Trip.* Nashville, TN: Abingdon Press, 1971.

JETSUN SAKYA CENTER (JSC)

U.S. Tibetan Buddhist group, originating with the Ngor sect of the Tibetan Sakya School. It was founded in 1977 by Dezhung Rinpoche in New York City and has been based there. Practices include meditation and yoga.
See also VAJRADHATU

JEWISH SCIENCE, SOCIETY OF

Also known as the Society for Applied Judaism, this group was founded by Morris Lichtenstein (1890–1938) in 1922 in New York City and developed as a Jewish equivalent of CHRISTIAN SCIENCE. The founder was born in Lithuania, came to the United States in 1907, and was ordained as a REFORM JUDAISM rabbi in 1916.

The origins of the group can be traced first to significant numbers of Jewish converts to Christian Science around the turn of the century and to attempts by Jewish leaders to counter that trend. In 1916, Alfred Geiger Moses, a Reform Judaism rabbi, published *Jewish Science*, which became the foundation of the group's doctrine. The Jewish Science affirmations state that, "The God consciousness in me expresses itself in Health, in Calmness, in Peace, in Power and in Happiness. I am calm and cheerful; I hate no one; I envy no one; there is no worry or

Moishe Rosen, founder of Jews for Jesus (courtesy Jews for Jesus).

fear in me; I trust in God all the time."
See also CHRISTIAN SCIENCE LIBERALS;
NEW THOUGHT

Source:
Meyer, D. *The Positive Thinkers*. New York:
Pantheon Books, 1980.

JEWS FOR JESUS

International Hebrew Christian evangelical
organization dedicated to spreading the
message of HEBREW CHRISTIANITY, that
is, the possibility of combining Jewish
identity and Christian beliefs of the Fundamentalist variety. The rituals combine Jewish and Protestant elements. Jesus Christ of
the New Testament is known as Yeshua or
Y'shua.

The group was founded in 1970 in
northern California by Moishe Rosen. In
1973 it was incorporated under the official
name Hineni Ministries. It officially
changed to Jews for Jesus in 1984. Branches
operate in major U.S. and Canadian urban
centers, as well as in Argentina, France,
Great Britain, Ukraine, Russia, and South
Africa.

Source:
Sobel, B.Z. *Hebrew Christianity: The Thirteenth Tribe*. New York: Wiley, 1974.

James Jershom Jezreel, see NEW AND
LATTER HOUSE OF ISRAEL
(JEZREELITES)

John, Bubba Free, see FREE DAIST
COMMUNION

JOHN FRUM (JON FRUM)

Melanesian syncretistic, millenarian movement (CARGO CULT) started on Tana Island, New Hebrides (now Vanuatu) in 1936.
Its doctrine combines the return of ancestor
worship with native separatism. The basic
belief is in the imminent appearance of the
savior John Frum (=Broom), who is presented either as a traditional deity or as the
"king of America" and who will deliver the
"cargo" (cars, machines, and other modern
products) by airplanes and get rid of the
Europeans. Followers worship before red-
painted images of the mythical John Frum,
red crosses, and red-painted airplanes.

A.C. Johnson, see CHURCH OF THE
LORD JESUS CHRIST OF THE APOSTOLIC
FAITH

Maurice M. Johnson, see "THE CHURCH
WHICH IS CHRIST'S BODY"

Steve Johnson, see NEW YORK
CHURCH OF CHRIST

Thomas O. Johnson, see TRUE GRACE
MEMORIAL HOUSE OF PRAYER

W.H. Johnson, see HOUSE OF THE LORD

JOHREI

Officially known as the Society of Johrei,
this Japanese monotheistic "healing" movement was founded in 1971 as a breakaway
group from SEKAI KYUSEI KYO (World
Messianic Association). It claims to follow
the original teachings of Mikichi Okada
(1882–1955), the founder of Sekai Kyusei
Kyo.

Johrei is "divine light transmitted to heal
sickness or affliction . . . channeled through
the palm of its administrator and accompanied by prayers." This is the major "healing"
procedure followed by the group. It also

promotes theories about "purification" of the body from "alien substances," nutrition, and "nature farming." Affiliated churches include Light of Salvation Church (Kyoto), Reimi Church (Kyoto, Tokyo), Mesia Kyokwe (Korea), and Templo Messianic Universal (Brazil).

T.M. Jolly, see GOSPEL ASSEMBLIES (JOLLY)

Francis Marion Jones, see CHURCH OF UNIVERSAL TRIUMPH/THE DOMINION OF GOD

Franklin Jones, see FREE DAIST COMMUNION

Jim Jones, see PEOPLE'S TEMPLE

Marc Edmund Jones, see SABIAN ASSEMBLY

Prophet Jones, see CHURCH OF UNIVERSAL TRIUMPH/THE DOMINION OF GOD

Vendyl Jones, see B'NAI NOACH

Jonestown, see PEOPLE'S TEMPLE

Clarence Jordan, see KOINONIA PARTNERS

JOYA HOUSES
U.S. Hindu group founded in the 1970s by Joyce Green, former "divine Mother" in the HANUMAN FOUNDATION.

JOY FARM
NEW THOUGHT group founded as a healing center in Connecticut after the death of Emma Curtis Hopkins in 1925.
See also HOPKINS ASSOCIATION, EMMA C.

William Quan Judge, see THEOSOPHY

Daniel C. Juster, see BETH MESSIAH CONGREGATION

K

KABBALISTIC ORDER OF ROSA CRUZ
International Rosicrucian group, active mainly in Latin America.
See also ROSICRUCIANS

KAGYU DRODEN KUNCHAB
Tibetan Buddhist center founded by Kalu Rinpoche and based in San Francisco. It has been associated with KAGYU KUNKHYAB CHULING.

KAGYU KUNKHYAB CHULING
North American Tibetan Buddhist group devoted to spreading the doctrines of the Tibetan Kagyu order in the West. It was founded around 1970 by Lama Kalu Rinpoche, a spiritual teacher of the Tibetan Buddhist Kargyudpa order.

Shlomo Kalo, see DA'AT

Kalu Rinpoche, see KAGYU DRODEN KUNCHAB; KAGYU KUNKHYAB CHULING

KARDECISM
Modern spiritualist doctrine named after Allan Kardec (1804–1869), French spiritualist who has influenced spiritualist movements all over the world. Born Hyppolyte Leon Denizard Rivail, he adopted the "Celtic" name Kardec following his "conversion." During a spiritualist seance he claimed to have had a revelation by a spirit named "Truth," who gave him the mission of founding one great universal religion based on spiritualism and belief in reincarnation. He had only a few followers during his lifetime, but his tomb at the Père-Lachaise Cemetery in Paris is still a place of pilgrimage and worship.

In Brazil Kardecism has been popular since the 19th century, and in 1957 the government issued a postage stamp bearing Kardec's portrait. The movement has especially influenced the UMBANDA movement of Brazil.
See also MARTINISM

KARGYUDPA ORDER
Tibetan group based in southern California and associated with KAGYU KUNKHYAB CHULING.

KARGYU DSAMLING KUNCHAB
Tibetan group based in New York City and associated with KAGYU KUNKHYAB CHULING.

Karma Dzong, see VAJRADHATU

KARMA KAGYU INSTITUTE
North American Tibetan Buddhist group devoted to spreading the doctrines of the Tibetan Karma Kagyu lineage in the West. It was founded around 1980 in Wood-stock, New York, by Jamgon Kongtrul Rinpoche, who claimed to be the "lineage holder" of Karma Kagyu.

KARMA TRIYANA DHARMACHAKRA (KTD)
Tibetan Buddhist group based in Woodstock, New York, devoted to the teachings of the Gyalwa Karmapa, head of the Kagyupa order of Tibetan Buddhism. Founded in 1976, the group is headed by Lama Tenzin Choney, aided by Lama Kathar and Lama Gangha. It operates a monastery in Woodstock and branches around the

U.S., which are known as Karma Thegsum Choling.

Karme-Choling, see VAJRADHATU

KARM LING
French Tibetan Buddhist group founded in the 1970s.

Mark Karras, see UNIVERSAL SHRINE OF DIVINE GUIDANCE

Hans Kary, see VEDIC CULTURAL CENTER

Jim Kaseman, see WORD OF FAITH MINISTRIES

Bunjiro Kawate, see KONKOKYO

KAYAVAROHAN
Hindu commune based in St. Helena, California, founded by Yogeshwar Muni in the 1970s. The group follows Hindu traditions and practices, including "yogic health" and meditation. Kayavarohan has operated the Santana Dharma Foundation, offering meditation training to nonmembers.

Amy Kees, see CHURCH OF TZADDI

Karl Kellner, see ORDO TEMPLARUM ORIENTALIS

Clarence Kelly, see SOCIETY OF ST. PIUS V

Grady R. Kent, see CHURCH OF GOD (JERUSALEM ACRES)

KERISTA VILLAGE
Commune founded in 1971 in San Francisco, based on the concept of polyfidelity in "multiple marriages." Its religion is based on "a benevolent Divinity that had no gender and wanted human beings to be free, fun-loving, equalitarian and rational."

Frederick Kettner, see BIOSOPHICAL INSTITUTE (BIOSOPHY)

Laurel Elizabeth Keyes, see ORDER OF FRANSISTERS AND FRANBROTHERS

Phez Khalil, see THE PROSPEROS

George Khambule, see CHURCH OF CHRIST, THE CONGREGATION OF ALL SAINTS OF SOUTH AFRICA

Pir Vilayat Inayat Khan, see ABODE COMMUNITY

T.R. Khanna, see MAHA YOGA ASHRAM

Gene Kieffer, see KUNDALINI RESEARCH FOUNDATION

Richard Kieninger, see STELLE COMMUNITY

Marl Kilgore, see ZION'S ORDER OF THE SONS OF LEVI

Frank Russell Killingsworth, see KODESH CHURCH OF IMMANUEL

KIMBANGUIST MOVEMENT
Known officially as L'Église de Jesus Christ par le Prophète Simon Kimbangu (Church of Jesus Christ on Earth through the Prophet Simon Kimbangu) or E.J.C.S.K., and otherwise known as ngunzism, SK, this African Christian millenarian movement was

founded in 1921 in the then Belgian Congo by Simon Kimbangu (1889–1951), an oil refinery worker from Bakongo. In 1915 he was baptized and was trained as a Baptist minister but failed to become a pastor. In April 1921, Kimbangu proclaimed the imminent departure of all whites and offered himself as a healer and savior. He soon became known as a charismatic preacher and "healer." Under Belgian colonial rule, Kimbangu was sentenced to death, then to life imprisonment; he died in prison after thirty years.

In addition to "healings," the movement promises a golden age soon to be attained, following the Second Coming. The doctrine and practices combine traditional ancestor worship with Christian rites and prayers. Members pray "in the name of the Father, the Son, and the Holy Ghost descended into Simon Kimbangu." His village of Nkamba has become known as the "New Jerusalem," a center of pilgrimage. Members believe that Kimbangu was sent to earth by Jesus Christ, and some expect his imminent return. Before the coming of independence in 1960 the movement was mainly anticolonialist; since then it has adopted an antiwitchcraft emphasis.

The church has become the largest independent church in Central Africa, with branches in Zaire and neighboring countries. The founder's three sons have been its leaders. In 1970 L'Église became a member of the World Council of Churches. In 1971 it was one of only four churches recognized by the government of Zaire. Many other groups claim to carry on the founder's legacy.

Sources:
Balandier, G. *Ambiguous Africa: Cultures in Collision*. New York: Pantheon Books, 1966.
MacGaffey, W. *Modern Kongo Prophets*. Bloomington: Indiana University Press, 1983.
Martin, M.L. *Kimbangu: An African Prophet and His Church*. Oxford: Basil Blackwell, 1975.

D.E. Kind, see NEW BEGINNINGS (EX-CHRISTIAN SCIENTISTS FOR JESUS)

KINGDOM FELLOWSHIP CHURCH

British-Israelist group founded in the 1930s by Robertson Orr, a former Presbyterian minister, in Long Beach, California.
See also BRITISH ISRAELISM

KINGDOM MESSAGE ASSOCIATION

British-Israelist group based in New York City, founded and headed by C. Lewis Fowler. Later Fowler headed the Kingdom Bible Seminary in St. Petersburg, Florida.
See also BRITISH ISRAELISM

Source:
Roy, J.L. *Apostles of Discord*. Boston: Beacon Press, 1953.

KINGDOM TEMPLE, INC.

U.S. British-Israelist group founded in 1935 by Joseph Jeffers, former Baptist preacher, in Los Angeles, California. In 1943 Jeffers announced that he was "the Christ." In 1945 he was sentenced to four years in a federal prison for violating a divorce settlement with his second wife. While Jeffers was in prison his third wife operated the Temple of Yahweh in Cabazon, California.

Source:

Roy, J.L. *Apostles of Discord*. Boston: Beacon Press, 1953.

Kirpal Light Satsang, see KIRPAL RUHANI SATSANG

KIRPAL RUHANI SATSANG

Known also as the Kirpal Light Satsang, this Western Sikh-inspired group with head-quarters in California claims to be the authentic successor to the RUHANI SATSANG led by Kirpal Singh (1896–1974). It was founded by his disciple Thakar Singh, known as "the present living Master, Sant Thakar Singh Ji." The group "... is devoted to communicating the truth about human existence, its nature and purpose as expressed by the Masters of the Yoga of Inner Light and Sound." Branches have operated in Western Europe and the United States. See also SANT BANI ASHRAM; SAWAN KIRPAL RUHANI MISSION

Kirpal Singh, see KIRPAL RUHANI SATSANG; RUHANI SATSANG; SANT BANI ASHRAM; SAWAN KIRPAL RUHANI MISSION

Kitamura Sayo, see TENSHO KOTAI JUNGU KYO

KITAWALA (Chitawala)

African syncretistic messianic movement started in the 1920s in Zaire (then Belgian Congo) by Nyirenda, who called himself Mwana Lesa ("son of God"), under the influence of JEHOVAH'S WITNESSES. The founder was executed in 1926. The movement's doctrine describes a divine family in which the eldest son is black but his birthright is stolen by a white brother. It promises a new age in which whites will be ruined and blacks restored to their divine position of seniority. The movement has become connected with the KIMBANGUIST MOVEMENT. Its branches have also operated among Africans in Western Europe.

Henry Knight, see BEIT IMMANUEL

KNIGHTS TEMPLAR NEW AGE CHURCH

Occultist group founded in the late 1980s by Duane Mantley and Charles Hamilton and based in Phoenix, Arizona. Describing itself as a "New Age/Eclectic Church," it practices Tarot divination and "rune readings."

Joel Kobran, see MARGARET FULLER CORPORATION

KODESH CHURCH OF IMMANUEL

African-American Conservative Protestant group founded in 1929 in Pittsburgh by Frank Russell Killingsworth. Members follow a strict behavior code, forbidding alcohol, tobacco, and "prideful" dress.

Ze'ev Kofsman, see HEBREW CHRISTIAN ASSEMBLY–JERUSALEM CONGREGATION

Koh-E-Nor University, see MOVEMENT OF SPIRITUAL INNER AWARENESS

KOINONIA

"Spiritual and educational community" founded in 1952 and located near Baltimore, Maryland. In Koinonia "many 'new age' and traditional paths and forms of worship meet and share the energy as the community strives to reverence and to experience the Universal Spirit in its many dancing manifestations."

KOINONIA PARTNERS
Christian commune founded in 1942 near Americus, Georgia, by Clarence Jordan as Koinonia Farm. The present name was adopted in 1968. The group adopted a radical stance vis-à-vis its environment, preaching and practicing racial integration, equality, and economic justice, all inspired by a radical interpretation of Christianity.

Komeito, see SOKA GAKKAI

Jamgon Kongtrul Rinpoche, see KARMA KAGYU INSTITUTE

KONKOKYO ("Golden Light Teaching")
Japanese Shinto-inspired new religion founded by Bunjiro Kawate (1814–1883), also known as Konko Daijin, following a religious experience at age forty-five (*i.e.*, in 1859). The group's syncretistic doctrine includes the notion of Tenchi Kane no Kami (Konjin), who is conceived of as the parent god of heaven and earth. The group leader is held to be a mediator between the believers and God through whom individual salvation is achieved. Unlike other Japanese new religions, it has taken a determined stance against political activity. Branches have operated in North America.

KOSMUNITY
Canadian religious commune in British Columbia, which claimed to follow "the Essene tradition of purity in diet, lifestyle, and spiritual learning."
See also UNIVERSAL FAITHISTS OF KOSMON

Kimi Kotani, see REIYU-KAI KYODAN

Kototama, see THIRD CIVILIZATION

Roger Kozic, see FRATERNITÉ "SALVE REGINA" DU FRÉCHOU

KRIPALU CENTER
Branch of KRIPALU YOGA ASHRAM started in the late 1970s; in 1983 it moved to Lenox, Massachusetts.

KRIPALU YOGA ASHRAM
Hindu commune based in Sumneytown, Pennsylvania, established in 1971 by Yogi Amrit Desai (1932–   ), an Indian who immigrated to the United States in 1960. The commune is devoted to the teaching of Shaktiput Kundalini Yoga and Kripalu Yoga. Desai advocates vegetarianism and occasional fasts.

Gopi Krishna, see KUNDALINI RESEARCH FOUNDATION

Ekkirala Krishnamacharya, see WORLD TEACHER TRUST

KRISHNAMURTI FOUNDATION
International organization founded in 1969 and based in Ojai, California, dedicated to spreading the teachings of Jiddu Krishnamurti (1895–1986). Krishnamurti was born in Madanapalle, India, to a Brahmin family and at the age of thirteen was discovered by Charles Webster Leadbeater and Annie Wood Besant, two leaders of the THEOSOPHICAL SOCIETY. It was Leadbeater who saw the boy bathing and realized that he was the "Vehicle of the next World Teacher," the avatar, "God incarnate." Krishnamurti's father, Jiddu

Jiddu Krishnamurti with his foster mother, Annie Wood Besant, leader of the Theosophical Society.

Narayana Aijer, was a devout Brahmin who also worked part time in the Theosophical Society office in Madras. After handing over his two sons to Mrs. Besant, he later tried to win them back through lawsuits, but lost.

The Order of the Star in the East was set up to promote the World Teacher in 1911. The boy and his brother were educated in England, and in 1923 Annie Besant announced that he was indeed the new World Teacher. In 1929, however, Krishnamurti rejected the role of an avatar, and the Order was dissolved. Nevertheless, Krishnamurti's writings before 1929 are still used by Theosophical groups around the world.

For the rest of his long life Krishnamurti acted as the non-Guru Guru for thousands, preaching a message of independence and a rejection of leaders, be they religious or secular. His religious faith was ecumenical and eclectic, combining East and West. He admitted Jesus Christ, Lao-tzu, and other great mystics to his list of "enlightened beings."

The British branch of the Foundation is known as the Krishnamurti Foundation Trust Ltd.

See also THEOSOPHY

Source:
Tillett, G. *The Elder Brother: A Biography of Charles Webster Leadbeater.* London: Routledge & Kegan Paul, 1982.

Swami Kriyananda, see ANANDA CO-OPERATIVE VILLAGE

Sri Goswami Kriyananda, see THE TEMPLE OF KRIYA YOGA

Arnoldo Krumm-Heller, see FRATERNITAS ROSICRUCIANA ANTIQUA

Elisabeth Kübler-Ross, see SHANTI NILAYA

Kabutaro Kubo, see REIYU-KAI KYODAN

Lucy Kudjo, see TRUE CHURCH OF CHRIST (NEW BETHLEHEM)

Kuka, see NAMDHARI

William Kullgren, see BEACON LIGHT MINISTRY

KUNDALINI RESEARCH FOUNDATION

Hindu-oriented group founded in 1970 in New York City by Gene Kieffer and other followers of Gopi Krishna (1903–1984). Kundalini, in Hindu lore, means sexual energy supposedly localized in the base of the spine. Kundalini yoga attempts to release this energy for use in the human brain.

KUROZUMI KYO

Japanese new religion founded in 1815 by Munetada Kurozumi (1780–1850), a Shinto priest who at the age of 35 had a mystical experience of union with the sun-goddess. Group practices include faith healing, as developed by the founder.

Source:
Hardacre, H. *Kurozumikyo and the New Religions of Japan.* Princeton: Princeton University Press, 1986.

L

LAMA FOUNDATION

Syncretistic religious commune near San Christobal, New Mexico, founded in 1967 by Steve Durkee. Practices stem from Buddhist, Christian, and Sufi traditions. The commune has hosted teachers of various traditions and published their teachings. In the 1970s one of the best-known visitors was Baba Hari Dass, a Hindu monk who practices continual silence and communicates by writing on a chalkboard. Since 1971 he has visited the Foundation several times.

See also SUFI ORDER IN THE WEST

LAMAIST BUDDHIST MONASTERY OF AMERICA

Tibetan Buddhist monastery founded by the Tibetan Lama Geshe Wangyal (1902–1983) in the 1960s. Geshe Wangyal went to the United States in 1955 to serve as lama to the Kalmuck-Mongolian community there. The monastery in Howell, New Jersey, is known as Labsum Shedrub Ling.

See also TIBETAN BUDDHIST LEARNING CENTER

Lama Kunga Thartse, Rinpoche, see EWAM CHODEN TIBETAN BUDDHIST CENTER

LAMA YESHE MOVEMENT

Tibetan Buddhist movement in the West founded by exiled Tibetan monks. The founder, Lama Yeshe, died in 1984. As of 1987 the group was reported to have thirty-three meditation centers around the world. In March 1987 a two-year-old Spanish boy, Osael Ita Torres, was selected as the reincarnation of Lama Yeshe.

Gary Lamb, see MARGARET FULLER CORPORATION

LAMB OF GOD

Charismatic communal group growing out of the CATHOLIC CHARISMATIC RENEWAL movement, founded in the early 1970s in Timonium, Maryland.

LAMB OF GOD CHURCH

U.S. PENTECOSTAL group founded in 1942 by Rose Soares. Based in Hawaii, it addresses itself to native Hawaiians.

George M. Lamsa, see NOOHRA FOUNDATION

LAODICEAN HOME MISSIONARY MOVEMENT

U.S. Adventist group started in 1955 by John W. Krewson as a result of a schism in the LAYMEN'S HOME MISSIONARY MOVEMENT. Krewson has been in dispute with Raymond Jolly of the Movement, and also with John J. Hoefle of the EPIPHANY BIBLE STUDENTS ASSOCIATION.

See also JEHOVAH'S WITNESSES

William Arnold Lapp, see CHURCH OF THE CHRISTIAN SPIRITUAL ALLIANCE

James F.A. Lashley, see AMERICAN CATHOLIC CHURCH ARCHDIOCESE

Zephirin Simon Lassy, see MISSION DE DIEU DU BOUGIE

LAST DAY MESSENGER ASSEMBLIES

Fundamentalist, Dispensationalist group

concentrated in the Western United States and Canada, founded by Nels Thompson in the 1920s in Oakland, California.

LATIN-RITE CATHOLIC CHURCH

International traditionalist Catholic movement led by Pierre Martin Ngo Dinh Thuc, former Archbishop of Hue, Vietnam. Thuc, who rejects the reforms introduced in the Roman Catholic Church after 1965, has ordained many leaders of dissenting Catholic groups in North and South America since 1975.

See also FRATERNITY OF ST. PIUS X; SERVANTS OF THE SACRED HEART OF JESUS AND MARY; UNION CATOLICA TRENTO

Latter Day Saints, Church of Jesus Christ of, see MORMONS

LATTER RAIN MOVEMENT

North American millenarian PENTECOSTAL movement started in 1946 in the Sharon Orphanage and School, North Battleford, Saskatchewan, Canada, following a schism in the local branch of the ASSEMBLIES OF GOD. It was led by George Hawtin and Percy Hunt. Faith healing and prophecies were practiced. The movement later developed into the MANIFEST SONS OF GOD, or "over-comers," and the CHRISTIAN GROWTH MINISTRIES. Several congregations in the United States have been committed to the Latter Rain vision while keeping their independence. Since the 1960s movement branches have operated in Europe.

Tommie Lawrence, see GOD'S HOUSE OF PRAYER FOR ALL NATIONS, INC.

R.C. Lawson, see CHURCH OF OUR LORD JESUS CHRIST OF THE APOSTOLIC FAITH

LAYMEN'S HOME MISSIONARY MOVEMENT (LHMM)

U.S. Christian Adventist group created by a schism in the Watch Tower Bible and Tract Society (JEHOVAH'S WITNESSES) in 1918. Paul S.L. Johnson, in dispute with J.R. Rutherford, left the movement with Raymond Jolly and joined in forming the PASTORAL BIBLE INSTITUTE (PBI). Later Johnson and Jolly withdrew and founded the Laymen's Home Missionary Movement.

The Movement follows the original teachings of Charles Taze Russell, which have been superseded among the Witnesses by the teachings of J.R. Rutherford. Following Johnson's death in 1950, Jolly succeeded to the leadership. Branches of the group have been operating in Europe. See also EPIPHANY BIBLE STUDENTS ASSOCIATION; LAODICEAN HOME MISSIONARY MOVEMENT

LDS SCRIPTURE RESEARCHERS

Dissident Mormon group, also known as "Believe God Society" and "Doers of the Word," founded by Sherman Russell Lloyd in Salt Lake City, Utah, in the 1950s. Members believe in the second coming of Joseph Smith and study the teachings of Swedenborg.

See also MORMONS; SWEDENBORG FOUNDATION

Charles Webster Leadbeater, see KRISHNAMURTI FOUNDATION; LIBERAL CATHOLIC CHURCH

LECTORIUM ROSICRUCIANUM

European Rosicrucian group founded in

Holland in 1924 by J. Van Rijckenborgh and other former members of the ROSICRUCIAN FELLOWSHIP. The group's doctrine combines Christian and Theosophical elements. It proposes that mankind's problem is overcoming the endless cycles of reincarnation and the separation from divine order. These will come to an end when humans model themselves after Jesus Christ. The group has had branches in Western Europe and North America.
See also ROSICRUCIANS; THEOSOPHY

LEDERER MESSIANIC MINISTRIES

Also known as the Lederer Foundation, this U.S. Hebrew-Christian group was founded in 1936 by members of the Lederer family in Baltimore, Maryland.
See also HEBREW CHRISTIANS

Marcel Lefebvre, see FRATERNITY OF ST. PIUS X

Legio Maria, see MARIA LEGIO

Ignatius Lekganyane, see ZION CHRISTIAN CHURCH

Frederick Lenz, see RAMA SEMINARS

LEROY JENKINS EVANGELISTIC ASSOCIATION

U.S. PENTECOSTAL-healing group led by Leroy Jenkins, a disciple of A.A. Allen. In 1979 Jenkins was convicted of conspiracy to commit arson and sentenced to twelve years in prison. Paroled in 1985, he has resumed his activities as a faith healer.
See also MIRACLE REVIVAL FELLOWSHIP

Source:
Randi, J. *The Faith Healers*. Buffalo: Prometheus Books, 1987.

LETUB

New Guinea nativist syncretistic movement (CARGO CULT) started in 1937 in Madang province. Its doctrine combined Christian and native beliefs, and it gradually became nationalistic and political. The movement adopted a combined traditional-biblical myth, according to which two brothers, Kilibob and Manup, created two separate human cultures. Kilibob was the ancestor of whites, who possessed the "cargo," whereas Manup and his descendants were dispossessed. Now the native ancestors were building new boats to deliver the "cargo," and all normal work stopped. The movement later was revived as the MADANG CULT.

Source:
Lawrence, P. *Road Belong Cargo*. Manchester: Manchester University Press, 1964.

Clifton Harby Levy, see CENTER OF CHRISTIAN SCIENCE

H. Spencer Lewis, see AMORC ROSICRUCIAN ORDER

Ralph Maxwell Lewis, see AMORC ROSICRUCIAN ORDER

Samuel L. Lewis, see SUFI ISLAMIA RUHANIAT SOCIETY

William A. Lewis, see HOUSE OF JUDAH

Faith healer Leroy Jenkins, founder of the Leroy Jenkins Evangelistic Association.

LIBERAL CATHOLIC CHURCH (LCC)

International Theosophical-Christian group founded in 1916 in London by Charles Webster Leadbeater, a British leader in the early Theosophical movement, and James Ingall Wedgewood, who served as its first presiding bishop. Leadbeater was forced to resign from the Theosophical Society in 1906 after being charged with immoral conduct. He was reinstated after the death of Theosophical Society President Henry Steel Olcott in 1907, when Annie Besant gained that position.

The group conducts regular church services and operates branches around the world. Its doctrine includes belief in reincarnation and interprets Christianity along Theosophical lines, viewing Christian mythology as part of a long chain of events tied to the Ascended Masters. "The world is the theatre of an ordered plan, according to which the spirit of man, by repeatedly expressing himself in varying conditions of life and experience, continually unfolds his powers." Special emphasis is placed on faith healing.

See also THEOSOPHY

Source:
Tillett, G. *The Elder Brother: A Biography of Charles Webster Leadbeater*. London: Routledge & Kegan Paul, 1982.

LIBERAL JUDAISM

Formally known as the Jewish Religious Union, this radical variety of REFORM JUDAISM was established in London in 1902 by Claude Montefiore and Lily Montague and is known only in Britain. Montefiore aimed at a new interpretation of Jewish heritage through the elevation of "prophetic" or "higher" Judaism over the legalistic, priestly tradition. That meant also recognizing the Jewish legacy in the New Testament. Services eliminated most elements of synagogue traditions and were marked by mixed seating for men and women and elimination of Hebrew and of the Torah-reading rituals. Its center has been the West London Synagogue of British Jews.

Sources:
Kessler, E., ed. *An English Jew: The Life and Writings of Claude Montefiore*. London: Valentine Michell, 1989.
Umansky, E.M. *Lily Montague and the Advancement of Liberal Judaism*. Lewiston, NY: Edwin Mellen, 1983.
Unterman, A. *Jews: Their Religious Beliefs and Practices*. London: Routledge & Kegan Paul, 1981.

LIBORISMO

Syncretistic Catholic-spiritualist movement in the Dominican Republic. Its origins date to a nativist movement in 1910 led by Liborio Mateo, who claimed to be God's messenger. Mateo was killed in 1922, but his ideas lived on. Followers go on pilgrimage to the village of Palma Sola.

LICHTCENTRUM BETHANIEN

Swiss Christian-spiritualist group founded in 1967 by Frieda Maria Lämmle (1907–   ). The founder claimed to have received messages from Jesus Christ.

Morris Lichtenstein, see JEWISH SCIENCE, SOCIETY OF

LIFE SCIENCE CHURCH

U.S. Protestant organization offering mail-order ordination as a minister.

LIFE-STUDY FELLOWSHIP

NEW THOUGHT group founded in 1939 in Noroton, Connecticut, which operates solely by mail.

Lifewave, see ISHVARA

LIGHTHOUSE UNIVERSAL LIFE CHURCH (LIGHTHOUSE ULC)

Also known as the Lighthouse Meditation Group, this Hindu-oriented group was founded in the late 1980s by Cathy Florida in Whitmore Lake, Michigan. It has collaborated with the JAIN MEDITATION INTERNATIONAL CENTER.

LIGHT OF THE UNIVERSE (L.O.T.U.)

Occultist-UFO group founded in the early 1960s in Tiffin, Ohio, led by a teacher known as Maryona. Its doctrine is based on the notion of the "soul's progress" through reincarnation. Meditation is practiced.

LIGHT OF TRUTH CHURCH

Known also as the Temple of Truth (TOT), this U.S. occultist group was founded in 1973 by Nelson H. White, a former member of the ORDO TEMPLI ASTRATE.

LIGHT OF YOGA SOCIETY

Hindu group founded in the 1960s by Alice Christensen, "a disciple of Swami Rama," and based in Cleveland, Ohio. The group is devoted to the spreading of Hindu teachings and practices, including yoga and meditation.

LINDISFARNE

Occultist group founded in the 1960s by William Irwin Thompson (1938–) in Southampton, New York (later moved to western Massachusetts), and devoted "to the study and realization of a new planetary culture." It promotes the teachings of the Russian Orthodox mystic Vladimir Soloviev and publishes his works.

Renee and Bill Linn, see NEW YORK SPIRITUAL CENTER, INC.

Malcolm Little (Malcolm X), see NATION OF ISLAM (NOI)

Warren Litzman, see WORLD RENEWAL, INCORPORATED

LIVE OAK GROVE

Neo-pagan U.S. group devoted to the Druid tradition, the religion of the ancient Celts in Gaul and Britain. The Druid religion was polytheistic and included human sacrifice. The mistletoe was considered sacred and a remedy for illness.

David Livingstone Missionary Foundation, see CHURCH OF THE CHRISTIAN CRUSADE

Jorge Angel Livraga, see NEW ACROPOLIS

Sherman Russell Lloyd, see LDS SCRIPTURE RESEARCHERS

LOCAL CHURCH MOVEMENT

Also known as Chu Hui So, the Little Flock, the Assembly Hall Churches, and the Witness Lee Movement, this Fundamentalist Christian group was founded in China in

Welsh druids, collecting the sacred mistletoe. (see p. 169)

1923 by Nee Shu Tsu, who after his conversion to Christianity used the name To Shen (Watchman) and is sometimes referred to as Watchman Nee. He founded about 200 churches in China between 1923 and 1950 in an early version of the JESUS MOVEMENT. In 1952 he was imprisoned by the Communist government, and he died in prison in 1972. The movement's center was moved to Taiwan.

The Western version of the movement was started in 1962 by Stephen Kuang, who came to the U.S. in 1954. In 1960 a close associate of Nee known as Witness Lee (1905–) came to the U.S. and settled in Los Angeles, becoming the group's leader. Nee was influenced by the PLYMOUTH BRETHREN and adopted DISPENSATIONALISM. The Local Church advocates a special role for women, who must be veiled during church meetings. The group proclaims all other religious organizations to be Satanic.
See also FUNDAMENTALISM

Charles and Ada Lochbaum, see APOSTOLIC FAITH

David Loden, see BEIT ASSAPH

LOGOS WORLD UNIVERSITY CHURCH

Christian-occultist group, sometimes described as an "interfaith church and meditation center," founded in 1983 by Anne Puryear and Herbert Bruce Puryear, former leaders of the ASSOCIATION FOR RESEARCH AND ENLIGHTENMENT. Its credo includes, "The central place of meditation to one's daily spiritual growth. The ability of every person to become their own priest…" Much of the group's work and beliefs have been inspired by Edgar Cayce and the Association for Research and Enlightenment. Headquarters are in Scottsdale, Arizona, with branches and affiliated groups all over the United States. The Church offers a variety of teachings, including spiritualism, Gurdjieff, meditation, and parapsychology. Its founders perform "life readings" and "psychic counseling."
See also GURDJIEFF GROUPS

Sadhu Loncontirth, see ATMANIKETAN ASHRAM

LONDON CENTRAL CHURCH

Sometimes called the Central London Church of Christ (CLCC), or the London Church of Christ, this is the London branch of the BOSTON CHURCH OF CHRIST, founded in the 1980s.
See also BODY OF CHRIST; CHRISTIAN GROWTH MINISTRIES; CHRISTIAN RESTORATION MINISTRIES; CROSSROADS CHURCHES OF CHRIST

Max Freedom Long, see HUNA RESEARCH ASSOCIATES

LORD'S COVENANT CHURCH, THE

British-Israelist group based in Phoenix, Arizona, and led by Sheldon Emry, a former vice-president of CHRISTIAN RESEARCH, INC. Emry is the author of many publications promoting the British-Israelist viewpoint. His radio program, known as "America's Promise," was broadcast all over the United States until his death in 1985. After Emry's death, Ben Williams took over as leader.
See also BRITISH-ISRAELISM

LORIAN ASSOCIATION

Occultist commune founded in the 1970s by David Spangler (1945–   ) near Madison, Wisconsin (now moved to Washington State). It is devoted to the teaching of Anthroposophical and Eastern ideas and is inspired by Findhorn.

See also ANTHROPOSOPHY; FINDHORN FOUNDATION

Arleen Lorrance, see LOVE PROJECT

Isabelo de los Reyes, Sr., see PHILIPPINE INDEPENDENT CHURCH

LOTHLORIEN

U.S. neo-pagan group started by Paul V. Beyerl, which claims to follow both Western Wiccan tradition and Tibetan Buddhist lore.

LOVE FAMILY

Also known as the Church of Armageddon, or the Church of Jesus Christ at Armageddon, this Christian commune was founded by Love Israel, formerly Paul Erdman (1940–   ), in Seattle, Washington, in 1969. The founder reportedly had a revelation that only he represented the authentic message of the New Testament. Members were considered Christians and the true Israelites and adopted both biblical names and names representing virtues (such as Integrity and Courage), which became permanent. They were enjoined to follow Old Testament dietary laws. The group adopted a new calendar with new names for days of the week and months, and a new clock.

The founder considered inhaling vapors of toluene (an industrial solvent) a religious ritual. The practice was stopped after two members were asphyxiated in 1972. The group still used hyperventilation, hallucinogens, and marijuana as aids to altering consciousness. Later cocaine was heavily used by Love Israel himself. Most members left the group in 1983, but a minority stayed on with the leader on a ranch in eastern Washington. The Church of Armageddon was officially disbanded in 1985, but the group was in existence as of 1991.

Source:
Allen, S. *Beloved Son.* Indianapolis: Bobbs-Merrill, 1982.

LOVE INN

JESUS MOVEMENT group founded in 1969 in Freeville, New York, by Scott Ross, a former disc jockey.

James A. Lovell, see UNITED ISRAEL WORLD FELLOWSHIP

LOVE PROJECT

U.S. Christian-occultist group founded in 1971 by Arleen Lorrance and Diana K. Pike. In 1972 it merged with the Bishop Pike Foundation, formerly known as the FOUNDATION OF RELIGIOUS TRANSITION

Lee Lozowick, see HOHM

Chuck Lucas, see CROSSROADS CHURCHES OF CHRIST

Gay Luce, see SAGE COMMUNITY

LUCIS TRUST

Umbrella organization that operates the Arcane School, occultist-Theosophical group founded in 1923 by Alice A. Bailey

(1880–1949) in New York City. She was aided by her husband, Foster Bailey. The Baileys were Theosophists who left the movement in the 1920s after a dispute with the official leadership.

Alice Bailey wrote twenty-four books, eighteen of which are claimed to be the result of telepathic collaboration with a Tibetan sage spirit, Djwal Khul, known sometimes as D.K. or the Tibetan Master.

The goal of the Arcane School is to develop "the science of soul contact." "The function of the school is to assist those at the end of the probationary path to move forward on the path of discipleship, and to assist those already on that path to move on more quickly and to achieve greater effectiveness in service. The training, which is conducted by correspondence, is based on three fundamental requirements—occult meditation, study, and service to humanity." The School proclaims the imminent coming of the Christ, as part of the Aquarian Age: "There is widespread expectation that we approach the 'Age of Maitreya', as it is known in the East, when the world Teacher and present head of the spiritual Hierarchy, the Christ, will reappear among men to sound the keynote of the new age."

The ARCANE SCHOOL also offers Goodwill Meditation, "a worldwide group of people who link together in thought each week at noon on Wednesday to meditate upon the energy of good-will . . . to stimulate and increase the use of goodwill in a troubled world." Spreading "goodwill" is carried out in Triangles; *i.e.*, groups of three who daily say the Great Invocation.

Functions of the Lucis Trust are the World Goodwill Information and Research Service, established in 1932, and the Triangles, founded in 1937; Radio Lucis, which

presents the group's doctrine through radio programs; *The Beacon* magazine; the Lucis Trust Library, Lucis Productions, and the World Service Forum.

See also AQUARIAN EDUCATIONAL GROUP; INSTITUTE FOR PLANETARY SYNTHESIS; SCHOOL OF ESOTERIC STUDIES; SERVERS OF THE GREAT ONES, INC.; THEOSOPHY; WORLD TEACHER

Source:

Judah, J.S. *The History and Philosophy of the Metaphysical Movements in America.* Philadelphia: Westminster, 1967.

Veronica Lueken, see OUR LADY OF THE ROSES

LUMPA CHURCH

Known sometimes as the Visible Salvation Church, this millenarian group of the Bemba tribe in northern Zambia was founded in 1953 by Alice Mulenga Lubusha (?–1978), who experienced what she described as death. When she was in heaven God handed her a copy of the true Bible and sent her back to earth to preach the true gospel. She then took the name Alice Lenshina ("Queen") and started a holy village in Kasomo, known as Sione or New Zion. The movement became very nationalistic and anti-Catholic. Her visions drew a popular following, especially in the Chinsali district, which was also the home district of Kenneth Kaunda, later to become Prime Minister, and whose brother, Robert Kaunda, became a Lumpa leader. The Church was in conflict with the British colonial authorities and then with the United National Independence Party (UNIP), which became the ruling party when Zam-

Lyndon Baines Johnson, former President of the United States, namesake of a Melanesian Cargo Cult.

bia gained independence. During the struggle for independence Alice Lenshina banned political activities by Church members, and in November 1963 thirty-seven "holy villages" were established for members. In July 1964 Lumpa members armed with spears and axes attacked a police station, and government troops killed 587 of them. Later in the year the Kaunda government banned the movement and in 1970 expelled its followers.

LUTHERAN BAPEDI CHURCH

South African separatist church founded in 1889 by J.A. Winter, a German missionary to the Bapedi tribe. The group was one of only eight churches recognized by the South Africa government in 1960.

Source:
Sundkler, B.G.M. *Bantu Prophets in South Africa*. London: Oxford University Press, 1961.

LYNDON B. JOHNSON

Melanesian syncretistic group (CARGO CULT) based in New Hanover and later spread to the coast of New Ireland, started in 1964 by Bosmailik. Members regarded Lyndon B. Johnson, United States President, as their leader and hoped to induce him to come to the island and bring them "cargo," *i.e.*, Western-made products and riches. The founder collected the sum of $83,000 in order to "buy" Lyndon B. Johnson.

Jessica Lynott, see YOGA INSTITUTE OF CONSCIOUSNESS

M

Edir Macedo, see UNIVERSAL CHURCH OF THE KINGDOM OF GOD

MADELEY TRINITY METHODIST CHURCH

Known originally as the Church of the Way, this small congregation of the Free Methodist Church, in Santa Ana, California, withdrew from the denomination in 1959 after the pastor was accused of deviations from official doctrine. The group kept growing in the 1960s and 1970s. Belief in demon possession of both humans and animals and the practice of exorcism became central in the 1970s. In the winter of 1979–1980 the group of over 100 members left California for Springfield, Missouri. In the spring the membership went into hiding and have been out of sight since then.

Mahasabha, see HINDU MAHASABHA

MAHASIDDHA NYINGMAPA

Tibetan Buddhist group based in western Massachusetts, founded in the late 1960s by Dodrup Chen, Rinpoche.

MAHA YOGA ASHRAM

Hindu commune near Boston, founded by Yogiraj Shri T.R. Khanna in the late 1960s. Its doctrine is based on "the principles and practices of the eightfold path of raja yoga."

MAHDI

In the Shiite Muslim tradition, the Mahdi is Muhammad ibn al-Hannifiya, who disappeared (or died) in 880 C.E. Shiite belief is that the Mahdi, known also as the Hidden Imam, has been in hiding and will come back one day to restore peace and justice.

Since the early 19th century there have been three Mahdist movements, combining messianism and anticolonialism, which rebelled against British rule: the Nigerian Mahdi, a Somalian Mahdi known as the Mad Mullah, and the Sudanese Madhi. When the term Mahdi is used today it usually refers to the third, Mohammed Ahmad Ibn Abdallah (1843–1885). His regime survived for fourteen years, during which he won major battles against the British until finally defeated in Omdurman. The figure of the Sudanese Mahdi still serves as an inspiration to Islamic movements around the world.

The Mahdiyah movement has survived as a political movement led by the Mahdi's descendants and still plays a major role in Sudanese politics.

See also NUBIAN ISLAAMIC HEBREWS

Source:

Holt, P.M. *The Mahdist State in the Sudan 1881–1898: A Study of Its Origins, Development and Overthrow.* Oxford: Clarendon Press, 1958.

Mahesh Prasad Varma, see TRANSCENDENTAL MEDITATION

MAHIKARI ("True Light")

Known also as Sekai Mahikari Bumei Kyodan, this Japanese new religion was founded in 1959 by Okada Yoshikazu (1901–1974), who took the name Okada Kotama (Jewel of Light) and is known to his followers as Sukui Nushi Sama (Lord Savior). The group's doctrine is borrowed mainly from SEKAI KYUSEI KYO, which in turn followed OMOTOKYO. It combines Eastern and Christian traditions, proclaims the coming millennium, and contains elements of Shinot (ancestor worship, veneration of the Emperor, and emphasis on purity), Buddhism ("karma" and reincarnation), and Japanese folk religion (miraculous healing).

The founder claimed to be God's emissary, a successor to Buddha and Jesus Christ of earlier traditions. He offered his own version of the myth of Jesus Christ, according to which Jesus was trained in Japan and did not die on the cross, but in old age in Japan. The true teaching of Jesus was that presented by Mahikari. The Japanese are the chosen people, and their language is divine. Mahikari offers immediate salvation in the form of health, harmony, and wealth. Spirit possession is the main cause of misfortune. A special doctrine addresses the magical causes and cures of illness: Illness is caused by possession by ancestral spirits, and healing through a special "light" that affects the spirits. Modern medical practices are rejected. The movement has spread to Western Europe, Africa, and the French Caribbean. A splinter group known as SUKYO MAHIKARI was started in 1978.

Source:

Davis, W. *Do-Jo: Magic and Exorcism in Modern Japan.* Stanford, CA: Stanford University Press, 1980.

MAI CHAZA CHURCH

Known also as Guta ra Jehovah ("City of Jehovah") after its Holy Village and headquarters, this African independent church was founded in 1954 in Zimbabwe (then Southern Rhodesia) by Mai ("Mother") Chaza (?–1960). The founder, a former Methodist, was reported to have "died," and following a "rebirth" claimed supernatural power. She then became a popular healer and exorcist. Since her death she has been known as Mai Chaza Jesus, or "a black messiah."

Maitreya, see WORLD TEACHER

Tsunesaburo Makiguchi, see SOKA GAKKAI

MAKOM OHR SHALOM

Jewish syncretistic group founded in the 1980s in southern California by Theodore G. Falcon. "Makom Ohr Shalom explores the rich heritage of Jewish mysticism and Kabbalah to meet the growing needs of these seeking the spiritual and meditative foundations of their identity and background."

MAKUYA (GENSHIFUKUIN-KAMI-NO-MAKUYA-KYOKAI)

Japanese indigenous Christian group, known also as the "Tabernacle of God" or the Original Gospel (Tabernacle) Movement. Founded by Abraham Ikuro Teshima, who became a Christian in 1948 following a "divine revelation," the group had its origins in the MUKYOKAI movement. It is PENTECOSTAL in doctrine and practices, with emphasis on faith healing. In addition, it has developed a special attachment to Judaism. It claims to follow authentic Judaic traditions, and its members demonstrate a thorough knowledge of modern Hebrew and contemporary Israeli culture. Branches have operated in North and South America.

Source:

Caldarola, C. *Christianity: The Japanese Way.* Leiden: E.J. Brill, 1979.

Ta Malanda, see MOUVEMENT CROIX-KOMA

Malcolm X, see NATION OF ISLAM (NOI)

Manalista, see IGLESIA NI CRISTO (MANALISTA, INC)

Felix Manalo, see IGLESIA NI CRISTO (MANALISTA, INC)

MANAV KENDRA

Western Sikh-inspired group that claims to represent the authentic RUHANI SATSANG led by Kirpal Singh. Its branches operate in Western Europe and the United States.
See also KIRPAL RUHANI SATSANG; SANT BANI ASHRAM; SAWAN KIRPAL RUHANI MISSION

MANDALA BUDDHIST CENTER

Center founded by Jomyo Tanaka in New York City in the 1980s. It claims to represent the tradition of Shingon Esoteric Buddhism as practiced in Japan. Shingon Buddhism is an occult tradition founded in Japan in the ninth century. Mandala Buddhist Center emphasizes the practice of meditation.

Manhattan Philosophical Center, see THEOCENTRIC FOUNDATION

MANIFEST SONS OF GOD

Sometimes known as "overcomers," this U.S. Christian millenarian group developed in the 1950s out of the Canadian LATTER RAIN MOVEMENT. The group parallels in many ways the movement known as CHRISTIAN GROWTH MINISTRIES.

Ma Nku, see ST. JOHN'S APOSTOLIC FAITH MISSION OF SOUTH AFRICA

Mildred Mann, see SOCIETY OF PRAGMATIC MYSTICISM

Duane Mantley, see KNIGHTS TEMPLAR NEW AGE CHURCH

Franco Manuel, see INTERNATIONAL CHRISTIAN CHURCHES

MARA LA ASPARA

UFO group founded by Enid Brady, minister of the Spiritualist Church in Holly Hills, Florida, who reported contacts with extraterrestrials in the late 1950s. In the late 1960s she started relaying messages from Mara la Aspara of Venus. She was joined by John Langdon Watts in the late 1960s. His teachings are similar to those of Edgar Cayce and the ASSOCIATION FOR RESEARCH AND ENLIGHTENMENT.

MARANATHA CAMPUS MINISTRIES (MARANATHA CHRISTIAN CHURCHES)

PENTECOSTAL group founded in 1972 by Bob Weiner at Murray State University in Paducah, Kentucky. Maranatha has operated as a campus ministry, its branches being attached to colleges and universities. It has also taken public stands on political issues, emphasizing the dangers of a Soviet invasion of the United States through Central America. Members are forbidden conventional dating of the opposite sex because marriages are supposed to be arranged in heaven. In the 1980s the group was criticized by parents of members, and several members were kidnapped and "deprogrammed."

Johane Maranke, see AFRICAN APOSTOLIC CHURCH OF JOHANE MARANKE

MARGARET FULLER CORPORATION

ANTHROPOSOPHY group founded in 1987 in New York State by Joel Kobran and Gary Lamb and devoted to propagation of the ideas of Rudolf Steiner.

MARIA LEGIO (OF AFRICA)

Known also as Legio Maria, this separatist African movement grew out of the Legio Maria, the Legion of Mary, an Irish Roman Catholic lay organization. It was founded in Kenya in 1963 by two Roman Catholic members of the Luo tribe, Simeon Ondeto (1910–   ) and Gaudencia Aoko. In doctrine, it combines Catholic and traditional African elements. Practices include speaking in tongues, faith healing, and exorcism. Structure follows that of the Roman Catholic Church, with pope and cardinals. The movement experienced impressive growth in its early years, but then declined.

MARIA LIONZA

Syncretistic African-Catholic spiritualist movement in Venezuela. It started early in the 20th century in the Sorte Mountains and spread to the cities after World War I. It is reminiscent of UMBANDA in Brazil, but includes a majority of local elements. Popular heroes from the history of Venezuela, especially Indians, including Maria Lionza herself, dominate the pantheon of spirits and saints.

Source:

Simpson, G.E. *Black Religions in the New World*. New York: Columbia University Press, 1978.

MARIA ROSA MYSTICA

Dissident Roman Catholic movement started in Brescia, Italy, in 1947, when a nurse claimed to have had apparitions of the Virgin Mary. European headquareters are in Germany, and branches were reported in the United States in the mid-1980s.

Frederick B. Marine, see EVANGELICAL BIBLE CHURCH

MARK-AGE METACENTER

U.S. spiritualist-Christian group founded in 1962 by Pauline Sharp (1925–   ), known as the "prophetess Nada-Yolanda." In her visions, Nada-Yolanda deals with "The relationships and the responsibilities between the angelic and the man kingdoms ... the actual words of the seven archangels ... spiritual guidelines for the Latter Days and the Second Coming" and plans for a new age of spiritual evolution. The prophetess is in touch with visitors from outer space. Many of the messages and the terminology follow Theosophical teachings.

See also THEOSOPHY

Dorothy Martin, see ASSOCIATION OF SANANDA AND SANAT KUMARA

MARTINUS INSTITUTE

International occultist, Theosophical, spiritualist movement founded by Martinus (1890–1981) in Copenhagen, Denmark, in the 1920s. It operates the Kosmos Holiday Centre and branches in Western Europe and the United States. The group teaches a "Science of the Spirit" based on belief in "immortal energy" and reincarnation.

H. Martyn, see INDEPENDENT THEOSOPHICAL SOCIETY

Maryona, see LIGHT OF THE UNIVERSE

MASA JEHOVAH

Also known as Gaan Tata, this nativist syncretistic group was started in the 1880s among the "Bush Negroes" of Saramaka, Djuka, and Boni living in the interior of Surinam and French Guiana. The doctrine combines strong Christian elements with indigenous traditions. In 1936 a prophet named Wensi led a reform movement in the group, pushing it toward stronger Christian emphasis. In 1972 another prophet, Akalali, led a similar movement.

MASOWE APOSTLES

Successively known as the Vapostori (apostles) of Johanes Masowe, the Basketmakers, the Hosannas, the Apostolic Sabbath Church of God, after 1964 the African Gospel Church, and since 1973 Gospel of God Church, this African syncretistic group was founded by John Masowe of the Shona tribe of Southern Rhodesia, now Zimbabwe. He was born Shoniwa in 1915. During the famine of 1932 he died and came back to life. He retired to the mountains for a few days and returned as Johanes Masowe, John the Baptist. In 1943 the group, then known as the Apostolic Sabbath Church of God, followed its leader to Port Elizabeth, South Africa, where they lived until 1962, known as the Korsten Basketweavers, a hard-working community.

In that year the 1,880 members were deported to Rhodesia. They then settled in Lusaka, Zambia. The founder died in 1973, and several schisms followed.

Johanes Masowe, somtimes called "the secret Messiah," told his followers that they would not die. He was believed to be the Son of God, Jesus returned, and Shona, his native tongue, the original language of mankind. The group is Sabbatarian and PENTECOSTAL in ritual. It has branches all over East Africa, with a strong presence in Kenya, Zimbabwe, Zambia, and Tanzania.

Source:

Dillon-Malone, C. *The Korsten Basketmakers: A Study of the Masowe Apostles, an Indigenous African Religious Movement.* Manchester: Manchester University Press, 1978.

Massjid al-Farah al Ashki, see HALVETI-JERRAHI ORDER OF NEW YORK

Robert Masters, see DROMENON

Roy Masters, see FOUNDATION OF HUMAN UNDERSTANDING

MATA AMRITANANDAMAYI MISSION

International Hindu movement led by Mata Amritanandamayi (1953–), who has been traveling in the West since 1987.

MATAGIRI

Commune based in Mt. Tremper, New York, founded in 1968 by Sam Spanier. It is devoted to spreading the Integral Yoga of SRI AUROBINDO.

Robert Jay Mathews, see THE ORDER

MATSOUANISM (MATSWA)

Initially known as Amicalism, this nativist African political-messianic movement in Zaire (then Belgian Congo) was started in 1926 by Andre Grenard Matswa (1899–1942) of the Sundi-Ladi tribe. He first founded, in Paris, the Association amicale des originaires de l'Afrique équatoriale française," known as Amicale Balali, or amicalisme, designed to protect the rights of Africans under French rule. It then moved toward resistance to French colonialism. Matswa was arrested and exiled in 1930; after his death in prison in 1942, the movement became messianic. Its doctrine is based on the expectation of the founder's return, and he is known as "Jesus-Matswa." In popular belief he is linked to Simon Kimbangu.

The group has survived as the Église Matsouaniste in Zaire and Congo.
See also KIMBANGUISM

Source:
Balandier, G. *Ambiguous Africa: Cultures in Collision.* New York: Pantheon Books, 1966.

Matswa, see MATSOUANISM

Wentworth Arthur Matthew, see COMMANDMENT KEEPERS CONGREGATION OF THE LIVING GOD

Woods Mattingly, see SEEKER'S QUEST

MAZDAZNAN

Western Zoroastrian renewal movement founded in 1902 by Otoman Zar-Adhust Hanish (1844–1936), and based in Los Angeles. Practices include a prescribed diet, exercises, special breathing techniques, and chanting. Branches have operated in Europe since 1911.

MBUETI

Known also as Bwiti, Église des Banzie (Church of the Initiates), or Religion d'Eboga, this African syncretistic movement combines Catholic beliefs and local ancestral cults. Started around 1910 among members of the Fang tribe of West Africa, it is especially strong in Gabon and Equatorial Guinea. Members are initiated through the use of the local drug called *eboga.*

Source:
Fernandez, J.W. *Bwiti: An Ethnography of the Religious Imagination in Africa.* Princeton: Princeton University Press, 1982.

Tolbert McCarroll, see STARCROSS MONASTIC COMMUNITY

John McClain, see CHRIST CENTER FOR POSITIVE LIVING

Samuel McComb, see EMMANUEL MOVEMENT

Peter McCormick, see FOUNDATION FAITH OF THE MILLENNIUM

Kip McKean, see BOSTON CHURCH OF CHRIST

Corinne McLaughlin, see SIRIUS COMMUNITY

Aimee Semple McPherson, see FOURSQUARE GOSPEL, INTERNATIONAL CHURCH OF

MEADOWLARK HEALING CENTER

Occultist commune devoted to the "inner spiritual healing process," founded in the 1970s in California.

MEDITATION GROUP FOR THE NEW AGE (MGNA)

Originally known as Meditation Mount and sometimes as the Group for Creative Medi-

Avatar Meher Baba.

tation, this international NEW THOUGHT group has headquarters in Ojai, California, and branches in Western Europe and Latin America. Founded in 1950 by Florence Garrique, it is in the Alice Bailey tradition. See also LUCIS TRUST

Lloyd Arthur Meeker, see EMISSARIES OF DIVINE LIGHT

MEGIDDO MISSION
Millenarian group founded in the late 19th century by L.T. Nichols. He operated a Mississippi River mission boat named *Megiddo*, which gave the group its name. In 1903 he started a community in Rochester, New York, which has been group headquarters since then. Doctrine is based on the imminence of the battle of Armageddon, which will be followed by the millennium.

MEHER BABA, FRIENDS OF
U.S. group devoted to the teachings of Meher Baba, born Merwan Sheheriarji Irani (1894–1969). He was born in Poona, India, of Persian parents. Many stories of miracles and of contacts with holy men and women are told about his early years. He started his career as a spiritual leader in India in 1921 and became known in the West in the early 1930s. In 1921 a Hindu teacher named Upasni Maharaj passed on his disciples to the young leader, who then became known by the name Meher Baba (best translated as "Compassionate Father"). He attracted more disciples, called *mandali*, and asserted that he was the Avatar ("God incarnate") of the Age, the last in this epoch that included Zoroaster, Krishna, Rama, Buddha, Jesus, and Muhammad. Meher Baba took a vow of silence in 1925, communicating by means of an alphabet

board and later through a system of hand gestures. In 1966 he broke his silence to communicate a last message to the world, before his death several months later.

Headquarters for Meher Baba's work, called Meherabad and Meherazad, are in Maharashtra State, India. His followers are often known as "Baba lovers." Besides Friends of Meher Baba, other U.S. groups are devoted to his teachings, including the Society for Avatar Meher Baba in New York City, SUFISM REORIENTED, and the BABA LEAGUE.
See also MEHER DURBAR, UNIVERSAL SPIRITUAL LEAGUE OF AMERICA

MEHER DURBAR
Formerly known as the Meher Baba House, this group based in New York City was founded in the late 1980s. It is devoted to the teachings of Meher Baba.
See also MEHER BABA, FRIENDS OF

MELECH ISRAEL
Canadian Hebrew-Christian organization based in Toronto.
See also HEBREW CHRISTIANITY

S. Pereira Mendes, see NEW THOUGHT SYNAGOGUE

Mesia Kyokwe, see JOHREI

Messiah's World Crusade, see ONE WORLD FAMILY

MESSIANIC ASSEMBLY OF ISRAEL
Israeli Hebrew-Christian group based in Jerusalem, founded in 1948 by Ze'ev Kofsman, who came to Jerusalem from France. The founder has been reported to

dispute some traditional Christian teachings, such as the canonical status of Paul's writings and the divinity of Jesus Christ. Nevertheless, he had contacts with Christian groups abroad, including the ASSEMBLIES OF GOD in the United States. The group has a PENTECOSTAL emphasis. Around 1970 it merged with two others to form the HEBREW CHRISTIAN ASSEMBLY—JERUSALEM CONGREGATION. See also HEBREW CHRISTIANITY

MESSIANIC HEBREW-CHRISTIAN FELLOWSHIP

Hebrew-Christian group founded in the 1980s in Harrisburg, Pennsylvania.

MESSIANIC JEWISH ALLIANCE OF AMERICA (MJA)

International Hebrew-Christian association founded in 1915 in Chicago as the Hebrew Christian Alliance of America. The name change, in 1975, reflected the appearance of MESSIANIC JUDAISM. It is a loose association of more than one hundred groups and congregations around the world, which maintain independence in many doctrinal matters.

MESSIANIC JUDAISM

Movement developed out of HEBREW CHRISTIANITY in the 1970s to counteract its missionary image and to change its character from Gentile Christian–oriented to more Jewish in tone. There is greater emphasis on Jewish nationalism and Jewish rituals. Separate Messianic Judaism congregations are promoted, as opposed to "assimilation" within Christian churches. Significant differences in doctrine and rituals exist among individual congregations.

Source:
Rausch, D. *Messianic Judaism: Its History, Theology, and Polity.* Lewiston, NY: Edwin Mellen Press, 1982.

Michael J. Metelica, see RENAISSANCE CHURCH-COMMUNITY

METROPOLITAN CHURCH ASSOCIATION, THE

Known also as the Burning Bush, this "HOLINESS" revivalist group was founded in Chicago in 1894.

METTANOKIT

Commune based on native American traditions, founded in Greenville, New Hampshire, in the late 1970s by Medicine Story.

A.M. Meyer, see HEBREW CHRISTIAN ALLIANCE

Ann Poter Meyer and Peter Victor Meyer, see SOCIETY FOR THE TEACHING OF THE INNER CHRIST, INC.

Masheikh Wali Ali Meyer, see SUFI ISLAMIA RUHANIAT SOCIETY

Enoch Mgijima, see "ISRAELITES"

Richard S. Mhlanga, see NATIONAL SWAZI NATIVE APOSTOLIC CHURCH OF AFRICA

MIDWEST PAGAN COUNCIL (MPC)

Organization of three pagan groups in the greater Chicago area, founded in 1976. It is committed to promoting a public perception of paganism as a religion.

Robert E. Miles, see MOUNTAIN CHURCH

Annie Rix Militz, see HOME OF TRUTH MOVEMENT

MILLENARIANISM
Religious movement that promises imminent collective salvation for the faithful in an earthly paradise that will rise following an apocalyptic destruction ordained by the gods.

Source:

Cohn, N. *The Pursuit of the Millennium* New York: Oxford University Press, 1970.

Harry Miller, see PEOPLE OF THE LIVING GOD

William Miller, see ADVENTISTS, SECOND

Mary L. Mills, see GOSPEL ASSEMBLIES (MILLS)

MIND AND BODY SCIENCE
Occultist group founded in the late 1960s in Scottsdale, Arizona, by Robert H. Frey. The group combined Western ocuult ideas with Eastern practices such as meditation.

Ministerial and Missionary Alliance of the Original Trinity Apostolic Faith, Inc., see FULL GOSPEL EVANGELICAL ASSOCIATION

MINISTRY OF UNIVERSAL WISDOM
UFO-Theosophical group based in California and founded by George Van Tassel in 1952. The founder has reported many messages from, and actual meetings with, extraterrestrials.

Mioshi, see TENSHO KOTAI JUNGU KYO

MIRACLE LIFE REVIVAL, INC.
PENTECOSTAL-healing group founded by Neal Vincent Frisby in 1967. It is based at Capstone Cathedral in Phoenix, Arizona.

MIRACLE REVIVAL FELLOWSHIP
Known until 1970 as A.A. Allen Revivals, Inc., this PENTECOSTAL-healing group was founded by Asa Alonzo Allen and is led since his death in 1970 by Don Stewart, who coined the current name. Allen earned a reputation as a "healer" in the 1940s and was active as a traveling healer all over the United States, especially in the South and the West. Despite his saintly reputation, he died of cirrhosis of the liver, an alcoholic's disease. The group is now active mainly as a licensing agency for ministers worldwide. See also LEROY JENKINS EVANGELISTIC ASSOCIATION

Mirokukai, see HONBUSHIN

Mirzais, see AHMADIYYA MOVEMENT

Rammurti Sriram Mishra, see ICSA (INTEGRAL CENTER OF SELF-ABIDANCE)

MISSIONARY CHRISTIAN AND SOUL WINNING FELLOWSHIP
Protestant evangelical group founded by Lee Shelley, former minister of the CHRISTIAN AND MISSIONARY ALLIANCE in Long Beach, California, in 1957. It conducts missionary campaigns aimed at Jews in California.

MISSION DE DIEU DU BOUGIE
Known also as Lassyism or Nzambi ya Bougie (God of the Candle), this African

nativist, syncretistic movement was started in 1953 by Zephirin Simon Lassy (1908–) of the Vili tribe in the Congo, in secession from the SALVATION ARMY. After traveling for thirty years in Europe and America, the founder joined the Army in 1946 but then started his own career as a visionary and "healer," claiming amazing success. His doctrines combine Salvation Army notions with traditional ideas about magical healing. The movement has spread to Angola.

MITA (Iglesia Mita)

Puerto Rican PENTECOSTAL group founded in 1940 by Juanita Garcia Peraga (?–1970), known as Mita, former member of the ASSEMBLIES OF GOD, who is considered a prophet and healer. It has branches in Latin America and in the United States, where the membership is drawn from Puerto Rican communities. The term Mita refers to the "Word of Life," which only believers receive through visions and dreams. The founder was considered the incarnation of the Holy Spirit, which then passed to her successor, Teofile Vargas Sein, known as Aaron.

Hulon Mitchell, see NATION OF YAHWEH (HEBREW ISRAELITES)

Gordon "Jack" Mohr, see CRUSADE FOR CHRIST AND COUNTRY

MOLOKANS

Russian Eastern Orthodox dissident sect founded in Czarist Russia in the late 18th century by Simeon Uklein, which grew out of the DUKHOBOR. Rejecting Dukhobor mysticism, Uklein preached for a return to earlier traditions in the Russian Orthodox Church. He claimed that the historical church fathers corrupted and diluted true Christianity by introducing pagan traditions, and he opposed all established church rituals. Members of the group drank milk during Lent, something forbidden in the Russian Orthodox Church, and so acquired the name of Molokans, or milk drinkers. Because of their pacifism and their religious ideas, members of the group have been persecuted. Some Molokan groups migrated to the United States in the early 20th century.

Source:

Moore, W.B. *Molokan Oral Traditions.* Berkeley: University of California Press, 1973.

Lily Montague, see LIBERAL JUDAISM

James A. Montandon, see CHURCH OF MERCAVAH

Claude Montefiore, see LIBERAL JUDAISM

MOODY CHURCH, THE

Fundamentalist group named for the evangelist Dwight Lyman Moody (1837–1899). This Chicago congregation symbolizes historical continuity with 19th-century Fundamentalism and Moody's historical role as its leader. Moody was a shoe salesman who organized Sunday Schools in his spare time and then became a lay preacher. In 1870 he started collaborating with Ira David Sankey (1840–1908), and they undertook preaching tours of the United States and Great Britain. These activities led to the founding of the Student Christian Movement (SCM).

The Moody Church is the successor to the Illinois Street Independent Church

Dwight Lyman Moody, founder of the Fundamentalist Moody Church.

founded in 1864 by Moody. The congregation is Dispensationalist and evangelical. The Moody Bible Institute, a major Fundamentalist teaching center, is also named for Dwight L. Moody.

See also DISPENSATIONALISM; FUNDAMENTALISM

Sources:

Curtis, R.C. *They Called Him Mr. Moody.* Garden City, NY: Doubleday, 1962.

Findlay, J.F. *Dwight L. Moody, American Evangelist, 1837–1899.* Chicago: University of Chicago Press, 1969.

Moonies, see UNIFICATION CHURCH

MOORISH SCIENCE TEMPLE OF AMERICA

African-American nationalist group founded in 1913 in Newark, New Jersey, by Timothy Drew (1886–1936), who adopted the name Noble Drew Ali. Drew wrote the *Holy Koran* (unrelated to the Islamic Koran) and claimed that African-Americans should be known as Asiatics, Moorish, or Moors and that their true nation is "Morocco." He denounced the common terms Negro and Ethiopian. Later he claimed that Islam was the religion of the Asiatics and defined his followers as Moslems. After his death, several followers claimed to be reincarnations of Noble Drew Ali.

Source:

Fauset, A.H. *Black Gods of the Metropolis.* Philadelphia: University of Pennsylvania Press, 1944.

Eugene Crosby Monroe, see SHILOH TRUST

G.H. Montgomery, see DEFENDERS OF THE CHRISTIAN FAITH, INC.

Sun Myung Moon, see UNIFICATION CHURCH

Victor Manuel Mora, see WESLEYAN PENTECOSTAL CHURCH

MORAL RE-ARMAMENT (M.R.A.).

Known also as the Oxford Group or Buchmanites, this international Christian revitalization movement was founded in 1921 in England by the American Lutheran minister Frank N.D. Buchman (1878–1961). Ordained in 1902, Buchman had a "vision of the Cross" in 1908. In 1929 the group became known as the Oxford Group when seven Oxford men carried its message to South Africa, and in 1938 the name was formally changed to Moral Re-Armament. The name change took place as the nations of Europe were energetically arming themselves in preparation for what turned out to be World War II. As M.R.A., it focused on political and social issues. From its beginnings, it cultivated its contact with affluent and well-known personalities, claiming connections in high places. During the late 1940s and early 1950s in the United States it was highly visible, with its strong anti-Communist orientation. Since the death of its founder, the group has been in sharp decline but still has branches around the world.

The movement operated through small groups cultivating the "four Absolutes" (honesty, purity, unselfishness, love). The main ritual was that of "sharing," a public confession of sin before the group at a houseparty. Complete surrender of the

Frank N. D. Buchman (second from left), founder of Moral Re-Armament.

human will was demanded and divine guidance expected on such occasions.

Sources:

Clark, W.H. *The Oxford Group: Its History and Significance.* New York: Bookman Associates, 1951.

Driberg, T. *The Mystery of Moral Re-Armament.* New York: Knopf, 1965.

Eister, A.W. *Drawing-Room Conversation: A Sociological Account of the Oxford Group Movement.* Durham, NC: Duke University Press, 1950.

MORMONS

Officially known as Church of Jesus Church of Latter Day Saints (LDS), and often as LDS or "Saints," this Christian millenarian group was founded in 1830 by Joseph Smith, Jr. (1805–1844) in northern New York State. At age fourteen Joseph Smith declared that he had spoken with God. Later he had other visions, during some of which an ancient book, written on four tablets, was given to him. He transcribed this text, which has become known as *The Book of Mormon* and has given its name to the Church. The book is the movement's main scripture, in addition to the Bible. On April 6, 1830, Smith and a group of followers founded the Church of Christ, and the name was later changed to the Church of Jesus Christ of Latter Day Saints. Smith announced to the world that he was "seer, translator, prophet, apostle of Jesus Christ, and elder of the church." In 1835 twelve apostles were appointed and sent to gain converts in the United States. In 1837 the first Mormon missionaries arrived in Great Britain.

In its early years the movement encountered much violence because of its unconventional beliefs and its advocacy of polygamy, which was rescinded in 1904. Opposition forced the group to move successively to Ohio, Missouri, and Illinois, where the city of Nauvoo was founded in 1840. In 1844 Joseph Smith and his brother were killed there by a mob. Again the members undertook a long trek away from the eastern United States, led by Brigham Young (1801–1877), and settled in Salt Lake City. In 1850 Young became the first governor of the territory of Utah, which became a state in 1895.

Mormon doctrine regards the church as a revival of the organization of the early Christian church and attributes a central role to America in history and eschatology. According to this doctrine, Jesus Christ was revealed to early immigrants in the U.S. and

The angel Moroni delivering the plates of the Book of Mormon to Joseph Smith.

Joseph Smith's Original Temple of Mormonism, at Nauvoo, Illinois.

will reveal himself again in Independence, Missouri, as Zion will be built on American soil. In addition, Mormons believe in the literal gathering of Israel and the "restoration of the Ten Tribes." Mormons reject the traditional Christian doctrines of original sin and salvation by grace. Upheavals and disasters are expected before the Second Coming, which will leave only the Mormons unharmed. This belief leads to a preoccupation with physical survival and the stocking of emergency supplies of food and water in Mormon homes.

Members avoid caffeine and tobacco. They do not drink Coca-Cola, alcoholic beverages, coffee, or tea. They tithe their income. Marriage is considered an eternal covenant. Glossolalia was practiced in the early years of the group. Non-Mormons are excluded from Mormon temples, but according to reports ceremonies include dramatic enactments of Mormon mythological narratives. Each Mormon receives a secret name for the purpose of temple work.
See also REORGANIZED CHURCH OF JESUS CHRIST OF LATTER DAY SAINTS; UNITED ORDER EFFORT

Sources:
Anderson, N. *Desert Saints*. Chicago: University of Chicago Press, 1966.
Arrington, L.J. *Brigham Young: American Moses*. New York: Knopf, 1985.
Arrington, L.J. & Britton, D. *The Mormon Experience*. New York: Knopf, 1979.
Brodie, F.M. *No Man Knows My History*. New York: Knopf, 1945.
Bushman, R.L. *Joseph Smith and the Beginnings of Mormonism*. Urbana: University of Illinois Press, 1984.
Gottlieb, R., and Wiley, P. *America's Saints: The Rise of Mormon Power*. New York: Putnam, 1985.
Hill, D. *Joseph Smith: The First Mormon*. Garden City, NY: Doubleday, 1977.
Leone, M. *Roots of Modern Mormonism*. Cambridge, MA: Harvard University Press, 1979.
Mullen, R. *The Latter-Day Saints: The Mormons Yesterday and Today*. Garden City, NY: Doubleday, 1966.
O'Dea, T. *The Mormons*. Chicago: University of Chicago Press, 1957.
Shipps, J. *Mormonism: The Story of a New Religious Tradition*. Urbana: University of Illinois Press, 1985.
Taves, E.H. *Trouble Enough: Joseph Smith and the Book of Mormon*. Buffalo: Prometheus Press, 1984.

MORNINGSTAR

Syncretistic commune founded in Sonoma County, California, in 1966 by the musician Lou Gotlieb. It was moved to Taos, New Mexico, in 1967.

E.J. Morris, see FREE CHURCH OF GOD IN CHRIST

Samuel Morris, see FATHER JEHOVAH

Bud and Carmen Moshier, see TODAY CHURCH

Mother Divine, see FATHER DIVINE MOVEMENT

MOUNTAIN BROOK

NEW THOUGHT group founded by William Samuel in Mountain Brook, Alabama, in 1968. It operates mainly by correspondence.

Robert E. Miles, former Grand Dragon of the Michigan Ku Klux Klan, arrives at court for arraignment on charges of conspiring to bomb school buses. He was later convicted and served a six-year sentence.

MOUNTAIN CHURCH OF JESUS CHRIST THE SAVIOUR, THE

Also known as The Mountain Church or the "Mountain kirk," this is a Christian Identity, white-supremacist, militarist group associated with the Ku Klux Klan. Founded by Robert E. Miles, former head of the Michigan Ku Klux Klan, it is based in Cohoctaw, Michigan.

Miles developed his own version of Identity, known as dualism, according to which Aryan history was divided into an early period in the North, worshipping the Norse gods, and a later period in West Asia, which produced Christianity. Humanity is divided into two races, whites of the "astral plane" and nonwhites. Another dualism is found in a battle between "God and Lucifer" or "Yahweh and Satan," who used to be equals. **Yahweh exiled Satan to earth**, and Satan, with the help of his allies the Jews, is trying to trick Caucasians.

In the 1970s Miles served six years in federal prison for bombing school buses used in integration programs. In 1988 he was charged by the U.S. government with seditious conspiracy and convicted. In April 1988 some members of the church were acquitted by a jury in Fort Smith, Arkansas, of plotting to overthrow the U.S. government.

See also BRITISH ISRAELISM; CHURCH

OF JESUS CHRIST CHRISTIAN—ARYAN NATIONS; IDENTITY MOVEMENT; THE ORDER

MOUVEMENT CROIX-KOMA (Nailed to the Cross)

African independent movement started in 1964 in the Congo by Ta Malanda (?–1976), a Roman Catholic layman of the Lari tribe. At first the founder stated that the movement was part of the Roman Catholic Church, but all links have since been severed. Doctrine emphasizes opposition to witchcraft in all its forms, and members are required to give up their magical objects in public ceremonies.

MOVEMENT OF SPIRITUAL INNER AWARENESS (MSIA)

NEW THOUGHT group founded by John-Roger Hinkins (1934–   ), known as John-Roger, in California in 1963. The founder, a former schoolteacher, was born Roger Delano Hinkins to Mormon parents in Utah. In 1963 he claimed to be possessed by a spirit known as "John the Beloved."

MSIA defines itself as "a group of loving people who come together in their common love for the God in their hearts, for the Mystical Traveler through John-Roger, and for one another." John-Roger is considered "the physical embodiment of the Mystical Traveler Consciousness," which visits earth only once every 25,000 years.

The group operates the Baraka Center for "holistic therapy"; the John-Roger Foundation, which offers "Insight Transformational Seminars"; Koh-E-Nor University, which offers "advanced degrees in Applied Human Relations with specialization in Consciousness Facilitating"; the Integrity Foundation, which awards the Interna-tional Integrity Awards; NOW productions, and the Heartfelt Foundation. It has offered the "Insight Transformational Seminars" as management-training courses to major corporations. The group also offers "Prosperity" training and expects its members to tithe.

On June 19, 1988, "John-Roger passed the keys to the Mystical Traveler Consciousness to John Morton." He also said that he still holds the "Mystical Traveler and Preceptor Consciousness." According to media reports, the various MSIA operations have accumulated a vast fortune, and John-Roger has achieved a unique degree of personal influence. In the mid-1980s, MSIA counted scores of celebrities among its followers. On August 10, 1988, a resolution was passed by the United States Congress declaring Sept 24, John-Roger's birthday, National Integrity Day; it was also sponsored by 200 cities and 46 states.

Muchabaya Momberume, see AFRICAN APOSTOLIC CHURCH OF JOHANE MARANKE

MU FARM

Syncretistic commune founded in 1971 near Yoncalla, Oregon, by Fletcher Fist. Doctrine is eclectic, combining Christianity, Hinduism, and Theosophy.

J.K. Mugonza, see SSERULANDA SPIRITUAL PLANETARY COMMUNITY

Elijah Muhammad, see NATION OF ISLAM (NOI)

Herbert D. Muhammad, see NATION OF ISLAM (NOI)

Silas Muhammad, see NATION OF ISLAM (NOI) (SILAS MUHAMMAD)

Waarith Deen Muhammad, see NATION OF ISLAM (NOI)

Wallace D. Fard Muhammad, see NATION OF ISLAM (NOI)

Wallace Delaney Muhammad, see NATION OF ISLAM (NOI)

Swami Muktananda Paramahansa, see SHANTI MANDIR TEMPLE OF PEACE; SYDA FOUNDATION

MUKYOKAI

Japanese indigenous Christian movement known as "nonchurch Christianity," started by Kanzo Uchimura (1861–1930), a former Methodist, in the early 20th century. Uchimura in 1891 rebelled publicly against the official status of Shinto as the Japanese national cult and then rebelled against Protestant foreign missions. The group operates in small Bible study groups, with no buildings or clergy.
See also MAKUYA

Source:
Caldarola, C. *Christianity: The Japanese Way.* Leiden: E.J. Brill, 1979.

Jerry Mulvin, see DIVINE SCIENCE OF LIGHT AND SOUND

Bob Mumford, see CHRISTIAN GROWTH MINISTRIES

Jon Mundy, see INTERFAITH FELLOWSHIP

Arnold Murray, see SHEPHERD'S CHAPEL

Jacqueline Murray, see ATLANTEANS

Murshid Sam, see SUFI ISLAMIA RUHANIAT SOCIETY

George J. Musey, see SERVANTS OF THE SACRED HEART OF JESUS AND MARY

MYSTIC CONNECTION/CHURCH OF LIGHT

Spiritualist group founded by Shari Sumrall in Florida in the 1980s.

N

John Nackabah, see TWELVE APOSTLES

Nada-Yolanda, see MARK-AGE METACENTER

Myoko Naganuma, see RISSHO KOSEI-KAI

Prem Nagar (Shri Hans Maharaj Ji), see DIVINE LIGHT MISSION

Tanja Nahoum, see UNIVERSAL SPIR-ITUAL TEMPLE OF THE NEW ERA—TEMPLE OF CELESTIAL LIGHT

Omiki Nakayama, see TENRIKYO

Nalanda Foundation, see VAJRADHATU

NAMDHARI

Known also as Kuka, this Sikh sect calls for renewal and reform and proclaims a continuing line of living gurus, which puts it in clear opposition to majority Sikh doctrine. It was founded in the mid-19th century by Balak Singh (1797–1862), who was succeeded by Ram Singh (1816–1885).
See also NIRANKARI

Source:
Khushwant Singh. *A History of the Sikhs.* Princeton: Princeton University Press, 1963–1966.

Jyotir Maya Nanda, see INTERNATIONAL SCHOOL OF YOGA AND VEDANTA

Georges de Nantes, see COMMUNION PHALANGISTE

NARAYANANDA UNIVERSAL YOGA TRUST

International Hindu group led by Pramukh Swami, active in several European countries especially Great Britain and Denmark, since the 1970s.

Source:
Williams, R.B. *A New Face of Hinduism.* Cambridge: Cambridge University Press, 1983.

NATIONAL COLORED SPIRITUALIST ASSOCIATION OF CHURCHES

U.S. spiritualist group founded in 1925, as African-American members of the NATIONAL SPIRITUALIST ASSOCIATION OF CHURCHES left because of its segregationist policies. Otherwise the group is identical to the N.S.A.C. in doctrines and practices.

NATIONAL INSTITUTE FOR SELF-UNDERSTANDING

U.S. organization related to the SELF-REALIZATION FELLOWSHIP. It offers "spiritual readings and counseling."

NATIONAL ISLAMIC ASSEMBLY

U.S. Islamic group founded in 1985, which has attempted to form an alliance of all Islamic-oriented groups among African-Americans.
See also NATION OF ISLAM (NOI)

NATIONAL SPIRITUAL ALLIANCE

U.S. spiritualist group started in 1913 by secession from the NATIONAL SPIRITUALIST ASSOCIATION OF CHURCHES over the issue of reincarnation. Belief in reincarnation was not a part of the N.S.A.C. Declaration of Principles, and the majority objected to its promotion. This issue was to lead to other secessions.

NATIONAL SPIRITUALIST ASSOCIATION OF CHURCHES (N.S.A.C.)

Spiritualist organization founded in Chicago in 1893 by Harrison D. Barrett and James M. Peebles, former Unitarian ministers. It is the largest and the oldest of U.S. spiritualist organizations. Several other groups were created over the years as a result of schisms within the N.S.A.C.

Its Declaration of Principles affirms belief in "Infinite Intelligence," which is expressed by the phenomena of nature, both physical and spiritual. It also affirms belief in the continuity of personal identity after "the change called death" and belief in communication with "the so-called dead."

It contains no references to reincarnation, the Bible, or traditional Christian concepts.

See also GENERAL ASSEMBLY OF SPIRITUALISTS; NATIONAL COLORED SPIRITUALIST ASSOCIATION OF CHURCHES; NATIONAL SPIRITUAL ALLIANCE

Sources:

Brown, S. *The Heyday of Spiritualism.* New York: Hawthorn Books, 1970.

Nelson, G.L. *Spiritualism and Society.* New York: Schocken Books, 1969.

NATIONAL SPIRITUAL SCIENCE CENTER

Spiritualist group founded in 1941 in Washington, D.C., by Alice W. Tindall, who had been a member of the SPIRITUAL SCIENCE CHURCH.

NATIONAL SWAZI NATIVE APOSTOLIC CHURCH OF AFRICA

South African "ZIONIST" church founded by Richard S. Mhlanga, who planned it as the national Swazi church. The founder believed in faith healing alone but was ready to tolerate the use of medicine in order to receive national status.

Source:

Sundkler, B.G.M. *Bantu Prophets in South Africa.* London: Oxford University Press, 1961.

NATION OF ISLAM (NOI)

Originally named the Lost-Found Nation of Islam in the West and popularly known as Black Moslems, this revitalization movement among African-Americans offers them an Islamic religious identity separating them from the surrounding culture. Naming members X, as was done in the early days of the movement, was a symbol of separation and separatism. The movement is supposed to have originated in the teachings of the mysterious Wallace D. Fard Muhammad (W.D. Fard), a man who preached in the black communities of the Midwest in the early 1930s and disappeared in 1934. Reportedly, Fard promulgated the view that African-Americans were in reality Moslems separated from their true identity. Elijah Muhammad (1897–1975), a former Baptist minister born Elijah Poole, who followed Fard and actually founded the NOI, regarded his teacher as a Mahdi, a divine Messiah and prophet. He led the movement from the 1930s to 1975 as it experienced significant growth, especially after World War II.

According to original NOI doctrine, Fard came to the U.S. from "Arabia" around

Malcolm X, an early leader of the Nation of Islam.

1930 and was actually an incarnation of Allah, and he appointed Elijah Muhammad as his prophet. The prophet taught that all humans were black until an evil genius named Yakub created a white race of devils on the island of Patmos. Following a world upheaval predicted for 1970, black people would assume control of the planet.

These beliefs clearly deviated from orthodox Islam. Malcolm X (Malcolm Little, 1925–1965), who was second in command to Elijah Muhammad, started a movement toward Sunni Islamic orthodoxy and changed his name to El Hajj Malik Shabbaz. After Malcolm X left the movement to found his own mosque, he was assassinated by members of NOI. Elijah Muhammad's son-in-law was also murdered by a rival faction. The group operated a security force known as the Fruit of Islam (FOI).

From its early years the NOI was active and successful in raising living standards of its members and saving them from lives of crime and drug addiction. They were taught a life-style of puritanism and hard work. Alcohol, tobacco, and other drugs were forbidden, as were gambling and dancing. The self-help doctrine preached by the founder led to self-reliance and pride.

The founder's son, Herbert D. Muhammad, took over the leadership in 1975, officially adopted the name Nation of Islam, or Bilalians, and opened the membership to all races. In 1977 leadership passed to another son, Wallace Delaney Muhammad, later known as Waarith Deen Muhammad (1934–   ), who moved the Nation toward Orthodox Islam and in 1976 changed its name to World Community of Al-Islam in the West. Later the name Muslim Community of America was adopted. In 1980 it was changed again to American Muslim Mission (AMM). The organization was dissolved in 1985, and Waarith Deen Muhammad resigned as leader. His declared intention was to let independent mosques run their affairs as part of the worldwide Sunni Muslim community. In 1986 he established an affiliation with the Council of Rabita, an Islamic group founded in 1978 in Mecca.

After 1975, when the founder died without a will, the group was hurt by suits and countersuits by his twenty-one children, in and out of wedlock, involving his property and the group's property, which was worth many millions.

Nation of Islam (NOI) now denotes, in

Elijah Muhammad, founder of the Nation of Islam.

most cases, a group headed by Abdul Haleem Farrakhan.

See also HANAFIS; NATION OF ISLAM (FARRAKHAN)

Sources:

Breitman, G. *The Last Year of Malcolm X.* New York: Schocken, 1968.

Breitman, G., Porter, I., and Smith, B. *The Assassination of Malcolm X.* New York: Pathfinder Press, 1976.

Essien-Udom, E.U. *Black Nationalism.* Chicago: University of Chicago Press, 1962.

Lincoln, C.E. *The Black Muslims in America.* Boston: Beacon Press, 1961.

NATION OF ISLAM (NOI) (FARRAKHAN)

Known also as The Nation, this African-American Moslem-inspired group was founded in 1977 by Abdul Haleem Farrakhan (Louis Eugene Wolcott, 1933–) as a breakaway group from what was then the World Community of Al-Islam in the West, successor to the NATION OF ISLAM. The declared aim of the new group was to revive the original Nation of Islam concept as promoted by Elijah Muhammad. Its doctrine emphasizes moral reawakening, economic self-help, and some Islamic beliefs. Its leader was known as Louis X in the early 1960s and was the minister in the Nation of Islam mosque in Boston. He then moved to the Harlem district of New York. Since the late 1970s he has taken an outspoken separatist stand regarding whites and often expressed anti-Semitic views. In 1985 his group organized People Organized and Working for Economic Rebirth (POWER), designed to achieve economic self-sufficiency for African-Americans.

NATION OF ISLAM (JEREMIAH SHABAZZ)

Islamic group founded by Jeremiah Shabazz in the late 1970s. Based in Philadelphia, it grew out of the NATION OF ISLAM (NOI). Before 1975 Shabazz was minister of the NOI Philadelphia Temple.

NATION OF ISLAM (SILAS MUHAMMAD)

Islamic group founded by Silas Muhammad in the late 1970s. Based on the West Coast, it grew out of the NATION OF ISLAM (NOI).

NATION OF YAHWEH (HEBREW ISRAELITES)

Known also as the Temple of Love or the Followers of Yahweh, this Black Judaism group was founded in the 1970s in Miami, Florida, by Hulon Mitchell, Jr. (1935–), former member of a PENTECOSTAL church and later a leader in the NATION OF ISLAM. In the late 1960s Mitchell reported having died and then risen from the dead to pursue a divine mission. By 1979 he was known as Brother Moses. Later he changed his name to Yahweh ben Yahweh and declared himself the son of God.

African-Americans, according to Yahweh ben Yahweh, are the lost tribe of Judah. Members are expected to change their names when joining and to adopt the name Israel. They wear white robes and turbans. They are expected to enjoy immortality. The group has achieved a measure of influence in Miami, and October 7, 1990, was declared Yahweh Ben Yahweh Day by the mayor. In November 1990 Yahweh Ben Yahweh and sixteen other members of the group were indicted in connection with fourteen cases of murder and other serious crimes.

Yahweh ben Yahweh, founder of the Nation of Yahweh, also known as the Hebrew Israelites and the Temple of Love.

NATIVE AMERICAN CHURCH (NAC)

Native American syncretistic revitalization movement combining Christian elements with native tradition, which has made the use of peyote psychedelic into its central ritual. It was started in 1906, and in 1909 the name Union Church was taken. In 1918 the group was incorporated under its present name. The First Born Church of Christ was later absorbed by the group. The use of peyote has involved the group in legal battles for generations, but it has won the right to use the drug. Public Law 91-513, the Comprehensive Drug Abuse Prevention and Control Act of 1970, as passed by the United States Congress, prohibits the use of peyote but makes an exemption for members of the Native American Church. A 1990 ruling against the exemption by the United States Supreme Court has cast doubt on the future of the group.

Sources:

Aberle, D.F. *The Peyote Religion among the Navaho*. Chicago: Aldine, 1966.

Anderson, E.F. *Peyote, The Divine Cactus*. Tucson: University of Arizona Press, 1980.

La Barre, W. *The Peyote Cult*. Hamden, CT: Shoe String Press, 1959.

Slotkin, J.S. *The Peyote Religion: A Study in Indian-White Relations*. Glencoe, IL: Free Press, 1956.

Nava Vidhana, see CHURCH OF THE NEW DISPENSATION

NAZARETHA (OR SHEMBEITES)

Officially known as the Nazarite Baptist Church, and as the Ama-Nazaretha or Nazarites, this South African syncretistic movement was founded in 1911 by the Zulu prophet Isaiah Shembe (1870–1935). As a young man Shembe had many visions in which he was told to repent and to leave his four wives. He started working as a healer and exorcist and in 1906 was baptized by Baptist missionaries.

In 1916 he established a village named Ekuphakameni, eighteen miles from Durban. Then he had a vision telling him to go to Nhlangakazi Mountain in Natal, which has become the Nazarite Holy Mountain. Nhlangakazi is the site of the annual January festival, and Ekuphakameni of the July festival. After the prophet's death, his mantle was inherited by his son, Johannes Galilee Shembe.

Group doctrine opposes modern medicine and until 1944 opposed all vaccination. Shembe rejected Jesus in favor of Jehovah and chose Sabbath to replace Sunday.

Shembe is considered the Black Christ, supposedly risen from the dead, and the Christian Bible is believed to have been written about him.

Source:

Sundkler, B.G.M. *Bantu Prophets in South Africa*. London: Oxford University Press, 1961.

Ndugumoi, see TUKA

NECEDAH SHRINE

Sometimes known as the Diamond Star Constellation, this independent Catholic group was founded by Mary Ann Van Hoof in Wisconsin in the 1960s. In the 1950s Mrs. Van Hoof reported apparitions of the Virgin Mary and "other celestials," which led to the publication of various revelations. The group operated the Seven Sorrows of Our

Emerson Jackson of the Native American Church performs a ceremony outside the Supreme Court Building in Washington, D.C. The Court ruled **to** exempt the sect from laws against use of peyote.

Sorrowful Mother Infants Home for unwed mothers. The home was the subject of investigations by authorities, and the group was forced to change its method of operation.

Watchman Nee, see LOCAL CHURCH MOVEMENT

John Oliver Nelson, see COMPANY AT KIRKRIDGE

Neo-Humanism, see ANANDA MARGA

NETIVYAH

Israeli Hebrew-Christian group founded in the 1950s in Jerusalem by Daniel Zion, former chief rabbi of Bulgaria. The founder's views are reported to have been unorthodox by Christian traditional standards.

The group is committed to preserving some Jewish rabbinical traditions.
See also HEBREW CHRISTIANITY

Nevada Slim, see INTERNATIONAL CHURCH OF SPIRITUAL VISION, INC.

THE NEVERDIES

Also known as Church of the Living or the Everlasting Gospel, this PENTECOSTAL group based in West Virginia believes in physical immortality. Among its leaders have been Ted Oiler and Henry Holstine.

NEW ACROPOLIS (N.A.)

International occultist-Theosophical group founded in 1956 in Buenos Aires by Jorge Angel Livraga (1930–), known as JAL, and his wife Ada Albrecht. Branches have developed all over Western Europe and in

Members of the Neverdies, also called the Church of the Living, hold a service expounding their belief in immortality.

Israel. The group offers many public lectures but also operates a parallel secret "Theosophical Society." Its doctrine includes belief in the reality of fairies, as well as plans for a new political order inspired by Plato's *Republic*. It teaches an array of Western occultist traditions, including alchemy, "Tibetan" and "Egyptian" lore, and the "cosmic laws of the microcosm and the macrocosm." Other tenets include reincarnation, astrology, and the secrets of ancient Greek culture. Followers are being prepared for the "Age of Aquarius" by being trained to become "supermen."
See also THEOSOPHY

NEW AGE CHRISTIANITY WITHOUT RELIGION

International Christian group founded by Hugh de Cruz in the 1970s. It has headquarters, known as Temple of Light, in the Canary Islands but has branches worldwide. The largest are in Spain, New Zealand, and Ghana. The doctrine recognizes various masters, chief among them Sandana, Jesus Christ of the Aquarian Age. Some Hindu ideas are also promoted.

NEW AGE CHURCH OF BEING

Group founded in 1988 in Harbin Hot Springs, California, based on the idea of ". . . being at peace with the natural and spiritual energies of the land, with the assistance of Shamans and teachers of Native American traditions." Activities include "Full Moon gatherings, equinox and solstice celebrations."

NEW AGE CHURCH OF TRUTH

PENTECOSTAL-occultist group founded in the 1960s by Gilbert N. Holloway (1915–)

in Deming, New Mexico. It operates the Christ Light Community.

NEW APOSTOLIC CHURCH

Initially known as the General Christian Mission, this European Fundamentalist group was created through a schism in the CATHOLIC APOSTOLIC CHURCH. Its German branch was started in 1860 by Heinrich Geyer; H. Niehaus became leader in 1863. The schism was started by members who doubted the official prediction of 1864 for the Second Coming. The new Church started growing after the turn of the century and spread to Switzerland and Austria. Three schisms created the APOSTELMAT JUDA in 1902, the REFORMED APOSTOLIC COMMUNITY in 1921, and the APOSTELMAT JESU CHRISTI in 1923.

The group has followed a policy of strict secrecy in regard to its doctrines. From headquarters in Dortmund, Germany, branches operate throughout Western Europe and Africa.

NEW BEGINNINGS

British-Israelist, white-supremacist group founded by Eldon D. Purvis in the 1960s and based in Waynesville, North Carolina. Its doctrine emphasizes traditional PENTECOSTAL beliefs in "healing" and "prophecy."
See also BRITISH ISRAELISM

NEW BEGINNINGS (EX-CHRISTIAN SCIENTISTS FOR JESUS)

Group started by former members of CHRISTIAN SCIENCE who have become evangelical Christians and have been fighting their former church. Founded in 1980 by D.E. Kind, it is based in Anaheim, California.

Members of the New Age Church of Being perform a ritual at the Giza Pyramids near Cairo, Egypt.

NEW CHRISTIAN CRUSADE CHURCH

Christian Identity, white-supremacist, militarist group founded in 1971 in Metairie, Louisiana, by James K. Warner, a former member of the American Nazi Party. The group's doctrine is\anti-Semitic. It is connected with the CHRISTIAN DEFENSE LEAGUE, and with the Sons of Liberty.
See also IDENTITY MOVEMENT

NEW COVENANT APOSTOLIC ORDER (NCAO)

Christian   Fundamentalist-millenarian group founded in 1975 by Jack Sparks and other former members of the Christian World Liberation Front in Berkeley, California. The group started on a voyage in search of an appropriate and stable religious identity. In 1979 it took the name Evangelical Orthodox Church (EOC), becoming part of the Eastern Orthodox tradition of Christianity and espousing the Eastern Orthodox emphasis on ritual and on belief in the Virgin Mary as the Mother of God. In 1987 the group joined the Antiochian Orthodox Christian Archdiocese of North America, an orthodox body founded in the 1930s.
See also JESUS MOVEMENT

NEW COVENANT CHURCH

Fundamentalist group founded in Orlando, Florida, in 1987 by Jim Bakker, to continue his television ministry earlier carried out through the Praise the Lord (PTL) organization. The founder was later sentenced to prison for mishandling funds contributed to Praise The Lord by followers.

NEW CREATION BIBLE STUDENTS

Known officially as the Christian Millenial Fellowship, this U.S. millenarian group was created by the 1910 schism in the Watch Tower Bible and Tract Society that also led to the founding of the CHRISTIAN BELIEVERS CONFERENCE. The group is made up of Italian-Americans and has had contacts with similar groups in Italy.
See also JEHOVAH'S WITNESSES

New Ecumenical Research Association (New ERA), see UNIFICATION CHURCH

NEW HARMONY CHRISTIAN CRUSADE

Identity group founded in Mariposa, California, in the 1970s by George Udvary, a native of Hungary who came to the United States in 1956.
See also IDENTITY MOVEMENT

NEW HISTORY SOCIETY

Bahai splinter group founded in New York City in 1929 by Mirza Ahmad Sohrab (1891–1958), who was excommunicated by the Bahais in the 1930s, and Lewis Stuyvesant Chanler.

NEW JERUSALEM FELLOWSHIP

British offshoot of JEHOVAH'S WITNESSES founded in 1920 by F.S. Edgell (?–1950).

NEW LIFE EVANGELISTIC CENTER

JESUS MOVEMENT group founded around 1970 in St. Louis, Missouri.

NEW REFORMED ORTHODOX ORDER OF THE GOLDEN DAWN

Neo-pagan witchcraft group started in the 1970s in the San Francisco Bay area.

NEW SALEM CHURCH (ALADURA)

African independent PENTECOSTAL group

founded in Nigeria in 1956 by Lucy Adeoti.

NEW TESTAMENT CHURCH OF GOD

U.S. "HOLINESS" group founded in Arkansas in 1942.

NEW THOUGHT

U.S. theistic, "mind healing," "positive thinking" movement started in the 19th century and inspired by the work of Phineas Parkhurst Quimby (1802–1866), who had also inspired Mary Baker Eddy, the founder of CHRISTIAN SCIENCE. Quimby died in 1866, but in the 1880s the movement developed under the leadership of Emma Curtis Hopkins, an associate of Mary Baker Eddy (and a former editor of the *Journal of Christian Science*), Ernest S. Holmes, Charles S. Fillmore, and Myrtle Fillmore.

"Free Thought" groups held national conventions in the U.S. starting in 1894, the International Metaphysical League was founded in 1899, the National New Thought Alliance in 1908, and the International New Thought Alliance in 1914. In Great Britain the movement has become known as The Higher Thought.

The New Thought doctrine is summed up in belief in "the infinitude of the Supreme One, the Divinity of man and his infinite possibilities through the creative power of constructive thinking and obedience to the voice of the Indwelling Presence which is our source of Inspiration, Power, Health, and Prosperity."

The movement combined the ideas of Quimby with those of Mary Baker Eddy. Healing through the power of mind and the ultimate sovereignty of the mind over material reality were the cornerstones of its ideology. Disease was "unreal" and so could be overcome by a right-thinking mind, but the existence of matter was never denied. Later an emphasis on the attainment of financial prosperity and the elimination of "unreal" poverty through "mind power" was added.

See also A COURSE IN MIRACLES; ACTUALISM; CHRISTIAN SCIENCE; CHURCH OF THE HEALING CHRIST (DIVINE SCIENCE); CRYSTAL CATHEDRAL; DIVINE SCIENCE CHURCH; ETERNAL FLAME FOUNDATION; HOME OF TRUTH MOVEMENT; HOPKINS ASSOCIATION, EMMA C.; RELIGIOUS SCIENCE INTERNATIONAL; RELIGIOUS SCIENCE, UNITED CHURCH OF; SCIENCE OF MIND CHURCH; UNITY SCHOOL OF CHRISTIANITY

Sources:

Braden, C.S. *Spirits in Rebellion*. Dallas: SMU Press, 1963.

Judah, J.S. *The History and Philosophy of the Metaphysical Movements in America*. Philadelphia: Westminster Press, 1967.

Meyer, D. *The Positive Thinkers*. New York: Pantheon Books, 1980.

Schneider, L., and Dornbusch, S. *Popular Religion*. Chicago: University of Chicago Press, 1958.

NEW THOUGHT SYNAGOGUE

Jewish variant of NEW THOUGHT founded in Los Angeles, California, in 1953 by S. Pereira Mendes.

NEW VRINDABAN

Officially known as the League of Devotees at New Vrindaban, and sometimes as the International Society for Krishna Consciousness of West Virginia, this Hindu group is an offshoot of the INTERNA-TIONAL SOCIETY FOR KRISHNA CON-SCIOUSNESS (ISKCON). In the late 1970s, under the leadership of Kirtanananda Swami Bhaktiphada (ne Keith Ham of Peekskill, New York), the group separated from the Society. In 1987 its leader was expelled by the ISKCON governing body because of "dishonesty" and "apparent approval of illegal activity." In May 1986 a former member, Steven Bryant, was found murdered in Los Angeles. Bryant had accused New Vrindaban leaders of many criminal offenses. Since 1986 there have been serious accusations and convictions of criminal involvement by the group and its leader, including murder of former members and drug smuggling. It has been strongly and repeatedly criticized by ISKCON.

Source:

Hubner, J., and Gruson, L. *Monkey on a Stick: Murder, Madness and the Hare Krishnas.* San Diego: Harcourt Brace Jovanovich, 1988

NEW WICCAN CHURCH
British neo-pagan group founded in the 1980s and attempting to unite various neo-pagan traditions.

NEW WORLD OF ISLAM
U.S. African-American Moslem organization started in the 1970s, an offshoot of the NATION OF ISLAM.

NEW YORK CHURCH OF CHRIST
Fundamentalist organization founded in 1982 by Steve Johnson. It is a branch of the CROSSROADS CHURCHES OF CHRIST and is structured according to the SHEPHERD-ING principle, which provides for authoritarian leadership and close supervision of members. This style has been the basis of the "shepherding movement," which includes the BODY OF CHRIST, CHRISTIAN GROWTH MINISTRIES, and CHRISTIAN RESTORATION MINISTRIES.

NEW YORK METAPHYSICAL SOCIETY
NEW THOUGHT group founded by Alexander Demaras in the 1970s.

NEW YORK SPIRITUAL CENTER, INC.
Spiritualist group founded in the 1960s by Renee and Bill Linn. It operates the Metaphysics and Parapsychology Institute, Inc.

NEW YORK UNITED SABBATH DAY ADVENT CHURCH
U.S. African-American, Adventist, Sabbath-keeping congregation. In 1956 it became, together with similar groups, THE UNIFICATION ASSOCIATION OF CHRISTIAN SABBATH KEEPERS.
See also SEVENTH-DAY ADVENTISTS

NICHIREN SHOSHU SOKA GAKKAI OF AMERICA (NSA)
Known popularly as Nichiren Shoshu, this is the U.S. branch of SOKA GAKKAI SOCIETY, a Japanese new religion that reached the U.S. in 1957. The first Soka Gakkai emissary in the United States, Masayasua Sadanaga, started to recruit members in Los Angeles. In 1963 he changed his name to George M. Williams, and the group's name to Nichiren Shoshu.

"The object of worship in Nichiren Shoshu Buddhism is the Dai-Gohonzon, inscribed by the founder, Nichiren Daishonin, on October 12, 1279, with the

American members of Nichiren Shoshu of America chant during a meeting.

aim of enabling all people to attain absolute happiness and bring about world peace. The Gohonzon literally means the most fundamental and respectable entity. It contains the life-force and the fundamental law inherent in the whole universe which is Nam-myoho-renge-kyo." By following the "fundamental law," the individual can achieve enlightenment and happiness.

L.T. Nichols, see MEGIDDO MISSION

NIRANKARI
Sikh sect calling for renewal and reform, started in Peshawar in the early 19th century by Baba Dayal (1783–1855). The group's doctrine calls for a return to the original teachings of Nanak. In addition, it assumes a continuing line of living gurus, which puts it in clear opposition to majority Sikh doctrine.

See also NAMDHARI

Source:

Khushwant Singh. *A History of the Sikhs.* Princeton: Princeton University Press, 1963–1966.

Swami Nityananda, see SYDA FOUNDATION

Nityananda, see SHANTI MANDIR TEMPLE OF PEACE

NITYANANDA INSTITUTE

U.S. Hindu group devoted to the teachings of Swami Rudrananda (1928–1973), popularly known as Rudi. Albert Rudolph (Rudi) was born and raised in Brooklyn, New York. He became renowned as a "spiritual teacher" and teacher of meditation, then was killed in a plane crash. Rudrananda was a disciple of Swami Nityananda (?–1961) and Swami Muktananda (1908–1982) but started his own ashram in India in 1969. This group was founded in 1973 by Swami Chetananda in Bloomington, Indiana, and later moved to Boston.

See also SHREE GURUDEV RUDRANANDA YOGA ASHRAM

Nivedita, see RAMAKRISHMA MATH AND MISSION

Nikkyo Niwano, see RISSHO-KOSEI-KAI

O.T. Nodrog, see ARMAGEDDON TIME ARK BASE

NOISE, THE

Melanesian syncretistic group (CARGO CULT) started in the Admiralty Islands in February 1947 (just three months after the start of PALIAU CHURCH) by Wapei, who reported a visit from Jesus Christ of the New Testament and predicted the imminent arrival of cargo. Wapei described cargo ships piloted by Jesus Christ on their way to the island. His followers stopped working, started fasting, and destroyed their property. When the prophecy failed, he was killed at his own request. Many of his followers later joined Paliau, but others continued to claim contact with Wapei's spirit.

Richard Nolen, see UNITED LEADERSHIP

Two avatars of the Italian occultist group Nonsiamosoli. (Top) Russian monk Grigori Efimovich Rasputin, favorite of Empress Alexandra at the time of World War I. (Bottom) Comte de Cagliostro, adventurer and charlatan, a figure at the court of Louis XVI of France. (see page 212)

COUNCIL OF HEBREW ISRAELITES

NON-DIGRESSIVE CHURCH OF GOD, THE

U.S. PENTECOSTAL group founded in the early 20th century.

NONSIAMOSOLI ("We are not alone")

Italian occultist "UFO" group founded in 1979 in Porto Sant'Elpidio by Giorgio Bongiovanni. Many of the group's ideas came from an earlier group, Fratellanza Cosmica, which was disbanded in 1978. The new group combines in its doctrine Catholic traditions and Western occultism, together with messages received from "extraterrestrials." Bongiovanni reported apparitions by the Virgin Mary of Fatima. Eugenio Siragusa (1919–), the founder of Fratellanza Cosmica, is believed by Nonsiamosoli to be the reincarnation of a priest from "Atlantis" and of Cagliostro and Gregory Rasputin.

NOOHRA FOUNDATION

Christian-NEW THOUGHT group founded in 1970 in California to promote the teachings of George M. Lamsa (1892–1975), who in 1927 founded the Aramaic Bible Society. Lamsa originated a theory according to which the New Testament was written in Aramaic and had to be interpreted according to ancient Aramaic language and traditions.

Allen Noonan, see ONE WORLD FAMILY

Ernest L. Norman, Ruth Norman, see UNARIUS—SCIENCE OF LIFE

NORTH AMERICAN OLD ROMAN CATHOLIC CHURCH (N.A.O.R.C.C.)

OLD CATHOLIC group founded in 1916 in Chicago by Carmel Henry Carfora (?–1958), who was born in Italy and came to the United States as a Roman Catholic priest. The group displayed doctrinal and ritualistic conservatism. Schisms followed Carfora's death, and the group came to the verge of complete disappearance.

NORTHEAST KINGDOM COMMUNITY CHURCH (Church at Island Pond)

Originally known as the Vine Christian Community, this Fundamentalist, PENTECOSTAL, communal group was founded by Gene Spriggs and Martha Spriggs in Chattanooga, Tennessee, in 1972. It grew out of the JESUS MOVEMENT of the early 1970s. Later the group moved to the Northeast, establishing communities in Vermont and Massachusetts. It has been involved in several controversies and legal disputes stemming from accusations of authoritarianism and child abuse.

Leah Novick, see CONGREGATION BEIT SHECHINAH

Claude Rex Nowell, see SUMMUM CHURCH

John Humphrey Noyes, see ONEIDA, PERFECTIONIST COMMUNITY OF

NUBIAN ISLAAMIC HEBREWS

Known also as the Community of Ansaar Affairs in America, or Ansaaru Islaam, this Islamic African-American group was founded in the 1970s in New York City by a

A member of the Northeast Kingdom Community Church in custody of police on charges of child abuse.

leader known as Al Imaam Issa Al Haadi Al Mahdi. The founder claims to be the great-grandson of the 19th-century Sudanese Mahdi, Mohammed Ahmad Ibn Abdallah (1843–1885), and to continue the Mahdi's mission. His brand of Islam, proclaimed to be the only authentic one, contains a conservative interpretation of the Koran. The group has operated several economic organizations designed to foster self-reliance and self-respect.

See also MAHDI; NATION OF ISLAM

NU YOGA
European Hindu-oriented group started in the 1970s by Sanatanananda.

Nyabingi, see RASTAFARIANS

Nyah, see ETHIOPIAN ZION COPTIC CHURCH

NYINGMAPA CENTER
Tibetan Buddhist group based in Berkeley, California, founded in 1969 by Tarthang Tulku Rinpoche. It represents the Tibetan Nyingmapa tradition.

Wilhelm A. Nyland, see INSTITUTE FOR RELIGIOUS DEVELOPMENT

Nzambi ya Bougie, see MISSION DE DIEU DU BOUGIE

Olumba Olumba Obu, see BROTHER-HOOD OF THE CROSS AND STAR

ODINISTS

North American neo-pagan group started in the 1960s, which follows Norse mythology and worships that pantheon. It has been affiliated with extreme right-wing political causes and groups and ideas of the racial superiority of the "Nordic Race."

Odoru-Shukyo, see TENSHO KOTAI JUNGU KYO

Salome Mamle Odum, see UNITED CHRISTIANS CHURCH

Samuel E. Officer, see YAHWEH'S TEMPLE

Koji Ogasawara, see THIRD CIVILIZATION

OHIO BIBLE FELLOWSHIP

U.S. Christian Fundamentalist group founded in 1968 by former members of the INDEPENDENT FUNDAMENTAL CHURCHES OF AMERICA, who felt that the latter was not sufficiently Fundamentalist.

Ted Oiler, see NEVERDIES

Mikichi Okada, see SEKAI KYUSEI KYO

Okada Kotama, see MAHIKARI

Shoken Okano, see GEDATSU

Adeniran Oke, see ETHIOPIAN NATIONAL CHURCH, NIGERIA

Henry Steel Olcott, see THEOSOPHY

OLD CATHOLIC

Term appearing in the names of numerous churches, signifying groups that have separated from the Roman Catholic Church at various times. The earliest such split was in 1724, creating the Dutch Church of Utrecht. In the 19th century a wave of schisms occurred when German, Austrian, and Swiss groups refused to accept the doctrine of papal infallibility, proclaimed in 1870. In some cases the schismatic movement was connected with earlier attempts to gain autonomy from Roman Catholic hierarchy.

Under the leadership of J.J. Döhlinger (1799–1890) of Germany, dissenters from Germany, France, Austria, and Switzerland met in a congress in Cologne in 1872. They adopted rules allowing marriage of priests and conduct of services in the vernacular. In Switzerland Old Catholics are officially known as the Christian Catholic Church.

Later, several East European groups, mainly Polish, refused to accept Roman Catholic authority. Old Catholic churches now operate all over the world. Following the Second Vatican Council of 1962–1965, a fourth wave of schisms created *traditionalist* Catholic groups that claim to preserve earlier Catholic rituals and traditions. Some Old Catholic groups have also been traditionalist in this sense, faithful to earlier customary rituals.

See POLISH MARIAVITE CHURCH; POLISH NATIONAL CATHOLIC CHURCH OF AMERICA

Sources:

Anson, P.F. *Bishops at Large.* London: Faber and Faber, 1964.

Pruter, K., and Melton, J.G. *The Old Catholic Sourcebook.* New York: Garland, 1983.

OLD CATHOLIC CHURCH IN AMERICA

OLD CATHOLIC group founded in 1917 by William Henry Francis Brothers (1887–1979). Following the founder's death, schisms and decline occurred.

OLD TIME FAITH, INC.

Fundamentalist group founded by Essie Binkley in the 1940s in Los Angeles. In 1949 Mrs. Binkley ordained Marjoe Gortner (1945–   ) as a minister. He performed marriages and became a well-known child preacher. In 1973 Gortner produced a film, *Marjoe*, about the life of a child preacher and the world of revival-tent evangelism and "faith healing."

Marjoe Gortner, former minister in the Fundamentalist Old Time Faith sect, who was ordained at the age of four.

Chester Olszewaski, see CHRISZEKIAL ELIAS

OMOTOKYO (OMOTO or OOMOTO)

Japanese millenarian, Shinto-inspired new religion, whose name is translated as "the Teaching of the Great Origin." It was founded in 1899 by Mrs. Nao Deguchi (1836–1918), a former KONKOKYO teacher. In January 1892 she became convinced of her possession by a divine power. She started acting as a faith healer and then joined Konkokyo. Later she began preaching a message of world reformation and the coming of the kingdom of heaven. Her adopted son, Onisaburo Deguchi (1870–1948), became the leader after her death, and the group, although successful, was subject to government persecution in the 1920s and 1930s. After World War II the group was revived and reorganized.

Omotokyo gave rise to several new movements, including SEKAI KYUSEI KYO, SEICHO NO IE, and ANANAIKO.

Simeon Ondeto, see MARIA LEGIO (OF AFRICA)

Edwin and Lois O'Neal, see CHURCH OF THE CHRISTIAN SPIRITUAL ALLIANCE (CSA)

ONE WORLD FAMILY

Also known as the Universal Industrial

Church of the New World Comforter or the Messiah's World Crusade, this communal movement was founded in 1966 in San Francisco by Allen Noonan (1918–), also known as Allen-Michael. The doctrine combines Christian ideas with belief in communication with extraterrestrial beings. Noonan claims to have traveled to outer space in 1947 and since then to having received messages from extraterrestrial beings as well as Christian-oriented revelations.

Ajijiro Onishi, see HONMICHI-KYO

Onishi Tama, see HONBUSHIN

Oomoto, see OMOTOKYO (OMOTO)

OPEN BIBLE CHURCH

U.S. British-Israelist group based in Baltimore, headed by Otis B. Read, Jr.
See also BRITISH ISRAELISM

OPEN BIBLE STANDARD CHURCHES, INC.

U.S. PENTECOSTAL group founded in 1935 by a merger of two groups, the Open Bible Evangelistic Association and the Bible Standard, Inc. The group's doctrine emphasizes healing and tithing.

ORAGE GROUP

New York Gurdjieff group under the guidance of A.R. Orage (1871–1932). Orage was a noted British literary critic in the 1920s, who left his work to become a Gurdjieff

Alan Berg, Denver talk-show host who was murdered by members of The Order, military wing of the Church of Jesus Christ Christian–Aryan Nations.(**see p. 218**)

disciple in France. He was sent as a missionary to the United States, where he spent the years 1924–1931. Orage was quite successful in his efforts and provided vital financial support, but he was removed by Gurdjieff himself, who disbanded the New York group. Orage returned to his work in literary criticism.

See also GURDJIEFF GROUPS

ORDEN FIAT LUX

Swiss Christian-spiritualist group founded in 1975 by Erika Bertschinger (known as Uriella), a former follower of the GEISTIGE LOGE. The founder reports receiving messages from Jesus Christ.

ORDER, THE

Also known as the Silent Brotherhood, this U.S. Christian Identity group was the military wing of the CHURCH OF JESUS CHRIST CHRISTIAN—ARYAN NATIONS. It was founded in 1983 by Robert Jay Mathews (1953-1984). In June 1984, two members murdered Denver radio personality Alan Berg. Later, group members obtained $3.6 million in an armed robbery. In December 1984 Mathews was killed in a shootout with FBI and other government agents in Whidbey Island, Washington.

Members of The Order have been convicted numerous times of conspiracy against the United States government, arson, and murder. They have been sentenced to prison terms of no less than forty years. Two other members were sentenced to 150 years in prison each for the murder of Alan Berg. The group ceased to exist after 1984.

See also IDENTITY MOVEMENT

Source:

Martinez, T., and Guinther, J. *Brotherhood of Murder*. New York: McGraw-Hill, 1988.

ORDER OF FRANSISTERS AND FRANBROTHERS

Group inspired by St. Francis of Assisi, founded in 1963 in Denver, Colorado, by Laurel Elizabeth Keyes. The group is "interreligious, embracing all faiths, East and West. The intentions of Fransisters and Franbrothers is identity with their Ideal, feeling that daily living is an offering of Love. It is important to do one's best and for Life to know that one of Its extensions is coming closer to Its Source. Teaching, healing, and retreats are main activities." The Order operates the Restorium retreat center.

ORDER OF ST. LUKE

U.S. group growing out of the Protestant Episcopalian Church, founded in the 1950s, and devoted to "spiritual healing."

ORDER OF THE CROSS

International Christian-Theosophical group founded in Great Britain in 1904 by John Todd Ferrier (1858–1942). The founder claimed to have received revelations that helped him recover the missing parts of the New Testament. The missing teachings include belief in reincarnation, complete opposition to the taking of life, and complete refusal to engage in violent action. Thus, members are vegetarians and pacifists.

ORDER OF THE INITIATES OF TIBET

Theosophical group founded in Washington, DC, in 1909.

A painting by Giovanni Bellini of Saint Francis of Assisi, inspiration of the group Fransisters and Franbrothers.

ORDO TEMPLI ASTRATE (OTA)

Occultist group founded in 1970 in Pasadena, California, and claiming to continue the traditions of the ORDO TEMPLI ORIENTIS.

ORDO TEMPLI ORIENTIS (O.T.O.)

International occultist, neo-pagan group founded in Germany in 1895 by Karl Kellner. In 1912 Aleister Crowley (1875–1947) became the head of its British branch. The group exists in two wings, one following Crowley and the other the original German tradition. There have been branches of both wings in the United States and in Western Europe.

(ORIGINAL) CHURCH OF GOD, INC.

PENTECOSTAL group founded in 1917 by Joseph L. Scott following a schism in THE CHURCH OF GOD (CLEVELAND, TENNESSEE). Tithing is practiced.

ORIGINAL PENTECOSTAL CHURCH OF GOD

PENTECOSTAL group noted for the occasional handling of snakes by members, popularly known as "snake handlers," outside services. It was founded in the early 20th century in rural Kentucky.

See also CHURCH OF ALL NATIONS; DOLLEY POND CHURCH OF GOD WITH SIGNS FOLLOWING

Moses Orimolade, see CHERUBIM

AND SERAPHIM (ETERNAL ORDER OF)

ORTHODOX PRESBYTERIAN CHURCH

Originally known as the Presbyterian Church in America, this Fundamentalist group was founded by J. Gresham Machen in 1937 in dissent from the Presbyterian Church in the U.S.A.

See also BIBLE PRESBYTERIAN CHURCH; FUNDAMENTALISM; WESTMINSTER BIBLICAL FELLOWSHIP

Juan Carlos Ortiz, see BODY OF CHRIST

S.B.J. Oschoffa, see CELESTIAL CHURCH OF CHRIST

J.O. Oshitelu, see ALADURA

OSIRIAN TEMPLE ASSEMBLY

Occultist group based in New Jersey that claims to follow ancient Egyptian teachings and temple services.

Kanichi Otsuka, see SHINREIKYO

A. Stuart Otto, see CHURCH OF THE TRINITY (INVISIBLE MINISTRY)

OUR LADY OF THE ROSES

Also known as the Virgin of Bayside Shrine, or the Mary Help of Mothers Shrine, this traditionalist Roman Catholic group was founded by Veronica Lueken (1923–) in New York City in 1970. The founder claims to have had visions since 1967, and to have received regular messages from the Holy Virgin, first at home in 1970, and later during apparitions near the Vatican Pavilion at the site of the 1964 World's Fair in Flushing Meadow. The messages call for a return to pre-Vatican II church rituals and rules and contain denunciations of modern "permissiveness," homosexuality, and "Satanic" groups involved in cannibalistic child sacrifice. In addition, they report on the alleged murder of Pope John Paul I and announce an imminent apocalypse, the destruction of the world monetary system, and the deaths of world leaders. Lueken's followers testify to numerous miracles at the site, referred to as "the Lourdes of America."

P.D. Ouspensky, see COOMBE SPRINGS; GURDJIEFF GROUPS

P

PACIFIC INSTITUTE OF SCIENCE AND HUMANITIES

Gurdjieff group founded by George and Mary Cornelius around 1975 and based in Oregon.

See also GURDJIEFF GROUPS

PADANARAM

Christian commune founded in 1966 in Indiana by Daniel Wright, who had a divine revelation of the spot where the settlement was to be founded. The group aims at reviving "the primitive lifestyle in the Book of Acts" of the New Testament. Its economic operations have been extremely successful.

Paik Moon Kim, see ISRAEL SOODO WON

Ian Paisley, see FREE PRESBYTERIAN CHURCH

Pak Subuh, see SUBUD

PALIAU CHURCH

Syncretistic movement (CARGO CULT) on Manus, of the Great Admiralty Islands in Melanesia, started by the prophet Paliau, a former policeman, in 1946. In 1954 it developed into a political movement and a Christian church. The doctrine was based on messianic Christianity and called for a rejection of polygamy and native rituals. Moreover, Paliau criticized the "cargo" movements, as well as traditional rank, clan, and tribe divisions and advocated economic planning and cooperation. The group, the first native church in Melanesia, grew out of the Roman Catholic Church and later developed close relations with Protestant churches, advocating national unity and modern agriculture.

See also THE NOISE

Source:

Mead, M. *New Lives for Old: Cultural Transformation, Manus, 1928–1953.* New York: William Morrow, 1956.

PALMARIAN CATHOLIC CHURCH

Sometimes known as the Holy Palmarian Church, this international Roman Catholic traditionalist group was founded in 1968 in Palmar de Troya, Spain, by Ferdinand Clemente Dominguez y Gomez (1946–   ), who failed in his aim to become a Catholic priest. The founder claimed many apocalyptic visions and predictions resulting from contacts with the Virgin Mary. These included predictions of a Communist takeover in Spain and of major schisms in the Roman Catholic Church. Members consider Francisco Franco, the dictator of Spain who died in 1975, to be a saint. They reject the authority of the Roman Catholic Church while claiming most of its traditions. In 1976 Dominguez and his followers were excommunicated from the Roman Catholic Church, and in 1978 he declared himself to be Pope Gregory XVII. The group operates the Order of the Holy Visage. It has collaborated with the RENOVATED CHURCH OF CHRIST and with the APOSTLES OF INFINITE LOVE.

PANACEA SOCIETY

Christian millenarian group based in Bedford, England, founded by Helen Exeter in 1916, inspired by the teachings of a long series of British visionaries including John Wroe, Joanna Southcott, and the SOUTH-

Generalissimo Francisco Franco of Spain, considered a saint by members of the Palmerian Catholic Church. (see p. 221)

COTTITES, since the early 19th century. Members believed that a sealed box left by Joanna Southcott when she died in 1814 contained writings of immense importance to Great Britain. They demanded that twenty-four bishops of the Church of England meet and open the box. The Society also expected a period of divine visitation and healing between 1923 and 1927. In 1924 it started offering water "of saving and healing virtue." The group expected the end of the "Adamic Age" in the year 2000 or even sooner. Those who survive the present troubles will live in the New Age, a perfect life in a perfect world. Those who partake of the saving water before the coming of the New Age will be healed and suffer less at their death.

Source:
Balleine, G.R. *Past Finding Out: The Tragic Story of Joanna Southcott and Her Successors.* New York: Macmillan, 1956.

PAN AFRICAN ORTHODOX CHRISTIAN CHURCH

Formerly known as the Shrine of the Black Madonna, this Christian African-American nationalist group was founded by Albert B. Cleage (who changed his name to Jaramogi Abebe Agyeman) in Detroit, Michigan, in the 1960s. The group's doctrine claims that events described in the Bible and biblical figures had to do with black history. The ancient Israelites were black, and all major religions, including Islam, Buddhism, and Christianity, were developed by black people. Whites have created only paganism. Christianity, in its black version, is designed to liberate black people in the United States.

PANSOPHIC INSTITUTE

Group devoted to spreading the ideas of Tibetan Buddhism, founded in 1973 by Simon Grimes in Reno, Nevada. It has operated the School of Universal Wisdom.

Paramananda, see ANANDA ASHRAMA

Paranjothi, see TEMPLE OF UNIVERSAL PEACE

Paras Rajneesh Meditation, see RAJNEESH FOUNDATION INTERNATIONAL

Charles Parham, see APOSTOLIC FAITH CHURCH (KANSAS)

Parishad, see VISHWA HINDU PARISHAD

Carl and Sandra Parks, see VOICE OF ELIJAH, INC.

PASTORAL BIBLE INSTITUTE (PBI)

International Adventist group founded in the early 1920s in the United States. Following the death of Charles Taze Russell in 1916, a dispute arose about his successor in the Watch Tower Tract and Bible Society. Joseph R. Rutherford was opposed by R.H. Hirsh, I.F. Hoskins, A.I. Ritchie, and J.D. Wright. When Rutherford gained the leadership position in 1918, his opponents left and started the PBI. Doctrinally, the group follows the original writings of Russell, which have been superseded by Rutherford's writings in the JEHOVAH'S WITNESSES movement.

PATHFINDER CHURCH

Christian Identity church founded by Karl

Schott in Spokane, Washington, in the 1980s.
See also IDENTITY MOVEMENT

PATHWORK, THE

Occultist group started in 1957 by Eva Broch (also known as Eva Pierrakos, ?–1979) in New York State. The group's teachings, known as the Guide Lectures, are claimed to have been delivered to Eva Pierrakos by "a spirit being of Light known as the Guide" through "the spiritual channel" between 1957 and 1979. The group offers the public "channelled spiritual teachings which outline a powerful and expansive process for observing and transforming our shadow side, while simultaneously cultivating our divinity." This belief system "is inspired by attunement to the Living Force (Inner Godself, Christ Consciousness) within each of us." In addition, meditation and faith healing are practiced. The group has operated the Institute for Core Energetics in New York City, the Phoenicia Pathwork Center in New York State, and the Sevenoaks community in Virginia. Its branches have been active around the United States.

George Patterson, see GEORGIAN CHURCH

PAUL BRUNTON PHILOSOPHIC FOUNDATION

Syncretistic group based in New York State, founded in the 1970s to ". . . seek a practical philosophy that will embrace but not merge the distinctive contributions of each system of thought in order to create a living synthesis of timeless truths." It distributes the teachings of Paul Brunton (1898–1981).

Earl P. Paulk, Jr., see GOSPEL HARVESTERS EVANGELISTIC ASSOCIATION

Norman Paulsen, see THE BUILDERS

Jerome Peartree, see TEMPLE OF THE ETERNAL LIGHT

James M. Peebles, see NATIONAL SPIRITUALIST ASSOCIATION OF CHURCHES

Mary Pendergast, see UNIVERSITY OF METAPHYSICS

PENTECOSTAL

Term denoting Christian groups that stress personal religious experience rather than doctrine and involve glossolalia or "speaking in tongues," "faith healing," and "prophecy." The term is used interchangeably with Charismatic. The term Classical Pentecostals refers to Christians who are followers of officially Pentecostal groups that were started in the early 20th century. The term Neo-Pentecostal refers to Christians committed to Charismatic practices while retaining membership in mainstream Protestant groups. Catholic Pentecostals are those who follow Charismatic practices while keeping membership in the Roman Catholic Church.

Modern Pentecostalism is said to have started in the winter of 1900–1901 in the Bethel Bible College in Topeka, Kansas, and then in the Azusa Street Mission in Los Angeles in 1906.
See also APOSTOLIC FAITH CHURCH (KANSAS); CATHOLIC CHARISMATIC RENEWAL

Sources:
Anderson, R.M. *Vision of the Disinherited:*

The Making of American Pentecostalism. New York: Oxford University Press, 1979.

Bradfield, C.D. *Neo-Pentecostalism: A Sociological Assessment*. Washington, DC: University Press of America, 1979.

Goodman, F.D. *Speaking in Tongues, A Cross-Cultural Study of Glossolalia*. Chicago: University of Chicago Press, 1972.

Hollenweger, W.J. *The Pentecostals*. London: SCM Press, 1972.

Kelsey, M.T. *Tongue Speaking*. Garden City, NY: Doubleday, 1968.

Kildahl, J.P. *The Psychology of Speaking in Tongues*. New York: Harper & Row, 1972.

Sneck, W.J. *Charismatic Spiritual Gifts*. Washington, DC: University Press of America, 1981.

PENTECOSTAL ASSEMBLIES OF THE WORLD

African-American PENTECOSTAL group based in Indianapolis, founded by G.T. Haywood in 1919. It was originally an integrated church, but most of its white members left in 1924 to found the PENTECOSTAL CHURCH, INC. A strict dress and conduct code is emphasized, and healing is practiced.

See also APOSTOLIC CHURCH OF JESUS CHRIST

PENTECOSTAL CHURCH OF GOD OF AMERICA

First known as the Pentecostal Assemblies of the U.S.A., this PENTECOSTAL group was started in 1919 by John C. Sinclair and George Brinkman. The current name was adopted in 1979. It is based in Joplin, Missouri.

PENTECOSTAL CHURCH OF ZION

PENTECOSTAL group operating in the Midwest, founded by Luther S. Howard in 1954. Howard was a minister of the Holy Bible Mission, which was dissolved around 1950 following the death of its founder. Some of its former ministers followed Howard. The group keeps many Old Testament commandments, including the avoidance of unclean meats, and believes in continuing revelation.

PENTECOSTAL EVANGELICAL CHURCH

U.S. PENTECOSTAL group founded in 1936. It is identical in doctrine and practices to the PENTECOSTAL CHURCH OF GOD OF AMERICA.

PENTECOSTAL FIRE-BAPTIZED HOLINESS CHURCH

U.S. PENTECOSTAL group formed in 1918 as a result of a schism in the Pentecostal Holiness Church. Doctrine is stricter, compared to the parent body, in regard to attire and entertainment. No jewelry for women nor neckties for men are allowed, nor is attendance at fairs or theaters. Disputes over dress standards led to a further schism and the founding of EMMANUEL HOLINESS CHURCH.

James Penton, see CHRISTIAN FELLOWSHIP INTERNATIONAL

PEOPLE OF PRAISE (POP)

Charismatic ecumenical group growing out of the CATHOLIC CHARISMATIC RENEWAL movement, founded in 1971 in South Bend, Indiana, by Paul Decelles and Kevin Ranaghan. It has operated twenty-five branches in North America and the Caribbean.

PEOPLE OF THE LIVING GOD

Christian PENTECOSTAL commune based in Tennessee, founded in 1932 by Harry Miller. Members practice economic equality and follow a simple life-style, saving most of their income for missionary work. The doctrine attacks all established churches as sectarian.

PEOPLE'S CHRISTIAN CHURCH

Church founded in 1916 in New York City by Elmer E. Franke (1861–1946) as an offshoot of the SEVENTH-DAY ADVENTISTS. Its beliefs resemble closely those of the SDA but deny the status of Ellen G. White as prophetess.

PEOPLE SEARCHING INSIDE (PSI)

Also known as the Kundalini Research Institute, this international Hindu-oriented group was founded in 1976 in Canada by Joseph F. Dippong, a follower of Gopi Krishna (1903–1984). Kundalini, in Hindu lore, means sexual energy supposedly localized in the base of the spine. Kundalini yoga attempts to release this energy for use in the human brain. PSI branches have operated in Canada and Britain.
See also KUNDALINI RESEARCH FOUNDATION

PEOPLE'S TEMPLE CHRISTIAN (DISCIPLES) CHURCH

Popularly known as the People's Temple, this Christian group was one of the most notorious religious movements of recent history, becoming the subject of worldwide horror when more than 900 of its members committed suicide. Founded in 1956 in Indiana as the Community National Church by Jim Jones (1931–1978), it started as a typical lower-class congregation. Jones practiced faith healing, and his followers attributed various miracles to him. He became an ordained minister of the DISCIPLES OF CHRIST in 1965 and then moved to San Francisco with 150 followers. Most members were poor African-Americans, but Jones was able to establish ties with political leaders in the area. Throughout its existence there, People's Temple was actually a mainline Protestant congregation, belonging to the Christian Church (Disciples of Christ).

In 1974 the group moved to Guyana, South America. In November 1978, 912 members died in a mass suicide on orders from Jones, who was among them. It should be noted that most of the members who died with Jones were African-American females.

Sources:
Kilduff, M., and Javers, R. *The Suicide Cult.* New York: Bantam, 1978.

Klineman, G., Butler, S., and Conn, D. *The Cult That Died: The Tragedy of Jim Jones and the People's Temple.* New York: Putnam, 1980.

Levi, K. *Violence and Religious Commitment: Implications of Jim Jones's People's Temple Movement.* London: Pennsylvania State University Press, 1982.

Naipaul, S. *Journey to Nowhere: A New World Tragedy.* New York: Simon & Schuster, 1981.

Juanita Garcia Peraga, see MITA MOVEMENT

Members of Jim Jones's People's Temple lie dead in Jonestown, Guyana, after their leader joined them in a mass suicide.

Harold M. Percival, see WORD FOUN-DATION

PERFECT LIBERTY KYODAN (P L KYODAN)

Japanese Shinto-inspired new religion founded in 1946 by Tokuchika Miki. It grew out of the Hitonomichi (Way of Mankind) branch of the SHINTO-TOKUMITSU-KYO movement, which was founded in 1912 by Tokumitsu Kanada (1863–1924). Hitonomichi was suppressed by the government in 1937 and was revived as P L KYODAN. The English name was adopted by the founder. The group is committed to monotheism, faith healing, and expectations of an upcoming total salvation.

Branches have operated on the West Coast since 1960.

Sources:

Bach, M. *The Power of Perfect Liberty.* Englewood Cliffs, NJ: Prentice-Hall, 1971.

Ellwood, R.S. *The Eagle and the Rising Sun.* Philadelphia: Westminster, 1974.

Russell Perkins, see SANT BANI ASHRAM

Troy D. Perry, see UNIVERSAL FELLOW-SHIP OF METROPOLITAN COMMUNITY CHURCHES

Rudolph H. Pestalozzi, see SOLAR CROSS FELLOWSHIP

Duane Peterson, see INTERNATIONAL CHRISTIAN MINISTRIES

PETITE ÉGLISE (VENDEENNE)

French Catholic group founded in 1801 by thirty-eight bishops who rejected the Concordat of July 15, 1801, reached by the Roman Catholic Church under Pope Pius VII and Napoleon's government. According to the agreement, known as "le concordat de l'an IX," the head of the secular government appointed French bishops, who then took an oath of loyalty to the government.

Phat Giao Hoa Hao, see HOA HAO

PHILIPPINE INDEPENDENT CHURCH (PIC)

Known also as the Aglipayan Church, and as the Iglesia Filipina Independiente, this schismatic Catholic movement operating in the Philippines and among Filipino communities overseas was started in 1890 and officially founded in 1902 by Isabelo de los Reyes, Sr. (1864–1938) and Gregorio Aglipay (1860–1940). Gregorio Aglipay was a Roman Catholic priest who initiated a secession from the Church with 45 percent of members. Since 1948 it has had close relations with the Protestant Episcopal Church, which consecrates its bishops. The PIC developed as part of the struggle for Filipino independence from Spanish and United States colonialism. It has emphasized liturgy in the vernacular and has canonized Filipino nationalist heroes. Clergy are allowed to marry. Many schisms in the PIC over the years have led to an estimated 120 new Philippine independent churches.

Magdalen Mabel Phillips, see ALPHA AND OMEGA PENTECOSTAL CHURCH OF GOD OF AMERICA, INC.

W.T. Phillips, see APOSTOLIC OVERCOMING HOLY CHURCH OF GOD

PHILOSOPHICAL RESEARCH SOCIETY

U.S. Theosophical-Rosicrucian group founded by Manly Palmer Hall (1901–) in 1934 and devoted to the teaching of all Western occult traditions. Hall's system is a eclectic combination of THEOSOPHY with other occult traditions.
See also ROSICRUCIANS

Eva Pierrakos, see PATHWORK

PILLAR OF FIRE

Conservative Protestant group, Fundamentalist and PENTECOSTAL, founded in 1901 in Denver, Colorado, as the Pentecostal Union by Alma White (1862–1946). It adopted the current name in 1917. In the 1920s the group supported the Ku Klux Klan, but throughout its existence it has supported women's rights. Missions have been operated in Europe, Asia, and Africa.

P L Kyodan, see PERFECT LIBERTY KYODAN

PLYMOUTH BRETHREN

Informally known as the Church of God, this Protestant millenarian movement was founded by John Nelson Darby (1800–1882) in 1830 in Plymouth, England. Darby

Members of the international faction of the Plymouth Brethren, who call themselves the Exclusive Brethren, arrive for a mass meeting in Surrey, England.

was a curate in the Episcopalian Church of Ireland until 1827, when he felt obliged to leave it. In Dublin he had followers who became known as Brethren. Darby declared that the essence of Christianity was the expectation of Christ's imminent return. He set himself the task of reformulating the one true church of Jesus Christ of New Testament tradition.

The Brethren are strongly opposed to any organization along church or denominational lines. They accept the Bible as divinely inspired, absolutely and completely. Teachings are influenced by Calvinism. There is no formal clergy. The belief in seven dispensations, or ages (Innocence, Conscience, Government, Promise, Law, Grace, and the Personal Reign of Christ) is basic.

The Plymouth Brethren have been divided into several small factions as the result of many schisms since the mid-19th century.

Sources:

Ehlert, A.D. *A Bibliographic History of Dispensationalism*. Grand Rapids, MI: Baker Book House, 1965.

Noel, N. *A History of the Brethren*. Denver: William F. Knapp, 1936.

PLYMOUTH BRETHREN (EXCLUSIVE: BOOTH—CONTINENTAL)

International faction of the PLYMOUTH BRETHREN movement, characterized by strict Fundamentalism, Dispensationalism, and an ascetic life-style.

P'NAI OR RELIGIOUS FELLOWSHIP

Originally known as B'NAI OR, this Jewish group was started in the 1960s in Philadelphia by Zalman Schachter-Shalomi. Its doctrine combines Jewish beliefs and practices with Hindu-style meditation, pacifism, and social concerns. The original name, which means "Sons of Light," was dropped because of its masculine gender. P'nai Or branches have operated in the United States and Europe.

POLISH NATIONAL CATHOLIC CHURCH

Catholic group in North America that had its beginnings in March 1897. It was officially formed in 1904 in Scranton, Pennsylvania, with Francis Hodur as founder and leader. It represents a movement for cultural autonomy among Polish immigrants in the United States, who resented being led by non-Polish priests. The dissent took the form of aligning with the OLD CATHOLIC movement, which rejects the authority of Rome while remaining loyal to Catholic liturgy and dogma. This is one of the few U.S. churches connected with the Old Catholic movement in Europe.

Elijah Poole, see NATION OF ISLAM

POSITIVE THINKING MINISTRY

Occultist group based in New York City, founded in the early 1980s by Kenneth G. Dickkerson. Practices include "Kirlian photography," psychic readings, and past-life revelations.

Harrison W. Poteat, see CHURCH OF GOD, THE HOUSE OF PRAYER

Pierre Poulain, see ÉGLISE DE LA SAINTE FAMILLE

POWER OF JESUS AROUND THE WORLD CHURCH

African independent PENTECOSTAL group started among the Luo of Kenya in 1955.

Swami Prabhavananda, see VEDANTA SOCIETY

A.C. Bhaktivedanta Prabhupada, see INTERNATIONAL SOCIETY FOR KRISHNA CONSCIOUSNESS

Praise the Lord (PTL), see NEW COVENANT CHURCH

Prajapita Brahma, see BRAHMA KUMARIS (RAJA YOGA)

Preaching Tabernacle, see CHONDOKWON

PREMA DHARMASALA AND FELLOWSHIP ASSOCIATION; PREMA WORLD COMMUNITY

Also known as World Community, this U.S. syncretistic communal group was founded in 1970 by Sri Vasudevadas, who combined the teachings of the Sufi Orders with those of Paramahansa Yogananda, founder of the SELF-REALIZATION FELLOWSHIP. The group, based near Virginia Beach, Virginia, also operates the Temple of Cosmic Religion.
See also SUFI ORDER IN THE WEST

Premananda, see SELF-REVELATION CHURCH OF ABSOLUTE MONISM

PRIMITIVE ADVENT CHRISTIAN CHURCH

Adventist group started in West Virginia as

a result of a schism in the ADVENT CHRISTIAN CHURCH.
See also ADVENTISTS

PRIMITIVE CHURCH OF CHRIST, SCIENTIST

Independent CHRISTIAN SCIENCE group founded by Leon Greenbaum in St. Louis, Missouri, following the death of Mary Baker Eddy in 1910.

Derek Prince, see CHRISTIAN GROWTH MINISTRIES

Mark and Irene Probert, see INNER CIRCLE KETHRA E'DA FOUNDATION

THE PROCESS, OR THE CHURCH OF THE FINAL JUDGMENT

Known officially as The Church of the Final Judgment and popularly as The Process, this occultist-Christian group was founded in 1963 in London by two members of SCIENTOLOGY, Robert Moore, also known as Robert de Grimston, and Mary Anne de Grimston. It was first known as Compulsions Analysis, or "The Family." By 1966 it had become The Process, designed to bring about unlimited personal development. Then a group of two dozen members moved to Mexico, turning to a more religious and less psychotherapeutic direction, drawing on the Rosicrucian tradition. Satan appeared in the doctrine in 1967, and it then developed a pantheon of four gods: Lucifer, Jehovah, Christ, and Satan. Doctrine stated that the world would end around the year 2000 but that members would be saved. Then the leader, Robert de Grimston, was expelled, and with him three of the four gods of the pantheon; only Jehovah was left. By 1972 the group was based in Toronto, Canada. In 1973 the group renamed itself The Foundation Faith; it later moved to New York City, and then to Arizona.
See also FOUNDATION FAITH OF GOD

Sources:
Bainbridge, W.S. *Satan's Power: Ethnography of a Deviant Psychotherapy Cult.* Berkeley: University of California Press, 1978.
Evans, C. *Cults of Unreason.* London: Harrap, 1973.

PROGRESSIVE JUDAISM

In Great Britain, a subgroup of REFORM JUDAISM. The term "progressive" is sometimes used in other countries, especially in Europe, to denote Reform Judaism.
See also LIBERAL JUDAISM

Elizabeth Clare Prophet, Mark Prophet, see SUMMIT LIGHTHOUSE

Prophet Cherry, see CHURCH OF GOD (BLACK JEWS)

Prophet Jones, see CHURCH OF UNIVERSAL TRIUMPH/THE DOMINION OF GOD

PROSPEROS, THE

Gurdjieff group founded by Thane Walker and Phez Khalil in Florida in 1956. It refers to itself as a Fourth Way School, based on a master-disciple relationship leading to "personal liberation."
See also GURDJIEFF GROUPS

Proutist International, see ANANDA MARGA

Prout Universal, see ANANDA MARGA

PROVIDENCE INDUSTRIAL MISSION

Independent African Christian movement founded by John Chilembwe in 1898 in Malawi (then Nyasaland). The founder was educated in the United States, became a JEHOVAH'S WITNESSES preacher, and then established the church as part of a move for independence from British rule. He died leading a rebellion in 1915. His main church was destroyed and the movement banned by the British, but it was revived in 1925. Since then it has undergone a schism but still exists in Malawi.

Source:

Shepperson, G., and Price, T. *Independent African: John Chilembwe and the Origins, Setting and Significance of the Nyasaland Native Rising of 1915.* Edinburgh: Edinburgh University Press, 1958.

Karl Pruter, see CHRIST CATHOLIC CHURCH (DIOCESE OF BOSTON)

W. Graham Pulkingham, see CHURCH OF THE REDEEMER COMMUNITY

PURGATORIAL SOCIETY, THE

Millenarian group started in New York in 1931 by Luci Mayer Barrow, who predicted the imminent coming of a new world order.

Benjamin and Mary Purnell, see HOUSE OF DAVID

Gottfried de Purucker, see UNIVERSAL BROTHERHOOD AND THEOSOPHICAL SOCIETY

Eldon D. Purvis, see NEW BEGINNINGS

Anne and Herbert Puryear, see LOGOS WORLD UNIVERSITY CHURCH

Q

Quadianis, see AHMADIYYA MOVE-MENT

Phineas P. Quimby, see NEW THOUGHT

QUIMBY CENTER

NEW THOUGHT group founded by Neva Dell Hunter (?–1978) in 1966 in Alamagordo, New Mexico. Doctrine is Hindu-inspired and includes belief in reincarnation. Practices include "spiritual healing" through "aura balancing," "karmic life readings," and "psychic counseling."

R

Swami Radha (Sylvia Hellman), see YASODHARA ASHRAM SOCIETY

RADHASOAMI SATSANG

Sikh revival group founded in 1861 by Tulsi Ram, better known as Siva Dayal Saheb or Soamiji Maharaj (1818–1878), in Agra, India. He left behind two books, one in prose and the other in poetry, both titled *Sar Bachan*. After his death came a succession of gurus and some disputes.

The movement claims to be a continuation of the Sant Mat tradition of northern India and appears to combine Hindu and Sikh elements. The holy name Radha Soami means "the Supreme Being"; it is also the name of the founder, who was the perfect incarnation of God. The guru, known as the Sant Satguru, occupies a central position in the doctrine. He is the source of all revelation and salvation and teaches secret meditation techniques to disciples. The pictures of gurus are worshiped. Membership is kept secret and may overlap with membership in other religious faiths. All religions are held to be equally true, but the group's faith is supreme.

Since the 19th century the movement has developed into independent branches including the small Radhasoami Satsang Soamibagh and Radhasoami Satsang Dayalbagh and the large RADHASOAMI SATSANG BEAS. In turn, the groups have inspired new movements. Branches of all the groups can be found in Western Europe and the United States.

See also RUHANI SATSANG

Source:
Farquhar, J.N. *Modern Religious Movements In India*. New York: Macmillan, 1919.

RADHASOAMI SATSANG BEAS

The largest and most influential of the RADHASOAMI SATSANG branches. Its leader, Baba Sawan Singh (1858–1948), was the master of both Charan Singh, who succeeded him, and Kirpal Singh, who started his own movement. He developed contacts with North American followers as early as 1911. The group's center is in Beas, Punjab, India. Western branches have operated in Europe and North America.

See also RUHANI SATSANG; SANT BANI ASHRAM; SAWAN KIRPAL RUHANI MISSION

RAËLIANS

Originally known as the Mouvement pour l'Accueil des Elohim Créateurs de l'Humanité (Madech), this international occultist group was founded in the 1970s in France by Claude Vorilhon (1946–), known to group members as Raël. The founder has claimed contacts with extraterrestrials who relayed messages about great danger to humankind that might be averted by group activities. The contacts include Sensual Meditation and "telepathic communication" with outer space. The group's doctrine calls for establishment of a "Geniocracy" on earth led by the superior white race. It operates the Mouvement pour la Géniocratie Mondiale, based in Geneva. Members are expected to tithe and deed their property to the group.

RAINBOW FAMILY OF LIVING LIGHT

U.S. pantheistic-occultist communal move-

Annual assembly of the Rainbow Family of Living Light, occultist communal movement that regards marijuana as sacramental.

ment founded by Barry Adams in the late 1960s. Its doctrine combines Christian ideas with pantheism, THEOSOPHY, and Hindu ideas. There are no formal rituals, but meditation and chanting are practiced. Marijuana is regarded as sacramental.

Raja Yoga, see BRAHMA KUMARIS

RAJNEESH FOUNDATION INTERNATIONAL (RFI)

Now known as Osho Meditation, initially known as Paras Rajneesh Meditation, and also known by the popular nicknames of the Orange people, Neo-Sannyasin Movement, Sannyasins, and Rajneesh Meditation, this Westernized Hindu group is the reflection and the creature of its founder. Bhagwan (meaning "god" or "The Blessed One") Shree Rajneesh was born on December 11, 1931, as Chandra Mohan in a small town in central India, of Jain background. Raj or Rajneesh was his nickname. He experienced "enlightenment" on March 21, 1953, while sitting under a maulshree tree. Between 1957 and 1967 he taught at the Raipur Sanskrit College and at the University of Jabalpur. In 1967 he resigned his academic position to devote his life to the "spiritual regeneration of humanity." In 1970 he started the Neo-Sannyas International Movement. In 1971 he took the name Bhagwan Shree Rajneesh and revealed the story of his 1953 "enlightenment" and of his incarnation as a great sage 700 years earlier. By 1972 he had about 50 Western followers, who donned ochre robes, changed their names, and carried his picture with them at all times. In 1974 the Shree Rajneesh Ashram and the Rajneesh Foundation were established in Poona, about 100 miles southeast of Bombay, by Rajneesh and seven disciples. Rajneesh Meditation Centers were established in the West during the 1970s. In 1979 the Ashram had about 200 residents, most of them foreigners. By the end of 1980 it had 1,500 residents and was prosperous and self-sufficient. Tensions with the surrounding Indian com-munity led to a decision to move.

In 1981 Rajneesh took a vow of silence and moved to the United States. He first settled in New Jersey; then, with 280 of his followers, he moved to Antelope, Oregon, founding the Rajneesh Neo-Sannyas International Commune, or Rajneeshpuram. By that time the movement had 200 branches worldwide. The development of the Oregon commune, which housed hundreds of active followers and covered 10,000 acres, led to increasing friction with its environment. In Europe the RFI opened communes, business corporations, discotheques, and restaurants, which enjoyed success in their initial stage (1981–1983) but had collapsed by 1986.

On October 27, 1985, Rajneesh was arrested by U.S. government agents and accused of several offenses, mainly immigration fraud. On November 14, 1985, Rajneesh confessed to two felonies, paid a fine of $400,000 in cash, and left the United States forever. Several of his associates pleaded guilty to attempted murder by poisoning. By January 1986 the commune was empty.

Several attempts by Rajneesh to enter countries in Europe failed as he became an international *persona non grata*, and he returned to India. In late 1989 he changed his name to Osho, and in January 1990 he died.

The movement's doctrine reflected its

Bhagwan Shree Rajneesh in custody on charges of immigration fraud. After confessing and paying a fine, he left the United States in 1985.

founder's personality and leadership. All initiates wore a necklace with a picture of Rajneesh at all times. Rajneeshism was apparently an unsystematic combination of "religious attitudes and methods for work on the self, eastern and western—from Krishna to Gurdieff, from Pantajali to Wilhelm Reich." At his ashram, various Western psychotherapy workshops were offered. The Rajneesh doctrine included belief in reincarnation and *karma* (destiny determined by behavior in past lives). Thus, beggars should not be helped because they are working out their past sins. A stated belief of Rajneesh and his followers was an expected cataclysm that would end life on earth. Only Rajneesh followers might survive, and even that was not certain. In 1983 Rajneesh predicted an earthquake that would devastate much of the West Coast. In 1984 he announced that AIDS was the scourge predicted by Nostradamus and that billions would die of it within the next decade. In 1985 RFI publications predicted floods, earthquakes, and nuclear war within the next decade.

Sources:

Belfrage, S. *Flowers of Emptiness*. New York: Dial, 1981.

Mangalwadi, V. *The World of Gurus*. New Delhi: Vikas Publishing House, 1977.

Mehta, G. *Karma Cola*. New York: Simon & Schuster, 1979.

Menen, A. *The Mystics*. New York: Dial Press, 1974.

Milne, H. *Bhagwan: The God That Failed*. New York: St. Martin's Press, 1988.

RAJ-YOGA MATH AND RETREAT

Hindu monastic group based in the State of Washington. Founded by Satchakrananda in the 1960s, it is devoted to the practice of various yoga techniques.

Rama (Frederick Lenz), see RAMA SEMINARS

Swami Rama, see HIMALAYAN INTERNATIONAL INSTITUTE OF YOGA SCIENCE AND PHILOSOPHY

RAMAKRISHNA MATH AND MISSION

Also known as the Ramakrishna Movement, this Hindu revival group is devoted to spreading the teachings of Sri Ramakrishna Paramahamsa (1834–1886), born Gadadhar Chatterji to poor Brahmin parents in the village of Karmarpukar in Bengal, India. Its namesake spent his life studying Christianity and Islam, in addition to being a devout Hindu, in an attempt to develop a syncretistic system. He is reported to have had visions of Hindu gods as well as of Muhammad and Jesus Christ. He was devoted to the goddess Kali, and then to Rama and Krishna, and so in 1864 adopted the name Ramakrishna. In 1874 he started to explore Christianity and had visions of Jesus Christ. During the last six years of his life, Ramakrishna formed a group of followers, and among them was Vivekananda, who was entrusted with the task of continuing the master's work.

The movement's actual founder, and best-known figure in addition to Ramakrishna himself, was Vivekananda (1863–1902), born Narendranath Datta to a high-class Calcutta family. Vivekananda was first a follower of BRAHMA SAMAJ, but then became a disciple of Ramakrishna. After Ramakrishna's death, Vivekananda renounced secular life and devoted himself to

A depiction of the Hindu deity Rama, worshiped as the seventh incarnation of Vishnu. This deity is claimed by various religious sects.

the master's teachings. In 1893 he traveled to the Parliament of Religions, held together with the World's Fair in Chicago. He became the focus of much publicity and interest and later made lecture tours in the U.S. and Great Britain. This was the beginning of the movement's overseas missionary work. Vivekanda again traveled to the U.S. and Europe in 1899–1900 and took part in the Congress of Religions in Paris in 1900. His best-known Western convert was Nivedita (Margaret E. Noble, 1867–1911), a British woman, converted in 1896, who devoted her postconversion life to charity and writing. She founded the Nivedita Girls' School, became Vivekananda's biographer, and edited his published teachings.

The Ramakrishna Mission was formally started by Vivekananda in 1897, and both the Math (monastery) and the Mission have been based since then in Belur, India.

The movement's doctrine expresses the basic unity of all religions, tolerance toward different faiths and practices, and the value of the meditative life. Practices include monastic living and selfless service to the poor and sick. A mission, which is devoted to social service, is attached to every Math.

Groups all over the world claim to be following the teachings of Sri Ramakrishna. His teachings have also influenced many Western writers and artists, such as Romain Rolland (1866–1944).

See also ANANDA ASHRAMA; VEDANTA SOCIETY

Sources:

Bassuk, D.E. *Incarnation in Hinduism and Christianity: The Myth of the Godman.* Atlantic Highlands, NJ: Humanities Press, 1986.

Isherwood, C. *Ramakrishna and His Disciples.* New York: Simon & Schuster, 1965.

RAMAKRISHNA VEDANTA CENTRE

British branch of the international VEDANTA SOCIETY, founded in London in 1948.

RAMAKRISHNA VEDANTA SOCIETY

Hindu group founded in Boston in 1926 by Swami Akhilananda (1894–1962), who served as its leader until his death. The Society is dedicated to spreading the Hindu message in the United States.

RAMAKARISHNA–VIVEKANANDA CENTER

New York City branch of the VEDANTA SOCIETY, founded in 1933.

RAMANA MAHARSHI

Ramana Maharshi (1879–1950) was a Hindu holy man who renounced the world at age seventeen and moved to the hill Arunachala. Four years later he moved into a nearby Virupaska Deva cave, where he lived for sixteen years. By 1903 Ramana had become known as Maharshi, and his fame spread throughout India and the West. He believed in the value of silence, and practiced it, granting only brief interviews to his disciples. He preached a search for perfection and self-knowledge. Though Ramana Maharshi never started a movement, his followers carry on activities devoted to the propagation of his teachings, which are represented by the following: "Divine Grace is essential for realization. It leads one to God-realization, but such Grace is vouchsafed only to him who is a true devotee or a yogin, who has striven hard on the path toward freedom."

See also ARUNACHALA ASHRAMA BHAGAVAN SRI RAMANA MAHARSHI CENTER, INC.

RAMA SEMINARS

Formerly known as Lakshmi Meditation, this meditation group is based in Malibu, California. Founded in 1979 by Rama (formerly Frederick Lenz), it promotes Eastern meditation techniques and traditions. Rama was a disciple of SRI CHIMNOY; he founded his own group after realizing that he was "one of the twelve truly enlightened beings on the planet."

Ram Dass (Baba), see HANUMAN FOUNDATION; SEVA FOUNDATION

Ram Mohan Roy, see BRAHMA SAMAJ

Ram Singh, see NAMDHARI

Kevin Ranaghan, see PEOPLE OF PRAISE (POP)

Pascal Beverly Randolph, see FRATERNITAS ROSAE CRUCIS

Michael Rapunzel, see RENAISSANCE CHURCH-COMMUNITY

RASHTRIYA SWAYAMASEVAK SANGH (RSS)

Hindu revitalization movement founded in 1925 by Kashavrao Baliram Hedgewar (1889–1940). One of the main conservative Hindu groups, it operates the Jana Sangh political party.

Source:
Baxter, C. *The Jana Sangh: A Biography of an Indian Political Party.* Philadelphia: University of Pennsylvania, 1969.

RASTAFARIANS

Overall name for a loosely defined messianic movement among poor Jamaicans that spread to Great Britain and the United States. It was started in 1930 under the influence of the "Back to Africa" movement of Marcus Garvey (1887–1940), and inspired by the coronation of Ras Tafari Makonnen (later known as Haile Selassie) as Emperor of Ethiopia. Haile Selassie (1892–1975) is regarded not only as the black Messiah coming to liberate all black people, who are the true Jews, but as Jah the living God. Christianity is rejected, but the Christian Bible is used and quoted and biblical symbols are used as inspiration. The Bible is regarded as black history, usurped and distorted by whites. April 1 is celebrated as the beginning of the year, and Ras Tafari's Coronation Day is another holiday. Haile Selassie visited Jamaica in 1966 but never commented on the Rastafarian beliefs. Some followers claim he is still alive.

In the 1930s the movement was led by Leonard Howell, a follower of Garvey, who for a while managed to create a commune of Rastafarians in which marijuana was raised, among other crops. Rastafarians have no houses of worship, but gatherings are frequent. Menstrual taboos are strictly observed, and women are segregated during their periods. Followers smoke marijuana (known as *ganja*) as a sacrament, which has led to difficulties with police in Britain and the U.S. reggae music has also been associated with the Rastafarians. In the 1970s the movement gained visibility thanks to its promotion by the reggae singer Robert Nesta (Bob) Marley (1945–1981).

Haile Selassie, at the time of his coronation as Emperor of Ethiopia. He was the inspiration of the Rastafarian movement.

Identified groups that have developed out of the movement include the AFRICAN CULTURAL LEAGUE, African Methodist Episcopal Church, Ethiopian Coptic Faith, Ethiopian National Congress, Ethiopian Orthodox Church, ETHIOPIAN ZION COPTIC CHURCH, Ethiopian Youth Cosmic Faith, Fraternal Solidarity of United Ethiopians, Nyabingi, Twelve Tribes of Israel, United Afro-West Indian Brotherhood, United Ethiopian Body, and Universal Black Improvement Organization. Membership is often informal, and group divisions are far from strict.

See also AFRICAN REFORM COPTIC CHURCH OF GOD IN CHRIST, THE FIRST FRUIT OF PRAYER, GOD'S ARMY CAMP

Sources:

Barrett, L. *The Rastafarians: Sounds of Cultural Dissonance*. Boston: Beacon Press, 1977.

Cashmore, E. *Rastaman: The Rastafarian Movement in England*. London: Allen & Unwin, 1985.

Cronon, E.D. *Black Moses: The Story of Marcus Garvey and the Universal Negro Improvement Association*. Madison: University of Wisconsin Press, 1955.

Simpson, G.E. *Black Religions in the New World*. New York: Columbia University Press, 1978.

Williams, K.M. *The Rastafarians*. London: Ward, Lock Educational, 1981.

RATANA CHURCH

Maori syncretistic religious-political movement founded in 1925 by Tahupotiki Wiremu Ratana (1873–1939). In 1918, acting as a "healer" during the influenza epidemic, he started having visions and promised his followers that angels from heaven would come to protect them. The sources of the Church's doctrine are mostly Christian, but Ratana is regarded as the main intermediary in members' relations with the supernatural world. The movement has been represented as a political party in the New Zealand parliament and is the strongest Maori group there.

See also RINGATU

Bulent Rauf, see BESHARA SCHOOL

Serge Raynaud de la Ferriere, see UNIVERSAL GREAT BROTHERHOOD A.U.M. SOLAR LINE

REBA PLACE FELLOWSHIP

Mennonite communal movement that, starting in 1957, created several communes in the Midwest including the Reba Place Fellowship in Evanston, Illinois, Plow Creek in Bureau County, Illinois, New Creation in Newton, Kansas, and Fellowship of Hope in Elkhart, Indiana.

RECONSTRUCTIONISM

Jewish radical renewal and reform movement developed out of CONSERVATIVE JUDAISM by Mordecai M. Kaplan (1881–1983), officially separating from the parent movement in 1922. Kaplan's view was that Judaism is a civilization, not just a religion. Today the smallest Jewish denomination in the United States, it has one theological seminary, in Philadelphia.

See also REFORM JUDAISM

Source:

Kaplan, M.M. *Judaism as a Civilization: Towards a Reconstruction of American-Jewish Life*. New York: Yoseloff, 1957.

B.E. Rediger, see FORT WAYNE GOSPEL TEMPLE

REFORMED CONGREGATION OF THE GODDESS

Neo-pagan group founded by Samantha River, known as Jade, in the 1970s in Madison, Wisconsin. It celebrates Halloween as New Year's Eve, follows a calendar that adds 8,000 years to any CE year, and admits only women.

REFORMED DRUIDS OF NORTH AMERICA

Neo-pagan group based in California, started in the 1960s.

REFORMED PRESBYTERIAN CHURCH, EVANGELICAL SYNOD

Fundamentalist group founded in 1965 through merger of the Reformed Presbyterian Church in North America, General Synod (formed in 1833), and the Evangelical Presbyterian Church formed in 1956 out of the BIBLE PRESBYTERIAN CHURCH. The new group opposed the separation of church and state and aspired to have the United States proclaimed a "Christian nation." In 1982 it became part of a larger conservative group, the Presbyterian Church in America.

See also ORTHODOX PRESBYTERIAN CHURCH

REFORMED ZION UNION APOSTOLIC CHURCH, THE

African-American "HOLINESS" Protestant group founded in Virginia in 1869.

REFORM JUDAISM

International Jewish renewal movement that rejects historical Jewish practices in

Isaac Mayer Wise, leader of Reform Judaism (courtesy of the UAHC Press).

favor of adjustments to modern life. First ideas of reforming Orthodox Judaism appeared in the late 18th century in Germany. In the 1840s conferences of modernist rabbis began to formalize the changes in liturgy and beliefs. The main thrust was against traditional rituals and practices. Jewish identity was to be preserved through emphasis on ethical beliefs rather than obedience to revealed truth.

The development of a strong Reform Judaism took place in the United States in the 19th century under the leadership of I.M. Wise (1819–1900). In the 1820s the Reformed Society of Israelites was formed but did not not survive long. The formal founding can be dated to 1885, when the Pittsburgh Platform was adopted by a conference of rabbis. The Platform rejected the Jewish Oral Tradition and ritual traditions. In 1935, in its Columbus Platform, the movement expressed a certain return to ritual and tradition.

See also CONSERVATIVE JUDAISM; LIBERAL JUDAISM; RECONSTRUCTIONISM

Sources:

Blau, J.L., ed. *Reform Judaism: A Historical Perspective.* New York: Ktav, 1973.

Meyer, M.A. *Response to Modernity: A History of the Reform Movement in Judaism.* New York: Oxford University Press, 1988.

Rudavsky, D. *Modern Jewish Religious Movements: A History of Emancipation and Adjustment.* New York: Behrman, 1967.

REIYU-KAI KYODAN (Spiritual Friends Association)

Japanese Buddhist revival movement coming out of the Nichiren Shu Buddhist tradi-

tion, founded in Tokyo in 1922 by Kimi Kotani (1901–1971) and Kabutaro Kubo (1892–1944). Doctrine emphasizes faith healing, the Lotus Sutra, ancestor worship, and patriarchal morality. The RISSHO KOSEI KAI group grew out of this movement. Branches of Reiyu-Kai Kyodan have operated in Europe, Asia, and the Americas. See also NICHIREN SHOSHU; SOKKA-GAKKAI

Source:

Hardacre, H. *Lay Buddhism in Contemporary Japan: Reiyukai Kyodan.* Princeton, NJ: Princeton University Press, 1984.

RELIGIOUS SCIENCE INTERNATIONAL

Originally known as the International Association of Religious Science Churches (IARSC), this NEW THOUGHT group was founded by Ernest Holmes (1887–1960) in 1948 in Los Angeles. Later it became a dissenting group from RELIGIOUS SCIENCE, UNITED CHURCH OF. In its credo, the group states: "We believe that the Universal Spirit, which is God, operates through a Universal Mind, which is the Law of God; and that we are surrounded by the Creative Mind, which receives the direct impress of our thought and acts upon it . . . We believe in the healing of the sick through the power of this Mind." In addition to ministers, the group ordains "licensed practitioners," who provide "personal spiritual mind treatment work" based on the "Science of Mind."
See also CHRISTIAN SCIENCE

Sources:

Braden, C.S. *Spirits in Rebellion.* Dallas: SMU Press, 1963.

Judah, J.S. *The History and Philosophy of the Metaphysical Movements in America.* Philadelphia: Westminster Press, 1967.

RELIGIOUS SCIENCE, UNITED CHURCH OF

NEW THOUGHT group founded in 1952 by Ernest Holmes (1887–1960) in Los Angeles. It grew out of the Southern California Metaphysical Institute, started in 1916, and the Institute of Religious Science and Philosophy, started in 1927. The group's credo is similar to that of RELIGIOUS SCIENCE INTERNATIONAL, which proclaims the ability of the subjective mind to heal and teaches a method of prayer known as "spiritual mind treatment."

Source:
Judah, J.S. *The History and Philosophy of the Metaphysical Movements in America.* Philadelphia: Westminster Press, 1967.

Charles Mason Remey, see BAHAIS UNDER THE HEREDITARY GUARDIANSHIP

REMNANT CHURCHES OF GOD

Caribbean African-American PENTECOSTAL group started in the 1920s.

RENAISSANCE CHURCH-COMMUNITY

Earlier known as the Brotherhood of the Spirit, and as the Renaissance Movement, this communal revitalization movement was started by Michael J. Metelica (1951–), known also in the groups as Michael Rapunzel, in western Massachusetts and officially incorporated in 1974. The doctrine combines traditional millenarian ideas with notions of the "Aquarian Age." The *Aquarian Gospel*, a 19th-century book, is at the basis of the group's religious beliefs, among which reincarnation is central. The founder is considered a reincarnation of Christ. Members are pioneers of the New Age, which is to start following a series of ecological disasters, earthquakes, and civil disorders. The movement has operated successful musical groups to spread its message.

Source:
Borowski, K. *Attempting an Alternative Society.* Norwood, PA: Norwood Editions, 1984.

RENOVATED CHURCH OF CHRIST (Église du Christ-Roi Rénovée)

Also known as the Renewed Church of Christ the King, this Western European dissenting Roman Catholic group was founded by Michel Collin (1905–1974), a Catholic priest from Dijon, France. Ordained in 1933, Collin was defrocked by the Church in 1951 following his claims of apparitions, revelations, and divine consecrations. In 1961 he named himself Pope Clement XV, and during the 1960s he collaborated with other dissenting OLD CATHOLIC and Roman Catholic groups, especially the APOSTLES OF INFINITE LOVE. Collin (or Clement XV) died after fasting for 100 days. Since his death, his followers have been active in Western Europe, sometimes collaborating with other dissenting Catholic groups.
See also MAGNIFICAT

Source:
Delestre, A. *Clement XV.* Nancy: Presses Universitaires, 1985.

The assassination of Joseph Smith, founder of Mormonism.

REORGANIZED CHURCH OF JESUS CHRIST OF LATTER DAY SAINTS (RLDS)

Originally known as the New Organization, this Mormon splinter group was created after the murder of Joseph Smith, Jr., the founder of Mormonism, in 1844. Following the founder's death, the movement split into several groups, each claiming Smith's legacy. It is estimated that twenty-five such groups are in existence today, and the largest is The Reorganized Church.

The Church was officially founded on April 6, 1860. Opposed to the leadership of Brigham Young, it has been led by lineal descendants of Smith since 1859, when Joseph Smith III became its President. It was always opposed to polygamy, which was one of its main differences with mainstream Mormonism. The Church has grown, and its base of strength is the Midwest. It has failed in its efforts to acquire the temple lot at Independence, Missouri, designated by Joseph Smith, Jr. as the site of the Second Coming, but its headquarters are across the street from the lot, which is owned by THE CHURCH OF CHRIST (TEMPLE LOT). Branches of this group have operated in Western Europe.

See also CHURCH OF JESUS CHRIST IN SOLEMN ASSEMBLY; CHURCH OF THE FIRST BORN OF THE FULLNESS OF TIMES; MORMONS; UNITED ORDER EFFORT

Francis X. Resch, see ARCHDIOCESE OF THE OLD CATHOLIC CHURCH IN AMERICA

RESTORATION MOVEMENT
North American Pentecostal movement started in the early 1980s, inspired by the LATTER RAIN MOVEMENT of the late 1940s. Restorationists believe that the period of the last 450 years has seen the restoration of the ancient Christian Church as evidenced by the PENTECOSTAL revival of the 20th century.

RESURRECTED CHURCH OF GOD
PENTECOSTAL African-American group started in Philadelphia in the 1950s. It has branches in Great Britain in West Indian communities.

Abihu Reuben, see ETHIOPIAN HEBREWS

Benito F. Reyes, see WORLD INSTITUTE OF AVASTHOLOGY

RHEMA BIBLE CHURCH
International Christian Charismatic church founded in the United States in the 1960s, with branches in southern Africa.

Keith Milton Rhinehart, see AQUARIAN FOUNDATION

Thomas Rich, see VAJRADHATU

Mira Richard, see SRI AUROBINDO

John E. Richardson, see GREAT SCHOOL OF THE MASTERS

Moses Rimolade, see CHERUBIM AND SERAPHIM (ETERNAL ORDER OF)

RISSHO KOSEI-KAI (Integrative Becoming)
Japanese new religion growing out of the Nichiren Buddhist tradition, founded in 1938 by two former members of REIYU-KAI, Nikkyo Niwano (1906–) and Myoko Naganuma (1899–1957). Worship practices focus on the Lotus Sutra, group counseling, and divination. Branches have operated in the United States, South America, and Asia since the 1960s.
See also NICHIREN SHOSHU; SOKKA GAKKAI

Sources:
McFarland, H.N. *The Rush Hour of the Gods.* New York: Macmillan, 1967.
Guthrie, S. *A Japanese New Religion: Rissho Kosei-Kai in a Mountain Hamlet.* Ann Arbor, MI: Center for Japanese Studies, University of Michigan, 1988.

Ritchings, Edna Rose, see FATHER DIVINE

Friedrich Rittelmeyer, see CHRISTIAN COMMUNITY CHURCH

Nicholas Roerich, see AGNI YOGA SOCIETY

S.B. Rohold, see CHRISTIAN SYNAGOGUE

ROOSEVELT SPIRITUAL MEMORIAL BENEVOLENT ASSOCIATION
U.S. spiritualist group founded in 1949.

ROOT OF DAVID MINISTRIES

Evangelical group founded in the late 1980s by Roger Abergal in Encino, California.

Moishe Rosen, see JEWS FOR JESUS

Roy A. Rosenberg, see TEMPLE OF UNIVERSAL JUDAISM

Joseph Rosenfarb, see BETH MESSIAH

ROSH PINA CONGREGATION

Hebrew-Christian group founded by Marvin Morrison in the 1970s and based in Baltimore.

ROSICRUCIAN FELLOWSHIP

Occultist group founded in 1908 in Columbus, Ohio, by Carl Louis van Grasshoff, also known as Max Heindel (1865–1919), who headed the Los Angeles Theosophical Lodge in 1904–1905. Heindel claimed to be "an authorized messenger of the Elder Brothers of the Rose Cross, who are working to disseminate throughout the Western world the deeper Spiritual meanings which are both concealed and revealed within the Christian religion." Within two years of its start the group had branches in Los Angeles and in Seattle, Portland, and North Yakima, Washington. For many years headquarters have been in Mount Ecclesia, Oceanside, California.

See also ROSICRUCIANS; THEOSOPHY

ROSICRUCIANS

Known also as the Order of the Rosy Cross, the movement's name is attributed to a legendary medieval brotherhood devoted to magic and alchemy. According to the legend, the founder was Christian Rosenkreutz (supposedly 1378–1484), who had brought his scientific and esoteric knowledge from the East.

Since the early 17th century, when the legend was first published in Germany in the form of three books purporting to have been written by Christian Rosenkreutz, various esoteric groups have claimed the mantle of medieval Rosicrucian origins. Their teachings include alleged ancient traditions, Christian ideas and symbols, and an amalgam of Western occult beliefs including alchemy and divination practices. The Rosicrucian tradition and ideas have affected hundreds of modern religious movements that do not always acknowledge such influence (*e.g.*, THEOSOPHY; EMIN SOCIETY).

See also AMORC ROSICRUCIAN ORDER; ANCIENT MAYANS, ORDER OF; AUSAR AUSET SOCIETY; FÉDERATION UNIVERSELLE DES ORDRES ET SOCIÉTÉS INITIATIQUES; FRATERNITAS ROSAE CRUCIS; LECTORIUM ROSICRUCIANUM; ORDER OF THE GOLDEN DAWN; ORDO TEMPLI ORIENTIS; ROSICRUCIAN ANTHROPOSOPHIC LEAGUE; ROSICRUCIAN FELLOWSHIP; SOCIETAS ROSICRUCIANA IN AMERICA

Source:
Yates, F.A. *The Rosicrucian Enlightenment.* London: Routledge & Kegan Paul, 1972.

Scott Ross, see LOVE INN

John Rossnner, see SPIRITUAL SCIENCE FELLOWSHIP

Georges Roux, see TÉMOINS DU CHRIST

Ram Mohan Roy, see BRAHMA SAMAJ

Rua Kenana Hepetika, see CHURCH OF TE KOOTI RIKIRANGI

Rudi (Albert Rudolph), see NITYANANDA INSTITUTE; SHREE GURUDEV RUDRANANDA YOGA ASHRAM

Swami Rudrananda, see NITYANANDA INSTITUTE; SHREE GURUDEV RUDRANANDA YOGA ASHRAM

RUHANI SATSANG

Also known in the West as the Fellowship of the Spirit and as the Science of Spirituality, this branch of the RADHASOAMI SATSANG movement was started in 1951 following a dispute over the succession to leadership in the RADHASOAMI SATSANG BEAS. Kirpal Singh (1896–1974), who lost the leadership in the BEAS group to Jagat Singh, started the new movement, which in turn gave rise to other groups.

See also ECKANKAR; KIRPAL RUHANI SATSANG; SANT BANI ASHRAM; SAWAN KIRPAL RUHANI MISSION

Charles Taze Russell, see JEHOVAH'S WITNESSES

Adam Rutherford, see INSTITUTE OF PYRAMIDOLOGY

Joseph Franklin Rutherford, see JEHOVAH'S WITNESSES

S

SABIAN ASSEMBLY

Occultist group founded in 1923 by Marc Edmund Jones in Los Angeles. Jones drew his ideas from THEOSOPHY, NEW THOUGHT, spiritualism, and Eastern traditions. He also claimed to follow the Kabbalah. Group practices have included Tarot readings and astrology.

Oliver C. Sabin, Jr., see EVANGELICAL CHRISTIAN SCIENCE CHURCH

SACRED NAME MOVEMENT

U.S. Protestant movement that advocates the use of supposedly Hebrew names for Christian deities, such as the name Yahweh for the biblical God, and the name Yehoshua for Jesus of the New Testament. See also ASSEMBLIES OF YAHWEH; ASSEMBLIES OF YAHWEH (MICHIGAN); ASSEMBLY OF YAHVAH (OREGON)

Masayasua Sadanaga, see NICHIREN SHOSHU SOKA GAKKAI OF AMERICA

Sadhanalaya Ashram, see HOLY SHANKARACHARYA ORDER

Bill Sadler, Jr., see URANTIA FOUNDATION

Sadr Anjuman-i Ahmadiyya, see AHMADIYYA MOVEMENT

SAGE COMMUNITY

U.S. faith healing group founded by Gay Luce in the late 1970s.

Sahaj Marg, see SHRI RAM CHANDRA MISSION

Mani Sahukar, see SATHYA SAI BABA

SAI BABA

Sai Baba of Shirdi (1856–1918) was an Indian holy man considered an avatar, the incarnation of God. He was so much admired that both Moslems and Hindus claimed him as their own. His ancestry is unclear. He settled in Shirdi, which became a place of pilgrimage, at age 23 and became known through thousands of miracle stories told of him. His disciple, Sri Upasani Baba, set up an ashram in Sakori, northern India.

Followers of Sai Baba abstain from meat and drugs of any kind. His many Indian devotees have built shrines in his name all over India, and there have been Western groups of admirers.
See also SATHYA SAI BABA

Saint Germain Foundation, see "I AM"

"Saints," see MORMONS

SAIVA SIDDHANTA CHURCH

Also known as the Wailua University of the Contemplative Arts, and as Subramuniya Yoga Order, this Hindu group was founded in 1957 in Hawaii by Subramuniya (1927–), a North American student of Hinduism. Meditation and yoga are practiced, and an ascetic life-style is advocated.

Sekiguchi Sakae, see SUKYO MAHIKARI

Jigdal Dagchen Sakya, Rinpoche, see SAKYA TAGCHEN CHOLING CENTER

SAKYA TAGCHEN CHOLING CENTER

Known also as the Monastery of Tibetan Buddhism, this Tibetan Buddhist group based in the State of Washington was founded in the 1970s by Jigdal Dagchen Sakya, Rinpoche. It is committed to the Sakya sect of Vajrayana Buddhism.

SALEM ACRES

Christian commune founded by Lester B. Anderson in the late 1960s near Rock City, Illinois. Doctrine emphasizes both Pentecostalism (speaking in tongues and faith healing) and the keeping of Old Testament commandments regarding the Sabbath and diet.

SALVATION ARMY, THE

International Christian Fundamentalist movement founded in 1878 in London by William Booth (1829–1912), a Methodist minister who left his church in 1865 to organize the Christian Mission, devoted to social service. In 1878 the Mission was organized along "military" lines and became the Salvation Army. Members of the Booth family have been active in leading the movement, including Mrs. Catherine Booth (1829–1890) and the founder's son, William Bramwell Booth (1856–1929), who was the leader between 1912 and 1929. He was followed by Edward Higgins (1929–1934), Evangeline Booth (1934–1939), G.L. Carpenter (1939–1946), Albert Osborn, and Eva Burrows.

The movement's doctrine is based on "personal justification," the personal experience of being "born again" through the acceptance of Jesus Christ. There are no sacraments, but Founder's Day (July 2) is a

General William Booth, founder of the Salvation Army.

memorial day for all dead Army members. The commitment to social service is based on the assumption that the satisfaction of basic needs must precede any religious awakening.

The Army has maintained social service programs that have become widely admired. These include the largest rehabilitation programs for alcoholics in the United States, thrift shops, and halfway houses, organized in over 3,000 local centers around the world. It also operates the largest program in the world for locating missing persons.

See also AMERICAN RESCUE WORKERS; RESCUE MISSION; VOLUNTEERS OF AMERICA

Evangeline Booth, daughter of the founder of the Salvation Army and commander from 1934 to 1939.

Sources:

Collier, R. *The General Next to God.* New York: Dutton, 1965.

Coutts, J. *The Salvationists.* London: Mowbrays, 1977.

McKinley, E.H. *Marching to Glory.* New York: Harper & Row, 1980.

Sandall, R. *The History of the Salvation Army.* London: T. Nelson, 1947–1973.

Sukui Nushi Sama, see MAHIKARI

William Samuel, see MOUNTAIN BROOK

SANTA ANITA CHURCH

NEW THOUGHT group based in California, founded in the 1970s by Margaret Stevens.

John Santamaria, Rocco Santamaria, see ITALIAN PENTECOSTAL ASSEMBLIES OF GOD

SANT BANI ASHRAM

North American Sikh organization founded in the 1970s in New Hampshire by Russell Perkins, devoted to the teachings of Ajaib Singh, a disciple of Kirpal Singh (1896–1974). The organization offers "initiation into the path of Surat Shabd Yoga [translated as the "yoga of the celestial sound"], a path of love and discipline that embraces the essence of the teachings of all True Masters."

See also KIRPAL RUHANI SATSANG; RADHASOAMI SATSANG; SAWAN KIRPAL RUHANI MISSION

SANTINIKETAN

Known as "The House of Peace," this Indian religious academy was founded by Rabindranath Tagore (1861–1941), poet, musician, Nobel laureate in literature, who attempted to develop a universal religion based on the notion of unity among all world faiths.

See also ARYA SAMAJ; BRAHMA SAMAJ

Ben Sebastian Sapio, see THE WAY, THE TRUTH AND THE LIFE

Sar Shalom, see CHOSEN PEOPLE MINISTRIES

Brahmananda Sarasvati, see ICSA (INTEGRAL CENTER OF SELF-ABIDANCE)

Dayanand Sarasvati, see ARYA SAMAJ

Prakashanand H.D. Saraswati, see INTERNATIONAL SOCIETY OF DIVINE LOVE

Sivananda Saraswati, see INTEGRAL YOGA INSTITUTE; INTERNATIONAL SCHOOL OF YOGA AND VEDANTA; SIVANANDA YOGA VEDANTA CENTERS INTERNATIONAL; SIVANANDA YOGA VEDANTA CHURCH

Haroutiun Saraydarian, see AQUARIAN EDUCATIONAL FOUNDATION

Prabhata Ranjana (P.R.) Sarkar, see ANANDA MARGA

SARVA DHARMA SAMBHAVA KENDRA

Sometimes known as the Chandra Group, after its leader, this international Hindu revival movement was founded in the 1970s in India by Nemi Chand Ghandi (1949–), known as Chandra Swami. The group opened branches in Western Europe in the

1980s, and the leader attracted much attention. In 1986 his name was linked in the media to financial scandals in Great Britain and India, which threw the movement into a serious crisis.

Sri Swami Satchidananda, see INTEGRAL YOGA INSTITUTE

Satchidananda Ashrams, see INTEGRAL YOGA INSTITUTE

SATHYA SAI BABA
Sathya Sai Baba (1926–   ) is one of India's leading gurus of the 20th century. He claims to be a reincarnation of Sai Baba of Shirdi. Born Sathya Narayana Raju in south India, at age fourteen he claimed for the first time to be the incarnation of Sai Baba. In 1963 he claimed to be an incarnation of the god Shiva. Sathya Sai Baba has predicted his own death, to take place in 2022. He is considered to have the largest following of any Hindu holy man in modern times. Groups of his followers operate in India and in many Western countries.

Source:
Bassuk, D.E. *Incarnation in Hinduism and Christianity: The Myth of the Godman.* Atlantic Highlands, NJ: Humanities Press, 1986.

SATHYA SAI BABA CENTRAL COMMITTE OF AMERICA
Hindu group based in California and devoted to the teachings of SATHYA SAI BABA.
See also SAI BABA

SATHYA SAI BABA NATIONAL HEADQUARTERS OF AMERICA
Hindu-inspired group based in California, devoted to the teachings of SATHYA SAI BABA. Its doctrine is expressed as follows: "The message of the 'Fatherhood of God and the Brotherhood of Man', which Jesus Christ proclaimed two thousand years ago, should become a living faith for the achievement of real peace and the unity of mankind."
See also SAI BABA

SATHYA SAI BABA SOCIETY
Hindu group, founded in 1961, based in California, and devoted to spreading the message of SATHYA SAI BABA. The Society has published at least 30 volumes of his teachings.
See also SATHYA SAI BABA CENTRAL COMMITTEE OF AMERICA

SATYANANDA ASHRAM
International Hindu movement devoted to the teachings of Swami Satyananda of Bihar and to the practice of "Tantric Yoga."

Jack Saunders, see FRAZIER CHAPEL

SAVITRIA
Occultist commune founded in 1969 in North Baltimore, Maryland, by Robert Hieronimus. Its aim is to prepare for the coming Aquarian Age, and its practices include meditation. A strict code of conduct is followed.

Swami Savitri Priza, see YOGA INSTITUTE OF CONSCIOUSNESS

Gene Savoy, see INTERNATIONAL COMMUNITY OF CHRIST

SAWAN KIRPAL RUHANI MISSION

Also known as Science of Spirituality, this international RADHASOAMI SATSANG group recognizes Sant Darshan Singh (1921–), the son of Kirpal Singh (1896–1974), as his father's true heir and claims that Sant Darshan Singh was trained by Hazur Baba Sawan Singh (1858–1948). The group's name combines the names of Hazur Baba Sawan Singh and of Sant Kirpal Singh. Its doctrine is based on Radhasoami Satsang traditions and the teachings of Kirpal Singh. "We can attain self-knowledge and God-realization through mystic experiences on the path of the Masters."
See RUHANI SATSANG; SANT BANI ASHRAM

Zalman Schachter-Shalomi, see P'NAI OR

Julius Schacknow, see BROTHER JULIUS

Solomon Schechter, see CONSERVATIVE JUDAISM

Raymond Schertenlieb, see EMIN SOCIETY

Charles P. and Dorothy Schmitt, see FELLOWSHIP OF CHRISTIAN BELIEVERS

Russell Paul Schofield, see ACTUALISM

SCHOOL OF ESOTERIC STUDIES

U.S. occultist splinter group formed by members of the Arcane School in 1956 after the death of its founder.
See also LUCIS TRUST

SCHOOL OF LIGHT AND REALIZATION (SOLAR)

Occultist group inspired by the teachings of Alice Bailey and THEOSOPHY, founded in 1969 by Norman Craemer near Traverse City, Michigan. The School prepares its students for the coming of the Christ and the beginning of the Aquarian Age.

SCHOOL OF PRACTICAL PHILOSOPHY

Occultist, syncretistic group founded in the 1960s and based in New York City. Combining a Gurdjieff approach with Hindu teachings, it claims to be guided by Shankara Charya, an Indian teacher.
See also GURDJIEFF GROUPS

SCHOOL OF THE PROPHETS

PENTECOSTAL group founded in the early 20th century in Louisville, Kentucky.

SCHOOL OF TRUTH

South African NEW THOUGHT group, originally known as the School of Practical Christianity, founded by Nicol C. Campbell in 1937 in Johannesburg. Its doctrine emphasizes adherence to Christianity, and members are expected to tithe. Branches have operated in Zimbabwe and the United States.

SCHOOL OF UNIVERSAL PHILOSOPHY AND HEALING

British spiritualist group founded by Gladys Spearman-Cook in London in the 1950s.

Francis K. Schuckardt, see CONGREGATION OF MARY THE IMMACULATE QUEEN

Helen Schucman, see A COURSE IN MIRACLES

Robert Schuller, see CRYSTAL CATHEDRAL

Jack Schwartz, see ALETHEIA PSYCHO-PHYSICAL FOUNDATION

SCIENCE OF MIND CHURCH
NEW THOUGHT group based in Los Angeles, founded by Frederick Bailes in the 1950s.

SCIENTOLOGY, CHURCH OF
Earlier known as the Hubbard Association of Scientologists International, and often advertised as Dianetics, this international organization claims to be a religion, although such claims must be doubted.

It was founded in the 1950s by Lafayette Ronald (L. Ron) Hubbard (1911–1986). May 9, 1950, the day when *Dianetics: The Modern Science of Mental Health* was published, is considered by many as Scientology's birthdate, although the Church of Scientology was founded only four years later. Together with March 13, Hubbard's birthday, the day is celebrated by Scientologists. *Dianetics* has been a best-selling book since it first came on the market. As recently as 1988 it appeared on the New York *Times* paperback best sellers list (classified under "Advice, How-to and Miscellaneous") for sixty-two consecutive weeks (it has been suggested that copies were bought by the group to inflate sales figures). Dianetics began as a secular psychotherapy movement but soon developed into a "religion" organized through local churches, which are tightly run by the Founding Church of Scientology, as the group's headquarters was incorporated.

The Church of Scientology has inspired probably more social science research and more media attention than any other similar group; its activities all over the world have been studied and reported widely.

Scientology has been involved in considerable litigation and criminal prosecutions. In 1958 the Internal Revenue Service revoked its tax-exempt status, and in 1963 the Food and Drug Administration seized materials used in Scientology "auditing," including books and E-meters. Scientology has failed in attempts to regain its tax-exempt status. In U.S. Courts, Scientology has been sued by former members, who in some cases have won damages for church practices.

In 1965 the group's activities were banned in Australia, and it changed its name to the Church of the New Faith, but in 1983 the ban was reversed by the Australian High Court. In 1984 an Australian court ruled that Scientology was a religion and therefore entitled to tax-exempt status.

On February 14, 1978, Hubbard (*in absentia*) and two associates were sentenced to prison terms and heavy fines by a French court in Paris. Hubbard himself received a sentence of four years and a fine of 35,000 francs. The sentences were upheld by an appellate court on February 29, 1980. The tax-exempt status of the group in France was revoked in 1985, after it had been determined that its aim was profit-making.

In July 1985 a court of appeals in Copenhagen decided that the Church of Scientology was a profit-making venture and must pay taxes on its income. In April 1986, the Danish Minister of Justice announced a decision to deport forty

L. Ron Hubbard, founder of Scientology, saying good-bye to his staff after having been ordered out of the country by the government of Rhodesia.

Scientologists who were running the European and African headquarters for the Church in Copenhagen.

In 1988 in Canada Scientology was charged with theft of government documents, and the group expressed readiness to donate $1 million to charity if charges were dropped.

In November 1988, court proceedings were initiated in Spain against Heber Janetch, the leader of the Church.

The official goal of Scientology, as stated by its founder, is to lead humankind "...to total freedom and truth" (see *What Is Scientology*, by L.R. Hubbard, published by the Church of Scientology in 1978). In the same volume (p. 209) Scientology is defined as "...the study of knowing how to know and deals with Man as a spirit separate from his mind and body... Scientology is used to increase spiritual freedom, intelligence, ability, to produce immortality." Hubbard claimed that in the course of his research he "came across incontrovertible scientifically-validated evidence of the existence of the human soul" (p. 4).

According to Scientology doctrine, the universe is populated by *thetans*, a large group of omnipotent, eternal beings. The *thetans* created the world as we know it. Later they gave up most of their powers, and that is how all human beings were created. All humans can return to the state of *thetan* if they follow Scientology and its procedures. The first step on the road to becoming a *thetan* is that of *clear*. One becomes *clear* through *auditing* or *processing* and then is totally free of psychosis, neurosis, compulsions, or inhibitions and does not suffer from any psychosomatic disease. His intelligence, as measured by IQ tests, is superior to normal. Scientology believes in reincarnation, and one who has become *clear* in this life will carry on his excellence to the next one. Hubbard in 1963 reported a visit to Heaven, where the grounds looked "like the Busch Gardens in Pasadena."

Scientology operates numerous front organizations such as the Alliance for the Preservation of Religious Liberty, Narconon, the Citizens Commission on Human Rights, the Committee on Public Health and Safety, American Citizens for Honesty in Government, the Committee for a Safe Environment, and the National Commission on Law Enforcement and Social Justice. In April 1977 Scientology in the United States joined with the UNIFICATION CHURCH and the CHILDREN OF GOD to form the Alliance for the Preservation of Religious Liberty (APRL). Religious Research Foundation (RRF) was a front organization to which revenues were channeled to avoid taxes.

A front organization created to operate within U.S. government institutions, and so claiming to be specifically nonreligious, is the Concerned Businessmen's Asso-ciation of America, which also operates the Way to Happiness Foundation. Scientology has reportedly offered "corporate innovation" programs to several U. S. corporations.

In addition to these well-known U.S. front organizations, Scientology has established scores of similar organizations in other countries.

See also DIANOLOGY AND EDUCTIVISM; DUGA

Sources:

Evans, C. *Cults of Unreason*. London: Harrap, 1973.

Croydon, B., and Hubbard, L.R., Jr. *L. Ron*

Hubbard: Messiah or Madman?. Secaucus, NJ: Lyle Stuart, 1987.

Malko, G. *Scientology: The New Religion*. New York: Dell, 1970.

Miller, R. *Barefaced Messiah: The True Story of L. Ron Hubbard*. New York: Holt, 1987.

Wallis, R. *The Road to Total Freedom: A Sociological Analysis of Scientology*. New York: Columbia University Press, 1976.

Joseph L. Scott, see (ORIGINAL) CHURCH OF GOD, INC.

SEAX-WICA SEMINARY

Neo-pagan group founded by Raymond Buckland in the early 1970s and based in Charlottesville, Virginia. It is devoted to what Buckland has called Saxon Witchcraft, which is the worship of the old Saxon deities Woden and Freya representing the male and female principles.

See also CHURCH OF WICCA CIRCLE; COVENANT OF THE GODDESS

SEEKER'S QUEST

Esoteric Christianity group founded in the 1950s in California by Woods Mattingly. In 1970 the group merged with the CHRIST MINISTRY FOUNDATION and Mattingly became the leader, but the groups separated again in 1972. Healing through "spiritual work" is a major practice.

SEICHO-NO-IE

Known sometimes as the Truth of Life, a Japanese Shinto-inspired new religion whose name means the House of Growth. Founded in 1930 by Masaharu Taniguchi (1893–1987), it grew out of the OMOTOKYO (OMOTO) movement, and it is influenced by NEW THOUGHT ideas and especially by RELIGIOUS SCIENCE. "The practice of shinsokan, a form of meditation, is the method by which members strive to realize the Truth, the Truth that one is a child of God, pure and sinless." Branches have opened in the United States and in Europe. The group has been involved in politics and promotes a right-wing ideology for Japan.

Sources:

Judah, J.S. *The History and Philosophy of the Metaphysical Movements in America*. Philadelphia: Westminster Press, 1967.

McFarland, H.N. *The Rush Hour of the Gods*. New York: Macmillan, 1967.

Thomsen, H. *The New Religions of Japan*. Rutland, VT: Charles E. Tuttle, 1963.

Teofile Vargas Sein, see MITA

SEKAI KYUSEI KYO (SKK, World Messianic Association)

Japanese Shinto-inspired new religion growing out of the OMOTOKYO movement. It was founded in 1950 as Sekai Meshiakyo (Church of World Messianity or C.W.M.) by Mikichi Okada (1882–1955), known to his followers as Meishu-sama. Okada became a member of Omotokyo in 1923 and a leader after 1926. He left the group in 1935 to found the Dai Nippon Kannon Kai. In 1948 he founded the Nippon Miroku Kyokai. Sekai Kyusei started as a healing movement with Buddhist orientation but has moved closer to Christianity. It teaches the coming of the Messianic age and the practice of faith healing. Branches

Paramahansa Yogananda, founder of the Self-Realization Fellowship.

operate in the United States, Latin America, and East Asia.
See also ANANAIKO; JOHREI; SEICHO NO IE; WORLD MESSIANITY

Sekai Mahikari Bumei Kyodan, see MAHIKARI

Sekai Meshiakyo, see SEKAI KYUSEI KYO

SELF-REALIZATION FELLOWSHIP (SRF)

Hindu group founded in 1935 in Los Angeles by Paramahansa Yogananda (1893–1952), who was born in India and studied under Swami Sri Yukteswar. In 1918

Yogananda founded the YOGODA SATSANGA SOCIETY in India. In 1920 he came to the United States and started teaching yoga in Los Angeles. The group offers "direct personal experience of God" through the practice of *kriya yoga*, a technique of "deep meditation affecting energy centers in the body." SRF also operates the Church of All Religions as well as centers and branches in forty-three countries.
See also SELF-REVELATION CHURCH OF ABSOLUTE MONISM

SELF-REVELATION CHURCH OF ABSOLUTE MONISM

U.S. Hindu group started by Paramahansa Yogananda in 1927 and later led by Swami Premananda. In addition to Yogananda teachings, the group emphasizes the teachings of Gandhi. The group operates the Swami Order of Absolute Monism for members who want to commit themselves to the monastic life, and one mission in India.
See also SELF-REALIZATION FELLOWSHIP (SRF)

Ernest William Sellers, see IGLESIA BANDO EVANGELICO GEDEON

Kehsab Chandra Sen, see BRAHMA SAMAJ; SADHARAN BRAHMO SAMAJ; CHURCH OF THE NEW DISPENSATION

Sonfuku Senge, see TAISHAKYO

SERVANTS OF THE LIGHT (SOL)

British Theosophical group whose members claim to follow "the mystery schools of the ancient Mediterranean world" and the "Bardic traditions of the West." Hindu ideas are also followed, as well as "psychic" messages.
See also THEOSOPHY

SERVANTS OF THE LIGHT

U.S. ecumenical community founded in Minneapolis, Minnesota, in the 1970s, which developed out of the CATHOLIC CHARISMATIC RENEWAL movement.

SERVANTS OF THE SACRED HEART OF JESUS AND MARY

Traditionalist Catholic group started in 1981 in Friendwood, Texas, by George J. Musey. It has been linked to several other traditionalist groups in the U.S.

SERVERS OF THE GREAT ONES, INC.

Occultist group based in Boston, founded in the 1960s. The doctrine is described as follows: "Eastern and Western techniques are used to develop receptivity to soul contact and the ability to channel spiritual energies toward those areas of the planet most in need; for example, to the United Nations, to any nations in conflict, to bring about racial harmony, and to humanity in general." Classes offered include meditation and "Qabbalah, tarot, I Ching, and the Path of Discipleship." "At the time of the full moon, we link up with meditation groups around the world by using the Great Invocation." Another activity is "the sponsoring of public gatherings annually on World Goodwill Day, the full moon of Gemini."
See also LUCIS TRUST

SEVA FOUNDATION

U.S. Hindu group founded by Ram Dass in the 1970s, devoted to the propagation of traditional Hindu teachings in the West.
See also HANUMAN FOUNDATION

SEVENOAKS COMMUNITY

U.S. commune founded in 1972 by Donovan Thesenga, committed to the PATHWORK "spiritual growth" philosophy.

SEVENTH-DAY ADVENTIST CHURCH (SDA)

International Adventist movement started in the United States in the mid-19th century. Its founder, Ellen Gould White, nee Harmon (1827–1915), was an early follower of William Miller, who predicted the Second Advent for 1844. White suggested that Miller was right in his calculations but wrong in his definition of the predicted event; what actually occurred in 1844 was the cleansing of the divine sanctuary rather than the earthly one, which Miller had predicted. This was revealed to her at age sixteen. Very early, Mrs. White and her followers adopted the keeping of a Saturday Sabbath as part of their strong Old Testament orientation. The name Seventh-Day Adventist Church was adopted in 1860. Other than the emphasis on the Sabbath and the Advent, the movement reflects a general Protestant tradition. Practices include baptism by immersion, a ban on use of alcohol or tobacco, and tithing. The Church operates the International Religious Liberty Association.
See also ADVENTISTS, SECOND; SEVENTH-DAY CHRISTIAN CONFERENCE; SEVENTH DAY CHURCH OF GOD; TWENTIETH CENTURY CHURCH OF GOD
Source:
Numbers, R. L. *Prophetess of Health, A Study of Ellen G. White*. New York: Harper & Row, 1976.

SEVENTH-DAY ADVENTIST REFORM MOVEMENT

International Adventist movement created

in 1923 by German Seventh-Day Adventists who felt that conscientious objection to military service should be a formal requirement of fellowship. When their demand was not met, they established the SDA Reform Movement. The Movement has had branches in Europe, North America, and Oceania.

See also SEVENTH-DAY ADVENTIST CHURCH

SEVENTH DAY PENTECOSTAL CHURCH OF THE LIVING GOD

U.S. PENTECOSTAL group founded by Charles Gamble, a former Roman Catholic and Baptist layman. Its doctrine adopts some Old Testament rules, including keeping Saturday as the Sabbath.

Valerie Seyffert, see CHURCH OF INTEGRAL LIVING

Jeremiah Shabazz, see NATION OF ISLAM (JEREMIAH SHABAZZ)

El Hajj Malik Shabbaz, see NATION OF ISLAM

Idries Shah, see INSTITUTE FOR CULTURAL RESEARCH

Natubhai Shah, see JAIN SAMAJ EUROPE

Shaker Church, see INDIAN SHAKER CHURCH

SHAKERS

Officially named the United Society of Believers in Christ's Second Appearing, this millenarian Christian communal group was popularly known as Shakers (or "Shaking Quakers") because of their custom of "shaking off the flesh," which started as ecstatic spasms during meetings and then developed into dances, accompanied by speaking in tongues. It was founded in 1774 in England by Ann Lee Standerin (1736–1787), known to her followers as "Mother Ann Lee" and "Mother of the New Creation," who formulated the group's ascetic ideals including complete celibacy. Ann Lee lost four infant children, and almost died giving birth to the last one. She then experienced a series of visions in which sexual contacts between Adam and Eve were seen as the source of all evil and suffering.

In 1758 Ann Lee joined the British group then known as the "French Prophets," which was made up of British Quakers inspired by the French Camisards. She and her followers left England, and around 1780 the group started communal settlements in the United States. At the height of their success they had fifty-nine communes with 2,400 members.

Shaker teachings included a belief in the duality of God as both male and female. The founder, Mother Ann Lee, represented the female principle, while Jesus Christ represented maleness.

She was also known as the Word, or Christ in His Second Coming. The group believed in converting the dead and thus claimed among its members such famous historical personages as George Washington, Napoleon, and Queen Elizabeth I. Prescribed celibacy was one step in a program designed to bring about the millennium.

Sources:
Andrews, E.D. *The People Called Shakers.*

Sister Mildred Barker, head of the Shaker colony at Sabbathday Lake, Maine, looks over items to be sold at an auction in 1972. **(see page 263)**

New York: Oxford University Press, 1953.

Desroche, H. *The American Shakers*. Amherst, MA: University of Massachusetts Press, 1971.

Faber, D. *The Perfect Life*. New York: Farrar, Straus and Giroux, 1974.

Melcher, M.F. *The Shaker Adventure*. Princeton: Princeton University Press, 1941.

Morse, F. *The Shakers and the World's People*. New York: Dodd, Mead, 1980.

Whitworth, J. *God's Blueprints*. London: Routledge & Kegan Paul, 1975.

SHALOM CENTER

JESUS MOVEMENT group founded in the early 1970s in Colorado Springs, Colorado.

Rina Shani, see ETZBA ELOHIM

Shanti Desai, see SHANTI YOGI INSTITUTE

SHANTI MANDIR TEMPLE OF PEACE

U.S. Hindu group founded in 1987 by Nityananda (1962–   ), a native of Bombay who in 1981 was appointed as cosuccessor, with his sister, Chidvilasananda (1958–   ), to Baba Muktananda Paramahansa (1908–1982), founder of the SYDA FOUNDATION. The succession was announced by Muktananda Paramahansa a few months before his death. Nityananda left the Syda movement in 1985 and founded his own group.

Shanti Mandir practices include chanting and meditation. "There is only one thing I would like to achieve: I want people to have the *experience* of God and *know* that they are God. With no doubt to have the full conviction, 'Yes, I am that Truth. I am that consciousness'." The group is associated with the Mahamandaleshwar ashram in India.

SHANTI NILAYA

Spiritualist group founded in 1979 in California by Elisabeth Kübler-Ross. Also focused on "healing," the doctrine includes the notion of out-of-body travel and the ethereal body.

Source:

Gill, D. *Quest: The Life of Elisabeth Kübler-Ross*. San Francisco: Harper & Row, 1980.

SHANTI YOGI INSTITUTE

Hindu group founded by Shanti Desai, known as Shanti Yoga, in 1973 in New Jersey. It is devoted to teaching "hatha yoga, raja yoga, and meditation following the path of surrender."

Eddie Brahmananda Shapiro, see INTERNATIONAL YOGA FELLOWSHIP IN AMERICA

Lee Shelley, see MISSIONARY CHRISTIAN AND SOUL WINNING FELLOWSHIP

Isaiah Shembe, see NAZARETHA (SHEMBEITES)

SHEPHERDING

Organizational style in several U.S. Fundamentalist organizations, marked by authoritarian leadership and close supervision of members. The style has been the basis of the "shepherding movement," "discipleship," House Church Movement, Total Commitment Movement, or "multiplying churches." Examples include the BODY OF CHRIST, CHRISTIAN GROWTH MINISTRIES, and CHRISTIAN RESTORATION MINISTRIES.

See also CROSSROADS CHURCHES OF CHRIST; NEW YORK CHURCH OF CHRIST

SHEPHERD'S CHAPEL

Identity group founded by Arnold Murray in the 1970s and based in Gravette, Arkansas.

See also IDENTITY MOVEMENT

SHERBORNE STUDIES GROUP

Gurdjieff group based in Beverly Hills, California, and associated with the CLAYMONT SOCIETY, which follows the teachings of John G. Bennett.

See also GURDJIEFF GROUPS; SHERBORNE SCHOOL

SHILOH TRUE LIGHT CHURCH OF CHRIST

U.S. Adventist group founded in 1870 by Cunningham Boyle (1831–1884), a Methodist layman. Based on his reading of the Bible, Boyle proclaimed the generation of 100 years, to end in 1970 with the coming of Jesus Christ. The group is based in North Carolina. Members follow an austere lifestyle; only plain attire is allowed, and television and movies are banned. The group is fiercely opposed to government control, and in 1971 it won the legal right to educate its children. In 1986 it was in legal difficulties for breaking child-labor laws, because male children were employed as bricklayers as part of its educational program.

SHILOH TRUST

PENTECOSTAL commune founded in the 1930s by Eugene Crosby Monroe (1880–1961), based in Sulphur Springs, Arkansas.

SHILOH YOUTH REVIVAL CENTERS

Communal, PENTECOSTAL, millenarian group founded in 1969 near Eugene, Oregon. In the early 1970s the group operated farms, a construction company, and medical clinics. In the late 1970s most of these activities ceased, and the group was in decline. In 1986 it was sued by the IRS for back taxes on its members' earnings outside the communal enterprises, and it was dissolved in the late 1980s.

Shinnyoen, see SHINYO-EN

SHINREIKYO

Japanese new religion founded by Kanichi Otsuka after World War II and focused on faith healing. Branches have operated in the United States since the 1960s.

Shinsokan, see SEICHO-NO-IE

SHINTO-TOKUMITSU-KYO

Shinto revival movement founded in 1912 by Tokumitsu Kanada (1863–1924). Its Hitonomichi branch, suppressed by the Japanese government in 1937, was revived in 1946 as P L Kyodan.

See also PERFECT LIBERTY KYODAN (P L KYODAN)

SHINYO-EN (Shinnyoen)

Japanese new religious movement of Buddhist origins, founded by Shinjo Ito in 1936. Doctrine is based on worship of the ground god and the sky god in order to control the evil influences of lost souls; members are promised supernatural powers.

Since the 1960s branches have opened in the United States, Europe, and Asia.

Rina Shomroni, see ETZBA ELOHIM

Shoniwa, see MASOWE APOSTLES

SHORESH YISHAI

Hebrew-Christian group founded in the 1970s as the Church of Jesus the Messiah and based in Long Island, New York. It developed out of a Lutheran congregation whose leaders came to believe that to practice true Christianity and follow Jesus Christ of the New Testament they had to practice traditional Judaism. Members have begun following the complete Orthodox Jewish rules of conduct and ritual.

David William Short, see UNIVERSAL CHRISTIAN SPIRITUAL FAITH AND CHURCHES FOR ALL NATIONS

SHOUTERS (SPIRITUAL BAPTISTS)

Caribbean syncretistic Afro-Christian movement started in the late 19th century in Trinidad, Grenada, and other Caribbean islands. Followers practice "possession by spirits" and "speaking in tongues." The British authorities banned the group in 1917 but repealed the order in 1961.

Source:
Simpson, G.E. *Black Religions in the New World.* New York: Columbia University Press, 1978.

SHREE GURUDEV ASHRAM CALIFORNIA

Siddha meditation center associated with the SYDA FOUNDATION.

SHREE GURUDEV RUDRANANDA YOGA ASHRAM

U.S. Hindu group devoted to the teachings of Swami Rudrananda (1928–1973), popularly known in the 1960s as Rudi (Albert Rudolph), an American renowned as a "spiritual teacher" and a teacher of meditation, who was killed in a plane crash. Rudrananda was a disciple of Swami Nityananda (?–1961) and Swami Muktananda (1908–1982), but then started his own ashram in India in 1969. The U.S. group started in the early 1970s. Rudrananda's faith is often summed up as "The total person must be consumed to support life in its depth—to allow for creative interchange between a human being and God."
See also NITYANANDA INSTITUTE

Shrine of the Black Madonna, see PAN AFRICAN ORTHODOX CHRISTIAN CHURCH

SHRI RAM CHANDRA MISSION (SAHAJ MARG)

International Hindu movement named after its founder, Shri Ram Chandraji Maharaj (1899–1983), with branches in Europe.

Shri Sarupanand, see DIVINE LIGHT MISSION

SHRI VISHVA SEVA ASHRAM

Hindu group founded by Swami Vishva Hitesehiji in 1980 and based in New York City.

SIDDHA YOGA

Hindu religious movement started in the 1950s in India. It has been connected with, and has inspired, several Western groups.

Siddha Yoga, see SYDA FOUNDATION

Siddha Yoga Dham, see SYDA FOUNDATION

Ike T. Sidebottom, see TIMELY MESSENGER FELLOWSHIP

Burt Aaron Siegel, see DOR HASHALOM; NEW SYNAGOGUE

Simplified Kundalini Yoga, see WORLD COMMUNITY SERVICE

Albert Benjamin Simpson, see CHRISTIAN AND MISSIONARY ALLIANCE

Charles Simpson, see CHRISTIAN GROWTH MINISTRIES

John C. Sinclair, see PENTECOSTAL CHURCH OF GOD OF AMERICA

Charan Singh, see RADHASOAMI SATSANG BEAS

Thakar Singh, see KIRPAL RUHANI SATSANG

SIRIUS COMMUNITY

Occultist commune started in 1978 by Gordon Davidson and Corinne McLaughlin, former members of the FINDHORN FOUNDATION, near Amherst, Masssachusetts. It is guided by "... a vision to attain the highest good in all levels of God's creation—field and forest, plants and animals, humans and angels, earth and stars. The spiritual understandings we strive to embody have been lived by visionaries in all cultures down through the ages: faith in God, love, truth, cooperation, honoring the oneness of all life, detachment from desire, meditation, and service to the world ... we serve the world through our meditation. We work to create positive thought-forms of peace and healing for the world, as we know that energy follows thought." Members follow the traditions of Findhorn, Yogananda, Alice Bailey, and others. The group believe in living in attunement to the *devas*, nature spirits, and in overcoming financial difficulties through positive attitudes.

Sivananda Ashram Yoga Ranch, see SIVANANDA YOGA VEDANTA CENTERS INTERNATIONAL

Swami Sivananda Radha, see YASODHARA ASHRAM SOCIETY

SIVANANDA YOGA VEDANTA CENTERS INTERNATIONAL (SYVC)

Hindu-inspired group with branches in Western countries including Canada, France, Germany, and United States, founded by Swami Vishnu-devananda (1927–) in 1957. It is devoted to the teachings of Swami Sivananda Saraswati (1887–1963), a renowned Hindu holy man. Sivananda in 1924 opened in a small free dispensary, which later became a hospital, and preached selfless service to humanity as the highest calling. In 1969 Swami Vishnu-devananda founded True World Order (TWO) to foster international peace and brotherhood.

The group's doctrine is based on combining and teaching all yoga techniques. Headquarters are at the Sivananda Ashram Yoga Camp in Val Morin, near Montreal. It operates the Sivananda Ashram Yoga Ranch in New York State and the Sivananda Dhanwantari Ashram in Neyyar Dam, India, among other centers.

See also INTEGRAL YOGA INSTITUTE

SIVANANDA YOGA VEDANTA CHURCH

Hindu-oriented group founded in the 1960s by Victoria Coanda in South Milwaukee, Wisconsin. It is devoted to the teachings of Swami Sivananda Saraswati (1887–1963), a noted 20th-century Hindu guru who was the teacher of Swami Satchidananda and Swami Vishnu Devananda.

See also INTEGRAL YOGA INSTITUTE;

Swami Sivananda Saraswati, Indian holy man who was the inspiration for numerous groups.

SIVANANDA YOGA VEDANTA CENTERS INTERNATIONAL

Sivanarayana Paramahamsa, see BORNHOS

John Skikiewicz, see CHURCH OF MARY MYSTICAL ROSE OF PERPETUAL HELP

Judith Skutch, see FOUNDATION FOR INNER PEACE

John Slocum, see INDIAN SHAKER CHURCH

Victor Smadja, see HEBREW CHRISTIAN ASSEMBLY—JERUSALEM CONGREGATION

Chuck Smith, see CALVARY CHAPEL

E.D. Smith, see TRIUMPH THE CHURCH AND KINGDOM OF GOD IN CHRIST

Enid Smith, see UNIVERSAL FAITH AND WISDOM ASSOCIATION

Gerald L.K. Smith, see CHRISTIAN NATIONALIST CRUSADE

Johann Oskar Smith, see SMITH VENNER

Murcie P. Smith, see ESP PICTURE PRAYERS

Theodore Smith, see CENTER FOR CONSCIOUSNESS

SMITH VENNER

Scandinavian Christian group founded in Norway in the early 20th century by Johann

Swami Vishnu-devananda, founder of the Sivananda Yoga Vedanta Centers. **(see page 268)**

Oskar Smith (1871–1943), with branches in Western Europe and the United States.

"Snake handlers," see CHURCH OF ALL NATIONS; DOLLEY POND CHURCH OF GOD WITH SIGNS FOLLOWING

Rose Soares, see LAMB OF GOD CHURCH

Jacob M. Sober, Miriam M. Sober, see CHURCH OF RELIGIOUS PHILOSOPHY

SOCIETAS ROSICRUCIANA IN AMERICA (SRIA)

Occultist group started in 1907 in Boston by Sylvester C. Gould, who died in 1909. The leadership passed to George Winslow Plummer (1876–1944).

SOCIETY OF CHRIST, INC.

Spiritualist-Christian group founded in Los Angeles in the 1970s.

SOCIETY OF PRAGMATIC MYSTICISM

NEW THOUGHT group founded by Mildred Mann (?–1971) in the 1940s in New York City. Its doctrine is summed up as follows: "Pragmatic Mysticism is a truth teaching based on the Bible and the eternal laws of God. It is the practice of the presence of God in everyday life with conscious effort and direction."

SOCIETY OF ST. PIUS V

Traditionalist Catholic group in the United States, created as an offshoot of the FRATERNITY OF ST. PIUS X and led by Clarence Kelly. Members believe that Archbishop Marcel Lefebvre and the Fraternity were too liberal. They oppose all recent reforms in the Roman Catholic Church and conduct services in Latin. The Society has operated a convent, St. Joseph's Novitiate, which follows the monastic rules that governed such institutions before the reforms of the 1960s.

Mirza Ahmad Sohrab, see NEW HISTORY SOCIETY

SOKA GAKKAI (SK)

Buddhist religious-political movement based in Japan, founded in 1930 by Tsunesaburo Makiguchi (1871–1944) and Josei Toda (1900–1958). In 1960 Daisaku Ikeda (1928–) was elected the third president of the movement. Its religious origins are in the NICHIREN SHOSHU movement, and it is today represented in politics through the Komeito (Clean Government) Party. Komeito was organized in 1964 and in 1970 formally separated itself from Soka Gakkai.

Soka Gakkai ("Value Creation Society") has become a true mass movement; it has been accused of being neofascist and of acting for the restoration of state Shinto in Japan. It is one of forty sects that claim to follow the teachings of Nichiren (1222–1282), who was the founder of Japan's first Buddhist native sect, known as Hokke-Shu (Lotus sect). The group offers its members happiness, which is "the attainment of enlightenment through perfection and the realization of all desires." This is achieved through chanting the Lotus Mantra Chant—*Nam Yoho Rengay Kyo*, formulated by Nichiren in 1253. Chanting twice a day in front of the Gohonzon, the sacred scroll, brings about material prosperity and happiness. The Dai-Gohonzon, inscribed by Nichiren Daishonin himself, is kept at the main temple in Japan.

"The object of worship in Nichiren Shoshu Buddhism is the Dai-Gohonzon, inscribed by the founder, Nichiren Daishonin, on October 12, 1279, with the aim of enabling all people to attain absolute happiness and bring about world peace. The Gohonzon literally means the most fundamental and respectable entity. It contains the life-force and the fundamental law inherent in the whole universe which is Nam-myoho-renge-kyo."

Sources:

Anesaki, M. *Nichiren the Buddhist Prophet*. Cambridge: Harvard University Press, 1916.

Brannen, N.S. *Soka Gakkai*. Richmond, VA: John Knox Press, 1968.

Dator, J. A. *Soka Gakkai: Builders of the Third Civilization*. Seattle: University of Washington Press, 1969.

Metraux, D. *The History and Theology of Soka Gakkai*. Lewiston, NY: Edwin Mellen Press, 1988.

Murata, K. *Japan's New Buddhism*. New York: Walker/Weatherhill, 1969.

White, J.W. *The Sokkagakkai and Mass Society*. Stanford, CA: Stanford University Press, 1970.

SOKA GAKKAI INTERNATIONAL

Organization of national NICHIREN SHOSHU groups founded in 1975, claiming to have members in 115 nations. It supports the United Nations, where it has nongovermental organization status (NGO).

SOLAR, see SCHOOL OF LIGHT AND REALIZATION

SOLAR CROSS FELLOWSHIP

UFO-Theosophical group based in Auburn, California, founded in the 1950s by Rudolph H. Pestalozzi and focused on communicating with "space brothers." The group merged with the SOLAR LIGHT CENTER in the 1960s.

SOLAR LIGHT CENTER

UFO-Theosophical group founded by Marianne Francis, also known as Aleuti Francesca, in the mid-1960s in Central Point, Oregon. Members believe in the Great White Brotherhood and reincarnation and expect the second coming of Jesus Christ soon. They communicate with various "spiritual masters" and "outer-space intelligence."

See also THEOSOPHY

Soldiers of God, see SOJA WE MWARI

Paul Solomon, see FELLOWSHIP OF THE INNER LIGHT

Vladimir Soloviev, see LINDISFARNE

SONS AHMAN ISRAEL (SAI)
Polygamist Mormon-syncretistic group started in 1981 by David Israel in Utah. Its doctrine combines traditional Mormon elements with ideas about "Kabbalah" and gnosticism and claims of recent revelations. The group has a European branch known as INDEPENDENT CHURCH OF JESUS CHRIST OF LATTER DAY SAINTS.
See also MORMONS

SONS OF FREEDOM
Officially known as the Christian Community of Universal Brotherhood (CCUB), and later as the Union of Spiritual Communities, popularly known as Freedomites or "svobodniki," this group was created by a split in the DOUKHOBORS, an anarchist religious group based in Canada. Its doctrine calls for the rejection of materialism, extreme vegetarianism, and opposition to all government regulation and government-sponsored education. Between 1960 and 1985 the group was involved in 130 violent incidents, including bombings and arson, directed at other Doukhobor groups and the Canadian government.

Source:
Holt, S. *Terror in the Name of God.* New York: Crown, 1965.

Geshe Lhundup Sopa, see GANDEN MAHAYANA CENTER

Judy Sorensen, see COMMUNITY OF JESUS

Southern California Metaphysical Institute, see RELIGIOUS SCIENCE, CHURCH OF

William Sowders, see GOSPEL ASSEMBLIES

Sam Spanier, see MATAGIRI

Gladys Spearman-Cook, see SCHOOL OF UNIVERSAL PHILOSOPHY AND HEALING

SPIRIT OF JESUS CHRIST
Japanese indigenous Christian church formed in 1937 in secession from the ASSEMBLIES OF GOD. Missions operate in North and South America.

SPIRITUAL FELLOWSHIP OF AMERICA
NEW THOUGHT group founded by Pat Fenske in the 1970s in Philadelphia.

SPIRITUAL FRONTIERS FELLOWSHIP (SFF)
U.S. spiritualist group whose membership has consisted of Protestant ministers and laymen affiliated with established churches, together with members of Theosophical and spiritualist groups. It was founded in 1956 by Albin Bro, Paul Higgins, and Arthur Ford, famous medium and former minister of the FIRST SPIRITUALIST CHURCH OF NEW YORK. The SFF has published journals promoting the combined Christian-Spiritualist point of view.

Its membership and activities have been

mostly concentrated in the Midwest.
See also INNER PEACE MOVEMENT

Source:

Wagner, M.B. *Metaphysics in Midwestern America.* Columbus: Ohio State University Press, 1983.

SPIRITUAL LIFE INSTITUTE

North American Christian mystical group founded by Teresa Bielecki around 1980. The group maintains monastic retreats in Colorado and Nova Scotia and teaches "concrete mystical practices."

SPIRITUAL SCIENCE CHURCH

Also known as Spiritual Science Mother Church, this spiritualist-Christian group was founded in 1923 by "Mother" Julia O. Forrest, who had been a CHRISTIAN SCIENCE practitioner. The Church combines some Christian traditions with Theosophy and Christian Science. There is emphasis on healing, and less attention is paid to spirit communication compared to other spiritualist groups.
See also ASSOCIATED SPIRITUALISTS; NATIONAL SPIRITUAL SCIENCE CENTER

SPIRITUAL SCIENCE FELLOWSHIP

North American spiritualist-NEW THOUGHT group based in Montreal, and founded by John Rossnner.

Gene Spriggs, and Martha Spriggs, see NORTHEAST KINGDOM COMMUNITY CHURCH

SPRING GROVE

"Spiritual community" founded in the 1980s in Marin County, California, by Bruce Davis. Its doctrine is based on combining Christian nysticism with "psychical healing" and shamanism. The founder claims to have begun his "spiritual training . . . in the company of psychic healers in the Philippines" and to have ". . . studied with an Eskimo shaman in Alaska, trained in the Christian-based mysticism of 'A COURSE IN MIRACLES'."

SPRINGHILL COMMUNITY

"Spiritual community" founded in the late 1970s in Asby, Massachusetts. Practices emphasize silent meditation and prayer.

Richard G. Spurling, see CHURCH OF GOD (CLEVELAND, TENNESSEE)

SRI AUROBINDO

International Hindu group inspired by Aravinda Ackroyd Ghose (1872–1950), Indian philosopher and mystic, who became known as Sri Aurobindo after devoting himself to a life of contemplation. After receiving both traditional and Western education, he became an extreme nationalist, seeing Indian nationalism as divine. Following a political career in the independence movement, he renounced all political pursuits and in 1910 founded an ashram in Pondicherry, India, which was then a French colony. Actually, his move toward spirituality began in 1903 with an experience of the "vacant infinite." In 1908 he met a yogi who taught him how to experience "the Absolute." Then in 1909, while in prison, he had a vision of Krishna, which convinced him that he should leave politics. On November 24, 1926, he was reported to have experienced "the Day of Siddhi," the point of contact with the "Supermind."

Aurobindo's ashram attracted both Indian and Western followers. His best-known convert was the French woman Mira

Mira Alfassa, partner of Sri Aurobindo and founder of the city of Auroville.

Conceived in 1967, this was the initial approach to the design of Auroville, the first international city devoted to human unity and world peace.

Richard, nee Alfassa (1878–1973), who first visited the ashram in 1914 and settled there permanently in 1920. Known as The Mother, she became a full partner of Aurobindo, whom she believed to be a divine being descended to earth. He in turn saw her as "Divine Consciousness." She became the administrative leader of the ashram and led it to growth and material wealth. On February 29, 1956, she announced her avatarhood, *i.e.*, her divinity, and became regarded as the "Divine Mother." In the 1960s she founded the New Age Association, and in 1968, in collaboration with UNESCO, she established the city of Auroville. Since then Aurobindo disciples have been building Auroville, the "City of Human Unity." Groups of Sri Aurobindo followers have operated in the West.

Aurobindo's teachings constitute an attempt to adapt Hinduism to modern life, influenced by Ramakrishna and Vivekananda. He advocated the use of yoga techniques and founded what he called Integral Yoga. Aurobindo is known for his conception of supraconsciousness, the final stage of human evolution that will transform material life and individual consciousness. This level will be achieved only by a small elite, the kernel of a new human race.

See also ATMANIKETAN ASHRAM; CALIFORNIA INSTITUTE OF ASIAN STUDIES; MATAGIRI; RAMAKRISHNA MATH AND MISSION

Sources:

Bassuk, D.E. *Incarnation in Hinduism and Christianity: The Myth of the Godman.* Atlantic Highlands, NJ: Humanities Press, 1986.

McDermott, R., ed. *The Essential Aurobindo.* New York: Schocken Books, 1963.

SRI AUROBINDO INTERNATIONAL CENTER FOUNDATION

U.S. group devoted to the teachings of SRI AUROBINDO, founded in 1953 in New York by Mrs. Moore Montgomery.

SRI CHIMNOY

Known officially as Aspiration-Body-Temple-Service, this international group is devoted to the teachings of Sri Chimnoy (Chimnoy Kumar Ghose), a Bengali author and former postal clerk, born in 1931. He has been based in New York City since the 1960s, teaching a form of Hinduism described as the "path of grace" and inspired by SRI AUROBINDO. The group states that "Through Divine Love, one-pointed devotion, and unconditional surrender to the highest, the disciple comes to the realization of his eternal oneness with the Supreme." Practices include "nondenominational meditation." Branches have been active in Western Europe.

SRI MA ANANDAMAYI ASHRAMS

Hindu 20th-century movement focused on the personality of the Hindu woman saint Sri Ma Anandamayi. The first ashram was founded in 1932 in Dehra Dun, India. Western branches have opened since the 1960s. See also ANANDAMAYEE CHARITABLE SOCIETY; SRI MA ANANDAMAYI MONASTERY

SRI MA ANANDAMAYI MONASTERY

Hindu monastic group founded in 1967 by Swami Nirmalananda Giri in Oklahoma City, Oklahoma. It is devoted to the memory and teachings of Sri Ma

Sri Chimnoy, leader of a Hindu sect bearing his name, prepares for a marathon race held in New York City in honor of his forty-eighth birthday in 1979. **(see page** 274**)**

Anandamayi (or Anandamayee), famous Hindu woman saint (1896–). Members practice mantra meditation.

Sri Mataji Nirmala Devi, see NIRMALA DEVI

SRI RAMA FOUNDATION

North American Hindu group founded in 1971 in California, devoted to the teachings of Baba Hari Dass. Practices focus on yoga.

SRI RAM ASHRAMA

Hindu commune founded in 1967 as the Ananda Ashrama by Swami Abhayananda. Based in Benson, Arizona, the group practices meditation and yoga.

J.N. Srivastava, see TRANSCENDENTAL MEDITATION

SSERULANDA SPIRITUAL PLANETARY COMMUNITY

Also known as the SSerulanda Nsulo Y'obulamu Spiritual Foundation, this Ugandan syncretistic group was founded in the 1970s by J.K. Mugonza (1937–), a former Roman Catholic trained in India by a RADHASOAMI master. To his disciples, Mugonza is known as Bambi Baaba, "Redeemer of the New Age." His doctrines combine Hindu and Sikh ideas with the vocabulary of THEOSOPHY and UFO lore. He also promotes the notion of Uganda as the chosen nation, destined to lead the world in "spiritual splendor."

George A. Stallings, see IMANI TEMPLE

STANDARD CHURCH OF AMERICA

North American conservative Protestant group founded in 1919 in Watertown, New York, by Ralph G. Horner. Headquarters are in Borchville, Ontario, Canada.

Ray Stanford, see ASSOCIATION FOR THE UNDERSTANDING OF MAN
Noel Stanton, see JESUS FELLOWSHIP CHURCH

STARCROSS MONASTIC COMMUNITY

U.S. mystical retreat community founded by Tolbert McCarroll in the late 1960s. The overall orientation is Christian, with special reference to medieval Christian masters, but Eastern traditions are also used, including meditation. Starcross operates the Humanist Institute, which offers meditation classes.

Starkyites, see AGAPEMONE

STAUFFER MENNONITE CHURCH

Protestant group founded in Lancaster County, Pennsylvania, in the late 1840s by Jacob Stauffer.

Rudolf Steiner, see ANTHRO-POSOPHICAL SOCIETY; CHRISTIAN COMMUNITY CHURCH; HOLISTIC COMMUNITY

STELLE COMMUNITY

Theosophical-occultist group founded by Richard Kieninger (1927–) in Chicago in 1953. Doctrine predicts a series of world catastrophes starting in 1976–1977, leading to nuclear war in 1999 and culminating in a major catastrophe on May 5, 2000, in which 90 percent of humanity will be destroyed. Members of the community will be among the 10 percent saved.
See also THEOSOPHY

Sally Stern, see INNER CIRCLE OF ENCHANTMENT INC.

Augusta Stetson, see CHURCH TRIUMPHANT

Margaret Stevens, see SANTA ANITA CHURCH

Don Stewart, see MIRACLE REVIVAL FELLOWSHIP

Gary Stewart, see AMORC ROSI-CRUCIAN ORDER

St. John the Vine, see CHURCH OF THE LIVING GOD

Loy and Louise Stone, see COVEN OF ARIANHU

STONEGATE CHRISTIAN COMMUNITY

Evangelical commune based in West Virginia, founded in the 1980s.

Frank E. Stranges, see INTERNATIONAL EVANGELISM CRUSADES

R.A. Straughn, see AUSAR AUSET SOCIETY

James R. Strole, see ETERNAL FLAME FOUNDATION

John Stroup, see PENTECOSTAL CHURCH OF CHRIST

Friend Stuart, see CHURCH OF THE TRINITY (INVISIBLE MINISTRY)

SUBUD

Western movement of Islamic-Hindu origins started by Pak Muhammad Subuh (1901–   ), known as Bapak ("father"), an Indonesian monk. Bapak had a divine revelation in 1925 and began teaching Subud in Java in 1933. It appeared in the West for the first time in England in 1957 through the efforts of John G. Bennett, a British follower of Gurdjieff, after meeting a disciple of Subuh. The name Subud supposedly comes from a combination of the Sanskrit terms *Susila, Buddhi, Dharma,* and is unrelated to the founder's name.

The central practice of Subud is *latihan*, an ecstatic exercise done in groups varying in size from a few to hundreds and leading to the experience of bliss. Disciples describe it as an inner awakening during which "the life force" enters the soul of the believer. The experience may also be used to help reach personal decisions through sensing true inner feelings. There is also the ritual of *salamatan*, which is a feast for the membership. Subud members change their names, not only for internal group occasions, but also in official documents. See also GURDJIEFF GROUPS; SUFI ORDER IN THE WEST

Source:
Needleman, J. *The New Religions.* Garden City, NY: Doubleday, 1970.

Pak Muhammad Subuh, see SUBUD

SUFI ISLAMIA RUHANIAT SOCIETY, THE

Sufi group founded in California in 1968 by Samuel L. Lewis (1896–1971), known as Murshid Sam or "Sufi Sam," reputedly a member of the Chisti Order of Sufis. He was succeeded by Murshid Moineddin Jablonski and Masheikh Wali Ali Meyer. The group practices and teaches Sufi meditation and dancing.

SUFI ORDER IN THE WEST

Known in German-speaking countries as Zenith Institute, this international Islamic-inspired group is devoted to teaching the tradition of Sufism, *i.e.,* Islamic mysticism together with Universal Worship, which pays respect to all major world religions and adopts Christian, Buddhist, and yogic traditions. Actually, it combines Hindu and Islamic elements, with practices that include meditation, recitation, rhythmic chanting, and dancing.

The group was founded in England in 1914 by Hazrat Inayat Khan (1881–1927), who was born in India to a family of Moslem musicians. Between 1903 and 1907 he was a disciple of a Sufi master. He then traveled as a pilgrim throughout India, Burma, and Ceylon while performing as a musician. In 1910 he visited the United States and Europe, performing and lecturing. Between 1914 and 1920 he was in London, building up the Sufi Movement. He then traveled in the West, founding Sufi centers wherever he went, until 1926, when he

Pir Vilayat Inayat Khan, leader and son of the founder of the Sufi Order in the West. **(see page 279)**

returned to India. Hazrat Inayat Khan, known as "Pir-o-Murshid," was succeeded as group leader by his son, Pir Vilayat Inayat Khan (1916–   ), who founded the ABODE OF THE MESSAGE in upstate New York, which now serves as headquarters.

SUFISM REORIENTED, INC.

Group based in San Francisco devoted to the teaching of MEHER BABA. Originally started as a Sufi group early in the 20th century, the group changed its orientation in 1952 when its leader, Ivy Oneita Duce (1895–   ), known as Murshida ("teacher"), first met Meher Baba. It has published English versions of Meher Baba's collections of messages.

See also BABA LEAGUE; MEHER DURBAR; SUFI ORDER IN THE WEST

SUKYO MAHIKARI

Splinter group growing out of MAHIKARI ("True Light") following the death of its founder, started in 1978 by Sekiguchi Sakae. Its doctrine is identical to that of Mahikari, but it claims to be more loyal to the founder's teachings.

SUMMIT LIGHTHOUSE

Also known as The Church Universal and Triumphant (CUT) or Summit International, this occultist Theosophical group was founded in 1958 in Washington, DC, by Mark Prophet (1918–1973) and Elizabeth Clare (Wolf) Prophet (1940–   ), sometimes known as Guru Ma or Mother, former members of THE BRIDGE TO FREEDOM, "on orders from the Ascended Master El Morya." The group proclaims a "Coming Revolution in Higher Consciousness." Its doctrine is based on the teachings of "I AM," combining Western occultist traditions with Hindu ideas, and of the Great White Brotherhood (White Light of the Aura) and "Saint Germain." The Bible and Christian traditions are also utilized.

"The Summit Lighthouse publishes the teachings of the ascended masters of the Great White Brotherhood as taught by Elizabeth Clare Prophet. Study, meditation, and the science of the spoken Word in decrees and mantras are an essential part of their program to help the individual realize his God-potential and soul freedom and to assist people of every race and religion to live in harmony with cosmic law." In her public appearances Mrs. Prophet has delivered "dictations from the Ascended Masters," including "Beloved Mother Mary" and Nicholas Roerich. In the 1980s the group offered both faith healing and vegetarian diets designed to protect the body from AIDS and cancer. In 1982 the group acquired a 12,000-acre ranch in Paradise Valley, Montana, and in early 1990 many members moved there in anticipation of a global catastrophe predicted by Mrs. Prophet. In the late 1980s Summit Lighthouse was sued by Gregory Mull, a former member, who was awarded $1.56 million after accusing the group of pressuring him to give up his life's savings. The group has operated overseas branches in Latin America, Europe, and West Africa.

See also THEOSOPHY

SUMMUM CHURCH

Occultist group founded in 1975 by Claude Rex Nowell in Salt Lake City, Utah. Its practices include meditation, pyramid building, and mummification.

SUNERGOS INSTITUTE, INC.

Religious commune in Jasper, Arkansas,

founded around 1970. Its doctrine is based on a combination of Western and Eastern ideas.

SUNRAY MEDITATION SOCIETY

Occultist group based in New York City that promotes native American traditions. Founded in the 1970s in Huntington, Vermont, it is led by Dhyani Ywahoo, "planetary teacher," "the 27th holder of the Ywahoo lineage and a member of the traditional Etawa Band of the eastern Tsalagi (Cherokee) Nation." The group operates the Sunray School of Sacred Studies.

Susan Lipowitz Foundation, see ALAMO CHRISTIAN FOUNDATION

"Svobodniki," see SONS OF FREEDOM

SWAMINARAYANA

Hindu group founded in the late 18th century. In 1802 the founder, Swami Ramananda (1781–1830), known also as Sri Swaminarayan, who claimed to be God himself, ceded his place to twenty-one-year-old Swami Sahajanand. The latter reformed the group and created a body of five hundred monks. In his book *Shikshapatri*, written in 1826, he specifies the rules of conduct for followers, which prohibit murder, theft, suicide, meat, wine, self-mutilation, adultery, gambling, tobacco, and the breaking of Hindu caste laws. Monks are forbidden any contact with women, or even to talk about them. The *Shikshapatri* is read daily by or to all members. Since the 1950s branches of this group have opened among Hindus living in the West.

Source:
Brent, P. *Godmen of India*. Chicago: Quadrangle Books, 1972.

SWAMI SHANTIANANDA CENTER

Hindu group based in Tennessee, founded by Swami Shantiananda around 1970 and devoted to the teaching of Hindu beliefs and practices, including meditation and yoga.

Swami Swanandashram, see YOGIRAJ

SWEDENBORG FOUNDATION

One of several organizations representing a worldwide movement of followers of Emanuel Swedenborg (1688–1772). A Swedish mystic, trained as a mining engineer, Swedenborg in 1743 started having visions of angels, heaven, and hell. He declared that for thirty years he had been in daily contact with the "spiritual world." According to his visions, the world is divided into three regions: the heavens, the hells, and the world of spirits.

Swedenborg's visions are cast within a Christian framework and proclaim a spiritual Second Coming of Jesus Christ rather than a physical one. The old Church, founded by Jesus Christ, came to its end in 1587, and Swedenborg is the divinely inspired messenger of the new one, the full name of which is the New Church Signified by the New Jerusalem in the Revelation.

Organizations promoting Swedenborg's ideas arose soon after his death. The best-known among them are the Church of the New Jerusalem ("New Church"), founded in 1782, and the Swedenborg Society of London, founded in 1810, which is the world center of the movement. Swedenborgian groups now exist in Sweden, throughout the English-speaking world, and in southern Africa.

John Chapman (1774–1845), known as

"Johnny Appleseed," was instrumental in spreading the message in the United States.

Sources:

Meyers, M.A. *A New World Jerusalem.* Greenwood Press, 1983.

Toksvig, S. *Emanuel Swedenborg, Scientist and Mystic.* New Haven: Yale University Press, 1948.

"Sweet Daddy Grace," see UNITED HOUSE OF PRAYER FOR ALL PEOPLE

SWORD OF CHRIST GOOD NEWS MINISTRIES

Christian Identity group founded in the 1970s in Arkansas by Ralph P. Forbes, a former leader in the American Nazi Party. See also IDENTITY

The grave of John Chapman, who as "Johnny Appleseed" spent much of his life planting apple trees and spreading the message of Emanuel Swedenborg in the United States.

Sword of the Spirt, see WORD OF GOD

SYDA FOUNDATION (SIDDHA YOGA DHAM ASSOCIATES)

International Hindu group founded in 1975 and promoting Siddha Meditation in the West. Siddha Meditation is a technique taught by followers of Swami Muktananda Paramahansa (1908–1982). Muktananda, whose home ashram, Sri Gurudev Siddha Peeth, is in Ganeshpuri, near Bombay, followed the devotional tradition that he had learned from Swami Nityananda. He was born on May 16, 1908, and at age fifteen started wandering after an alleged first meeting with Swami Nityananda. He became Swami Nityananda's disciple only at age thirty-nine, settled in Ganeshpuri in 1956, and in 1961, when Swami Nityananda

Emanuel Swedenborg.

died, inherited his mantle. In the 1970s he spent two years in the U.S. In 1981 Nityananda (1962–) was appointed co-successor, with his sister Chidvilasananda (1958–), to Baba Muktananda Paramahansa. This succession was announced by Muktananda Paramahansa a few months before his death. Nityananda left the Syda movement in 1985 and founded his own group. Since 1985 the movement has been led by Swami Chidvilasananda, known to her followers as Gurumayi.

The underlying traditions of Syda are Vedanta and Kashmir Shaivism, and the practices are of kundalini yoga. Siddha Yoga offers a process of quick enlightenment known as *shaktipat*. "Shaktipat is a subtle spiritual process by which the Guru transmits his divine power into the aspirant either by touch, word, look or thought." "... Through chanting, meditation, and adherence to spiritual discipline," a seeker can cut through "the dramas of the mind" and experience the "joy and divinity of the Self that lies within."

Branches of this group in the United States are known as Siddha Yoga Dham. See also SHANTI MANDIR TEMPLE OF PEACE

Source:

Brent, P. *Godmen of India*. Chicago: Quadrangle Books, 1972.

T

"Tabernacle of God," see MAKUYA

Pak T'ae-son, see CHONDOKWON

Debendranath Tagore, see BRAHMA SAMAJ

Rabindranath Tagore, see SANTINIKETAN

Tahupotiki Wiremu Ratana, see RATANA

Jomyo Tanaka, see MANDALA BUDDHIST CENTER

Masaharu Taniguchi, see SEICHO-NO-IE

Tara Center, see WORLD TEACHER

"TARO CULT"

New Guinea syncretistic movement (CARGO CULT) started in 1914 by Buninia, of the Orokaiva people. Following a vision of his father's spirit, he developed magical practices for improving the taro crops. Taro spirits are worshiped and expected to provide believers with European goods ("cargo") or massive crops. Rituals include ecstatic dancing and spirit possession.

Source:
Williams, F.E. *Orokaiva Magic.* London: Oxford University Press, 1928.

Gaan Tata, see MASA JEHOVAH

TATAGATAS

U.S. commune founded by Ed Dalton in the 1960s, combining Western and Buddhist-inspired beliefs and practices, including meditation.

Richard Tate, see GOSPEL ASSEMBLIES (TATE)

Robert Taylor, see FIRST COMMUNITY CHURCH OF AMERICA

TAYU FELLOWSHIP

Neo-pagan homosexual group founded in the 1970s in California by Daniel Inesse. Its doctrine refers to the ancient Greek gods as guides.

TEACHING OF THE INNER CHRIST, INC.

Formerly known as the Society for the Teaching of the Inner Christ and as the Brotherhood of Followers of the Present Jesus, this Christian-Hindu-occultist group was founded in 1965 in San Diego by Ann Poter Meyer and Peter Victor Meyer. Its inspiration is drawn from the "master teachers Jesus and Babaji," and its practices include meditation and spiritual healing.
See also INTERNATIONAL BABAJI KRYIAN YOGA SANGAM

TEILHARD CENTRE, THE

British Christian group founded in 1965 in London to promote the teachings of the Jesuit Pierre Teilhard de Chardin, who tried to interpret evolution within the framework of Christianity. It is affiliated with the FONDATION TEILHARD DE CHARDIN and the ASSOCIATION DES AMIS DE PIERRE TEILHARD DE CHARDIN in Paris. See also AMERICAN TEILHARD ASSOCIATION

Luisa Teish, see YORUBA LACUMI

TÉMOINS DU CHRIST REVENU (Christ's Witnesses)

French Christian group founded in 1950 by Georges Roux (1903–1981), a mailman in Montfavet, in the department of Var. Roux claimed to be a reincarnation of Jesus Christ, became known as "Christ de Montfavet," and offered healing services through laying on of hands. The group's dietary rules forbid coffee, tobacco, tea, canned foods, and deep frying; members are promised a life span of 120 years if they avoid the "five poisons." Another rule forbade the use of normal medicine. This led to the death by neglect of three children of members in 1954, to legal proceedings, and to an outcry against the group, which at one point adopted the name of "Église Chrétienne Universelle." Roux predicted the disappearance of all "forces of evil" from earth on January 1, 1982, but he died on December 26, 1981. In the late 1980s the group adopted the name Alliance Universelle. Branches have operated in Western Europe.

Placide Tempels, see JAMAA

Temple Lot Church, see CHURCH OF CHRIST (TEMPLE LOT)

Pierre Teilhard de Chardin during World War I.

TEMPLE OF COSMIC RELIGION

International Hindu movement devoted to spreading Hindu teachings in the West. Founded by Satguru Sant Keshavadas as the Dasashram International Center in 1967, the movement emphasizes yoga and meditation.

TEMPLE OF KRIYA YOGA

U.S. Hindu group founded in the 1950s by Melvin Higgins, also known as Sri Goswami Kriyananda. Kriyananda was a student of Paramahansa Yogananda of the SELF-REALIZATION FELLOWSHIP and started the Temple after Yogananda's death in 1952. The Temple operates the College of Occult

Sciences. Activities included "Classes, counseling, and individual instruction in yoga, meditation, mystical philosophy, the spiritual sciences, and sane, joyous living."

TEMPLE OF THE ETERNAL LIGHT, INC.

Christian-occultist-pagan group, described as "an Omni-Denominational religious fellowship," founded by Jerome Peartree and Karen DePolito in 1985 in New York City. It offers "self-improvement through Magick," teaching "...Caballa, Tarot, Crystals, Wicca." Wiccan festivals are celebrated, as well as a "Gnostic Mass."

TEMPLE OF THE GODDESS WITHIN

Neo-pagan feminist association of covens, founded by Ann Forfreedom and based in Sacramento, California.
See also COVENANT OF THE GODDESS

TEMPLE OF UNIVERSAL JUDAISM

Known also as Congregation Daat Elohim, this Jewish reform group, with an ecumenical emphasis, was founded in New York City in 1975 by Roy A. Rosenberg. Doctrine emphasizes the commonality of world religions and a universalism in moral concerns.
See also REFORM JUDAISM

TEMPLE OF UNIVERSAL LAW

U.S. spiritualist-Theosophical group founded in 1936 in Chicago by Charlotte Bright.

TEMPLE OF UNIVERSAL PEACE

Hindu revival group founded in Madras, India, in 1935 by Swami Paranjothi. It is devoted to the practice of kundalini yoga, which assumes the presence and utilization of female energy within the human body.
See also WORLD COMMUNITY SERVICE

Osel Tendzin, see VAJRADHATU

Tenri Honmichi, see HONMICHI

Tenri Kenkyukai, see HONMICHI

TENRIKYO ("Heavenly Reason Teaching")

Japanese messianic syncretistic movement, originating in Shinto tradition, but including also Buddhist and Christian elements, founded by Mrs. Omiki Nakayama (1798–1887). The founder came from a prosperous farming family belonging to the Jodo Buddhist sect. She was married at age twelve to Zenbei Nakayama, a farmer, and had six children in her early twenties. At age forty she had her "first revelation," namely, that she was possessed by the god Tenri, and so the movement regards 1838 as the date of its founding. In 1862 a group was formed. The group scripture is known as Ofudesaki. Mrs. Nakayama is considered the Messiah, and many stories of miracles performed by her are told by members in support of their belief that God has chosen to manifest himself through her to save humankind. Mrs. Nakayama is considered the Temple of God and His mediator on earth. Tenrikyo doctrine also promises the imminent coming of the heavenly kingdom, which is its eventual goal.

The movement is sometimes referred to as the Japanese CHRISTIAN SCIENCE because of the beliefs it shares with that group. Its basic tenet in that connection is that the root of suffering and sickness is in the mind. Those who manage to overcome anger, selfishness, and other negative feelings may live to age 115 free of sickness and worry. This, and eternal life, will be everyone's lot when the messianic age comes.

After World War II, Tenrikyo began to take an active part in Japanese politics. Branches have operated among Japanese in North America and in Brazil.
See also HONMICHI

TENSHO KOTAI JUNGU KYO
Known also as Mioshi or Odoru-Shukyo ("Dancing Religion"), this Japanese syncretistic movement of Shinto origins was founded in 1945 by Kitamura Sayo (1900–1967), known to her followers as Ogamisama ("the goddess"). In 1943 she had experiences of being possessed by the Shinto god Tensho Kotai Jungu. Later she claimed to be Jesus Christ and Buddha. Group practices include "healing" and ecstatic dancing. Doctrine calls for getting rid of the root evils, the human weaknesses of regret, desire, love, and hatred. Branches operate in Hawaii and California in the United States, as well as in all continents.

John David Terry, see EMMANUEL CHURCH OF CHRIST ONENESS PENTECOSTAL

Abraham Ikuro Teshima, see MAKUYA

Vimala Thakar, see VIMAL PRAKASHAN TRUST

Eleanore Mary Thedick, see CHRIST MINISTRY FOUNDATION

THE HOLY EARTH ASSEMBLY (T.H.E.A.)
U.S. "pagan church" founded in the 1980s to perform "legal handfastings" ("pagan weddings") and training programs for pagan clergy.

William Theiford, see A COURSE IN MIRACLES

THEOCENTRIC FOUNDATION
Occultist-Theosophical group founded in 1959 in Phoenix, Arizona. It is the successor to the Shangrila Missions, the Eden Foundation, the Manhattan Philosophical Center, and the Theocentric Temple. The group teaches "Hermetic theology."

THEOCRATIC COMMUNE NATURAL HEALTH SERVICE
Christian healing commune founded in Detroit in the 1970s by Raymond Allen Archer (1940–   ). Archer advocated a strict diet of raw fruits and vegetables. In 1978 he was charged with manslaughter after his two children died of malnutrition.

THEOSOPHICAL ORDER OF SERVICE (T.O.S.), THE
British Theosophical charity organization founded in London in 1908 by Annie Besant.
See also THEOSOPHY

THEOSOPHICAL SOCIETY IN AMERICA
Theosophical group founded in 1895 by William Q. Judge following a dispute with Annie Besant, the leader of the Theosophical Society in Adyar, India. Most American Theosophists followed Judge and joined the new group.
See also THEOSOPHY

THEOSOPHY

Founded in 1875 at 46 Irving Place, New York City, Theosophy is in many ways the prototype for the Western new religion. It combines occult traditions, Eastern ideas, and ideals of self-improvement, leading the way to hundreds of similar and subsidiary groups.

The Theosophical Society was founded in 1875 in New York City by Helena Petrovna Blavatsky (1831–1891), aided by Henry Steel Olcott (1832–1907), William Quan Judge (1851–1896), Gerry Brown, and twelve followers. Madame Blavatsky, who first attracted public attention in the 1870s as a medium, claimed to have spent forty years traveling in the East, especially Tibet, and meeting the Masters of Wisdom, as well as taking part on the side of Garibaldi in the Italian wars of independence. Actually, she was born in Russia (nee Hahn), married General Blavatsky at seventeen, and a year later ran away. There is no proof of early travels to India, but she is known to have founded a spiritualist group in Cairo around 1870. In 1874 she came to the United States and gained some attention as a defender of spiritualism. Theosophy first started as a spiritualist group and drew its adherents from among New York spiritualists, but later it developed a distinct doctrine. The Theosophical Society sought contact with Indian groups; in 1878 it established a short-lived alliance with the ARYA SAMAJ and became known for four years as the Theosophical Society of the Arya Samaj.

Theosophy became an important force in the life of the intellectual elite in Great Britain and in India through the activities of Annie Wood Besant (1847–1933), who in 1898 founded the Benares Central Hindu College as a Theosophical misssionary institution. Besant was chosen by Blavatsky as her successor as head of the Theosophical Society.

In 1911 Besant proclaimed Jiddo KRISHNAMURTI (1895–1986) to be the coming "World Teacher," the avatar. Krishnamurti rejected this assignment in 1929. The Theosophical Society has maintained world headquarters in Adyar, India, since 1877. It maintains educational centers and publishing outlets in many countries, such as the Krotona Institute of Theosophy in Ojai, California.

"Theosophy, wisdom-religion, asserts the unity of everything in the universe and the existence of a knowledge at once scientific, philosophical and religious." Theosophical beliefs are expounded in *Isis Unveiled* (1877) and *The Secret Doctrine: The Synthesis of Science, Religion, and Philosophy* by H.P. Blavatsky. Madame Blavatsky stated that she had been chosen by a Buddha incarnation named Tsong-kha-pa to be guided by two secret masters in the Himalayas, the Mahatma Morya and the Mahatma Koot Hoomi, to save the world.

Theosophical doctrine claims to be based on esoteric knowledge and to embody the eternal truths supposedly basic to all world religions. It claims to offer a synthesis of religion, philosophy, and science and to investigate "laws of nature" and powers latent in human beings. It is a syncretistic collection of occultist beliefs, combined with ideas supposedly derived from ancient Egypt and some from Hinduism. Western occult traditions such as astrology are revered and upheld, and there still exists an Astrological Lodge of the Theosophical Society. There is belief in a Universal Spirit

Helen Petrovna Blavatsky, famous mystic and founder of the Theosophical Society.

and a hierarchy of perfected beings (the White Brotherhood, the Adepts, the Masters, the Mahatmas) who really supervise the evolution of the world. Reincarnation is regarded as part of evolution. The number seven is considered the key to understanding the universe, as there are seven basic forces in nature, seven planes of reality (Divine, Spiritual, Intuitional, Mental, Emotional, Etheric, Physical), and seven human races in evolutionary order, of which the Aryans are the fifth, the most highly evolved. In the future the sixth and seventh races will appear.

Many schisms have occurred in the Theosophical movement, starting with a Theosophical Organization founded by W.Q. Judge in 1895. A schism in European Theosophy led in 1912 to the founding of ANTHROPOSOPHY by Rudolf Steiner.

See also ANTHROPOSOPHY; KRISHNAMURTI; LIBERAL CATHOLIC CHURCH; THEOSOPHICAL ORDER OF SERVICE; UNITED LODGE OF THEOSOPHISTS; UNIVERSAL BROTHERHOOD AND THEOSOPHICAL SOCIETY

Sources:

Campbell, B.F. *Ancient Wisdom Revived.* Berkeley: University of California Press, 1980.

Meade, M. *Madame Blavatsky, The Woman Behind the Myth.* New York: Putnam, 1980.

Nethercot, A.H. *The First Five Lives of Annie Besant.* Chicago: University of Chicago Press, 1960.

Nethercot, A.H. *The Last Four Lives of Annie Besant.* Chicago: University of Chicago Press, 1963.

Williams, G.M. *Priestess of the Occult.* New York: Knopf, 1946.

Donovan Thesenga, see SEVENOAKS COMMUNITY

THIRD CIVILIZATION

Japanese new religion founded by Koji Ogasawara. It is based on a new interpretation of the Shinto scriptures and on the Kototama Principle, which is the origin and end of all human life. This principle will lead the world to the Third Civilization and the coming of the messiah. Branches have operated in Europe and the United States.

THIS TESTIMONY

Also known as Testimony Book Ministry, this Fundamentalist group is the U.S. branch of the HONOR OAK CHRISTIAN FELLOWSHIP CENTRE, an organization founded around 1920 by T. Austin Sparks. In doctrine it is closely related to the LOCAL CHURCH MOVEMENT with one exception: This Testimony follows the teachings of Watchman Nee, the founder, but not of Witness Lee, his successor.

John Thomas, see CHRISTADELPHIANS

David Thompson, see ALL FAITHS CHURCH/SCIENCE OF MIND

A.D. Thorington, see URERSA REFLECTIVE CENTER

Dennis W. Thorn, see FULL GOSPEL CHURCH ASSOCIATION

Robert Thornton, see CHRIST'S GOSPEL FELLOWSHIP

Thubten Yeshe, Thubten Zopa, see VAJRAPANI INSTITUTE FOR WISDOM CULTURE

Pierre Martin Ngo-Dinh-Thuc, see LATIN-RITE CATHOLIC CHURCH

TIBETAN BUDDHIST LEARNING CENTER (TBLC)

Center for the teaching of Tibetan Buddhism founded in 1958 in Washington, New Jersey, by Leshe Wangyal (1902–1983). Its aim is to develop "a Buddhism that is culturally American." It has engaged in many activities in connection with the XIV Dalai Lama (1935–   ), designed to make Tibetan Buddhism better known. It is connected with the LAMAIST BUDDHIST MONASTERY OF AMERICA, known also as Labsum Shedrub Ling.

TIMELY MESSENGER FELLOWSHIP

Informal association of Fundamentalist, Dispensationalist Christians based in Fort Worth, Texas, founded by Ike T. Sidebottom in 1939. It publishes *The Timely Messenger* and offers radio programs.
See also DISPENSATIONALISM; FUNDAMENTALISM; GRACE GOSPEL FELLOWSHIP

Katherine Tingley, see UNIVERSAL BROTHERHOOD AND THEOSOPHICAL SOCIETY

Tiruvannamalai, see RAMANA MAHARSHI

Josei Toda, see SOKA GAKKAI

TODAY CHURCH

Originally known as the Academy of Mind Dynamics, this NEW THOUGHT group was founded by Bud and Carmen Moshier in Dallas, Texas, in 1969.

Tokuchika Miki, see PERFECT LIBERTY

A.J. Tomlinson, see CHURCH OF GOD (CLEVELAND, TENNESSEE); CHURCH OF GOD OF PROPHECY

Homer Tomlinson, see CHURCH OF GOD (WORLD HEADQUARTERS)

Milton A. Tomlinson, see CHURCH OF GOD OF PROPHECY

TRADITIONAL CHRISTIAN CATHOLIC CHURCH

International traditionalist Catholic movement with its world center in Quebec and missions in the United States, Europe, and Hong Kong. Its ideology is based on religious and political conservatism, and it opposes all innovations in the Roman Catholic Church since the Second Vatican Council. The church was founded by Thomas Fehervary and a group of Hungarian immigrants, who came to Quebec after the Hungarian revolt of 1956.

Stewart Traill, see CHURCH OF BIBLE UNDERSTANDING

TRALEG TULKU

Western Tibetan Buddhist group, based in Melbourne, Australia, and led by Traleg Rinpoche, who claimed to be the 9th Traleg Tulku meditation master. Devoted to propagating Tibetan Buddhist teachings in the West, it was founded around 1980.

TRANSCENDENTAL MEDITATION (TM)

Officially known today as the World Plan Executive Council, this Western Hindu movement is dedicated to promoting both Hindu doctrines and traditional Hindu meditation techniques. The movement and its various affiliated organizations have been founded by a native of India known as the Maharishi Mahesh Yogi, whose real name is said to be either J.N. Srivastava or Mahesh Prasad Varma, born on October 18, 1911 (or 1918). A former Hindu monk, the Maharishi is reputed to have studied with a famous teacher named Brahmanda Sarasurati, or Swami Krishanand Saraswati, or Guru Dev. It was Guru Dev who was taught the special meditation technique that became known as TM. In 1958 the Maharishi left India on a mission to the West and arrived in the United States in 1959. The Spiritual Regeneration Movement Foundation, the early organizational form of Transcendental Meditation, was incorporated by the Maharishi and others in Los Angeles in 1959. In the late 1960s and early 1970s many affiliated organizations were created to spread the teaching of TM, including universities and international student movements such as the Spiritual Regeneration Movement (SRM).

The religious nature of TM teachings has been a matter of legal dispute in the United States since the early 1970s. The matter was brought to court before Federal Judge H. Curtis Meanor, at the U.S. District Court for the District of New Jersey. Judge Meanor's ruling, on October 19, 1977, stated that "The SCI/TM and the teaching thereof, the concepts of the field of pure Creative Intelligence, Creative Intelligence, and Bliss-Consciousness...and the puja ceremony, are all religious in nature within the context of the establishment clause of the First Amendment of the United States Constitution..." On February 2, 1979, this ruling was upheld by the U.S. Court of Appeals for the third circuit, sitting in Philadelphia. The TM organization never appealed that ruling. Thus, the view that TM activities are religious in nature has stood rather rigorous legal tests.

When we deal with the actual involvement of individuals in TM activities, it is necessary to differentiate between two levels. The first is that of the daily meditation technique, which does not usually mean a real religious involvement. Graduates of the daily meditation training are often unaware of the religious nature of the puja (graduation) ceremony and are unconcerned about the religious background of the technique. The second level is that of advanced meditation techniques and more esoteric beliefs, and persons committed to those are clearly disciples of a religion.

In 1976 Transcendental Meditation initiated its Siddhi Program, which promises its participants such abilities as levitation and invisibility. The advanced "Siddhi" techniques include more intensive meditation, as well as levitation, or "flying." The advanced meditators, or "Governors of the Age of Enlightenment," are capable of creating amazing effects, operating in relatively small numbers. TM doctrine speaks of a "unified field" of nature that is affected by advanced meditation by advanced meditators, known as Sidhas. Simultaneous meditation by the square root of 1 percent of the world population (about 7,000 people) would lead to cosmic changes, resolving political conflicts, lowering crime rates, and boosting stock market prices.

The World Government announced in January 1979 that its governors had restored peace to the five most troubled areas of the world: Central America, southern Africa,

Maharishi Mahesh Yogi, founder of Transcendental Meditation.

the Middle East, Iran, and Southeast Asia. In 1983 the World Government stated that it had in its possession an "invincible defense" through the "unified field" that "will neutralize the destructive capabilities of all those who possess the power of destruction found at the electronic and nuclear levels." This was followed by an invitation to (other) world governments "to contract on the basis of the Age of Enlightenment to solve their problems on the basis of cost reimbursement after the target is reached...every government already knows what must be achieved, and the World Government has already developed techniques to fulfill any requirement."

TM has also offered "immortality... through this unified field based approach to health."

The historical origins of the Maharishi's teachings are said to be in the tradition founded by Sankaracharya, a Hindu reformer of the Middle Ages who led a movement that revived Hinduism.

In 1980 Transcendental Meditation opened a center in India and later started promoting Ayurveda medicine, an ancient Indian tradition based on the use of fruits, and prayers. In the 1980s the movement established the Maharishi University of Natural Law (MUNL) in Great Britain.

A view of the 7,000 practitioners of Transcendental Meditation gathered at the Maharishi International University in Iowa in 1983. It is their belief that simultaneous meditation by the square root of 1 percent of the world population (about 7,000 people) would bring about cosmic changes.

after her death in 1814. Joanna claimed that she was pregnant with a divine child, but died before delivery. Turner claimed that the child, Shiloh, was born and would reappear on October 16, 1820, and then set a second date, April 10, 1821. Turner died after the prophecy failed to materialize. See also CHRISTIAN ISRAELITES

Source:

Balleine, G.R. *Past Finding Out: The Tragic Story of Joanna Southcott and Her Successors.* New York: Macmillan, 1956.

Turtle Heart (Anishinabe), see CENTER OF FIRST LIGHT

TWELVE APOSTLES

Known commonly as Nackabah and officially as the Church of the Twelve Apostles, this Christian syncretistic movement in Ghana was founded by Grace Tani, John Nackabah, and John Hackman in 1914 as a result of a revival movement led by William Wade Harris. Leadership has passed to the sons of John Nackabah. Doctrine is officially tied to the Methodist Church but in reality has an overwhelming emphasis on healing and prophecy. Pork and tobacco are prohibited, and fasts are recommended. See also HARRIS MOVEMENT

Source:

Baeta, C.G. *Prophetism in Ghana.* London: SCM Press, 1962.

Twelve Tribes of Israel, see RASTAFARIANS

TWENTIETH CENTURY CHURCH OF GOD

Adventist group founded in dissent from the WORLDWIDE CHURCH OF GOD by Al Carrozzo in 1974. The group has headquarters in Vacaville, California, and circulates several publications.

Paul Twitchell, see ECKANKAR

TWO-BY-TWO'S, THE

Known also as the Christian Fellowship, People on the Way, Disciples of Jesus, Friends, "go-preachers," or "Cooneyites," this Fundamentalist evangelical group grew out of the British 19th-century Faith Mission movement. It was founded in Ireland in 1900 by William Irvine (1863–1947) and in 1903 reached the United States. Edward Cooney was one of the most active early members, giving his name to the group. Members become wandering preachers, living off the proceeds of collection plates. Group doctrine advocates a lifestyle of extreme simplicity and poverty.

U

Kanzo Uchimura, see MUKYOKAI

UMBANDA

Syncretistic spiritualist movement in Brazil combining strong African and Catholic elements together with native Indian rituals and components of the spiritualist KARDECISM school. The first Umbanda group was founded in 1907, and thousands more have been started. Umbanda is loosely organized, but formal organization began to emerge in the 1920s in Rio de Janeiro and São Paulo.

According to Umbanda doctrine, spirits form armies known as "phalanxes," headed by African gods or Roman Catholic saints. The supreme God is surrounded by lesser deities, each of whom commands a "phalanx." Spirits are also divided by social class and race. A more successful reincarnation is promised believers who obey their personal deities.

Source:

Simpson, G.E. *Black Religions in the New World.* New York: Columbia University Press, 1978.

UNARIUS EDUCATIONAL FOUNDATION (UNARIUS—SCIENCE OF LIFE)

UFO-Theosophical group founded in 1954 by Ernest L. Norman in El Cajon, California. The name is an acronym of *UN*iversal *AR*ticulate *I*nterdimensional *U*nderstanding of *S*cience. The doctrine is eclectic, combining ideas from all Western occult traditions of modern times. The founder is characterized as "Ernest L. Norman, the

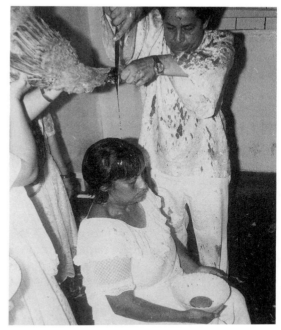

Priest José Paiva performing an ancient African Brazilian ritual believed to cure illness.

Archangel Raphael, incarnated 2,000 years ago as Jesus of Nazareth. He also lived the life of the Pharaoh Akhenaton 3,500 years ago. He was the historically famous teacher Anaxagoras, about 500 B.C."

Group doctrine predicts that by 2001 "An interstellar Starship carrying 1,000 space scientists from the Planet Myton, in the Starcluster of the Pleiades—the Constellation Taurus—will arrive on Earth and land on the raised portion of Atlantis in the Caribbean Sea." In the meantime group members are aided by "Space Brothers—Advanced Beings who live on the higher Spiritual Worlds."

The group, which has been headed by Ruth Norman (known as URIEL—*U*niversal

*R*adiant *I*nfinite *E*ternal *L*ight) since her husband's death, operates the Academy of Parapsychology, Healing and Psychic Sciences. "Past life therapy" is also provided. See also THEOSOPHY

UNDENOMINATIONAL CHURCH OF THE LORD, THE

"HOLINESS" group founded in 1918 in southern California by Jesse N. Blakeley. It operates missions in India and Africa.

UNDERSTANDING, INC.

UFO-Theosophical group founded in 1955 by Daniel Fry. Based in Tonapah, Arizona, it merged in the early 1970s with the UNIVERSAL FAITH AND WISDOM ASSOCIATION.

UNIFICATION ASSOCIATION OF CHRISTIAN SABBATH KEEPERS, THE

African-American Sabbath-keeping Adventist organization founded in 1956 in New York City by Thomas I.C. Hughes. It incorporated several existing African-American congregations in the greater New York area. The organization has maintained missionary outposts in Africa and the Caribbean. Over the years it has developed a much larger membership base overseas as the number of U.S. members decreased.

UNIFICATION CHURCH (UC)

Commonly known as "Moonies," officially called the Holy Spirit Association for the Unification of World Christianity (HSA–UWC), sometimes known as Pioneers of the New Age, the Unified Family (in Korea it is known as Tong Il; in Europe it is sometimes known as the Tongil Family), and by the names of many front organizations, this Christian millenarian group was founded on May 1, 1954, in Seoul, Korea.

Its founder, Sun Myung Moon, was born on January 6, 1920, in Korea to Presbyterian parents as Yong Myung Moon; he changed his name later. In his early years he was influenced by various Pentecostal and millenarian groups, and at age sixteen he had a "divine revelation" that changed the course of his life. According to Moon's claims, he was trained in Japan as an electrical engineer and arrested in 1946 in Pyongyang by the Communist regime of North Korea. Many of the claims regarding his imprisonment and trials are very much in dispute. It is asserted by nonchurch sources that most of his legal entanglements stemmed from morals charges.

The Unification Church first appeared as a religious group in Korea between 1951 and 1954. Its scripture, the *Divine Principles,* was published in 1957. In 1965 Moon made his first global tour, traveling to forty countries.

Unification Church theology combines Christianity with Oriental, especially Buddhist, ideas. Moon divides human history, which he asserts means only 6,000 years (since the creation of Adam) into four periods: From Adam to Abraham, 2,000 years of night, from Abraham to Jesus, 2,000 years of education, from Jesus to the 20th century, 2,000 years of development, leading to the fourth era, that of Perfection, about to start now with establishment of the Kingdom of Heaven on earth under the new Messiah. The doctrine holds that mankind will be redeemed by a perfect human being, married to a perfect woman, and having perfect children. God gave mankind a first chance to achieve that with the creation of Adam and Eve, and a second chance in

The Reverend Sun Myung Moon and his wife, Hak Ja Han, officiate at a mass wedding in Madison Square Garden, New York.

Unification Church founder Sun Myung Moon and his wife sprinkle newlyweds with water during a mass wedding in Seoul, South Korea.

Jesus, but in neither case was the Perfect Family created. The 20th century is another chance, with the perfect man appearing on earth.

This man, according to Moon's calculations, should have been born between 1917 and 1930. Moon once predicted the coming of the Christian millennium in 1967. According to another Unification Church calculation, 1981 was to be the year of "final victory," twenty-one years after the Marriage of the Lamb, that is the marriage of Sun Myung Moon to Han-hak-ja, the "New Eve," in 1960. Moon and his wife, Hak Ja Han (second or fourth wife, according to differing counts), are known as the True Parents. Members refer to Moon as "Father" or "Master." Although Moon has not clearly proclaimed himself the Messiah, it is apparent that Church members consider him just that.

According to UC theology, Korea is the "New Israel" (while Japan is the "Eve nation"), and Korean will be the language of the divine kingdom on earth in the future. One version of the doctrine is presented as "Godism," a set of beliefs consisting of belief in God, life after death, and the "sanctity of the individual."

This Church is among the best known of the new religions and competes only with SCIENTOLOGY in the controversy surrounding it and the research done on it. The Unification Church has been involved in a number of lawsuits. It has sued several newspapers, including the *New York Times,* for libel, but has lost every case. In 1982, Moon was sentenced by a U.S. District judge in New York City to eighteen months in prison and a $25,000 fine for income tax evasion. He was actually incarcerated during 1984–1985.

The UC has operated scores of profitable business corporations in Korea, Japan, the United States, and Latin America. It owns New World Communications, which operates several newspapers including the *Washington Times* and publishing houses. In Austria the Church founded a political party known as Neue Mitte. Among the leaders of the movement is Bo Hi Pak, military attaché at the Korean Embassy in Washington in 1961–1964. Home Church Program has been associated with right-wing political groupings and causes all over the world. In Bolivia it was involved in 1980 in the overthrow of the elected government by General Garcia Mesa, and in Honduras it was involved in supporting General Gustavo Alvarez in 1983. Neither leader stayed in power long.

The church operates scores of front organizations, which sometimes hide their religious connections behind a variety of titles and acronyms. These include the American Freedom Coalition (AFC), the Assembly of World Religions (AWR), CARP (Collegiate Association for the Research of Principles), CAUSA (Confederation of Associations for the Unification of American Societies), Freedom Leadership Foundation, Global Congress of World's Religions (for 1993), International Conference on the Unity of the Sciences (ICUS), International Cultural Foundation (ICF), International Federation for Victory over Communism (Victory over Communism or V.O.C), International Middle East Alliance, International Security Council, International Religious Foundation, National Council for the Church and Social Action, New Ecumenical Research Association (New ERA), New Educational Development Systems, Inc. (NEDS), New Hope Singers International,

One World Crusade, Professors World Peace Academy, Project Unity, Project Volunteer, the Washington Institute for Values in Public Policy, World Festival of Culture, and the Youth Seminar of World Religions (YSWR).

Sources:

Barker, E. *The Making of a Moonie.* Oxford: Basil Blackwell, 1984.

Boettcher, R. *Gifts of Deceit.* New York: Holt, Rinehart & Winston, 1980.

Bromley, D.A., and Shupe, A.D., Jr. *"Moonies" in America.* Beverly Hills, CA: Sage, 1979.

Horowitz, I.L. *Science, Sin, and Scholarship: The Politics of Reverend Moon and the Unification Church.* Cambridge, MA: MIT Press, 1979.

Kim, C.S. *Rev. Sun Myung Moon.* Washington, DC: University Press of America, 1978.

Lofland, J. *Doomsday Cult.* New York: Irvington Publishers, 1977.

UNION CATOLICA TRENTO

Mexican traditionalist Catholic movement founded in 1981 by Moises Carmona and Adolfo Zamora, who were consecrated by Pierre Martin Ngo-Dinh-Thuc of the LATIN-RITE CATHOLIC CHURCH. The movement rejects all reforms introduced into the Roman Catholic Church after 1965.
See also SERVANTS OF THE SACRED HEART OF JESUS AND MARY

UNION OF APOSTOLIC CHRISTIANS

International Christian group founded in 1954 in secession from the NEW APOSTOLIC CHURCH.

UNION OF MESSIANIC JEWISH CONGREGATIONS (UMJC)

International Hebrew-Christian organization founded in 1979, loosely drawing together numerous groups from all over the world. It has headquarters at BETH MESSIAH CONGREGATION in Gaithersburg, Maryland.
See also HEBREW CHRISTIANITY; MESSIANIC JEWISH ASSEMBLY OF AMERICA; MESSIANIC JUDAISM

UNIS

U.S. Gurdjieff group founded in the 1960s and based in New Jersey.
See also GURDJIEFF GROUPS

UNITED CHRISTIAN CHURCH AND MINISTERIAL ASSOCIATION

PENTECOSTAL group founded by H. Richard Hall in 1956 in Cleveland, Tennessee. Its main activity is the ordination of Pentecostal ministers by mail.

UNITED CHRISTIAN SCIENTISTS

CHRISTIAN SCIENCE offshoot founded in 1975, based in San Jose, California. Its members have criticized the official Christian Science leadership for its authoritarian rule. In 1987 the group won a legal battle to publish its own version of *Science and Health with Key to the Scriptures* by Mary Baker Eddy.

UNITED CHRISTIANS CHURCH

Ghanaian independent Christian PENTECOSTAL church founded in 1940 by Salome Mamle Odum (c.1900–), a former member of the Presbyterian Church of Ghana.

UNITED CHURCH AND SCIENCE OF LIVING INSTITUTE

U.S. NEW THOUGHT group founded in 1966 by Frederick Eikerekoetter II, former Baptist minister, also known as Reverend Ike. Most members are African-Americans. The doctrine, known as "Science of Living," emphasizes not only healing but also material prosperity. Reverend Ike speaks to followers through radio and television and reaches wide audiences.

UNITED EVANGELICAL CHURCHES

PENTECOSTAL group in California founded in 1960 by members of mainline Protestant churches in the United States who joined the neo-Pentecostal revival.

UNITED HOLY CHURCH OF AMERICA

African-American PENTECOSTAL group originating in Method, North Carolina, in 1886. After many organizational changes that involved various name changes (Big Kahara Holiness Association, the Holy Church of North Carolina and Virginia), it moved north and is based on the East Coast.

UNITED HOUSE OF PRAYER FOR ALL PEOPLE

Originally known as the House of Prayer for All the People, this U.S. African-American PENTECOSTAL group was founded in 1925 by Marcelino Manoel de Graca (1884–1960), popularly known as "Sweet Daddy Grace." The group was built and functioned

Reverend Ike (right), founder of the United Church and Science of Living, talks with members of his group.

around the leader's flamboyant personality. Grace referred to himself as God and promised "salvation by Grace only." Members donated as much as they could for the leader's benefit, and then bought Daddy Grace products that included soap, toothpaste, and shoe polish. A strict code of conduct was enforced. Following the founder's death, leadership disputes brought about a schism leading to formation of the TRUE GRACE MEMORIAL HOUSE OF PRAYER.

Source:

Fauset, A.H. *Black Gods of the Metropolis*. Philadelphia: University of Pennsylvania Press, 1944.

UNITED ISRAEL WORLD FELLOWSHIP

British-Israelist group founded by James A. Lovell (1908–   ) in 1946 and based in Fort Worth, Texas. Before founding the group, Lovell, who was born in Texas and served as a Baptist minister, founded two British-Israelist churches in California.

See also BRITISH ISRAELISM

Source:

Roy, R.L. *Apostles of Discord*. Boston: Beacon Press, 1953.

UNITED ISRAEL WORLD UNION (UIWU)

U.S. Jewish group with some features of BRITISH-ISRAELISM, founded by David Horowitz in 1943. It believes that the "message of the Hebrew Bible" is meant for all nations and that some gentiles are descendants of the "ten lost tribes of Israel." Horowitz claimed to have received instructions from Moshe Ghibbory, who was considered a divine messenger. Ghibbory reportedly lived in a cave in Jerusalem in the 1920s, when Horowitz met him. The group has been active in missionary work among non-Jews in Latin America and Africa.

See also HOUSE OF ISRAEL-ZION

UNITED LEADERSHIP COUNCIL OF HEBREW ISRAELITES (ULCHI)

"Black Jews" federation founded in Chicago in 1967 by Robert Devine, James Hodge, and Richard Nolen.

UNITED LODGE OF THEOSOPHISTS (U.L.T.)

International Theosophical group with headquarters in the United States, founded in 1909 by Robert Crosbie when he was ejected by Katherine Tingley from the UNIVERSAL BROTHERHOOD AND THEOSOPHICAL SOCIETY.

See also THEOSOPHICAL SOCIETY

UNITED MISSIONARY CHURCH

Christian evangelical group founded in Potsdam, Ohio, in 1947.

UNITED ORDER EFFORT

Group of conservative Mormons who believe in and practice polygamy as it was practiced in 19th-century MORMONISM. Despite many efforts to suppress polygamy, it still exists in this group and several others. The doctrine also forbids sexual relations during pregnancy, lactation, and menstruation. The group was started in the early 1930s in Utah. Members are concentrated in the Utah-Arizona border area.

See also CHURCH OF CHRIST (TEMPLE

A Mormon family of the 1870s: two wives and nine children. Polygamy is still practiced by at least one Mormon group in Utah, the United Order Effort.

LOT); CHURCH OF JESUS CHRIST IN SOLEMN ASSEMBLY; CHURCH OF THE FIRST BORN OF THE FULLNESS OF TIMES; REORGANIZED CHURCH OF JESUS CHRIST OF LATTER DAY SAINTS

Source:
Bradlee, B. Jr., and Van Atta, D. *Prophet of Blood*. New York: Putnam, 1981.

UNITED PENTECOSTAL CHURCH

U.S. PENTECOSTAL group formed in 1945 through a merger of the Pentecostal Assemblies of Jesus Christ and the Pentecostal Church, Inc. A strict dress code is observed, and modesty and avoidance of worldly amusements are emphasized.

UNITED PENTECOSTAL FAITH CHURCH

Canadian PENTECOSTAL group emphasizing healing and mission work overseas, affiliated with the FULL GOSPEL FELLOWSHIP OF CHURCHES AND MINISTRIES INTERNATIONAL.

UNITED SEVENTH-DAY BRETHREN

Adventist Sabbatarian group founded in 1947 in Oklahoma. Its doctrine emphasizes an Old Testament orientation and denial of the immortality of the soul.
See also ADVENT CHRISTIAN CHURCH; SEVENTH-DAY ADVENTIST CHURCH

UNITY SCHOOL OF CHRISTIANITY

Originally known as the Unity Society of

Practical Christianity, this NEW THOUGHT-Christian group was founded in 1903 by Charles Fillmore (1854–1948), who was influenced by Emma Curtis Hopkins and spiritualism. The group teaches "practical Christianity," which means that it follows Christian tenets such as biblical authority and the divinity of Jesus Christ, but also espouses reincarnation as a step toward immortality. All persons are considered to be potentially divine.

See also CHRISTIAN SCIENCE; DIVINE SCIENCE; HOPKINS ASSOCIATION, EMMA C.; RELIGIOUS SCIENCE

Sources:

Braden, C.S. *Spirits in Rebellion*. Dallas: SMU Press, 1963.

D'Andrade, H. *Charles Fillmore: Herald of the New Age*. New York: Harper & Row, 1974.

UNIVERSAL APOSTOLIC CHURCH OF LIFE

North American OLD CATHOLIC group started in 1955.

UNIVERSAL BROTHERHOOD

Theosophical group founded by Ureal Vercilli Charles, who heads the First Church of Spiritual Vision in New York City. The group claims to be guided by the Great White Brotherhood.

UNIVERSAL BROTHERHOOD AND THEOSOPHICAL SOCIETY

Theosophical organization founded in 1898 by Katherine Tingley (1847–1927) after a dispute with Ernest Hargrove, president of the Theosophical Society in America. In 1897 Mrs. Tingley organized the International Brotherhood League, which was active in charity and welfare work and gained much publicity during the Spanish-American War. Mrs. Tingley also founded the Point Loma community and school in San Diego, California, which was in existence from 1897 to 1942, graduating 2,500 students. Gottfried de Purucker was Tingley's successor as head from 1929 until 1942, when he died. He changed the organization's name to the Theosophical Society. After 1942 headquarters was moved to Covina, near Los Angeles, and then in 1951 to Altadena, near Pasadena. The UNITED LODGE OF THEOSOPHISTS was founded in 1909 by Robert Crosbie, who was ejected from the Brotherhood by Mrs. Tingley.

See also THEOSOPHY

Source:

Greenwalt, E.A. *The Point Loma Community in California, 1897–1942: A Theosophical Experiment*. Berkeley: University of California Press, 1955.

UNIVERSAL CHRIST CHURCH

Spiritualist group founded in 1970 in Los Angeles by Anthony Benik.

UNIVERSAL CHRISTIAN SPIRITUAL FAITH AND CHURCHES FOR ALL NATIONS

African-American PENTECOSTAL church founded in 1952 through a merger of the National David Spiritual Temple of Christ Church Union (Inc.) U.S.A., St. Paul's Spiritual Church Convocation, and King David's Spiritual Temple of Truth Associa-

An exorcism is performed in a service of the Universal Church of the Kingdom of God, a Brazilian movement with branches in the United States.

tion. David William Short, who founded the National David Spiritual Temple of Christ Church Union in 1932, became leader of the new body. The group emphasizes faith healing, but puts less emphasis on speaking in tongues.

UNIVERSAL CHURCH OF SCIENTIFIC TRUTH

NEW THOUGHT group founded in the 1950s by Joseph T. Ferguson in Birmingham, Alabama, in the 1950s, and affiliated with the Institute of Metaphysics. It offers "metaphysical healing" and the attainment of a "superconscious mind."

UNIVERSAL CHURCH OF THE KINGDOM OF GOD

Brazilian PENTECOSTAL evangelical group founded in Rio de Janeiro, Brazil, in 1977 by Edir Macedo (1945–). The group practices faith healing and exorcism for persons "possessed by malignant spirits" and the Devil. North American branches were opened in 1986, when Macedo moved to the United States.

UNIVERSAL CHURCH OF THE MASTER (UCM)

Spiritualist group founded in Los Angeles in 1908 by Robert Fitzgerald.

See also GENERAL ASSEMBLY OF SPIRITUALISTS; NATIONAL COLORED SPIRITUALIST ASSOCIATION OF CHURCHES; NATIONAL SPIRITUAL ALLIANCE; NATIONAL SPIRITUALIST ASSOCIATION OF CHURCHES

UNIVERSAL CHURCH, THE MYSTICAL BODY OF CHRIST

PENTECOSTAL, millenarian group founded in the 1970s by R.O. Frazier of Saginaw, Michigan. The doctrine calls for the creation of a Christian government on another continent to prepare for the end of time. A strict code of conduct is followed, and faith healing is practiced.

UNIVERSAL FAITH AND WISDOM ASSOCIATION

Theosophical group founded by Enid Smith in Tonapah, Arizona. In the early 1970s it merged with UNDERSTANDING, INC.

UNIVERSAL FAITHISTS OF KOSMON (U.F.K.)

Known also as Universal Brotherhood of Faithists or just Faithists, this messianic communal movement was founded in 1883 in New York City by John Ballou Newbrough (1828–1891), a dentist and spiritualist. In 1882 Newbrough published *OAHSPE: A New Bible*, which he said was dictated to him by angels. It contained a 78,000-year history of the earth, as well as "occurrences in the spiritual world." During the Kosmon Era, which began in the 19th century, the world will be transformed into a heavenly kingdom. "The OAHSPE Bible is not a destroyer of old systems or religions, but reveals a new one adapted to this age wherein all mortals can be brothers and sisters. It speaks of the life and destiny of mankind, and unfolds the Character and Person of the Creator, along with those called Sons and Daughters of GOD..." Followers have attempted to establish communes in the United States, Canada, and Great Britain. They are vegetarian and believe in nonviolence and "extrasensory vision." Subsidiary organizations have included the Kosmon Library, the Essenes of Kosmon, and the Faithist Farm.

See also ELOHISTS; KOSMON MOVE-
MENT

Source:
Goodspeed, E.J. *Modern Apocrypha*. Boston: Beacon Press, 1956.

UNIVERSAL FELLOWSHIP OF METROPOLITAN COMMUNITY CHURCHES (UFMCC or MCC)

Christian-homosexual group founded in
1968 in Los Angeles by Troy D. Perry, a
former minister of the CHURCH OF GOD
OF PROPHECY. Branches have operated
in Latin America, Europe, Africa, and
Australia.

UNIVERSAL GREAT BROTHERHOOD A.U.M. SOLAR LINE, THE

International Theosophical group with
headquarters in Mexico City, founded in
1948 by Serge Raynaud de la Ferriere
(1916–1962). "Its goal is the re-education of
humanity toward world peace through a
synthesis of science and religion, emphasizing the techniques of yoga, meditation,
cosmobiology, t'ai chi, I-Ching, karate,
Qabbalah, psychology, and art." Branches
have operated in the United States and
Mexico.
See also THEOSOPHY

UNIVERSAL HAGAR'S SPIRITUAL CHURCH

African-American spiritualist group
founded by George Willie Hurley (1884–
1943). Hurley's teachings combined Christianity, spiritualism, astrology, and other aspects of occultism. He also claimed that
African-Americans (referred to as "Ethiopi-

ans") were the true Jews, descendants of
the biblical Israelites.

Source:
Baer, H.A. *The Black Spiritual Movement:
A Religious Response to Racism*.
Knoxville: University of Tennessee
Press, 1984.

UNIVERSAL HARMONY FOUNDATION

U.S. spiritualist group founded in 1942 by J.
Bertran and Helene Gerling. It was first
known as the Universal Psychic Science
Association. It is based in Seminole, Florida,
where it operates a seminary.
See also GENERAL ASSEMBLY OF SPIR-
ITUALISTS; NATIONAL COLORED SPIR-
ITUALIST ASSOCIATION OF CHURCHES;
NATIONAL SPIRITUAL ALLIANCE; NA-
TIONAL SPIRITUALIST ASSOCIATION OF
CHURCHES

UNIVERSAL LIFE (Universelles Leben)

Also known as the Homebringing Mission
of Jesus Christ, this international Christian
group was founded in 1975 and officially
incorporated in 1984 by Gabrielle Wittek,
known as the teaching prophetess of the
Lord. She was born in Germany in 1931 to a
Catholic family. Following her mother's
death in 1970, she began having visions and
hearing voices; from 1975 she reported
messages from God and his angels, as well
as from the New Testament figure of Jesus
Christ. In addition to Christianity, Hindu
ideas such as karma have been adopted.
Universal Life teaches "holistic medicine"
and operates its own treatment center.
Members practice meditation and "healing." The group operates the Inner Spirit-of-
Christ Churches (ISOCC). Branches have

opened in South Africa, Australia, the United States, Israel, Italy, and Spain.

UNIVERSAL LIFE CHURCH

U.S. mail-order "church" founded in the 1960s by Kirby J. Hensley, offering ordination to all interested persons.

UNIVERSAL LINK

British Christian-spiritualist group started in a revelation experienced by Richard Grave of Worthing, England, in April 1961. In this experience Grave saw a "Christlike figure," and a series of messages proclaiming the Second Coming followed. At one point an exact date of Christmas 1967 was given. Followers study these revelations and expect the millennium soon.

UNIVERSAL PEACE INSTITUTE

NEW THOUGHT group founded in Mount Rose, Pennsylvania, in 1934 by Lillian K. Daniel.

UNIVERSAL SHRINE OF DIVINE GUIDANCE

U.S. Christian-occultist group founded by Mark Karras in 1966.

UNIVERSAL SPIRITUALIST ASSOCIATION

U.S. spiritualist group founded in 1956 by Clifford Bias and others after a schism in the Spiritualist Episcopal Church. In doctrine the new group is similar to the old one, namely Christian spiritualism.

UNIVERSAL SPIRITUAL LEAGUE OF AMERICA, THE

Informally known as "Meher Baba Lovers," this U.S. group devoted to the personality and the teaching of Meher Baba had its beginnings in the 1930s, when North Americans first came in contact with the movement in India. The group has been active in publishing Meher Baba literature. See also BABA LEAGUE; MEHER BABA, FRIENDS OF; MEHER DURBAR; SUFISM REORIENTED

UNIVERSAL SPIRITUAL TEMPLE OF THE NEW ERA—TEMPLE OF CELESTIAL LIGHT

Also known as Luz Celestial, Inc., this Christian-occultist group was founded in the 1980s by Tanja Nahoum in New York City. Practices include "channeling" and receiving messages from "Master Jesus, Master Saint Germain, Master El Morya and others."

UNIVERSAL TRUTH FOUNDATION

Syncretistic group based in Phoenix, Arizona, founded in the early 1970s and combining Western and Hindu traditions. Practices focus on Hindu meditation.

UNIVERSAL WORLD CHURCH

PENTECOSTAL group based in Los Angeles, founded in 1952 by O.L. Jaggars. The group has operated the University of the World Church.

UNIVERSARIUN FOUNDATION

UFO-Theosophical group founded in 1958 in Portland, Oregon, by Zelrun Karsleigh. Messages are reported from the spirit world and from ascended masters. Group doctrine is similar to that of "I AM."

UNIVERSITY BIBLE FELLOWSHIP (UBF)

U.S. Fundamentalist group started in the 1970s. It has been accused of severely curtailing member contacts with family and friends.

UNIVERSITY OF LIFE CHURCH

Occultist group based in Phoenix, Arizona, founded in the early 1960s by Richard Ireland. The founder first claimed to be able to communicate with souls of the dead and gave public demonstrations of "telepathy." In the 1970s the group started offering meditation classes.

UNIVERSITY OF METAPHYSICS

NEW THOUGHT group founded by Mary Pendergast and based in Portland, Oregon. The group is a continuation of the activities of Albert C. Grier, the founder of the CHURCH OF TRUTH.

UNIVERSITY OF THE SCIENCE OF SPIRIT

Dissident CHRISTIAN SCIENCE group started around 1890 in Chicago by Edward J. Arens.

UNIVERSITY OF THE TREES

Mystical group founded by Christopher Hills and based in Boulder Creek, Calfornia. Beliefs and practices were a combination of Christian, Hindu, and Tibetan Buddhist traditions.

University of the World Church, see UNIVERSAL WORLD CHURCH

URANTIA FOUNDATION

Also known as the Urantia Brotherhood, this Christian-occultist group is headquartered in Chicago. Its teachings are contained in the 2,097-page *Urantia Book*, published in 1955 by Bill Sadler, Jr. Before the Foundation was formally incorporated in 1955, a group had studied the 196 papers that make up the *Urantia Book*, starting in 1934.

The book is supposed to complete the Christian New Testament. It describes the history of the Earth (Urantia), the galaxy around it, and the life of Jesus Christ of the New Testament. It suggests a universe of seven levels, headed by a Trinity of Trinities. The center of the universe is the Isle of Paradise. All celestial and terrestrial beings are in a process of evolving into a "universal consciousness."

Members of this group usually retain their membership in established Christian churches. Related organizations include the Second Society Foundation and the Jesusonian Foundation. Branches have operated in Europe.

URERSA REFLECTIVE CENTER

California branch of the URANTIA FOUNDATION, founded by A.D. Thorington in Encino in the 1960s.

Uriella, see ORDEN FIAT LUX

V

VAJRADHATU

Sometimes known as the Vajradhatu International Buddhist Church, this North American Tibetan Buddhist group is officially descended from the Tibetan Kargyupa, Kagyu, and Nyingma sects of Vajrayana Buddhism. It was founded in 1973 by Chogyam Trungpa, Rinpoche (1939–1986), also known as Vidyadhara. Leaving Tibet in 1959, Trungpa settled in the United Kingdom. In 1967 he became the head of a monastery in Scotland and in 1970 moved to the United States. Vajradhatu was officially formed in 1973. In 1974 Trungpa founded the Naropa Institute (named for the medieval Buddhist holy man Naropa), a teaching center for disciples and the general public operated by the Nalanda Foundation (named for the legendary medieval Buddhist University of Nalanda). The Naropa Institute granted B.A. and M.A. degrees for the first time in 1977.

In 1976 Trungpa named a successor, Thomas Rich, who took the name Osel Tendzin. Tendzin became the leader, or "dharma heir of Vidyadhara," upon Trungpa's death in 1986. In March 1989, Osel Tendzin was accused of having sexual relations with disciples and knowingly transmitting to them the AIDS virus. He died in 1990.

Vajradhatu has offered a Westernized version of Tibetan Buddhism, created by its founder, and was quite eclectic. Contrary to the widely held image of the Buddhist monk, Trungpa was visibly noncelibate, drank alcohol quite heavily, enjoyed meat, and smoked tobacco. He objected to the use of marijuana for spiritual reasons.

Trungpa was believed by followers to be an incarnation of Trungpa Tulku, an old Tibetan master.

Vajradhatu headquarters are known as Karma Dzong, and regional centers are known as Dharmadhatus or Dharma Study Groups (DSG). The group's retreat center in Vermont is known as Karme-Choling (formerly Tail of the Tiger). Vajradhatu has operated the Maitri Center for Psychology, which used Tibetan meditation techniques, known as Maitri, for the treatment of psychological disorders. In the 1970s the group operated more than 150 business enterprises, including law firms, medical clinics, and investment corporations.

Source:

Clark, T. *The Great Naropa Poetry Wars.* Santa Barbara: Cadmus Editions, 1980.

VAJRAPANI INSTITUTE FOR WISDOM CULTURE

International Tibetan Buddhist group, "under the guidance of Lama Thubten Yeshe and Lama Thubten Zopa Rinpoche," with branches in Europe and the United States.

Mary Ann Van Hoof, see NECEDAH SHRINE

J. Van Rijckenborgh, see LECTORIUM ROSICRUCIANUM

George Van Tassel, see MINISTRY OF UNIVERSAL WISDOM

Teofile Vargas Sein, see MITA MOVEMENT

Mahesh Prasad Varma, see TRANSCENDENTAL MEDITATION

A.F. Varnell, see BETHEL MINISTERIAL ASSOCIATION

Sri Vasudevadas, see PREMA WORLD COMMUNITY

VEDANTA SOCIETY

Known in the United States as the American Vedanta Society and internationally as the Ramakrishna Mission in the West, this is an international Hindu revival movement. The name Vedanta literally means the concluding portions of the ancient Hindu Veda scriptures, and more broadly all literature and tradition derived from the Vedas. The group is made up of Western followers of ancient Hindu traditions.

The Vedanta Society was founded in the United States by Swami Vivekananda, who attended the World Congress of Religions held in Chicago in 1893. It was formally started in 1894 in New York City by Vivekananda and Francis (later Lord) Leggett. It is actually the Western branch of the RAMKRISHNA MATH AND MISSION, founded in India in the 19th century, and its strongest base is in California. Its best-known Hindu leader was Swami Prabhavananda, and its best-known Western members were Aldous Huxley and Christopher Isherwood.

"The fundamental truths of Vedanta are that the Godhead, the underlying reality, is omnipresent within each of us, within every creature and object, so man in his true nature is God; it is the purpose of man's life on earth to unfold and manifest this Godhead, which is eternally existent within him, but hidden; and truth is universal in that men seek the Godhead in various ways, but what they all seek is the same." The Vedanta Society in the United States is officially

under the guidance of the Ramakrishna Order of India. Other branches operate in Argentina, France, Switzerland, and Great Britain.

See also ANANDA ASHRAMA; RAMAKRISHNA VEDANTA CENTRE

Sources:

Damrell, J. *Seeking Spiritual Meaning: The World of Vedanta*. Beverly Hills, CA: Sage, 1977.

Isherwood, C. *Ramakrishna and His Disciples*. New York: Simon & Schuster, 1965.

VEDIC CULTURAL CENTER

Sometimes known as the Vedantic Cultural Society, this Hindu group incorporating the former ISKCON temple in Berkeley, California, was founded by Srila Hansadutta

Aldous Huxley, noted English writer, who was a member of the Hindu Vedanta Society.

Swami Prabhavananda, leader of the California-based Vedanta Society.

Swami, formerly Hans Kary, after his ex-communication from ISKCON in 1983. The reason for his expulsion was his advocacy of the use of weapons and his continuing possession of weapons, which led to his arrest in 1980. Hansadutta was arrested again in 1983 after being involved in a shooting incident.

Venkatesananda, see CHILTERN YOGA FOUNDATION

VENTURISM

U.S. belief system created by members of the American Cryonics Society, Inc. in the 1980s. Cryonics refers to the practice of freezing a dead body to preserve it for revival at some future date. Venturism is committed to the elimination of death.

Vethathiri Maharaj, see WORLD COM-MUNITY SERVICE

Victory over Communism, see UNIFI-CATION CHURCH

Joseph Rene Vilatte, see AMERICAN CATHOLIC CHURCH; GALLICAN CHURCH

Pir Vilayet Khan, see SUFI ORDER IN THE WEST

Dadaji Vimalananda, see YOGA HOUSE

VIMAL PRAKASHAN TRUST

Also known as the Friends of Vimala Thakar or Vimala Thakar Foundation, this interna-tional, Western-oriented Hindu group was founded in the 1960s by Vimala Thakar and

dedicated to spreading her teachings. Thakar has been close to KRISHNAMURTI, and her beliefs are similar to his. Branches have operated in the United States and Europe.

VINEYARD INTERNATIONAL

U.S. Fundamentalist group started in the 1980s as an offshoot of CALVARY CHAPEL, with branches in North and South America.

Raymond P. Virgil, see APOSTOLIC CHURCH OF JESUS

Virgin of Bayside Shrine, see OUR LADY OF THE ROSES

Vivekananda, see RAMAKRISHMA MATH AND MISSION; VEDANTA SOCIETY

VOICE OF CALVARY

Christian Fundamentalist commune founded in the 1970s in Mississippi.

VOICE OF ELIJAH, INC.

Evangelical, millenarian group founded in 1970 in Spokane, Washington, by Carl and Sandra Parks, who were inspired by the contemporary JESUS MOVEMENT.

VOLUNTEERS OF AMERICA

U.S. Christian Fundamentalist group founded in 1896 by Ballington and Maud Booth, son and daughter-in-law of William Booth, founder of the SALVATION ARMY. The group follows the doctrine and prac-tices of the Army and provides social service programs throughout the United States.

Claude Vorilhon, see RAËLIANS

WAKORINO

Group of African independent Christian PENTECOSTAL churches formed among the Kikuyu of Kenya from the 1920s to the 1960s. Members mostly wear white turbans and in the HOLY SPIRIT CHURCH OF ZAYUN red or blue turbans. The churches developed out of the Watu wa Mungu and the Aroti movements. The Wakorino group includes the African Mission of the Holy Ghost Church; Chosen Church of the Holy Spirit of Kenya; Christian Holy Ghost Church of East Africa; Holy Ghost Church of East Africa; and the Kenya Foundation of the Prophets Church.

WALDORF INSTITUTE

ANTHROPOSOPHY group based in Spring Valley, New York. It operates the Threefold Educational Foundation and the Fellowship Community.

THE WALK (CHURCH OF THE LIVING WORD)

Fundamentalist, occultist "New Testament Church" based in California, founded in 1954 by John Robert Stevens (1919–1983). The founder, known as the Apostle, was raised in Washington, Iowa, by a FOURSQUARE GOSPEL CHURCH family. The group has regularly published revelations received by the Apostle and dealing with "psychic experiences," "auras," astrology, and spiritualism. Its doctrine emphasizes the imminence of the Second Coming.

Thane Walker, see THE PROSPEROS

Orville Wallace, see GOSPEL ASSEMBLIES (WALLACE)

James Donald Walters, see ANANDA COOPERATIVE VILLAGE

Geshe Wangyal, see LAMAIST BUDDHIST MONASTERY OF AMERICA

Leshe Wangyal, see TIBETAN BUDDHIST LEARNING CENTER

Wapei, see THE NOISE

Gloria and Kenneth Wapnick, see FOUNDATION FOR "A COURSE IN MIRACLES"

James K. Warner, see NEW CHRISTIAN CRUSADE CHURCH

WATCHMAN HEALING MISSION

Also known as Church of the Watchtower, People of the Watchman (Bamulonda), and the People of Jehovah and Michael, this Zambian independent Christian communal movement was started in 1937, inspired by the WATCH TOWER MOVEMENT of Elliot Kamwana in Malawi. Its members live in communal villages.

Watchman Nee, see LOCAL CHURCH MOVEMENT

WATCHTOWER

Known sometimes as the Independent Watchtower, this African millenarian movement was founded by Jermiah Gondwe, leader of a "holy village" in Zambia (then Northern Rhodesia) around 1940. The movement has spread to the Congo (now Zaire) and Rhodesia (now Zimbabwe). The movement caused native rebellions in what were then the European colonies of Northern Rhodesia, Nyasaland, and Belgian Congo.

Charles E. Waters, Sr., see TRUE FELLOWSHIP PENTECOSTAL CHURCH OF GOD OF AMERICA

John Langdon Watts, see MARA LA ASPARA

WAY INTERNATIONAL, INC., THE

Sometimes known as the Way Bible Research Institute, this U.S. Fundamentalist group was founded by Victor Paul Wierwille (1918–1985) in 1953, when he started teaching a course called Power for Abundant Living (PFAL), based on his reinterpretation of the New Testament. Officially, the group dates its existence from 1942, when Wierwille claimed he had a divine revelation. In 1951 he spoke in tongues for the first time, but until 1957 he remained a minister in the United Church of Christ. In the early 1950s he started to practice faith healing and led sessions in speaking in tongues. In the late 1960s Wierwille was active in California and gained followers there. In October 1982, L. Craig Martindale (1950–) became the second president of the organization, and Wierwille retired.

Defined as a "Biblical research and teaching ministry," the group has headquarters in New Knoxville, Ohio, and branches all over the United States and the world. It is especially active in Latin America, Great Britain, and Western Europe.

The group's practices include speaking in tongues. Its doctrines differ from Ortho-dox Christianity in many details, including the text of the New Testament. Wierwille did not believe in the divinity of Jesus Christ; he stated that Jesus Christ, "the Promised Seed," was born on Wednesday, September 11, 3 BCE, between the hours of 6:15 and 7:45 p.m. He also expressed strong anti-Communist, anti-Catholic, and anti-Semitic views, resulting in several public controversies.

Members are encouraged to live communally. They are charged for participating in the thirty-six-hour Power for Abundant Living courses, which include materials and ideas taken from Dale Carnegie and aerobic exercises.

In 1979 The Way International was listed by Dun & Bradstreet as a "well-established business." In 1980 it was reported to have assets in excess of $12 million, including a corporate jet used in world-wide travel.

WAY OF THE CROSS CHURCH

African-American PENTECOSTAL group founded in 1927 by Henry C. Brooks and based in Washington, D.C.

THE WAY, THE TRUTH AND THE LIFE

Fundamentalist commune founded in North Carolina in the late 1960s by Ben Sebastian Sapio (1930–). The group left North Carolina in 1978.

James Ingall Wedgewood, see LIBERAL CATHOLIC CHURCH

Bob Weiner, see MARANATHA CAMPUS MINISTRIES

WENI MWANGUVU

Known also as the Miracle Revival Fellowship Pente Church, this African independent PENTECOSTAL group was founded in 1948 in secession from the Anglican Church.

Wensi, see MASA JEHOVAH

WESLEYAN PENTECOSTAL CHURCH
PENTECOSTAL group in Chile, founded in 1970 by Victor Manuel Mora, who was also active in the Socialist Party of Chile.

WESTERN BIBLE STUDENTS ASSOCIATION
Group based in Seattle, Washington, the West Coast branch of the CHRISTIAN BELIEVERS CONFERENCE.

WESTMINSTER BIBLICAL FELLOWSHIP
U.S. Fundamentalist group founded in 1969 when a group of members left the BIBLE PRESBYTERIAN CHURCH in protest against the leadership of Carl McIntire.

WESTMORELAND CHAPEL
Fundamentalist congregation based in Los Angeles, a branch of the HONOR OAK CHRISTIAN FELLOWSHIP CENTRE. Its founder, Carl B. Harrison, served earlier with the Honor Oak Centre.
See also THIS TESTIMONY

Samael Aun Weur, see GNOSTIC ASSOCIATION OF ANTHROPOLOGY AND SCIENCE

Christian Weyand, see TRUE CHURCH OF CHRIST, INTERNATIONAL

Alma White, see PILLAR OF FIRE

Nelson H. White, see LIGHT OF TRUTH CHURCH

Ruth White, see BAHAI WORLD UNION

WHITE EAGLE LODGE
Sometimes known as the Church of the White Eagle Lodge, this international spiritualist, occultist-Christian group based in England was founded in 1934 by Grace Cooke (?–1979). The leader served as a medium for messages from the spirit world of White Eagle, a "Red Indian" and a member of the White Brotherhood, who teaches five cosmic laws: reincarnation, cause and effect, opportunity, correspondence, and equilibrium. Messages, published in several books since the 1950s, are also received from the "Interplanetary Brotherhood." Members practice astrology and faith healing. Branches have operated in Europe, North America, and Africa.

WHITE STAR
UFO group based in Joshua Tree, Calfornia, founded in 1957 by Doris C. LaVesque. Messages from the spirit world and from UFO command centers are reported.

Victor Paul Wierwille, see WAY INTERNATIONAL

Clark Wilkerson, see INSTITUTE OF COSMIC WISDOM

Herbert F. Wilkie, see AMERICAN CATHOLIC CHURCH (SYRO-ANTIOCHEAN)

Ben Williams, see THE LORD'S COVENANT CHURCH

Daniel Powell Williams, see APOSTOLIC CHURCH

George M. Williams, see NICHIREN SHOSHU SOKA GAKKAI OF AMERICA

Smallwood E. Williams, see BIBLE WAY CHURCH OF OUR LORD JESUS CHRIST WORLD WIDE

Bernese Williamson, see CHURCH OF THE FULLER CONCEPT

Arthur Winkler, see CONGREGATIONAL CHURCH OF PRACTICAL THEOLOGY

Gerald B. Winrod, DEFENDERS OF THE CHRISTIAN FAITH, INC.

J.A. Winter, see LUTHERAN BAPEDI CHURCH

WISDOM INSTITUTE OF SPIRITUAL EDUCATION (WISE)

NEW THOUGHT group founded by Frank and Martha Baker in Dallas, Texas, in the 1950s. It offers "perfection of the spirit, mind, and body."

WISDOM'S GOLDENROD CENTER FOR PHILOSOPHIC STUDIES

U.S. Theosophical syncretistic group founded in 1972 by Anthony Damiani.

Gabrielle Wittek, see HOMEBRINGING MISSION OF JESUS CHRIST

Louis Eugene Wolcott, see NATION OF ISLAM (FARRAKHAN)

Elizabeth Clare (Wolf), see SUMMIT LIGHTHOUSE

Elwood Worcester, see EMMANUEL MOVEMENT

WORD FOUNDATION

U.S. occultist group founded in 1950. It is devoted to distributing the revelations of Harold M. Percival (1868–1953), an early Theosophist, who began having them in 1893.

WORD OF FAITH MINISTRIES

U.S. Christian, NEW THOUGHT group founded by Jim Kaseman in the 1970s. The group promotes "Positive Thinking," which is supposed to counter the effects of "Satan's work" in this world. It is connected with the WORD OF LIFE CHURCH in Sweden.

WORD OF GOD

Fundamentalist group growing out of the CATHOLIC CHARISMATIC RENEWAL movement, founded by Steve Clark and Ralph Martin, former Catholic activists, in Ann Arbor, Michigan, in 1967. The group practices SHEPHERDING or "discipleship," which provides for authoritarian leadership and close supervision of members. The style has been the basis of the "shepherding movement," which includes the BODY OF CHRIST, CHRISTIAN GROWTH MINISTRIES, and CHRISTIAN RESTORATION MINISTRIES. In the early 1970s Word of God became connected with the Christian Growth Ministries. Members, who mostly come from Roman Catholic backgrounds, are required to tithe. Exorcism, known as "deliverance" is often practiced. Members are also urged to prepare for a coming apocalypse, and some of them have committed themselves to celibacy.

Word of God operates the Sword of the

Spirit, an international subsidiary formed in 1983, with branches around the world. Through its own subsidiaries, the Sword of the Spirit is said to support various right-wing political causes.

See also BOSTON CHURCH OF CHRIST; NEW YORK CHURCH OF CHRIST

WORD OF LIFE CHURCH (Livets Ord)

Swedish Christian-NEW THOUGHT group founded in 1983 by Ulf Ekman, a former Church of Sweden minister. The group emphasizes "Positive Thinking" and believes in faith healing and exorcism. There is also a strong emphasis on material prosperity through faith. The group's inspiration comes from Norman Vincent Peale, Robert H. Schuller, Yongi Cho, and Kenneth Hagin. It has engaged in missionary work in Eastern Europe.

See also "FAITH" MOVEMENT

The Work, see GURDJIEFF GROUPS

WORKERS TOGETHER WITH ELOHIM

Group founded in 1975 by Charles Andy Dugger, son of A.N. Dugger, founder of the CHURCH OF GOD (JERUSALEM). Following the elder Dugger's death, the son was accused of both doctrinal deviation and adultery and was removed from his father's church.

WORK OF CHRIST

Communal group growing out of the CATHOLIC CHARISMATIC RENEWAL movement, founded in the early 1970s in Lansing, Michigan. It is connected with the WORD OF GOD group.

WORLD CATALYST CHURCH

Occultist group founded in 1967 in Butte, Montana. Its practices focus on meditation.

WORLD COMMUNITY SERVICE

Hindu revival group founded in Madras, India, in 1958 by Vethathiri Maharaj. It is devoted to the practice of kundalini yoga, which assumes the presence and utilization of female energy within the human body. The founder has developed new techniques known as Simplified Kundalini Yoga (SKY). Branches have operated in North America.

See also TEMPLE OF UNIVERSAL PEACE

WORLD CONGRESS OF FAITHS (WCF)

British ecumenical group founded in 1936 by Francis Younghusband. It "...brings together the committed followers of the great religions, as well as those who are 'seekers', in an international movement of all who cherish spiritual values."

WORLD INSIGHT

Group founded by Kenneth Storey and Gary Arvidson in 1974 as a result of schisms in the WORLDWIDE CHURCH OF GOD.

WORLD INSTITUTE OF AVASTHOLOGY

Theosophical group founded by Benito F. Reyes in Ojai, California, in the 1980s.

See also THEOSOPHY

WORLD MESSIANITY

U.S. branch of SEKAI KYUSEI KYO (World Messianic Association), a Japanese new religion whose doctrine is monotheistic and expects imminent world salvation. Faith healing is practiced.

WORLD RENEWAL, INCORPORATED

Initially known as the Berean Fellowship International, this PENTECOSTAL group was founded in 1963 by Warren Litzman in Dallas, Texas. The group doctrine emphasizes speaking in tongues. Mission centers are operated overseas.

WORLD TEACHER, THE

Also known as the Tara Center, and informally as Christ Maitreya, this British occultist group was started in 1980 by Benjamin Creme (1922–), a follower of the Arcane School from the 1950s. According to Creme, Maitreya, or "The Christ" (or "the Messiah, Krishna, the Imam Mahdi, the 5th Buddha"), appeared in this world on July 19, 1977, and has been living in Great Britain "…as an apparently ordinary man in the Asian community of London." The Masters of Wisdom have been leaving their retreats in the Himalayas to guide the world in the new Aquarian Age. The World Teacher, known as The Christ or Maitreya, made known his intention to return to the world in June 1945 and was supposed to reveal himself in 1982.

See also LUCIS TRUST

WORLDWIDE CHURCH OF GOD

U.S. Christian Fundamentalist group founded by Herbert W. Armstrong (1893–1986), which has long been identical with the founder's personality and developing beliefs. Originally, Armstrong was ordained in the Oregon Conference of the Church of God (Seventh-Day) in 1931. In 1934 he formed the Radio Church of God, in Eugene, Oregon, and started publishing *The Plain Truth* magazine, distributed free of charge and known by now to millions around the world. His broadcast "The World Tomorrow" has been among the first in the emerging field of electronic media preaching. In 1947 the church founded Ambassador College, located at church headquarters in Pasadena, California.

In doctrine, the Worldwide Church of God has emphasized Old Testament law and the rejection of major Christian holidays (Christmas and Easter) as pagan. The Christian idea of the Trinity is also rejected. Moreover, the church celebrates the presumed seven Old Testament feasts of Passover, Pentecost, Trumpets, Atonement, Tabernacles, the Last Great Day, and the First Day of the Sacred Year. The founder referred to himself as "God's Chosen Apostle." Quite early, he also adopted BRITISH ISRAELISM, the belief that the mythological "ten lost tribes" of the Old Testament were the ancestors of "Anglo-Saxon peoples." Members were told to avoid modern medicine and to tithe. Until 1976, Armstrong taught that remarried members of the Church should divorce their second spouse and remarry the first. After this teaching was repealed, he married a divorced woman.

In the early 1970s the church was torn by schisms, and at least seven splinter groups were formed. Herbert W. Armstrong was accused of financial corruption. Garner Ted Armstrong, his son and righthand man, was accused of sexual immorality. In 1978 he was excommunicated and founded the CHURCH OF GOD, INTERNATIONAL. In 1978 the Worldwide Church was the subject of government investigations and a lawsuit by the State of California, after dissidents complained about the handling of financial contributions. After the Church went into receivership in 1979, the charges were dropped.

Members of the Worldwide Church of God stage a sit-in demonstration in California during legal disputes over financial contributions.

See also ASSOCIATED CHURCHES OF GOD; CHURCH OF GOD (CLEVELAND, OHIO); CHURCH OF GOD SEVENTH ERA; CHURCH OF GOD, THE ETERNAL; GENERAL CONFERENCE OF THE CHURCH OF GOD; TWENTIETH CENTURY CHURCH OF GOD; WORLD INSIGHT

Daniel Wright, see PADANARAM

XAT AMERICAN INDIAN MEDICINE SOCIETY

U.S. group devoted to the preservation and propagation of Native American religious traditions. It operates THE CENTER OF FIRST LIGHT.

Y

Yahweh ben Yahweh, see NATION OF YAHWEH (HEBREW ISRAELITES)

YAHWEH'S TEMPLE
Known until 1981 as the Jesus Church, this PENTECOSTAL group was founded in 1947 in Cleveland, Tennessee, by Samuel E. Officer, a former member of the CHURCH OF GOD (CLEVELAND, TENNESSEE). Its doctrine combines Adventist, Sabbatarian, and SACRED NAME MOVEMENT elements.

YALIWAN'S MOVEMENT
New Guinea indigenous movement (CARGO CULT) started by Matthias Yaliwan, or Yeliwan (1930–), in the Wewak region, near Sepik, Papua New Guinea. In 1971 he led 60,000 followers to a mountaintop in the expectation of finding a buried cargo. In March 1972 he was elected to the Papua New Guinea House of Assembly by a vote of 7,200 to 435. The leader since then has disavowed any "cargo" beliefs.

Yarr, see ISHVARA

YASODHARA ASHRAM SOCIETY
North American Hindu group founded in 1956 by Sylvia Hellman (1911–), also known as Swami Sivananda Radha, a disciple of Swami Sivananda Saraswati in the Sivananda Ashram in Rishikesh, India. The group's doctrine centers around various yoga traditions. It is based in British Columbia and built around a core of disciples committed to the monastic life. Branches, known as Shambalah Houses, have operated in North America and England.

Yeliwan, see YALIWAN'S MOVEMENT

YELLOW EMPEROR RELIGION
Nationalist-religious movement in Taiwan, combining Chinese nationalism with ancient Confucian and Taoist doctrines. The Yellow Emperor or Ancestor, Huang Ti, is a legendary Chinese ruler known from quotations originating in a lost book and found in Taoist teachings. Huang Ti is considered the forefather of God, but also a Chinese Emperor, who followed Fu Hsi, the Conqueror of Animals, and Shen Nung, the Divine Husbandman.

YESHE NYINGPO
Tibetan Buddhist group founded in 1976 in New York City. It is devoted to the teachings of its founder, known as His Holiness Dudjom, Rinpoche, "head of the Nyingmapa order of Tibetan Buddhism."

Finis E. Yoakum, see CHRIST FAITH MISSION

YOGA HOUSE
U.S. Hindu group founded by Dadaji Vimalananda (1942–) in the 1970s. Practices include meditation and chanting.

YOGA INSTITUTE OF CONSCIOUSNESS
U.S. Tibetan Buddhist-oriented group founded in the 1960s by Jessica Lynott (1930–), known also as Swami Savitri Priza.

Paramahansa Yogananda, see SELF-REALIZATION SOCIETY; YOGODA SATSANGA SOCIETY

YOGI GUPTA ASHRAM, INC.

Hindu group founded in 1954 and based in New York City. It is devoted to spreading the teachings of Yogi Gupta, also known as Swami Kailashnanada, founder of the Kailashnanada Mission in Rishikesh, India. Doctrine stresses the practice of yoga exercises and vegetarianism.

YOGIRAJ

U.S. Hindu group devoted to the teachings of Swami Swanandashram (1921–), which focus on the practice of yoga exercises. The group became part of the HOLY SHANKACHARYA ORDER in the late 1970s.

YOGODA SATSANGA SOCIETY

Hindu group founded in 1918 in India by Paramahansa Yogananda (1893–1952) and based on the Yogoda yoga technique developed by him. Yogananda later founded the SELF-REALIZATION FELLOWSHIP in the United States.

YORUBA LACUMI

U.S. group founded by Luisa Teish in the 1970s, which claims to maintain African traditions of Yoruba magic and religion.

June Young, see ARISING SUN IFO

Sai Young, see KRISHNA YOGA COMMUNITY

Francis Younghusband, see WORLD CONGRESS OF FAITHS

YOUR HERITAGE

British-Israelist, white-supremacist group founded by Bertrand L. Comparet and based in San Diego, California.
See also BRITISH ISRAELISM

Swami Sri Yukteswar, see SELF-REALIZATION FELLOWSHIP

Yogi Yukteswar Sri Bbajhan, see JALA SANGHA

Dhyani Ywahoo, see SUNRAY MEDITATION SOCIETY

Z

C.C. Zain, see CHURCH OF LIGHT

Adolfo Zamora, see UNION CATOLICA TRENTO

Robert S. Zeiger, see AMERICAN OR-THODOX CATHOLIC CHURCH

Tim Zell, see CHURCH OF ALL WORLDS

Hermann Zimmer, see BAHAI WORLD UNION

Aubrey Zinn, see CHRISTIAN SERVICE, INC.

Daniel Zion, see NETIVYAH

ZION CHRISTIAN CHURCH (Z.C.C.)

South African nativist "ZIONIST" church founded in 1925 by Ignatius Lekganyane (?–1948) near Pietersburg, Northern Transvaal. The founder was known as a miraculous healer and respected as a god. He named his first son Jesus.

Z.C.C. has become the leader among independent South African churches, and its festivals at Zion City Moriah are occasions for visits by government leaders. Branches have operated in other southern African nations.

Sources:
Sundkler, B.G.M. *Bantu Prophets in South Africa.* London: Oxford University Press, 1961.
Sundkler, B.G.M. *Zulu Zion and Some Swazi Zionists.* London: Oxford University Press, 1976.

"ZIONIST"

Collective term denoting numerous (2,500 by some estimates) syncretistic movements in South Africa, noted for their practices of faith healing, speaking in tongues, and traditional African purification rites, as well as the central role of their founders-prophets. Many use the terms "Zion," "Apostolic," "Pentecostal," and "Faith" in their names. Historically, these churches are all linked to the influence of the CHRISTIAN CATHOLIC APOSTOLIC CHURCH IN ZION, which carried out mission work in South Africa around the turn of the century.
See also "ETHIOPIANS"

ZION MESSIANIC FELLOWSHIP

Canadian Hebrew-Christian group started in the 1960s and based in Vancouver.

ZION'S ORDER OF THE SONS OF LEVI

Dissident Mormon group founded in 1951 by Marl Kilgore, a former member of the AARONIC ORDER, in Bicknell, Utah, and later based near Mansfield, Missouri. Doctrine is based on standard Mormon teachings and additional revelations through Kilgore.
See also MORMONS

Zion Ward, see SHILOHITES

SYNOPTIC INDEX

How to use the synoptic index

The Synoptic Index groups entries by common attributes, such as religious origins or geographical location. Thus, if you are looking for information about new religious movements in Korea, or about organizations connected to Tibetan Buddhism, you will find them grouped under those headings.

ADVENTISTS:
ADVENT CHRISTIAN CHURCH
ADVENTISTS, SECOND
ADVENT SABBATH CHURCH
ASSEMBLIES OF YAHWEH
ASSEMBLIES OF YAHWEH (MICHIGAN)
ASSEMBLY OF YAHVAH
BODY OF CHRIST
BRANCH DAVIDIANS
    (BRANCH SEVENTH DAY ADVENTISTS)
CHURCH OF GOD (ABRAHAMIC FAITH)
CHURCH OF GOD, BODY OF CHRIST
CHURCH OF GOD (CLEVELAND, OHIO)
CHURCH OF GOD, INTERNATIONAL
CHURCH OF GOD (SABBATARIAN)
CHURCH OF GOD (SEVENTH-DAY,
    SALEM, WEST VIRGINIA)
CHURCH OF GOD SEVENTH ERA
CHURCH OF GOD, THE ETERNAL
DAVIDIAN SEVENTH-DAY ADVENTIST
    ASSOCIATION
END TIME MINISTRIES
EPIPHANY BIBLE STUDENTS
    ASSOCIATION
FOURSQUARE GOSPEL, INTERNATIONAL
    CHURCH OF
GENERAL CONFERENCE OF THE
    CHURCH OF GOD (SEVENTH DAY)
GENERAL COUNCIL OF THE CHURCHES
    OF GOD
HOUSE OF PRAYER FOR ALL PEOPLE
INTERNATIONAL CHURCH OF SPIRITUAL
    VISION, INC.
JEHOVAH'S WITNESSES
LAODICEAN HOME MISSIONARY
    MOVEMENT
LAYMEN'S HOME MISSIONARY
    MOVEMENT
MEGIDDO MISSION
NEW YORK UNITED SABBATH DAY
    ADVENT CHURCH
PEOPLE'S CHRISTIAN CHURCH
PRIMITIVE ADVENT CHRISTIAN CHURCH
SEVENTH-DAY ADVENTIST CHURCH
SEVENTH-DAY ADVENTIST REFORM
    MOVEMENT
SHILOH TRUE LIGHT CHURCH OF
    CHRIST
TWENTIETH CENTURY CHURCH OF GOD
UNITED SEVENTH-DAY BRETHREN
WORLD INSIGHT
WORLDWIDE CHURCH OF GOD

AFRICAN GROUPS:
CHURCH OF THE ANCESTORS
HARRIS MOVEMENT
KIMBANGUIST MOVEMENT
KITAWALA
LUMPA CHURCH
MALAGASY PROTESTANT CHURCH
MARIA LEGIO (OF AFRICA)
MASOWE APOSTLES
MATSOUANISM (MATSWA)
MBUETI
MISSION DE DIEU DU BOUGIE
MOUVEMENT CROIX-KOMA
PROVIDENCE INDUSTRIAL MISSION
SOJA WE MWARI
WENI MWANGUVU
See also **Ghana, Kenya, Nigeria, South
    Africa, Zaire, Zambia**

AFRICAN-AMERICAN GROUPS:

ADVENT SABBATH CHURCH

AFRICAN METHODIST EPISCOPAL
CHURCH (A.M.E.)

AMERICAN CATHOLIC CHURCH
ARCHDIOCESE

ANTIOCH BAPTIST CHURCH

APOSTOLIC CHURCH OF JESUS CHRIST

APOSTOLIC OVERCOMING HOLY
CHURCH OF GOD

AUSAR AUSET SOCIETY

BELIEVERS IN THE COMMANDMENTS OF
GOD

BETH BNAI ABRAHAM

BIBLE WAY CHURCH OF OUR LORD
JESUS CHRIST WORLD WIDE

CHRIST'S SANCTIFIED HOLY CHURCH

CHURCHES OF GOD, HOLINESS

CHURCH OF CHRIST (HOLINESS) U.S.A.

CHURCH OF GOD (BLACK JEWS)

CHURCH OF GOD IN CHRIST,
CONGREGATIONAL

CHURCH OF GOD IN CHRIST,
INTERNATIONAL

CHURCH OF THE LIVING GOD

CHURCH OF THE LIVING GOD,
CHRISTIAN WORKERS FOR
FELLOWSHIP

CHURCH OF THE LIVING GOD, GENERAL
ASSEMBLY

CHURCH OF UNIVERSAL TRIUMPH/THE
DOMINION OF GOD

COMMANDMENT KEEPERS
CONGREGATION OF THE LIVING GOD

EMBASSY OF THE GHEEZ-AMERICANS

ETHIOPIAN HEBREWS

FATHER DIVINE MOVEMENT

FIRE BAPTIZED HOLINESS CHURCH OF
GOD OF THE AMERICAS

FREE CHRISTIAN ZION CHURCH OF
CHRIST

FREE CHURCH OF GOD IN CHRIST

HANAFI MADH-HAB CENTER

HOUSE OF GOD WHICH IS THE CHURCH
OF THE LIVING GOD, THE PILLAR AND
GROUND OF TRUTH WITHOUT

CONTROVERSY

HOUSE OF ISRAEL

HOUSE OF JUDAH

HOUSE OF THE LORD

IMANI TEMPLE

ISRAELI SCHOOL OF U.P.K.

KODESH CHURCH OF IMMANUEL

MOORISH SCIENCE TEMPLE OF AMERICA

NATIONAL COLORED SPIRITUALIST
ASSOCIATION OF CHURCHES

NATION OF ISLAM (NOI)

NATION OF ISLAM (NOI) (FARRAKHAN)

NATION OF ISLAM (NOI) (SILAS
MUHAMMAD)

NATION OF ISLAM (NOI) (JEREMIAH
SHABAZZ)

NATION OF YAHWEH (HEBREW
ISRAELITES)

NEW YORK UNITED SABBATH DAY
ADVENT CHURCH

NUBIAN ISLAAMIC HEBREWS

PENTECOSTAL ASSEMBLIES OF THE
WORLD

REFORMED ZION UNION APOSTOLIC
CHURCH

RESURRECTED CHURCH OF GOD

ST. PAUL'S SPIRITUAL CHURCH
CONVOCATION

TRIUMPH THE CHURCH AND KINGDOM
OF GOD IN CHRIST

TRUE FELLOWSHIP PENTECOSTAL
CHURCH OF GOD OF AMERICA

TRUE GRACE MEMORIAL HOUSE OF
PRAYER

UNIFICATION ASSOCIATION OF
CHRISTIAN SABBATH KEEPERS

UNITED HOLY CHURCH OF AMERICA

UNITED HOUSE OF PRAYER FOR ALL
PEOPLE

UNITED LEADERSHIP COUNCIL OF
HEBREW ISRAELITES (ULCHI)

UNIVERSAL CHRISTIAN SPIRITUAL FAITH
AND CHURCHES FOR ALL NATIONS

UNIVERSAL HAGAR'S SPIRITUAL CHURCH

WAY OF THE CROSS CHURCH

YORUBA LACUMI
"BLACK JEWS":
  BETH BNAI ABRAHAM
  BLACK HEBREWS (THE KINGDOM OF
    GOD NATION)
  CHURCH OF GOD (BLACK JEWS)
  COMMANDMENT KEEPERS
    CONGREGATION OF THE LIVING GOD
  ETHIOPIAN HEBREWS
  HOUSE OF ISRAEL
  HOUSE OF JUDAH
  ISRAELI SCHOOL OF U.P.K.
  UNITED LEADERSHIP COUNCIL OF
    HEBREW ISRAELITES
BRAZIL:
  UMBANDA
  UNIVERSAL CHURCH OF THE KINGDOM
    OF GOD
BRITISH-ISRAELISM:
  ANGLO-SAXON FEDERATION OF
    AMERICA
  BIBLE PATTERN CHURCH FELLOWSHIP
  CALVARY FELLOWSHIP, INC.
  CHRISTIAN CONSERVATIVE CHURCHES
    OF AMERICA
  CHRISTIAN NATIONALIST CRUSADE
  CHRISTIAN RESEARCH, INC
  CHRIST'S GOSPEL FELLOWSHIP
  CHURCH OF ISRAEL
  CHURCH OF JESUS CHRIST-CHRISTIAN
  CHURCH OF THE COVENANTS
  DESTINY OF AMERICA FOUNDATION
  FULL GOSPEL TABERNACLE
  HOUSE OF PRAYER FOR ALL PEOPLE
  JAPPA TABERNACLE
  KINGDOM FELLOWSHIP CHURCH
  KINGDOM MESSAGE ASSOCIATION
  KINGDOM TEMPLE, INC.
  LORD'S COVENANT CHURCH
  NEW BEGINNINGS
  NEW CHRISTIAN CRUSADE CHURCH
  OPEN BIBLE CHURCH
  UNITED ISRAEL WORLD FELLOWSHIP
  UNITED ISRAEL WORLD UNION
  WORLDWIDE CHURCH OF GOD

YOUR HERITAGE
BUDDHISM:
  INSIGHT MEDITATION SOCIETY
  MANDALA BUDDHIST CENTER
  NISHIREN SHOSHU
  SOKA GAKKAI
  TATAGATAS
  See also **Tibetan Buddhism**
CARGO CULTS:
  ETOISM
  GHOST DANCE
  JOHN FRUM (JON FRUM)
  KAROEM
  LETUB
  LYNDON B. JOHNSON
  THE NOISE
  PALIAU CHURCH
  "TARO CULT"
  YALIWAN'S MOVEMENT
CHRISTIAN IDENTITY, see **Identity
  Movement**
COMMUNAL GROUPS, 19TH CENTURY:
  AMANA CHURCH SOCIETY
  SHAKERS
  UNIVERSAL FAITHISTS OF KOSMON
COMMUNAL GROUPS, 20TH CENTURY:
  AMMAL'S GARDEN
  AQUARIAN RESEARCH FOUNDATION
  AUM CENTER FOR SELF-REALIZATION
  BEAR TRIBE
  BROTHERHOOD OF THE WHITE TEMPLE
  BRUDERHOF
  BUILDERS
  CENTER OF LIGHT COMMUNITY
  CHINOOK COMMUNITY
  CHRIST BROTHERHOOD
  CHRISTIAN COMMUNITY OF BOSTON
  CHRIST'S CHURCH
  CHURCH OF THE SAVIOUR
  CIRCLE OF ANGELS
  COLONY
  COVENANT, THE SWORD, THE ARM OF
    THE LORD
  DEVA COMMUNITY
  FARM, THE

FISHERFOLK COMMUNITIES OF
  CELEBRATION
GANIENKAH
HEART CONSCIOUSNESS CHURCH
HIMALAYAN ACADEMY
HOLISTIC COMMUNITY
HOUSE OF DAVID
KAYAVAROHAN
KERISTA VILLAGE
KOINONIA
KOINONIA PARTNERS
KOSMUNITY
KRIPALU YOGA ASHRAM
KRISHNA TEMPLE
LAMA FOUNDATION
LAMB OF GOD
LORIAN ASSOCIATION
LOVE FAMILY
MAHA YOGA ASHRAM
MATAGIRI
MEADOWLARK HEALING CENTER
METTANOKIT
MORNINGSTAR
MU FARM
NORTHEAST KINGDOM COMMUNITY
  CHURCH
ONE WORLD FAMILY
PADANARAM
PEOPLE OF THE LIVING GOD
PREMA DHARMASALA AND FELLOWSHIP
  ASSOCIATION; PREMA WORLD
  COMMUNITY
RAINBOW FAMILY OF LIVING LIGHT
RAJ-YOGA MATH AND RETREAT
REBA PLACE FELLOWSHIP
RENAISSANCE CHURCH-COMMUNITY
SALEM ACRES
SAVITRIA
SEVENOAKS COMMUNITY
SHILOH TRUST
SHILOH YOUTH REVIVAL CENTERS
SIRIUS COMMUNITY
SPRINGHILL COMMUNITY
SPRING GROVE
SRI RAM ASHRAMA

STELLE COMMUNITY
STONEGATE CHRISTIAN COMMUNITY
SUNERGOS INSTITUTE, INC.
TATAGATAS
THEOCRATIC COMMUNE NATURAL
  HEALTH SERVICE
UNIVERSAL BROTHERHOOD
UNIVERSAL FAITHISTS OF KOSMON
VOICE OF CALVARY
WAY, THE TRUTH AND THE LIFE
WORK OF CHRIST
FRANCE:
AMIS DE LA CROIX GLORIEUSE DE
  DOZULÉ
COMMUNION PHALANGISTE
ÉGLISE DE LA SAINTE FAMILLE
EVADISME
FAMILLE DE NAZARETH (COMMUNE DE
  NAZARETH)
FOUNDATION TEILHARD DE CHARDIN
  and ASSOCIATION DES AMIS DE
  PIERRE TEILHARD DE CHARDIN
FRATERNITÉ "SALVE REGINA" DU
  FRÉCHOU
GALLICAN CHURCH
PETITE ÉGLISE (VENDEENNE)
TEMOINS DU CHRIST REVENU (Christ's
  Witnesses)
TROIS SAINTS COEURS (Three Holy
  Hearts)
GHANA:
HOLY TRINITY HEALING CHURCH
TRUE CHURCH OF CHRIST (NEW
  BETHLEHEM)
TWELVE APOSTLES
UNITED CHRISTIANS CHURCH
GURDJIEFF GROUPS:
CAFH SPIRITUAL CULTURE SOCIETY
CIRCLE OF ANGELS
CLAYMONT COURT
COOMBE SPRINGS
FELLOWSHIP OF FRIENDS
GURDJIEFF FOUNDATION
GURDJIEFF GROUPS
INSTITUTE FOR CULTURAL RESEARCH

INSTITUTE FOR RELIGIOUS
  DEVELOPMENT
INSTITUTE FOR THE COMPARATIVE
  STUDY OF HISTORY, PHILOSOPHY,
  AND THE SCIENCES
INSTITUTE FOR THE HARMONIOUS
  DEVELOPMENT OF THE HUMAN
  BEING
ORAGE GROUP
PACIFIC INSTITUTE OF SCIENCE AND
  HUMANITIES
PROSPEROS
SCHOOL OF PRACTICAL PHILOSOPHY
SHERBORNE STUDIES GROUP
SUBUD
UNIS

HEBREW-CHRISTIAN GROUPS:
AMERICAN MESSIANIC FELLOWSHIP
ARIEL MINISTRIES
BETH YESHUA
CHOSEN PEOPLE MINISTRIES
CHRISTIAN SYNAGOGUE
EMMANUEL MESSIANIC CONGREGATION
FIRST HEBREW PREBYTERIAN CHRISTIAN
  CHURCH
FRIENDS OF ISRAEL
HEBREW CHRISTIAN ASSEMBLY–
  JERUSALEM CONGREGATION
HEBREW CHRISTIAN PRAYER UNION
INTERNATIONAL HEBREW CHRISTIAN
  ALLIANCE OF AMERICA
JEWS FOR JESUS
LEDERER MESSIANIC MINISTRIES
MELECH ISRAEL
MESSIANIC ASSEMBLY OF ISRAEL
NETIVYAH
ROSH PINA CONGREGATION
SHORESH YISHAI
ZION MESSIANIC FELLOWSHIP
See also **Messianic Judaism**

**HINDU, HINDU-ORIENTED, and HINDU-
  INSPIRED INTERNATIONAL AND
  WESTERN GROUPS:**
AGNIHOTRA–THE PURIFYING FIRE
AKHANANANDA SARASWATI, SWAMI

ANANDA ASHRAMA
ANANDA COOPERATIVE VILLAGE
ANANDA MARGA
ARUNACHALA ASHRAMA BHAGAVAN SRI
  RAMANA MAHARSHI CENTER, INC.
ATMANIKETAN ASHRAM
BRAHMA KUMARIS (RAJA YOGA)
CENTER FOR SPIRITUAL AWARENESS
CHILTERN YOGA FOUNDATION
CHINMAYA MISSION
CHURCH OF THE CHRISTIAN SPIRITUAL
  ALLIANCE
CULTURAL INTEGRATION FELLOWSHIP
DIVINE LIGHT MISSION
EAST-WEST CULTURAL CENTER
FOUNDATION OF REVELATION
HAIDAKHAN SAMAJ
HANUMAN FELLOWSHIP
HANUMAN FOUNDATION
HIMALAYAN ACADEMY
HIMALAYAN INSTITUTE
HIMALAYAN INTERNATIONAL INSTITUTE
  OF YOGA SCIENCE AND PHILOSOPHY
HINDU AMERICAN RELIGIOUS INSTITUTE
HOHM
HOLY SHANKARACHARYA ORDER
I AM ASHRAM
ICSA (INTEGRAL CENTER OF SELF-
  ABIDANCE)
INTEGRAL YOGA INSTITUTE
INTERFAITH TEMPLE or INTERFAITH,
  INC.
INTERNATIONAL BABAJI KRIYA YOGA
  SANGAM
INTERNATIONAL SCHOOL OF YOGA
  AND VEDANTA
INTERNATIONAL SOCIETY FOR KRISHNA
  CONSCIOUSNESS (ISKCON)
INTERNATIONAL SOCIETY OF DIVINE
  LOVE
INTERNATIONAL YOGA FELLOWSHIP IN
  AMERICA
ISHVARA
JALA SANGHA
JOYA HOUSES

KAYAVAROHAN
KRIPALU CENTER
KRIPALU YOGA ASHRAM
KRISHNAMURTI FOUNDATION
KUNDALINI RESEARCH FOUNDATION
LAMA FOUNDATION
LIGHTHOUSE UNIVERSAL LIFE CHURCH
LIGHT OF YOGA SOCIETY
MAHA YOGA ASHRAM
MATA AMRITANANDAMAYI MISSION
MATAGIRI
NARAYANANDA UNIVERSAL YOGA
  TRUST
NATIONAL INSTITUTE FOR SELF-
  UNDERSTANDING
NITYANANDA INSTITUTE
NU YOGA
PRASURA INSTITUTE
PREMA DHARMASALA AND FELLOWSHIP
  ASSOCIATION
RAJNEESH FOUNDATION
  INTERNATIONAL
RAJ-YOGA MATH AND RETREAT
RAMAKRISHNA MATH AND MISSION
RAMAKRISHNA VEDANTA CENTRE
RAMAKRISHNA VEDANTA SOCIETY
RAMAKRISHNA–VIVEKANANDA CENTER
RAMANA MAHARSHI
RAMA SEMINARS
SAHAJA YOGA
SAI BABA
SAIVA SIDDHANTA CHURCH
SARVA DHARMA SAMBHAVA KENDRA
SATHYA SAI BABA
SATHYA SAI BABA CENTRAL COMMITTE
  OF AMERICA
SATHYA SAI BABA NATIONAL
  HEADQUARTERS OF AMERICA
SATHYA SAI BABA SOCIETY
SCHOOL OF PRACITCAL PHILOSOPHY
SELF-REALIZATION FELLOWSHIP
SELF-REVELATION CHURCH OF
  ABSOLUTE MONISM
SEVA FOUNDATION
SHANTI MANDIR TEMPLE OF PEACE

SHANTI YOGI INSTITUTE
SHREE GURUDEV ASHRAM CALIFORNIA
SHREE GURUDEV RUDRANANDA YOGA
  ASHRAM
SHRI RAM CHANDRA MISSION (SAHAJ
  MARG)
SHRI VISHVA SEVA ASHRAM
SIVANANDA YOGA VEDANTA CENTERS
  INTERNATIONAL
SIVANANDA YOGA VEDANTA CHURCH
SRI AUROBINDO INTERNATIONAL
  CENTER FOUNDATION
SRI CHIMNOY
SRI MA ANANDAMAYI ASHRAMS
SRI MA ANANDAMAYI MONASTERY
SRI RAM ASHRAMA
SRI RAMA FOUNDATION
SUBUD
SYDA FOUNDATION (SIDDHA YOGA
  DHAM ASSOCIATES)
TEACHING OF THE INNER CHRIST, INC.
TEMPLE OF COSMIC RELIGION
TEMPLE OF KRIYA YOGA
TRANSCENDENTAL MEDITATION
UNIVERSAL TRUTH FOUNDATION
UNIVERSITY OF THE TREES
VEDANTA SOCIETY
VEDIC CULTURAL CENTER
VIMAL PRAKASHAN TRUST
YASODHARA ASHRAM SOCIETY
YOGA HOUSE
YOGI GUPTA ASHRAM, INC.
YOGIRAJ
YOGODA SATSANGA SOCIETY
HINDU REFORM AND REVIVAL GROUPS:
ANANDA MARGA
ARYA SAMAJ
BRAHMA KUMARIS (RAJA YOGA)
BRAHMA SAMAJ
CHINMAYA MISSION
CHURCH OF THE NEW DISPENSATION
DEVA SAMAJ
GUPTA SABHA
HINDU MAHASABHA
PRARTHANA SAMAJ

RAMAKRISHMA MATH AND MISSION
RAMANA MAHARSHI
RAMA RAJYA PARISHA
RASHTRIYA SWAYAMASEVAK SANGH
SADHARAN BRAHMO SAMAJ
SAI BABA
SANTINIKETAN
SARVA DHARMA SAMBHAVA KENDRA
SIDDHA YOGA
SRI AUROBINDO
SUBBA RAO
SWAMINARAYANA
TEMPLE OF UNIVERSAL PEACE
WORLD COMMUNITY SERVICE
YOGODA SATSANGA SOCIETY

**IDENTITY MOVEMENT (CHRISTIAN
IDENTITY):**
ASSEMBLY OF CHRISTIAN SOLDIERS
CHRISTIAN CONSERVATIVE CHURCH OF
AMERICA
CHRISTIAN DEFENSE LEAGUE
CHRISTIAN PATRIOTS DEFENSE LEAGUE
CHURCH OF ISRAEL
CHURCH OF JESUS CHRIST
CHURCH OF JESUS CHRIST CHRISTIAN–
ARYAN NATIONS
COVENANT, THE SWORD, THE ARM OF
THE LORD
CRUSADE FOR CHRIST AND COUNTRY
MOUNTAIN CHURCH OF JESUS CHRIST
THE SAVIOUR
NEW CHRISTIAN CRUSADE CHURCH
NEW HARMONY CHRISTIAN CRUSADE
THE ORDER
PATHFINDER CHURCH
SHEPHERD'S CHAPEL
SWORD OF CHRIST GOOD NEWS
MINISTRIES

INDIA:
BORNHOS
BRAHMA SAMAJ
CHURCH OF THE NEW DISPENSATION
GUPTA SABHA
PARAMAHAMSA SABHA
RAMAKRISHNA MATH AND MISSION

RAMANA MAHARSHI
RASHTRIYA SWAYAMASEVAK SANGH
SANTINIKETAN
SARVA DHARMA SAMBHAVA KENDRA
SATHYA SAI BABA
SIDDHA YOGA
SWAMINARAYANA
YOGODA SATSANGA SOCIETY

ISLAM:
AHMADIYYA ANJUMAN ISHA'AT ISLAM
AHMADIYYA MOVEMENT
BABISM
BAHAISM
DEATH ANGELS
FIVE PERCENTERS
GURU BAWA FELLOWSHIP
HALVETI-JERRAHI ORDER OF NEW YORK
HANAFI MADH-HAB CENTER
MAHDI
NATIONAL ISLAMIC ASSEMBLY
NEW WORLD OF ISLAM
NUBIAN ISLAAMIC HEBREWS
SUBUD

ISRAEL:
BEIT ASSAPH
BEIT IMMANUEL
BETHESDA
CAFH
DA'AT
EMIN SOCIETY
ETZBA ELOHIM (THE FINGER OF GOD)
HEBREW CHRISTIAN ASSEMBLY–
JERUSALEM CONGREGATION
MESSIANIC ASSEMBLY OF ISRAEL

ITALY:
CHIESA CRISTIANA MILLENARISTA
CHIESA GUIRISDAVIDICA
CHIESA UNIVERSALE GUIRIS-DAVIDICA
DAMANHUR
NONSIAMOSOLI

JAMAICA:
ASSEMBLIES OF THE FIRST-BORN
BLACK ISRAELITES
CHURCH OF THE FIRST-BORN
ETHIOPIAN ZION COPTIC CHURCH

RASTAFARIANS
RAS TAFARI MELCHIZEDEK ORTHODOX
   CHURCH
REVIVAL ZION

JAPAN:
ANANAIKO
AUM SUPREME TRUTH
BUSSHO GOHNEN KAI
BYAKKO SHINKOKAI
GEDATSU-KAI
HONBUSHIN
HONMICHI-KYO
IESU FUKUIN KYODAN
ITTOEN
IZUMO-TAISHAKYO
JOHREI
KONKOKYO
KUROZUMI KYO
MAHIKARI
MAKUYA (GENSHIFUKUIN-KAMI-NO-
   MAKUYA-KYOKAI)
MARUYAMAKYO
MUKYOKAI
NICHIREN SHOSHU SOKA GAKKAI OF
   AMERICA
OMOTOKYO (OMOTO)
PERFECT LIBERTY KYODAN (P L
   KYODAN)
REIYU-KAI KYODAN
RISSHO KOSEI-KAI
SEICHO-NO-IE
SEKAI KYUSEI KYO
SHINREIKYO
SHINTO-TOKUMITSU-KYO
SHINYO-EN (Shinnyoen)
SOKA GAKKAI (SK)
SPIRIT OF JESUS CHRIST
SUKYO MAHIKARI
TENRIKYO
TENSHO KOTAI JINGU KYO
THIRD CIVILIZATION
WORLD MESSIANITY

JEHOVAH'S WITNESSES (and related
   groups):
ASSOCIATION FRANÇAISE DES LIBRES
ÉTUDIAN...
BEREAN BIBL...
BIBLE FELLOWS...
INSTITUTE OF PY...
KITAWALA
LAODICEAN HOME ...
   MOVEMENT
LAYMEN'S HOME MISSI...
   MOVEMENT (LHMM)
NEW CREATION BIBLE STU...
NEW JERUSALEM FELLOWSH...
PASTORAL BIBLE INSTITUTE
PROVIDENCE INDUSTRIAL MISS...
WATCHMAN HEALING MISSION
WATCHTOWER
WESTERN BIBLE STUDENTS
   ASSOCIATION

JESUS MOVEMENT:
AVALON COMMUNITY
CHILDREN OF GOD
CHURCH OF BIBLE UNDERSTANDING
FELLOWSHIP OF CHRISTIAN PILGRIMS
HOLY GHOST REPAIR SERVICE, INC.
INTERNATIONAL CHRISTIAN MINISTRIES
KOINONIA COMMUNITY
LOVE INN
NEW LIFE EVANGELISTIC CENTER
SHALOM CENTER
ZION'S INN

JUDAISM (and related groups):
AQUARIAN MINYAN OF BERKELEY
B'NAI NOACH ("Children of Noach")
CONGREGATION BEIT SHECHINAH
CONSERVATIVE JUDAISM
DOR HASHALOM
EMMANUEL
FRAZIER CHAPEL
INTERFAITH TEMPLE or INTERFAITH,
   INC.
JEWISH SCIENCE, SOCIETY OF
LIBERAL JUDAISM
MAKOM OHR SHALOM
NEW THOUGHT SYNAGOGUE
P'NAI OR RELIGIOUS FELLOWSHIP
PROGRESSIVE JUDAISM

REC...
REFO...
TEM...
TRE...
KEN...
A...
A...
C...

CONSTRUCTIONISM
REFORM JUDAISM
TEMPLE OF UNIVERSAL JUDAISM
TREE OF LIFE
KENYA:
AFRICA GOSPEL UNITY CHURCH
APOSTOLIC HIERARCHY CHURCH
CHRISTIAN HOLY GHOST CHURCH OF
EAST AFRICA
CHRISTIAN THEOCRATIC HOLY CHURCH
OF GOD
MARIA LEGIO (OF AFRICA)
POWER OF JESUS AROUND THE WORLD
CHURCH
VOICE OF PROPHECY CHURCH
WAKORINO
KOREA:
FULL GOSPEL CENTRAL CHURCH
ISRAEL SOODO WON (Israel Monastery)
JEUNGSAN
UNIFICATION CHURCH (UC)
MAORIS:
RATANA CHURCH
MESSIANIC JUDAISM:
BEIT ASSAPH
BEIT IMMANUEL
BETH MESSIAH
BETH MESSIAH
BETH MESSIAH
BETH MESSIAH CONGREGATION
CONGREGATION OF THE MESSIAH
JEWS FOR JESUS
MESSIANIC HEBREW-CHRISTIAN
FELLOWSHIP
MESSIANIC JEWISH ALLIANCE OF
AMERICA
UNION OF MESSIANIC JEWISH
CONGREGATIONS
See also **Hebrew Christian Groups**
MELANESIA:
BOUGANVILLE MOVEMENT
ETOISM
JOHN FRUM (JON FRUM)
KAROEM
LYNDON B. JOHNSON

THE NOISE
PALIAU CHURCH
See also **Papua New Guinea**
MORMONS:
AARONIC ORDER
APOSTOLIC UNITED ORDER
CHURCH OF CHRIST (BIBLE AND BOOK
OF MORMON TEACHING)
CHURCH OF CHRIST (FETTINGITE)
CHURCH OF CHRIST (TEMPLE LOT)
CHURCH OF CHRIST AT HALLEY'S BLUFF
CHURCH OF CHRIST WITH THE ELIJAH
MESSAGE
CHURCH OF THE FIRST BORN OF THE
FULLNESS OF TIMES
CHURCH OF THE LAMB OF GOD
CONFEDERATE NATIONS OF ISRAEL
LDS SCRIPTURE RESEARCHERS
REORGANIZED CHURCH OF JESUS
CHRIST OF LATTER DAY SAINTS
SONS AHMAN ISRAEL
UNITED ORDER EFFORT
ZION'S ORDER OF THE SONS OF LEVI
NEO-PAGAN:
ATHANOR FELLOWSHIP
CALUMET PAGAN TEMPLE
CHURCH OF ALL WORLDS
CHURCH OF THE ETERNAL SOURCE
CIRCLE SANCTUARY
COVENANT OF THE GODDESS
COVEN OF ARIANHU
DENVER AREA WICCAN NETWORK
(DAWN)
DIANIC WICCA
EARTHSPIRIT COMMUNITY
FANSCIFIAROAN CHURCH OF WICCA
FELLOWSHIP OF ISIS
FERAFERIA
GEORGIAN CHURCH
GLAINN SIDHR ORDER
GLASTONBURY COMMUNITY
HOUSE OF THE GODDESS
LIVE OAK GROVE
LOTHLORIEN
MIDWEST PAGAN COUNCIL (MPC)

337

AMERICAN CATHOLIC CHURCH (SYRO-
ANTIOCHEAN)
AMERICAN ORTHODOX CATHOLIC
CHURCH
ARCHDIOCESE OF THE OLD CATHOLIC
CHURCH IN AMERICA
CHRIST CATHOLIC CHURCH (DIOCESE
OF BOSTON)
CHRISZEKIAL ELIAS
CHURCH OF MARY MYSTICAL ROSE OF
PERPETUAL HELP
GALLICAN CHURCH
NORTH AMERICAN OLD ROMAN
CATHOLIC CHURCH
OLD CATHOLIC CHURCH IN AMERICA
POLISH MARIAVITE CHURCH
POLISH NATIONAL CATHOLIC CHURCH
UNIVERSAL APOSTOLIC CHURCH OF LIFE
PAGANISM, *see* **Neo-Pagan**
PAPUA NEW GUINEA:
GHOST WIND
KUKUAIK
LETUB
"TARO CULT"
YALIWAN'S MOVEMENT
See also **Melanesia**
PHILIPPINES:
EQUIFRILIBRICUM WORLD RELIGION
IGLESIA NI CRISTO (MANALISTA, INC)
PHILIPPINE INDEPENDENT CHURCH
PHILIPPINE UNITARIAN CHURCH
ROMAN CATHOLICS, TRADITIONALIST,
see **Traditionalist Roman Catholics**
ROSICRUCIANS:
AMORC ROSICRUCIAN ORDER
ANCIENT MAYANS, ORDER OF
AUSAR AUSET SOCIETY
FRATERNITAS ROSAE CRUCIS
LECTORIUM ROSICRUCIANUM
ORDO TEMPLI ORIENTIS
ROSICRUCIAN ANTHROPOSOPHIC
LEAGUE
ROSICRUCIAN FELLOWSHIP
SOCIETAS ROSICRUCIANA IN AMERICA
(SRIA)

SABBATH-KEEPING GROUPS:
ADVENT SABBATH CHURCH
ASSEMBLIES OF YAHWEH (MICHIGAN)
BELIEVERS IN THE COMMANDMENTS OF
GOD
CHURCH OF GOD, BODY OF CHRIST
CHURCH OF GOD (SABBATARIAN)
CHURCH OF GOD (SEVENTH-DAY,
SALEM, WEST VIRGINIA)
GENERAL CONFERENCE OF THE
CHURCH OF GOD (SEVENTH DAY)
GENERAL COUNCIL OF THE CHURCHES
OF GOD
NEW YORK UNITED SABBATH DAY
ADVENT CHURCH
PEOPLE'S CHRISTIAN CHURCH
SEVENTH-DAY ADVENTIST CHURCH
SEVENTH-DAY ADVENTIST REFORM
MOVEMENT
SEVENTH DAY PENTECOSTAL CHURCH
OF THE LIVING GOD
UNIFICATION ASSOCIATION OF
CHRISTIAN SABBATH KEEPERS
UNITED SEVENTH-DAY BRETHREN
VOICE OF PROPHECY CHURCH
SCIENTOLOGY:
ABILITISM
ADVANCED ABILITY CENTER
DIANOLOGY AND EDUCTIVISM
PROCESS, OR THE CHURCH OF THE
FINAL JUDGMENT PROCESS
SCIENTOLOGY, CHURCH OF
SIKHISM:
ECKANKAR
HEALTHY, HAPPY, HOLY
ORGANIZATION
KIRPAL RUHANI SATSANG
MANAV KENDRA
NAMDHARI
NIRANKARI
RADHASOAMI SATSANG
RADHASOAMI SATSANG BEAS
RUHANI SATSANG
SANT BANI ASHRAM
SAWAN KIRPAL RUHANI MISSION

"SNAKE HANDLERS":
    CHURCH OF ALL NATIONS
    DOLLEY POND CHURCH OF GOD WITH
      SIGNS FOLLOWING
    ORIGINAL PENTECOSTAL CHURCH OF
      GOD

SOUTH AFRICA:
    AI ZION ELECTED CHURCH
    APOSTOLIC HOLY ZION MISSION OF
      SOUTH AFRICA
    BANTU NEW CHRISTIAN CATHOLIC
      APOSTOLIC CHURCH
    CHRISTIAN APOSTOLIC FAITH CHURCH
      IN ZION
    CHURCH OF CHRIST, THE
      CONGREGATION OF ALL SAINTS OF
      SOUTH AFRICA
    "ETHIOPIANS"
    "ISRAELITES"
    LUTHERAN BAPEDI CHURCH
    NATIONAL SWAZI NATIVE APOSTOLIC
      CHURCH OF AFRICA
    NAZARETHA (OR SHEMBEITES)
    REVELATION APOSTOLIC CHURCH IN
      ZION
    SCHOOL OF TRUTH
    ZION CHRISTIAN CHURCH
    "ZIONISTS"

SPIRITUALISTS:
    AGASHA TEMPLE OF WISDOM
    AQUARIAN FOUNDATION
    ASSOCIATED SPIRITUALISTS
    ASSOCIATION FOR THE
      UNDERSTANDING OF MAN
    ASTARA FOUNDATION
    ATLANTEANS
    BAPTIST MOVEMENT OF DIVINE
      HEALING-MEDIATION
    FELLOWSHIP OF THE INNER LIGHT
    FIRST SPIRITUALIST CHURCH OF NEW
      YORK
    FIRST UNIVERSAL SPIRITUALIST CHURCH
      OF NEW YORK CITY
    FOUNDATION CHURCH OF DIVINE
      TRUTH

GENERAL ASSEMBLY OF SPIRITUALISTS
GREATER WORLD CHRISTIAN
    SPIRITUALIST LEAGUE
INDEPENDENT SPIRITUALIST
    ASSOCIATION
INNER CIRCLE KETHRA E'DA
    FOUNDATION
INTERNATIONAL GENERAL ASSEMBLY
    OF SPIRITUALISTS
INTERNATIONAL SPIRITUALIST
    FEDERATION
KARDECISM
LICHTCENTRUM BETHANIEN
MARK-AGE METACENTER
MARTINUS INSTITUTE
MYSTIC CONNECTION/CHURCH OF
    LIGHT
NATIONAL COLORED SPIRITUALIST
    ASSOCIATION OF CHURCHES
NATIONAL SPIRITUAL ALLIANCE
NATIONAL SPIRITUALIST ASSOCIATION
    OF CHURCHES
NATIONAL SPIRITUAL SCIENCE CENTER
NEW YORK SPIRITUAL CENTER, INC.
ORDEN-FIAT LUX
ROOSEVELT SPIRITUAL MEMORIAL
    BENEVOLENT ASSOCIATION
SCHOOL OF UNIVERSAL PHILOSOPHY
    AND HEALING
SHANTI NILAYA
SOCIETY OF CHRIST, INC.
SPIRITUAL FRONTIERS FELLOWSHIP
SPIRITUAL SCIENCE CHURCH
SPIRITUAL SCIENCE FELLOWSHIP
TEMPLE OF UNIVERSAL LAW
UMBANDA
UNIVERSAL CHRIST CHURCH
UNIVERSAL CHURCH OF THE MASTER
UNIVERSAL HAGAR'S SPIRITUAL CHURCH
UNIVERSAL HARMONY FOUNDATION
UNIVERSAL LINK
UNIVERSAL SPIRITUALIST ASSOCIATION
UNIVERSAL SPIRITUAL TEMPLE OF THE
    NEW ERA–TEMPLE OF CELESTIAL
    LIGHT

WHITE EAGLE LODGE

SUFISM:

ABODE OF THE MESSAGE

BABA LEAGUE

BESHARA TRUST

HALVETI-JERRAHI ORDER OF NEW YORK

HEALING ORDER OF THE SUFI ORDER

INSTITUTE FOR CULTURAL RESEARCH

INSTITUTE FOR RESEARCH ON THE
    DISSEMINATION OF HUMAN
    KNOWLEDGE

MEHER BABA, FRIENDS OF

MEHER DURBAR

PREMA DHARMASALA AND FELLOWSHIP
    ASSOCIATION; PREMA WORLD
    COMMUNITY

SUFI ISLAMIA RUHANIAT SOCIETY

SUFI ORDER IN THE WEST

SUFISM REORIENTED

UNIVERSAL SPIRITUAL LEAGUE OF
    AMERICA

THEOSOPHY GROUPS:

AGNI YOGA SOCIETY

AMERICAN UNIVERSALIST TEMPLE OF
    DIVINE WISDOM

ANTHROPOSOPHY

AQUARIAN EDUCATIONAL
    FOUNDATION

AQUARIAN FOUNDATION

ASTARA FOUNDATION

BRIDGE CENTER FOR SPIRITUAL
    STUDIES

BRIDGE TO FREEDOM

BROTHERHOOD OF THE WHITE TEMPLE

CHIROTHESIAN CHURCH OF FAITH

CHURCH OF RELIGIOUS PHILOSOPHY

CONCEPT-THERAPY INSTITUTE

DEVA COMMUNITY

FELLOWSHIP OF DIVINE TRUTH

GNOSTIC ASSOCIATION OF
    ANTHROPOLOGY AND SCIENCE

GNOSTIC SOCIETY

GREAT SCHOOL OF THE MASTERS

HERMETIC SOCIETY

"I AM"

INDEPENDENT THEOSOPHICAL SOCIETY

INTERFAITH TEMPLE or INTERFAITH,
    INC.

INTERNATIONAL COMMUNITY OF
    CHRIST

KRISHNAMURTI

LIBERAL CATHOLIC CHURCH

MARK-AGE METACENTER

MARTINUS INSTITUTE

MINISTRY OF UNIVERSAL WISDOM

ORDER OF THE CROSS

ORDER OF THE INITIATES OF TIBET

PHILOSOPHICAL RESEARCH SOCIETY

SCHOOL OF LIGHT AND REALIZATION
    (SOLAR)

SERVANTS OF THE LIGHT

SOLAR CROSS FELLOWSHIP

SOLAR LIGHT CENTER

STELLE COMMUNITY

SUMMIT LIGHTHOUSE

TEMPLE OF UNIVERSAL LAW

THEOCENTRIC FOUNDATION

THEOSOPHICAL ORDER OF SERVICE

THEOSOPHICAL SOCIETY IN AMERICA

THEOSOPHY

UNARIUS EDUCATIONAL FOUNDATION
    (UNARIUS–SCIENCE OF LIFE)

UNDERSTANDING, INC.

UNITED LODGE OF THEOSOPHISTS

UNIVERSAL BROTHERHOOD AND
    THEOSOPHICAL SOCIETY

UNIVERSAL FAITH AND WISDOM
    ASSOCIATION

UNIVERSAL GREAT BROTHERHOOD
    A.U.M. SOLAR LINE

UNIVERSARIUN FOUNDATION

UNIVERSITY OF THE TREES

WISDOM'S GOLDENROD CENTER FOR
    PHILOSOPHIC STUDIES

TIBETAN BUDDHISM:

DORJE KHYUNG DZONG

EWAM CHODEN TIBETAN BUDDHIST
    CENTER

GANDEN MAHAYANA CENTER

GELUG-PA ("Yellow Hat")

JETSUN SAKYA CENTER
KAGYU DRODEN KUNCHAB
KAGYU KUNKHYAB CHULING
KARGYUDPA ORDER
KARGYU DSAMLING KUNCHAB
KARM LING
KARMA KAGYU SAMYE-LING
KARMA TRIYANA DHARMACHAKRA
LAMAIST BUDDHIST MONASTERY OF
   AMERICA
LAMA YESHE MOVEMENT
MAHASIDDHA NYINGMAPA
NYINGMAPA CENTER
SAKYA TAGCHEN CHOLING CENTER
THARPA CHOELING
TIBETAN BUDDHIST LEARNING CENTER
TRALEG TULKU
UNIVERSITY OF THE TREES
VAJRADHATU
VAJRAPANI INSTITUTE FOR WISDOM
   CULTURE
YESHE NYINGPO
YOGA INSTITUTE OF CONSCIOUSNESS

TRADITIONALIST ROMAN CATHOLICS:
APOSTLES OF INFINITE LOVE
CONGREGATION OF MARY THE
   IMMACULATE QUEEN
FRATERNITY OF ST. PIUS X
LATIN-RITE CATHOLIC CHURCH
OUR LADY OF THE ROSES
PALMARIAN CATHOLIC CHURCH
RENOVATED CHURCH OF CHRIST (Église
   du Christ-Roi Rénovée)
SERVANTS OF THE SACRED HEART OF
   JESUS AND MARY
SOCIETY OF ST. PIUS V
TRADITIONAL CHRISTIAN CATHOLIC
   CHURCH
UNION CATHOLICA TRENTO

"UFO" GROUPS:
AETHERIUS SOCIETY

ARISING SUN IFO (IDENTIFIED FLYING
   OBJECTS)
ARMAGEDDON TIME ARK BASE (A.T.A.
   BASE)
BO AND PEEP
COSMIC CIRCLE OF FELLOWSHIP
COSMIC STAR TEMPLE
EXTRA-TERRESTRIAL COMMUNICATIONS
   NETWORK
LIGHT OF THE UNIVERSE
MARA LA ASPARA
MARK-AGE METACENTER
MINISTRY OF UNIVERSAL WISDOM
NONSIAMOSOLI
RAËLIANS
SOLAR CROSS FELLOWSHIP
SOLAR LIGHT CENTER
UNARIUS EDUCATIONAL FOUNDATION
   (UNARIUS–SCIENCE OF LIFE)
UNDERSTANDING, INC.
UNIVERSARIUN FOUNDATION
WHITE STAR

VIETNAM:
CAO DAI
HOA HAO

WEST AFRICA, *see* **African Groups,**
   Nigeria

WICCA, *see* **Neo-Pagan**

WITCHCRAFT, *see* **Neo-Pagan**

ZAIRE:
JAMAA
KIMBANGUIST MOVEMENT
KITAWALA (Chitawala)
MATSOUANISM (MATSWA)

ZAMBIA:
LUMPA CHURCH

ZIMBABWE:
AFFIRCAN APOSTOLIC CHURCH OF
   JOHANE MARANKE
FIRST ETHIOPIAN CHURCH
MAI CHAZA CHURCH